DATE DUE

MY 27'97			
JY 9'97			
MY 8			
DE 20'00			
DE 12 01			
JE 10'02			
JE 2'04			

DEMCO 38-296

DISPLACEMENTS

DISPLACEMENTS: Cultural Identities in Question

is Volume 15 in the series

THEORIES OF CONTEMPORARY CULTURE
Center for Twentieth Century Studies
University of Wisconsin–Milwaukee

General Editor, KATHLEEN WOODWARD

DISPLACEMENTS
Cultural Identities in Question

edited by Angelika Bammer

Indiana University Press

Bloomington and Indianapolis

The paper used in this publication meets the minimum require-
ments of American National Standard for Information Sciences—
Permanence of Paper for Printed Library Materials, ANSI
Z39.48-1984.

Manufactured in the United States of America

Library of Congress Cataloging-in-Publication Data

Displacements: cultural identities in question / edited by Angelika
Bammer.
     p. cm.—(Theories of contemporary culture; v. 15)
    Includes index.
     ISBN 0-253-31138-1.—ISBN 0-253-20897-1 (pbk.)
     1. Acculturation. 2. Ethnicity. 3. Culture conflict.
    I. Bammer, Angelika. II. Series.
    GN366.D57 1994
    303.48'2—dc20   94-1182

I 2 3 4 5 00 99 98 97 96 95 94

To my parents

Contents

Introduction

Angelika Bammer

THE SEPARATION OF people from their native culture either through physical dislocation (as refugees, immigrants, migrants, exiles, or expatriates) or the colonizing imposition of a foreign culture—what I am calling here displacement[1]—is one of the most formative experiences of our century. By all counts, the numbers are staggering. To take only one instance—the displacement of people as a result of Nazi policies and World War II—it is estimated that during the years of Hitler's rule over 30 million people were uprooted and forcibly moved, while the final redistribution of population in Europe alone after the end of the war resulted in the "permanent migration of another twenty-five million" (Kulisher 305). All in all, World War II is estimated to have effected the greatest displacement of human population ever recorded in world history.

Refugee counts tell a similar story. In addition to wars and so-called natural disasters, the combination of colonial and imperialist practices carried out on an international scale, and state-sanctioned ethnic, religious, and racial discrimination practiced intra-nationally have made mass migration and mass expulsion of people a numbingly familiar feature of twentieth-century domestic and foreign policy. With an estimated 60–100 million refugees worldwide since 1945, the conclusion that "the refugee crisis . . . is a dilemma belonging uniquely to the twentieth century" seems unhappily warranted (Sutter 1).[2]

In the case of people who are not expelled from but displaced *within* their native culture by processes of external or internal colonization, no comparable counts or estimates exist. Obviously not all of the 23 million who lived under French imperial rule in Indochina, say, or the 340 million British imperial subjects from the Indian subcontinent can be said to have been displaced by colonial rule, even if one extends the meaning of "displacement" metaphorically. (Some, no doubt, were in many ways even less displaced than the by-law and in-name dominating colonizers.) What is certain, however, is that the cumulative effect of colonial and imperialist policies—the expropriation of land that often left indigenous peoples with merely a small, and mostly poorer, portion of their own land; the pass laws that controlled and regulated their physical movement; the economic shifts that forced them into the new centers of imperial employment thus creating new patterns of migratory labor; the presence of a foreign ruling power that disappropriated local cultures[3]—effected massive displacements of indigenous peoples in ways that cannot be added up in numbers and that did not end with official decolonization.

In light of these figures, it is not surprising that displacement has played such a prominent role in the operative theoretical paradigms with which we have attempted to understand and explain the human condition and conditions of knowledge in our time. For in a generalized sense we are all, as people of the twentieth century, marked by this experience. Thus, it is again not surprising that displacement often appears as the equally defining feature of the two main periods into which the cultural history of our century is typically divided: modernism and postmodernism.

According to Fredric Jameson, modernism as it took shape in Western Europe between World War I and World War II is precisely predicated upon the structural displacement of significant parts of the Western world and sense of self into parts "located elsewhere . . . in colonies over the water whose own life experience and life world . . . remain unknown and unimaginable for the subjects of the imperial power." This simultaneously split and doubled existence—stretched across the multiple ruptures between "here" and "there"—constitutes the "new and historically original problem" of modernism: "the inability to grasp the way the system functions as a whole" (51). Salman Rushdie reflects on this history from the other way around, as it were: the perspective of those displaced by the presence of power "located elsewhere." Yet the link he establishes between the structures of colonialism, the culture of modernism, and the experience of displacement is much the same as that charted by Jameson: "[T]hose of us who have been forced by cultural displacement to accept the provisional nature of all truths, all certainties," he concludes, "have perhaps had modernism forced upon us" (13).

In the present, so-called *post*modern time, this sense of palpable, yet "unknown and unimaginable" contingencies, has become, if anything, even more foregrounded. As the "post-" designations proliferate, defining us in terms of what we supposedly no longer are (post-modern, post-colonial, post-feminist, etc.), and as we ever more obsessively attempt to specify our precise locations (the familiar "I am a [fill in the blanks]" recitation), our sense of identity is ineluctably, it seems, marked by the peculiarly postmodern geography of identity: both here *and* there and neither here *nor* there at one and the same time. It is in this sense and for this reason that marginality and otherness increasingly figure as the predominant affirmative signifiers of (postmodern) identity. Indeed, it would appear, almost by definition, that to "be" in the postmodern sense is somehow to be an Other: displaced.[4]

The problem with this notion of displacement is that differences, thus universalized, disappear. What is more, the historical experience of difference on the basis of such socially constructed categories of discrimination as race, class, gender, sexuality, or religious, ethnic, or cultural affiliation, is appropriated for the purposes of elaborating a new, postmodernistically hip version of the universal subject.[5] It is this generalizing, difference-blurring notion of displacement that this volume is set against. Instead, individually and collectively, the texts assembled here set out to chart the meaning of displacement in particular, concrete terms in order to more adequately grasp its multivalent complexity.

As the plural of the title of the volume indicates, the multiple resonances of displacement are both point of departure and site of inquiry for this project. An underlying question throughout is the nature of the relationships among displacement as a theoretical signifier, a textual strategy, and a lived experience. In this sense, this volume is part of the larger inquiry into (post)modern experiences of reality and their (post)modernist representations. Accordingly, displacement as I use the term here carries resonances of both Freud and Derrida. For Freud, displacement — *Verschiebung* (literally, "pushing aside") — was central to the operation of dream-work, the process by which uncomfortable thoughts and feelings ("latent dream-thoughts") are transferred to the safe remove of representational symbols ("manifest dream-content"): "*[I]n the course of the dream-work the psychical intensity passes over from the thoughts and ideas to which it properly belongs on to others which in our judgement have no claim to any such emphasis*" (154–55). Displacement (*Verschiebung*) was thus, for Freud, similar to repression (*Verdrängung*). In both cases, something was pushed aside, as it were, only in the latter case more forcefully and permanently. For Derrida, the critical move in the interpretive (that is, meaning-making) process is also a form of pushing aside: the deconstructive labor of desedimenting layers of meaning in the course of which meaning becomes *différance* — infinitely dispersed, indefinitely deferred. In both cases, that of Freud and Derrida, what is displaced — dispersed, deferred, repressed, pushed aside — is, significantly, still there: *Dis*placed but not *re*placed, it remains a source of trouble, the shifting ground of signification that makes meanings tremble.

One of the primary impulses of this book is to uncover some of that ground. For me this has meant regrounding the discussion of displacement in the history of our time, a history of displaced persons and peoples. Put another way, the intent of this volume is to refocus attention on that which too abstracted and metaphorized a notion of displacement has displaced, if not repressed, and that is history. In this regard, its agenda, and the assumptions on which that agenda is based, are different from related work in which terms of displacement such as exile or homelessness are used as metaphors for outsiderness and alienation. In so doing, the purpose is not to effect a displacement of another kind, much less to replace "theory" with "history." Rather, my intent has been to bring to the surface the material ground of culture and community within which the work of theory takes shape: to put the "place" back into "displacement."[6]

At issue in the materials assembled here is the relationship between the experience of cultural displacement and the construction of cultural identity. It is thus marked by the tension of the historically vital double move between marking and recording absence and loss[7] and inscribing presence. In this sense, this volume marks and is part of a recent shift among certain circles within the humanities from deconstructive critiques of the metaphysics of presence to critical analyses of the politics of identity.[8] This shift in attention and emphasis, which in recent academic practice has not infrequently coincided with a shift in (or at least expansion of) institutional affiliation from literature and philosophy to history and anthropology, is manifested in the surge of interest of late in issues of identity and difference.[9] These analyses are framed, on the one hand, by studies of identity formation on the level of the state and national culture and, on the other hand, by debates over "identity politics" on the level of individuals and groups constructed around such categories as race, ethnicity, gender, sexuality, and their various intersections. No longer, as in the sixties and seventies, the locus of political opposition from the extra-institutional stance of the mobilized, disenfranchised "counterculture," the politics of identity have entered the academy in what sometimes appears as the contradictory form of an at once critical, intra-institutional opposition and a criticism-defusing celebration of multiculturalism.

From another perspective, however, this contradiction is merely a symptom of what has always been the necessary dual strategy of an oppositional politics: negative systems critique and affirmative practical politics.[10] It is in this sense not unrelated to the deconstructive dilemma of needing to step outside and remain inside the same systems. Translated into a critical textual practice, this might mean that we should read history and its texts similarly: from the inside out and the outside in. For example, we could read a text like "The Ends of Man" against documents from the same period in which "Man" had a considerably different meaning.[11] Or, to take a related example, we could read Derrida's recent reflections on European cultural identity, *The Other Heading*, in which the "Other" is no longer the unspoken end (that which comes after "Man") but the central term, the focal signifier, in conjunction with texts like *"Race," Writing, and Difference*, in which one of the primary terms of culturally marked otherness—race—has been parenthetically suspended.

This volume aims at such a doubled reading by continually putting the categories "us" and "them" in tension. Colonialism is about the colonized and the colonizers both; home is about separation and commitment; and identity is at times about what we are essentially not, but are also not free to dispense with. The politics of identity, in short, is a constant process of negotiation.[12] As Toni Morrison points out in her study of the relationship between whiteness and blackness in the American cultural imaginary, we are often as inseparable from as incommensurable to one another. This relationality—different agendas joined within the same contested historical space—is central to the concept of identity as I am using it here.

Beyond these categories of opposition, however, there is another way to think of cultural identity. Just as psychoanalytic paradigms teach us to think of family in vertical terms as the relationship between parents and children, so the national "family" ("our" culture) is typically also presented in terms of a vertical lineage: a tradition with a past to which "we" belong and to which "they," by definition, are foreign. This paradigm has been challenged and subjected to critical revision of late by those who point out that this tradition in relation to which "we" supposedly cohere has never been singular, homogeneous. Rather, it has always been an amalgam of disparate and heterogeneous parts, the plural traditions of different peoples and groups whose complex and shifting interactions make up the actual shape of what we then imagine as a nation.[13]

Some go a step further to suggest that there is another—not linear, but horizontal—way to think of a cultural community. Taking the situation of Indian writers in England as a concrete case in point, Salman Rushdie, for example, suggests that these writers are not just negatively marked (neither "English" nor "Indian") but "have access to a second tradition." This tradition, he proposes, is one of cross-connections, not roots—"the culture and political history of the phenomenon of migration, displacement, life in a minority group"—that constitutes its own community cross- and intraculturally. And the life of such communities, he concludes, is undoubtedly "one of the central themes of this century of displaced persons" (124).

Indeed, in light of the facts and figures with which I began, we might well assume that this "migrant sensibility" of which Rushdie speaks is in large parts of the world already more the norm than the exception. Perhaps it even will (as it already in many ways has) replace the old concept of "cultural identity." What we are witnessing, globally and locally, I would venture to say, is in part the struggle over this very issue. It is in this context that Derrida begins his recent reflections on today's Europe with the question, "[I]s 'cultural identity' a good word for 'today'?" (*The Other Heading* 13). He concludes by answering in the negative. For, as he maintains,

> Whether it takes a national form or not, a refined, hospitable or aggressively xenophobic form or not, the self-affirmation of an identity always claims to be responding to the call or assignation of the universal. There are no excep-

tions to this law. No cultural identity presents itself as the opaque body of an untranslatable idiom, but always, on the contrary, as the irreplaceable *inscription* of the universal in the singular. (72–73)

In the present period of instability and contest over questions such as these— sometimes presented in the form of intellectual debate over "the canon" or "multiculturalism," sometimes enacted in the form of armed hostilities—this contest warrants careful scrutiny. How do "home" and "cultural identity" become sites of struggle over place? How are "foreignness" and "at-homeness" deployed strategically? What are the stakes? Who gains? Who loses? Seldom has the urgency of such questions been more palpable.

One of the issues around which debate, hopes, and hostilities often crystallize is language. And not surprisingly. For, at once carrier of national and familial traditions and emblem of cultural and personal identity, language functions equally as an identity-grounding home under conditions of displacement and a means of intervention into identity-fixing cultural agendas.[14] It is for this reason that the present volume is framed by two texts—one by Abdelfattah Kilito, the other by Theresa Hak Kyung Cha—that foreground this issue and highlight its complexity. The questions they raise are taken up and refracted in a number of ways by the other pieces. In the process, the texts assembled here cut across both generic and disciplinary boundaries as they bring literary, personal, scholarly, and political materials and perspectives to bear on the particular inquiry at hand.

The first section, "Power and Authorities," acknowledges the fact that identities, cultural or otherwise, are constructed and lived out not just in intrapsychic or metatheoretical realms but in the material space of differently authorized and institutionally vested powers. Often referred to as the "real world," this is the space in which the *discursive* nature of cultural formations is often eclipsed by the palpable experience of their force. The two middle sections, "(Re)Locating 'Home' and 'Community' " and " 'Natives,' Empires, and the Contingencies of Race," are framed by the acknowledgment of contingency in both its broadest and most literal sense.[15] Taking into account our various contingencies highlights the fact that each issue we raise touches on many others on all sides, just as the experience of displacement, both cause and effect of our contingent existences, forces upon us a heightened awareness of our simultaneously necessary and fragile connectedness. In this light, the contributions in these two sections reflect on such historically weighty and overdetermined terms as "home," "race," "Englishness," or "Jewishness," asking: What do they mean? How are they mobilized? What histories are constructed in their name? The last section, "Options and Exigencies," is designed as a counter to the undue, and I suspect often placatory, haste with which multiculturalism these days is celebrated.[16] In light of the degree to which discriminatory policies and practices continue unabated and often unchecked, this volume concludes with a reminder of the fact that identities are always constructed and lived out on the historical terrain between necessity and choice, the place where oppression and resistance are simultaneously located.

My work on this project was enabled and facilitated by support from a variety of sources whom I wish to thank here: the National Endowment for the Humanities for a Summer Grant in 1989 that provided valuable seed money; the National Humanities Center in North Carolina for a Fellowship, partially funded by The Rockefeller Foundation, that enabled me to spend the academic year 1989–90 in an almost utopian space of freedom from institutional obligations; the Emory University Research Council for a grant that released me from teaching responsibilities during the fall semester 1990. The Center for Twentieth Century Studies at the University of Wisconsin–Milwaukee played a particularly important role in bringing this project from ideas to book reality: A two-week residency at the Center in the spring of 1991 and a Center-sponsored conference on the topic that April enabled me to formulate, for the first time publicly, what this project was about and provided me with a vital forum for public dialogue on the issues. Out of this dialogue the core of the book evolved; some of the essays included in this volume were first presented as papers at the Center conference. Thus to the women and men at the Center for Twentieth Century Studies my abiding gratitude for their material, intellectual, and personal support at every phase of this project. I thank Kathleen Woodward for her strong and unfailing support, for the acuity of her editorial insight at critical stages, and for her ability to intervene with warmth and good humor at just the right moments; I thank Carol Tennessen for the integrity, clarity, and good sense with which she charted a path for the book and kept us on it; I thank Barbara Obremski, Paul Kosidowski, Nicole Cunningham, Brent Keever, and Cathy Egan for the care and professionalism with which they managed the technical and adminstrative details. I thank Elizabeth Soilis of the Emory University German Studies Department for her scrupulous, empathetic, and generous help with every aspect of this project. I thank the students, both in the Modern Studies program at the University of Wisconsin–Milwaukee and in the program in Comparative Literature at Emory University, with whom I worked on the issues (and, in some cases, texts) represented here for the excitement and energetic critiques with which they responded. I thank my friends who listened as I obsessed about the issues raised in this book for what sometimes must have seemed like a lifetime. Of course, for many of us who came together in our work on this book, it has been precisely that: a lifetime. For the sharing of those histories and for the rich and sustaining bonds of comradeship and friendship that developed in the process, I am deeply grateful. Finally, I thank my parents, whose histories taught me the necessity of asking the questions that led to this book. And I thank my partner,

DeWitt Whitaker, for giving me a place of security from which I could live with the questions—and the answers.

Notes

1. I find myself in unexpected agreement here with the logic of the Library of Congress cataloguing system whose placement of "migration" between "colonialism" and "immigration" suggests a similar concept of displacement.

2. As Sutter reports, in a single year (1988), according to a survey of the US Committee of Refugees, the refugee count was over 14,000,000: 4,000,000 in Africa; 9,000,000 in the Middle East; 280,000 in Latin America and the Caribbean; 625,000 in East Asia and the Pacific; 350,000 in Europe.

3. For both a particularly powerful description of the violence of cultural colonization and an eloquent argument for a cultural politics of resistance, see Ngũgĩ wa Thiong'o.

4. The particular ways in which this is so and the historical reasons why have been the subject of inquiry of late from a variety of different perspectives, most notably in the field of postcolonial cultural studies and Holocaust studies. For the former, the work of Spivak (see, for example, *The Post-Colonial Critic*) and Bhabha (see, for example, "Interrogating Identity") have played a particularly formative role. See also Trinh. For the latter, see, among others, Santner, Friedlander, Felman and Laub.

5. An example of the problematic blurring of these differences is Kristeva (see *Strangers*). Homi Bhabha's repeatedly elaborated distinction between "difference" and "diversity" offers an important counterstrategy. For a concise and lucid articulation of this distinction, see Bhabha and Rutherford.

6. This is precisely the move with which Derrida, also at critical moments, grounds his philosophical interventions in the historical contingencies at hand. "The Ends of Man" offers a pertinent example. Presented at an international philosophy and anthropology colloquium in New York in the fall of 1968, Derrida sets this inquiry into the status of "Man" as defined within Western metaphysical humanism into the context of colonial warfare: the violent encounter with the Other, the palpable notice of whose presence historically marked the beginning of the end referred to in the essay's title. For, as Derrida reminds his audience, the year in which this philosophical colloquium takes place had begun with a staggering escalation of the war in Vietnam; that same year, Martin Luther King, Jr. had been assassinated in Memphis; and universities from Paris to Prague to Berkeley to Mexico City had been the site of massive protests against all forms of colonization and imperialism. It is this context that defines the dilemma inherent in his proposed deconstructive strategy. For, while "[a] radical trembling can only come from the *outside*," the "force and efficiency of the system" is such that it "regularly change[s] transgressions into 'false exits.' " In this light, Derrida concludes, the only choice we have is to do two things at once: "To attempt . . . a deconstruction *without changing terrain* . . . and to *change terrain* . . . by *brutally* placing oneself outside" (134–35; my emphasis).

7. In this respect displacement might be thought of as another instance of the practice of "dissing." I thank Lisa Pertillar Brevard for the following definition:

> **dis** (verb): usually, to insult or ignore. A Black American slang term created and initially used by young Black American males who are part of the "hip-hop," i.e., rap

music, crowd. Often used in various forms in place of longer words, such as "disen-franchise(d); "dismiss(ed); or "disrespect(ed)."

8. It is perhaps in this respect symptomatic that exactly a decade ago a volume with much the same main title as the present one was published in the same Theories of Contemporary Culture series. The contribution of *Displacements: Derrida and After* was to take stock of the work of the philosopher who, as the editor, Mark Krupnick, wrote, "has done most to displace the metaphysics of presence" (1). A decade later, in the context of a more historically differentiated cultural studies, greater attention is being devoted to that which earlier fell outside of, or was itself displaced within, the purview of deconstruction.

9. To give merely a few examples: Bhabha, "Interrogating Identity;" Todorov; Mohanty; Rutherford; Balibar and Wallerstein; Parker et al.; Appiah and Gates; and Lavie and Swedenburg.

10. In a short (and to my knowledge) unpublished essay, "Women and Theory," Teresa de Lauretis spells out and explains the reasons for such a dual strategy from the perspective of feminism.

11. One could read, in this context, essays and speeches of Martin Luther King, Jr. or other documents of the American Civil Rights movement. For example, the organizing slogan of Operation Push was "I Am a Man." In the Memphis Sanitation Workers' strike, which was the occasion of Martin Luther King's visit to Memphis in 1968 when he was killed, the notion of "Man" was radically politicized in light of American race and class politics.

12. It is in this respect that I often find some of the fashionable "post-" designations not only politically problematic, but historically imprecise. For example, some of us may not be living in a colonial empire anymore, but others of us in the global political economy still are, for all practical purposes.

13. In this respect, Benedict Anderson's notion of the nation as an "imagined community" could be turned virtually on its head. For what is imagined is not just the nation as a projection of community, but the coherence and (comm)unity on which nationhood is then predicated.

14. On these issues, see Adorno, particularly "Words from Abroad" but also "On the Question."

15. Contingency, from the Latin *contingere*: to touch on all sides.

16. See, in this context, Todorov, *Nous et les autres*, in particular "Remarques sur le croisement des cultures."

Works Cited

Adorno, T. W. "Words from Abroad." *Notes to Literature*. Vol. 1. Ed. Rolf Tiedemann. Trans. Shierry Weber Nicholsen. New York: Columbia UP, 1991. 185–99.

———. "On the Question: 'What is German?' " Trans. Thomas Y. Levin. *New German Critique* 36 (1985): 121–31.

Anderson, Benedict. *Imagined Communities: Reflections on the Origin and Spread of Nationalism*. Rev. ed. New York: Verso, 1991.

Appiah, Kwame Anthony, and Henry Louis Gates, Jr., eds. *Identities*. Special issue of *Critical Inquiry* 18.4 (1992).

Balibar, Etienne, and Immanuel Wallerstein. *Race, Nation, Class: Ambiguous Identities.* London: Verso, 1991.

Bhabha, Homi K. "Interrogating Identity." *The Real Me?* 5–11.

Bhabha, Homi K., and Jonathan Rutherford. "The Third Space." Rutherford 207–21.

Brevard, Lisa Pertillar." 'Fight(ing) the Power': Power, (Dis?)placement and Cultural Identity among Young Black American Males in the Hood." Unpublished manuscript.

de Lauretis, Teresa. "Women and Theory." Unpublished essay. Midwest Modern Language Association Annual Meeting, 1983.

Derrida, Jacques. "The Ends of Man." *Margins of Philosophy.* Trans. Alan Bass. Chicago: U of Chicago P, 1982. 109–36.

———. *The Other Heading: Reflections on Today's Europe.* Trans. Pascale-Anne Brault and Michael B. Naas. Bloomington: Indiana UP, 1992.

Felman, Shoshana, and Dori Laub, eds. *Testimony: Crises of Witnessing in Literature, Psychoanalysis, and History.* New York: Routledge, 1992.

Freud, Sigmund. "On Dreams." *The Freud Reader.* Ed. Peter Gay. New York: Norton, 1989. 142–72.

Friedlander, Saul, ed. *Probing the Limits of Representation: Nazism and the "Final Solution."* Cambridge: Harvard UP, 1992.

Gates, Henry Louis, Jr., ed. *"Race," Writing and Difference.* Chicago: U of Chicago P, 1985.

Jameson, Fredric. "Modernism and Imperialism." *Nationalism, Colonialism, and Literature.* Ed. Terry Eagleton, Fredric Jameson, and Edward Said. Minneapolis: U of Minnesota P, 1990. 43–66.

Kristeva, Julia. *Strangers to Ourselves.* Trans. Leon Roudiez. New York: Columbia UP, 1991.

Krupnick, Mark, ed. *Displacement: Derrida and After.* Bloomington: Indiana UP, 1983.

Kulisher, Eugene M. *Europe on the Move: War and Population Changes, 1917-47.* New York: Columbia UP, 1948.

Lavie, Smadar, and Ted Swedenburg, eds. *Displacement, Diaspora, and Geographies of Identity.* Durham: Duke UP, forthcoming.

Mohanty, Satya P. "Us and Them." *New Formations* 8 (1989): 55–80.

Morrison, Toni. *Playing in the Dark: Whiteness and the American Literary Imagination.* Cambridge: Harvard UP, 1992.

Ngũgĩ wa Thiong'o. *Decolonising the Mind: The Politics of Language in African Literature.* London: Heinemann, 1986.

Parker, Andrew, Mary Russo, Doris Sommer, and Patricia Yeager, eds. *Nationalisms and Sexualities.* New York: Routledge, 1992.

The Real Me? Post-Modernism and the Question of Identity. ICA Documents 6. London: Institute of Contemporary Arts, 1987.

Rushdie, Salman. *Imaginary Homelands: Essays and Criticism 1981-1991.* New York: Viking, 1991.

Rutherford, Jonathan, ed. *Identity: Community, Culture, Difference.* London: Lawrence, 1990.

Santner, Eric L. *Stranded Objects: Mourning, Memory and Film in Postwar Germany.* Ithaca: Cornell UP, 1990.

Spivak, Gayatri Chakravorty. *The Post-Colonial Critic: Interviews, Strategies, Dialogues.* Ed. Sarah Harasym. New York: Routledge, 1990.

Sutter, Valerie O'Connor. *The Indochinese Refugee Dilemma.* Baton Rouge: Louisiana State UP, 1990.

Todorov, Tzvetan. *Les morales de l'histoire.* Paris: Grasset, 1991.

———. *Nous et les autres: La reflexion française sur la diversité humaine.* Paris: Seuil, 1989.

Trinh T. Minh-ha. *Woman, Native, Other.* Bloomington: Indiana UP, 1989.

Dog Words

Abdelfattah Kilito
Translated by Ziad Elmarsafy

Translator's Introduction

Abdelfattah Kilito's "Les mots canins" was written for a conference on bilingualism held at Rabat University, Morocco in November 1981. The subject was as close to Kilito as it was to most of the participants, all of whom were fluent if not native speakers of at least one language in addition to French. Kilito's approach, to put it mildly, is unorthodox: he compares the lot of the bilingual person to a lost traveler. This comparison acts as a point of departure for a playful narrative full of lacunae and labyrinthine digressions, constituting an ever-expanding allegorical web that eventually brings its own moment of composition within its compass. This ludic dimension is very much in the classical Arabic tradition of the *adīb*, the producer of texts whose cursory movement seems to lack direction but whose overall economy manages to contain a vast and substantial array of information. (The fact that Kilito's presentation had a very real point of reference was borne out when, in the subsequent discussion, Jacques Hassoun translated the image of the lost traveler into his own plight as an exiled Egyptian Jew.)

At issue in "Les mots canins" are language and identity, how one creates the other, and how the act of speaking a different language threatens to strip the speaker of his or her self. Which is not to say that Kilito gives uniformity the upper hand. On the contrary, this essay shows Kilito enjoying himself *qua* polyglot. Like his two points of reference—the lost traveler and the twelfth-century *adīb* Al-Jāḥiz—Kilito's text is nothing if not peripatetic and elusive, constantly taking delight in its ability to pass from one possibility to another (and thus contain them both), from one theme to another (and thus treat them both), from one idiom to another (and thus command them both). Rather than reiterate the commonplace argument that Arab francophone writers are necessarily alienated and that authenticity is only possible in a monolingual universe, Kilito is quite happy to let his ideas play themselves out in the space of linguistic and literary heterodoxy. In this respect, he approaches an ideal once described by Roland Barthes: Kilito, it seems, is the last happy (Arab) writer (94 *et passim*).

⤫⤫⤫

Quick, what does a bedouin do when he loses his way at night in the desert? What stratagem does he use to find human habitation, and therefore find himself?

You will probably never guess the answer, cat will inevitably get your tongue. Then again, what would such a seductive animal do with your tongue? Another riddle, one that does not translate very well into a feline idiom. If I were you, though, I would keep my tongue to myself and fight the cat's claws tooth and nail, for cats are visibly inhabited by the devil. You will, moreover, have to resign yourselves to hearing little more than miaows and caterwauls for the rest of this talk. How indeed is one to speak of language, of bilingualism, without evoking, quoting, and invoking animals? Is there not an inarticulate cry lurking behind every articulate word? That is why I shall refer in what follows to a bestiary, *The Book of Animals*, by the ninth-century Arabic writer Al-Jāḥiz, a man with bulging eyes (whence his surname).[1] I would like to think that the bulging of his eyes was due to his prolonged contemplation of the marvels of creation and his close scrutiny of animal behavior: eyes do, after all, open wide when we are amazed and when this astonishment is extreme they would probably come out of their sockets and stay open. (Jāḥiz did make a point of mentioning frogs, with whom he had at least one physical feature in common on this count.)

Let us not get lost in the animal kingdom, despite our theme of loss, deprivation, diminution, or, in a word, metamorphosis. So, a man is lost at night in the desert and must find his clan at any price. During the day he may well have left a trail of stones along the way, and his feet probably made prints in the sand. At night, however, neither stones nor footprints are easily perceived. The lost wanderer probably has good eyes, even bulging eyes, but they are not the eyes of a cat. What does he do? Taking his cue from the monkey, he resorts to a rather simian ploy: he starts barking (incredible but true). The Arabic word *mustanbih* means "he who imitates the dog's bark."[2] As he walks about, then, our nocturnal itinerant emits a few scattered barks. If there are any dogs in the area they will start to bark in turn and indicate human habitation to the traveler (dogs generally haunt camps and settlements). One must bark in order to find one's way; in order to become human one must first turn into a dog.

The barker is certainly very clever, and dogs are easily tricked. He barks out of necessity; there is no other way out of the situation in which he finds himself caught. The dogs think that one of their own kind is close by, addressing them in their own language. They waste no time in heeding the call. Their barking echoes the simulacrum of a bark, it is the echo of an echo, a copy of a copy. The bark does not, in fact, emanate from a member of the genus *canis*, but from an anthropomorphic creature who, in the dark night, pretends to be a dog, from a lost mimic who has temporarily renounced his idiom for that of the dogs. Thus he kills two birds with one stone: he finds people and cheats dogs. Necessity and playfulness go hand in hand. The ludic element plays a very important part in this situation: as a hypocritical simulator, the player finds his way by pretending to be a dog. Eventually he will no longer need to bark, having returned to his mother tongue, the same one that he had to twist and turn in order to produce the sounds of the canine language.

Is it certain, though, that he will find his own kinsfolk, people who speak his language? Has it been established that his steps and barks will lead him back to his own language? We should not be hasty with our reply, for the situation of our nocturnal wanderer is quite complex. Complex enough, quite possibly, to surpass even his own evaluation: he may overestimate the impact of his ploy and his influence, if any, on the dogs. In any case, he runs a big risk by barking, all the more so in view of his nocturnal solitude. What if, upon finding his tribe, he did not find his language? What if he could only bark in response to their questions? What if he were no longer capable of using the language of his family, this language grown so familiar from his days in the cradle, if not before, this other language that he learned by imitating the movement of his mother's lips? The possibility cannot be discounted, its unlikelihood notwithstanding. Nighttime is, as you all know, the time of magic, full of witchcraft and sorcery. It would come as no surprise, then, if under the influence of some strange spell, the man changed into a dog or if the barker, having lost sight of the rules of the game (and therefore of himself) were to start barking in earnest. Nobody imitates with impunity: just think of all the disputes that take place between actors. Mimicry and dealing in shadows are dangerous undertakings: shadows can harden and counterfeit barks could displace articulate language. Just imagine: a man is imitating a dog. He grows tired of this game at a certain point, decides that he has had enough and wants to return to his former seriousness (one does not spend all of one's time imitating dogs, after all). So our player decides to stop the game, but is unpleasantly surprised to find that he cannot utter the words that he could once pronounce. He concentrates his efforts, coughs, clears his throat (assuming, of course, that he is still capable of performing such gestures), shakes himself, breathes heavily, and repeats the entire experiment several times to no avail. He cannot speak; the sounds that leave his mouth are barks, irrevocably.

How, then, would his tribe react? His case is rather strange, and they have never seen anything like it: none of the myths and tales that circulate within the tribe deals with a man who starts barking one day and then. . . . Weary with despair (sometimes they tell themselves that it is better just to laugh about it), they surround their wayward son and lament his fate. Eventually, however, irritation gains the upper hand. They do not disown him, of course; he is still one of them, they maintain a certain solidarity (up to a point) with his misfortune, they put their hand on their heart and proclaim that they will never ever leave him to his fate. Little by little, however, a certain *malaise* takes over, and he becomes the sole topic of conversation (it is worth pointing out that nothing has ever warranted such extensive discussion in the tribe; everyone sets out to prove that he or she is not a barker). Troubling symptoms appear: our sad hero spends a great deal of time with dogs,[3] takes a liking to gnawing bones and develops an intense hatred of cats. He still understands what he is told, of course, and what people say to each other, but since he can only express himself in barks he forces himself to modulate. His barks vary according to time and place: he shouts, groans, yaps, screams, makes voices. When his kinsfolk discuss serious matters, he expresses his opinion in an improper, profane yapping that troubles even the most sacred ceremonies. The sorcerer is especially irritated by his inability to cure or exorcise the canine demons that possess our hero's body. Since he cannot own up to his failure (much less so when his professional prestige is at stake), he offers the following explanation as he points an accusing finger at our hero: "This individual is a mimic who bears our tribe ill-will." The accusation does not quite come off with the galvanizing effect he had anticipated (the sorcerer, of course, blames the reticent whom he accuses of suffering from canine influences). The barker is not put to death, nor is he chased out of the settlement and stoned. Instead his jaws (his snout?) are kept shut during ritual ceremonies: two men keep his head locked between their strong arms and thus keep him from yapping.

All of this is only a hypothesis, however. I should stop playing with words and barks, threading animal metaphors, tracing nocturnal walks, and weaving a discourse whose thread threatens to divide indefinitely in view of the immense number of possible combinations.

Then again, can I leave the barker all alone in the thick of the night? My heart won't let me. Besides, I have to know what will happen to him, I have to know how the story will end.

Let us begin again. Dogs designate human habitation to the lost traveler. All he has to do now is confidently direct himself toward his kinsfolk, guided by these promising barks. Actually I am being too optimistic in saying that the tribe he finds will be his own. There are dogs barking everywhere and those he hears are not necessarily the right ones. Everything could, in fact, be decided differently, by a most improbable roll of the dice, a move leading to the possibility of unfamiliar dogs. The fate that I would personally choose for the nocturnal wanderer does not count; his itinerary has a logic of its own and I cannot do anything to help him. The best I can do is try to predict the possibilities available to his steps and to this speech.

There are only two possibilities at first sight (nocturnal visibility notwithstanding) and therefore two possible epilogues: the itinerant will either find his own kinsfolk or he will happen upon a bunch of strangers. Other endings will prove necessary, however, especially in view of the established fact that every epilogue is a prologue.

Here, then, is one of the possibilities, one that you could not possibly have imagined: the dogs that answer the traveler's call might not be real. They could be lost bedouin who in turn are imitating dogs in order to find their way. If that is the case then a double trap is being set: mimicry is being resorted to on both sides, real dogs are thought to exist on both sides and, finally, only make-believe dogs are known to exist on both sides. At a certain moment they will meet, all will be undeceived and the search will have to start all over again.

Assuming that the dogs that answer the call are real, there is no guarantee that they are close to human habitation. They could be lost dogs. Dogs do get lost: despite their instinct, their alertness, these vigilant animals have been known to get lost. They make mistakes in any case, as witness their mistaking a false bark for a real one and a man for a dog.

Fake dogs, real dogs, and other narrative possibilities tempt me, but I will have to leave them by the way for the time being; I have other fish to fry.[4] So, as he hears the dogs bark, the wanderer says to himself, "I will either find strangers or my own people. Dogs are monolingual; the ones that I know bark in the same way as those that I don't know. At night all dogs bark in the same way." Still feeling optimistic, I will leave him to direct his steps toward the sounds he hears, knowing full well that he will find neither the rest nor the security that he so ardently desires. A great surprise awaits him. He approaches, his heart beats, he sees his kinsfolk and realizes that the unimaginable has come to pass: instead of speaking the language that they usually speak, they are, in fact, barking. Their desire to find their lost child was so extreme that they started barking to signal their presence and the location of the settlement. There he is among them, then, greeted by barks instead of words of welcome. What happened to him, or rather what almost happened to him, what could have happened to him, what should have happened to him has now happened to his clan.

Unless of course the entire settlement has lost its way, is looking for the camp and its fires which, at this remove, are about as useless as stars; unless the entire settlement has gone out in search of the language that was squandered so inconsiderately, the language that they treated so contemptuously and wiped out so gradually to the point where little remains apart from a bark that reverberates in vain.

Campfires are burning somewhere and it is probably their reflection that they see in the sky. The members of the tribe have deserted the settlement and have gone in search of the lost child and the lost idiom. They bark as they stray, and their straying will necessitate their consulting the stars on the location of their camp. The latter, too, is lost or, alternatively, is inhabited by strangers. The wanderer quickens his step during this time, under the mistaken impression that he has found what he was looking for: the dogs have barked, and just around the corner campfires have added to the evidence. Displays of emotion will not, as you may have guessed, take place: on one hand those that he likes are gone, and on the other hand the new settlers are not particularly hospitable (let me add that they will put out their campfires in order to discourage their unwelcome guest).

Here I need to digress slightly in order to prepare you for what is about to follow (what you will hear is quite extraordinary). I have to retrace my steps back to my starting point and to the word *mustanbih*, a word that connotes wandering and the hope of provoking barks as well as campfires. Barking by itself is not enough as a designation of human dwelling-places. As a sign of human presence, it is necessary but inconclusive (given that lost dogs exist). Its purpose is to lead to another irrefutable index: flames and smoke. Now, if the people that he is about to meet are inhospitable, how are they to put out the fire? They ask their mother to urinate on it.[5] She straddles the hearth and releases a thin stream of urine (nothing particularly copious since, being a stingy mother with stingy children, she does not willingly part with her own urine). The poet does not tell us if this parsimonious quantity of liquid is enough to put out the fire (then again the fire itself must have been quite weak; those who retain their urine do not squander their firewood) or if the results of the mother's compromise are satisfactory. The wanderer, in any case, will not be received. I would advise him, moreover, to move on as quickly as possible before he is torn to shreds by the starved dogs of the miserly (hungry and thirsty) tribe.[6]

He risks a different but no less disappointing destiny if his would-be hosts turn out to be generous. There are dogs on the prowl in the vicinity, but they are cowardly dogs who no longer bark. Their masters find themselves entertaining more often than not, and in the constant comings and goings these dogs lose their sense of direction, inundated as they are by an uninterrupted flow of vertical beings requesting food and shelter. They have been called to order so often that they have lost the habit of emitting canine sounds; besides they are usually too busy eating the abundant scraps that the guests give them. They are, in other words, as charitable as their masters, even though their motives are different. This idyllic scene leaves me feeling skeptical, however, leaves me begging for more. First of all, dogs who no longer bark, dogs who have been condemned to silence, dogs who merely open their mouths for eating: are these still dogs? I would also like to believe the generosity of their owners, but how am I to find these people if no bark indicates the campsite? I also suspect them of a parsimony deeper than that of the miserly tribe we have just left behind: the latter did not, after all, muzzle their dogs, and even though they put out their fires I still felt their reassuring presence, I knew that there were people there and that they communicated their presence to me through the mediation of their dogs. Communication with those who have kept their dogs from barking, on the other hand, is impossible. Imagine, if you will: I pass by them and not one aural sign guides me toward them. I keep telling myself that they are there and that every step I take takes me farther away from their camp. I bark in vain, there are no responses.

All the time, we will assume that our wanderer sees the campfires of a foreign tribe; we will assume that these foreigners are speakers and that the barker finds his tongue once again as he approaches them. What now? No matter what he does, he will be seen as an animal. When two languages meet, one of them is necessarily linked to animality. Speak like me or you are an animal. I would have to speak from a position of strength in order to speak in this way, otherwise I would be considered an animal. There is no way that we can speak of conflict in this case: for a conflict to arise the two opponents must be on equal, or at least comparable, footing. Lions fight tigers, but are quite content to simply devour rabbits or dogs. The state of bilingualism does not evoke the image of two adversaries approaching one another, armed with nets and tridents. In this case, one of the gladiators is already on the ground and is getting ready to receive the death blow. (In the annals of Rome, none of the Caesars took pity on a grounded gladiator.)

Our hero will soon discover all of this at his own expense. The strangers, whose language he does not speak, mistake him for an animal, not necessarily a dog (he has stopped barking in their presence) but a monkey. A monkey imitating not the language of dogs but the barking of foreigners. As long as he does not speak like them, he is considered a monkey. He knows himself to be a monkey, and an asthmatic one at that. Every time he opens his mouth, he must exert a significant effort, an effort that sets him apart from the others who speak comfortably, like people playing themselves, who speak as they breathe, and whose breathing is calm and regular. It is the effort that marks him as a monkey and mimic. There is no such thing as an effortless imitation. The monkey, who is none other than our recent wanderer, tries to get rid of his simian character in order to be seen as one of his human interlocutors. If they, who regard him with a mixture of curiosity and sickness, were on a footing equal to his he would not have had to resort to imitation: he imitates because he *is not* those that he imitates, he imitates what he cannot be, a fact of which he is well aware. The others, too, know, or eventually discover, that imitation does not make a man (as opposed to the dogs who, as we have seen, are easily tricked in games of imitation). The paradox of mimicry resides in the fact that the mimic wants to belong but in the end marks his or her own separation. Only what one is not is reproduced; "like" does not make an identity. Imitation lives on the rupture between being and seeming. An imitation, even if it attains perfection, will never abolish the difference that occasions it in the first place.[7]

On the other side of the mirror the interlocutors—the monkey's audience—are in an enviable situation. They have nothing to hide, they appear as what they are, they act in broad daylight, in the noonday sun (the one that casts no suspicious shadows). The monkey, on the other hand, is a born hypocrite; he always hides something, an entirely disavowed shadow zone goes with him everywhere. What he hides is not what he shows. Let us not forget that he was once lost at night in the desert, and that he is now lost among people, all because he is a mimic, because he dissimulates.

Curiously enough the monkey's observers like to play at this game of imitation from time to time. Monkeys are amusing animals after all and everybody mimics a mimic. They therefore spend their spare time imitating the appearance, rather than the essence, of the monkey. Now, the appearance of the monkey is an image of what they are, since the monkey forces himself to imitate them. In reproducing his image, therefore, they reproduce their own, slightly deformed, but theirs all the same.

I shall refer once again to Jāḥiz, not the Jāḥiz of the *Book of Animals* but rather the later one, the one who wrote the *Book of Eloquence*. Trust me, I shall continue to speak of non-anthropomorphic creatures, because neither he (Jāḥiz) nor I are capable of deliberating eloquence without evoking animals. Eloquence is always discussed in relation to the animal.

Jāḥiz wrote that an author cannot be proficient in two languages (*Animals* 1: 76–7). I suspect that he himself was monolingual, even though he uses foreign words on occasion. Scholars have gone (and still go) through a great deal of trouble to decide whether or not he spoke Farsi, as if it mattered. The fact of the matter is that Jāḥiz did not need to know any language other than Arabic, for the simple reason that there was, in his time, only one language, namely Arabic. All the rest was mere noise, a vast cacophony of yelps, neighs, and caterwauls. Jāḥiz was a happy writer.[8] He liked to laugh and his laughter was honest, unencumbered by afterthought. There were times when he experimented on real animals, such as snakes and flies (*Animals* 4: 113; 3: 349–50). He also had occasion to observe individual cases of people who spoke like animals, or rather who did not speak and therefore resembled animals. As proof let me mention this page in the *Book of Eloquence* where we see some domestic animals, a blind man, some hybrid creatures, and a mimic grouped together (69–70).

Why did they meet and what are they going to do together? The mimic (*ḥākiya*), says Jāḥiz, reproduces the dog's barking and the braying of the donkey; he also reproduces the attitude and gestures of the blind man, and finally he mimics the faulty pronunciation of non-Arab ethnic groups. Imitation makes us laugh at the expense of the other and reconfirms our sense of "ourselves." It presupposes a certain complicity between imitator and spectator, both of whom are present. The object of their mimicry, however, is "absent," elsewhere, confined to the trap of the third person (see Benveniste 228), even if he or she seems to say "I" through the voice of the performer and produces the semblance of a "you" for the spectator's benefit. Imitation is only made possible by the feeling of superiority that the spectators feel vis-à-vis the character portrayed.

You will have noticed that each of the imitated creatures suffers from a certain lack or deficiency. The dog and donkey lack articulate language, the blind man lacks sight, and the non-Arab the ability to pronounce guttural sounds. Jāḥiz points out that a given individual was recognized as being from Sind, from Khurāsān, or from Ahwāz from their Arabic pronunciation, because each group had its own set of idiosyncrasies (*Eloquence* 1: 69). Under these conditions, opening one's mouth amounts to self-betrayal, the revelation of one's difference and one's lack. It would be much simpler to walk on in silence with clenched teeth wherever people are to be found. But would a poet resign himself to silence in an age where poetry was not only written and read but recited and heard? There is a story told on this subject regarding two poets (Abū ʿAṭāʾ Al-Sindī and Ziyād Al-Aʿjam) whose pronunciation was deficient and who, in order to avoid embarrassment, hired slaves to recite their poems. Imagine: before an important figure, the poet stays silent while a representative recites his poem. The poem itself is thus entrusted to two people successively: the composer who creates it in the form of a quiet murmur, and the performer who ex-presses and presents it on the platter that is his tongue. During ceremonies the poet hears his own poem uttered by someone else. He needs a speaker in order to speak.

Severed tongues and ruptured eardrums are two phenomena with analogous consequences. Remember the deaf musician who was allowed, from time to time, to conduct the orchestra that played his compositions. The first time, the experiment produced little more than sonic discord. Eventually, however, the matter was resolved: a second conductor was appointed and kept hidden from the audience. They saw a musician who was merely playing the part of a conductor as he directed his own inner music. We have, therefore, two conductors, two audiences, and two scores, one audible and the other inaudible. The latter is heard only by the deaf composer who plays it to himself (the orchestra refuses to play along with him) and is thus kept out of step with its audible counterpart. The poet with no tongue is always a step ahead. If you watch his lips closely you will see them moving, mapping out the words that the speaker prepares to pronounce.

Severed tongues are castrated tongues. As you leaf through the seven volumes that compose the *Book of Animals*, do not be surprised if you run into castrati, creatures of questionable gender, neither male nor female (1: 105, 108) or animals whose status is complex and whose complexion complicated. To lose one's tongue is to lose one's linguistic aptitude. Losing one's language is unfortunate but not irreparable. On the other hand, losing language *per se*, losing one's tongue, the muscle lodged in one's mouth; such a loss is insurmountable. One of the questions that Jāḥiz neglects in his chapter on dogs, surprisingly enough, is whether or not dogs need tongues to bark. Is a tongue as necessary to the barking of a dog as it is to human speech?

But whatever became of our nocturnal wanderer? He has followed his trajectory, barking all the while. He is perhaps in a place abandoned even by its dogs (canine deserters *do* exist). If that is the case, he will bark all night to no avail.

As he writes these lines, the author is suddenly struck by a very disturbing possibility. What if, as he writes about dogs, he suddenly finds himself transformed into one? What if, in speaking about animals, he were to lose his tongue (or rather his tongues, since he speaks several languages)? What if, all of a sudden, he started barking? This risk is shared by the reader, who is no longer immune, and risks opening his mouth to produce, not phonemes and morphemes, not distinctive and significant units, but rather bark after identical bark.[9] If this possibility is a strong source of anguish, just clench your teeth, put your hand on your mouth, and think about something else.

Notes

"Les mots canins" from *Du bilinguisme*. Ed. Abdelkebir Khatibi. Paris: Denoël, 1985. 205–18.

1. Abū ᶜUthman ᶜAmr ibn Baḥr ibn Maḥbūb al-Kinānī al-Baṣrī (c. 776–869 AD), one of the most prolific Arabic prose writers of the First ᶜAbbasid period (749–940). Al-Jāḥiz's ugliness was proverbial, and his name ("the pop-eyed") derives from the Arabic verb *jaḥaza* (to bulge) and refers to the rather extreme protrusion of his eyes. His works cover a wide range of themes and a great deal of paper. Best known among them are *Kitāb al-Ḥayawān* (*The Book of Animals*), where observations of animal psychology and physiology coexist with passages on philosophy, anthropology, and literary history, and *Kitāb al-Bayān wa al-Tabyīn* (*The Book of Eloquence and Exposition*), a polemical rhetoric and selective inventory of the Arabic literary canon extant in the ninth century AD.—Trans.

2. Or rather, "he who provokes the barking of dogs by imitating them." See Al-Jāḥiz, *Animals* 379.

3. We ought to mention, in passing, the massive problems that he thus creates for the canine community.

4. Kilito uses the French equivalent of this expression; "j'ai d'autres chats à fouetter," literally, "I have other cats to whip." He goes on to exploit the issue paronomastically; "des chats dont j'ai déjà caressé le pelage électrique et dont il faudra maintenant coincer la queue dans une porte" ("cats whose fur I have already rubbed the wrong way and whose tail will now find itself trapped in a door").—Trans.

5. I swear that I am not making things up. I am only paraphrasing two lines by the poet Al-Akhṭal, the first of which is quoted by Jāḥiz in *Animals* (1: 384).

6. The dogs might even be rabid: Jāḥiz points out that a man bitten by a rabid dog himself starts barking (*Animals* 2: 10–11).

7. Kilito's language here is strongly reminiscent of Mallarmé's: "Une imitation, quand bien même elle atteindrait un très haut degré de perfection, jamai n'abolira la différence" recalls the central sentence of *Un coup de dés:* "Jamais, quand bien même lancé du fond d'un naufrage, un coup de dés n'abolira le hasard." —Trans.

8. There were numerous "bilingual" writers during the first four centuries after the *Hegira* (622 AD, the date of the Prophet Muḥammad's flight from Mecca to Medina and the starting point of the Muslim calendar). I find it hard to believe that they were all miserable. Misery is, on the other hand, the common lot of today's Arab francophone writers (whether they write in French or in Arabic) who speak of the hiatus, fracture, and fissure attached to their condition.

9. It is of course possible that not all of the barks will be identical. Remember the actor at Stanislavski's Moscow Theater who managed to create forty different messages from the expression, "good evening," by varying his expressive tint (mentioned in Jakobson 23).

Works Cited

Al-Jāḥiz. *The Book of Animals.* [*Kitāb al-Ḥayawān.*] Ed. ᶜAbd Al-Salām Muḥammad Hārūn. Vol. 1. Cairo: 1939.
———. *The Book of Eloquence.* [*Kitāb al-Bayān wa al-Tabyīn.*] Ed. ᶜAbd Al-Salām Muḥammad Hārūn. Vol. 1. Cairo: 1960.
Barthes, Roland. "Le dernier des écrivains heureux." *Essais critiques.* Paris: Seuil, 1964. 94–100.
Benveniste, E. *Problèmes de linguistique générale.* Paris: Gallimard, 1966.
Jakobson, R. "Linguistics and Poetics." *Selected Writings III.* Ed. Stephen Rudy. The Hague: Mouton, 1981.

Power and Authorities

Interrupted Journeys
The Cultural Politics of Indian Reburial
Pemina Yellow Bird and Kathryn Milun

I. Interrupted Journeys

INSIDE THE CIRCULAR *house made of earth and timber, the sounds of grieving are heard. It is early afternoon; a mother prepares her warrior son's torn body for burial. His father is wracked with sorrow, he is going through his belongings, seeking the things his man-child will need on his journey to the Spirit World. Neither speaks: they know what must be done for this child of theirs as he makes his way to the Creator's Land.*

His body is gently undressed and bathed with sage water. He is then marked with sacred paint so that his clan relatives will know he is coming and will watch for him. He is dressed in a finely beaded shirt and leggings, moccasins and robe. His hair is washed and braided, and his father attaches a wooden knife to a small braid on top of his head to acknowledge his death in hand-to-hand combat with the enemy. Upon seeing this, the mother breaks out in fresh tears and, wailing, cuts her hair and smears ashes from the fireplace on her face. In the onset of her grieving, she had severed her littlest fingers at the first joint; she feels pain only from her broken heart, however, and ignores the bleeding stumps.

Together, mother and father place in the robe weapons their son's medicine received on his first vision quest, the chokecherry pegs he used at the Sundance and the long strings of beads he loved to wear around his neck. Together, they sew shut the beautiful beaded buffalo robe and carry their son's body out to the burial grounds.

The entire village silently falls in behind them. Only sounds of grieving are heard. They are met by the keeper of the people's sacred pipe and bundle. By the natural laws of their living religion he is fed, given water for his journey and told he is no longer of this world. It is time to begin his journey to the world of the spirits. Prayers for his safe passage are said; a going home song is sung for him by his male relatives. Anguish and sorrow, pain and loss hang in the air and on the faces of the people as they give up this young man so full of promise and hope. A ball of sage is given to each of the relatives to cleanse themselves with, and after he is placed in the receiving breast of Mother Earth and covered with her, the sage is thrown in the direction he is to travel. As his spirit begins his journey, a gust of wind marks his leaving. His inconsolable parents stay with him for four days, fasting and praying, calling on relatives already in the Spirit World to watch for him and make the crossing with him.

Centuries later, the peaceful sounds of the prairie wind blowing through the cottonwoods and the songs of the meadowlarks are disrupted by the sound of an approaching car. The car stops at the edge of the burial grounds, and a man and a woman climb out. From the trunk of the car they produce rope, shovels, screens, and brushes. After carefully measuring and marking the ground, they begin to remove the layer of prairie grasses contained within their rope-boundary. With hand-shovels they carefully and slowly remove the earth layer by layer until they encounter what they have come for: the earthly remains of a young man.

The woman squeals with delight when she sees the belongings of the young man. "Look! This medicine bundle is still intact! And look—hundreds of those old glass beads! These will look great in that new display we're doing next week!" The man is more interested in the body. He is painstakingly brushing away the remaining dirt and hide remnants. He glances at the pile of soil samples they have gathered and decides to take some more, just in case this one proves interesting enough to mention in the paper he will be giving next fall at the Plains Historical Conference.

They spend the rest of the afternoon robbing the grave of the young man. They do so without qualms: they have a permit, this is State land, the dead body and the personal belongings of this Indian are State property, they are free to do with them as they wish. The law is on their side and they know it; they helped write it: "Unmarked Indian graves will be protected and preserved as a first priority. When preservation cannot be achieved, or when it is proven that excavation will advance American science, unmarked graves may be excavated only by a qualified archeologist who has been issued a permit by the State Historic Preservation Officer. All contents of the grave become the property of the State and must be analyzed by state-of-the-art methods. Human remains and burial artifacts will be curated in perpetuity by the State for the edification and benefit of its citizens."

While packing up their things, they make plans for the next day's work: they will go to the older section of the burial grounds in hopes of finding some pre-Columbian artifacts. Excited with the possibilities ahead, they laugh and joke on the walk back to the car. They do not see the young man whirling above them, desperately trying to understand what has happened, knowing only that he was pulled from the Spirit World to witness the appropriation of his body and belongings. He is crying, begging them to put back the things they stole, to leave him alone. He feels himself being pulled along with them as they drive away, and the pulling does not stop until he is stored in a box and placed on a shelf in a room filled with hundreds of others like himself: crying, pleading spirits, lost and pitiful.

When many, many years have passed a woman is awakened from a sound sleep by four angry warrior spirits who repeatedly beg her to hurry, hurry and get their bodies away from the white man's museum and back in the earth, for they are tired of whirling, lost and pitiful, and they long to return to the land of light, of goodness and love . . .

II. The Case of North Dakota

Pemina Yellow Bird spent a number of years fighting to get the dead bodies and grave goods of her Indian ancestors repatriated from the North Dakota State Historical Society and properly reburied. She speaks here with Kathryn Milun about that experience, beginning by talking about where she grew up . . .

Yellow Bird: For the most part I was born and raised on Fort Berthold Reservation in Western North Dakota. Parts of my childhood were lived elsewhere but we always came home. My mother participated in the relocation program . . .

Milun: What's a relocation program?

Yellow Bird: During the fifties the Feds tried one last major attempt at assimilation and they instituted what was known as the relocation program where they would give money to Indians to leave the reservation and travel to urban areas to look for work. So my mother tried this but we ended up coming home. So that is for the most part where I grew up. After school I lived in Denver for a few years, kicked around there, then came back to North Dakota. That's where I met my husband, Michael, in Grand Forks. My involvement with politics began when I was working as an administrative assistant for our tribal chairwoman (for the Three Affiliated Tribes). This was after I had already married and had my children and Michael was working as our tribe's human resources administrator.

Milun: It's a complicated story but eventually you were appointed by the Governor of North Dakota, a man who wanted to see the state's Indian population better represented in state government, to serve on the board of the North Dakota State Historical Society (SHS). You were the second Indian ever to be appointed to the board of that institution. What had you heard about the SHS before this time?

Yellow Bird: Well, all I knew of the State Historical Society was that it was a repository. They had archives and a museum. That was it. I had never even been to their museum.

Milun: So this was a repository for North Dakota's history. What did that mean to you?

Yellow Bird: Their version of North Dakota's history. The version of the indigenous peoples' history as written by the conquerors.

Milun: How did you come to find out that the State Historical Society was also holding so many of your dead ancestors?

Yellow Bird: Let's see. My appointment began in July of 1985. Sometime in the following November I got a letter from the executive director of the North Dakota Indian Affairs Commission.[1] She told me that a meeting was being held at the State Historical Society because some Indian remains had been brought up from under the ground. In accordance with a prior agreement with North Dakota's Indian tribes, the SHS staff had agreed to report such incidents to the Indian Affairs Commission. She wanted me to attend that particular meeting and hear the report on what had happened, so I went there and members of the SHS staff, specifically the state and assistant state archeologist, were showing the SHS board members and others from the Indian Affairs Commission a slide show about Indian burial mounds and different things. They mentioned an incident at a village that the archeologists call Double Ditch but we call Village of Yellow Earth where two non-Indian men evidently were poking around at a site and claimed that they "found" two skulls lying by the edge of the Missouri River. Someone saw these individuals leave with the skulls, wrote down their license number and turned it in to the police. The police tracked them down and found the skulls in these guys' homes still wet with shellac.

Milun: I've heard about this sort of thing. The skulls get used as book ends or end up on someone's coffee table as a conversation piece.

Yellow Bird: Well, when I heard about that I was shocked. I just could not believe that anybody would do that. To me it was just so alien, so unthinkable. So after the meeting I got hold of the state and assistant state archeologist and asked where the skulls were now. And they said, Well they're over there in the lab. The lab? Oh yeah, you know in the lab, in the Heritage Center [where the State Historical Society is housed]. So I said, Well what are you going to do with them? And they said, Well, we'll just put them in the vault with the others. The others? Yeah you want to see? And I thought geez, what do they mean "the others?" So I said, Yeah I want to see. So we went to the Heritage Center and down into the basement where an armed guard was standing next to a vault. He took a card and inserted it into the wall. It was like a bank vault door: a big handle that you have to spin and then the door pops open. They lead me into this warehouse-like room that was filled from the floor to the ceiling with boxes and boxes of remains of dead Indian people. And I said at that time—you know I was just shocked, it knocked the wind out of me—Are these all Indian people? And they go, Yup, they're all Indians. The non-Indians get reburied but we bring the Indians here for study. For study? What do you mean for study? Well, we don't actually study them much yet because we don't have the funds. There were numbered drawers just filled with Indian bodies.

There was one box that said "forty-four pieces of human skeletal remains." And I looked at that and I said to the state archeologist, Is that forty-four pieces of one person or forty-four different people? And he said, Or any combination in between. We have no idea what or who we have here. We haven't had the time or the money or the staff to analyze them. And I said, These have to go back into the ground. The minute I said that I felt coming from outside of me a feeling of fear that I have never known before or since. It was unearthly. I just felt all this fear. And then that quickly changed to anger and then to a dismal, heartbreaking kind of sadness and I just cried and cried. And I put out tobacco—they brought me an old coffee can or cup or something to burn it in and I faced my tobacco to the west and I made those old ones a promise that I would put them back in the ground. I felt so bad for them because I could feel how they were feeling. You see it was their feelings I was picking up on and that's why I felt the fear and anger and then finally that bottomless sadness. I knew they were not happy there. I knew that. So after we came out of there, within a couple of weeks, the board of the State Historical Society met. We had our agenda all fixed out and I waited until we got to new business and I raised my hand, stood up, and told all the board members and whatever staff was present that those remains that were in the basement had to go back into the earth. I said that those people down there were suffering, that the way we believed was that when you take them out of ground like that—something which is to us unthinkable and horrifying—they can't stay in the spirit world because they're no longer at rest. They can't stay in our world either because they don't have a body. They wander between the two worlds pitiful and lost and crying. So I told them all these things. I told them, They have to go back into the ground, this is wrong. And everybody sort of looked everywhere else but at me; they coughed and felt uncomfortable and squirmed. By the time I had finished I was crying so I sat down. There wasn't a word said. Finally someone said, Any other new business? Nothing? O. K. This meeting is adjourned. And everyone got up and left. The minutes came in the mail a few weeks later. Not a single remark of mine was contained in those minutes. It was as if I had never spoken. The next board meeting three months later the same thing happened. I waited until new business, got up and said the same thing. It never appeared in the minutes.

Milun: So if we looked at the minutes of the State Historical Society we'd never find a record of this conflict.

Yellow Bird: That's right. Nothing. So a solid year goes by. Four board meetings and I do the same thing at the end of each one, standing up and saying this is wrong, it's got to change. So I'm starting to feel frustrated. The last time I said something about it I added, And why is it that my remarks never appear in the minutes? I notice that the least little comment made by my non-Indian fellow board members appears in your minutes but I can talk and talk and talk about these ancestors of ours and not a word appears in the minutes. I said, Are not my words as good as theirs? Again everybody began to cough and look everywhere else but at me. Well it was very quiet for a long time after I said that. I was starting to get very angry. One board member finally raised his hand and made a motion that we direct the staff [of the State Historical Society] to write a discussion paper on the issue of reburial to edify the board so that the board could form an opinion on it. The staff directed to do that were the state and assistant state archeologist. Around the time of the next board meeting, the position paper came to us in the mail. I read it. I went ballistic. I was incensed. The entire paper was written utterly in the interests of science, academia, and the museum world. It not only did not represent Indian interests, but the few times Indian people were mentioned in there I found insulting and offensive. Such as "if the board does decide to rebury, they better be prepared to pay medicine men because they expect payment for the things they do."

Milun: Up until that time had you heard of other efforts by Indians across the country to see their ancestors in museums reburied?

Yellow Bird: Yes. I had talked to different people. I knew that there were some elders in my tribe who were aware that these remains were there. They were not aware, however, that there was anything they could do about it. They felt the same way I did but they felt that their hands were tied. They didn't think that they had any resources[2] or the ability to go after them. Also the North Dakota Indian Affairs Commission, five years prior to my discovery of these remains being stored in the State Historical Society, had passed a resolution directing the State Historical Board to rebury these remains. This came out because the assistant state archeologist with the assistance of a state legislator from Jamestown who calls himself a "lay archeologist" dismantled five mounds that were apparently endangered for some reason. According to information I got from another archeologist who was opposed to dismantling the burial mounds, the assistant state archeologist could (and should) have followed the law that was in place at the time and avoided disturbing the mounds. But the state agents chose to dismantle them.

Milun: By "dismantle" you mean they take the mounds apart, dig up the graves, and send the bones to the State Historical Society?

Yellow Bird: Yes. They destroyed those mounds. And according to the assistant state archeologist's account these mounds "yielded seventy-five individuals." One of the women they dug up they discovered had been suffering at the time from tuberculosis. And this was supposed to be such a major scientific discovery that Indian people suffered from tuberculosis prior to contact with Europeans. And it thus made all of those dead Indian "individuals" precious beyond compare. So at that time the Indian Affairs Commission said they wanted those remains reburied. They also made the agreement I spoke of earlier which was that they wanted to be notified and consulted whenever Indian graves were opened or otherwise "endangered" in the State of North Dakota. But this resolution was sent three times to the State Historical Society and it was ignored each time. They never responded to it. My problem with that resolution was that it never questioned what was done to these ancestors while they were being "scientifically" studied. But it didn't matter because the State Historical Society ignored them anyway. Five years later then this issue sort of exploded when the tribes and everybody became aware of how bad it was. We learned that there were literally hundreds of Indian bodies involved. The SHS had originally given me a very conservative estimate of anywhere between two and eight hundred individuals. But as it turned out, the state archeologist estimated that it could be upwards of a thousand.

Milun: In that vault in the State Historical Society's basement?

Yellow Bird: Yes. All Indians, he told me. So it was when the discussion paper came out that the war was on. The tribes united and formed a unified position on reburial with the unwavering support of the Governor and his staff. Our tribal councils then created the North Dakota Intertribal Reinterment Committee who officially represented the tribal governments of their respective tribes on the issue of reburial and repatriation. This committee was formed in 1988 and we have worked for reburial ever since. It took us all together from the very beginning five years. In January of 1990 we reburied what remained of the North Dakota State Historical Society's—and I'm quoting—"anthropological collection," once the pride of the SHS. There are still twenty boxes plus two bags of ancestors remaining and we are currently negotiating with the United States Corps of Engineers to get them back for reburial hopefully this summer [1992]. We reburied the ancestors that were returned to us without any further analysis,[3] without having to prove to anybody that we were related to these ancestors, which I don't think has ever been repeated in any other state. To my knowledge, in all other instances tribes have had to bear the burden of proof, to prove to state or local or federal authorities that these individuals are indeed their relatives. And the remains in all other cases I'm aware of did undergo a certain amount of analysis before reburial occurred. So you see our case is quite unique in this respect. In North Dakota we reburied everything, all of their belongings, everything that came out of the ground with them, even bits of earth, went back to the earth with them. In January of 1990, hundreds of our ancestors were reburied. In the meantime other reburials have occurred in the state where we have gotten back ancestors from local or private individuals. And the work continues.

III. Imperialist Nostalgia: The Cultural Politics of Indian Reburial

In the past few years, under enormous pressure from Native American groups throughout the country, major museums and university departments of anthropology have begun returning thousands of Native America's dead—both the bodies and funeral objects—to Indian tribes for reburial. The number of bodies involved is staggering: the Smithsonian has 18,500 Native American human remains; Harvard's Peabody Museum has another 5,000; the National Park Service has perhaps as many as 20,000. The Native American Rights Fund estimates that there might be as many as 2.5 million such Indian remains in museums, state historical societies, universities, and private collections in the United States—and these figures do not include the number of grave goods or sacred objects that are either held by such institutions or are bringing in a fine penny on the antiquities market (see Preston).

The conflict over the return and reburial of Native American dead, as we shall see, raises important issues for postcolonial politics today. Most people do not realize that until very recently, Indian graves have not received the same legal protection as those of non-Indian ancestry: up until the fall of 1990, when Congress finally passed a conservative version of the many bills Native American groups have been lobbying for on this issue (Public Law 101-601, Native American Grave Protection and Repatriation Act), Indian bones either excavated from a burial mound or discovered in the course of construction became the immediate property of the federal government. Even in cases in which relatives of the deceased were known, these descendants had no right under federal law to demand that the remains of their relations and the sacred objects that accompanied them be returned to the ground.

Since the early seventies, Indian groups in seventeen states have fought for and won legislation to end what we see as racist graverobbing.[4] (This has occurred, of course, only at the state, not the federal level.) Indian groups have faced greater difficulties, however, when attempting to recover for reburial the remains of their ancestors and sacred burial objects from museums. In both cases, seeking the return of their ancestors has meant winning a certain amount of public support for their cause.[5] For many Native Americans, speaking about their dead ancestors in courtrooms, in front of state legislators, and on TV goes against a deeply felt sense of the proper way to relate to the dead. Demanding the return of their "old ones" invariably has meant and continues to mean debating the treatment of their dead in mainstream sites dominated by non-Indian cultural practices. Thus, to the extent that they have been driven to engage in general public discussion on this issue, Amerindian leaders, in many cases, have been compelled to create a hybrid form of cultural practice to deal with the misapprehensions of powerful mainstream institutions regarding Native American culture.

A. *Translating Indians for Mainstream Cultural Consumption*

How has mainstream America perceived its indigenous peoples? We offer the following examples from recent American history. In both the early seventies and the late eighties, the environmentalist movement used Indians as symbols of the proper attitude one should adopt toward the environment. Earth Day's first posters displayed native peoples canoeing up rivers of industrial waste with tears running down their faces. White counterculture youths in both periods looked to the American Indian as a symbol of "authenticity." The headbands and fringed leather jackets of the late sixties were inspired by traditional native clothing. Carlos Casteneda's books on the teachings of Don Juan, the Yaqui medicine man, circulated a popularized version of "Indian spirituality" inspiring many "wanna-bes" to set off on pilgrimages to the closest reservation and hang out with real Indians. In a similar although much more commodified form, New Age philosophies marketed shamanism and a variety of Indian spiritual teachings to fill in the experiential vacuum heightened by the adrenal exhaustion of (eighties) consumerism. Such "quickfix" commercial remedies for spiritual crises have produced a variety of New Age Indian imitations that many Native Americans find downright degrading. Upon hearing that sweat lodges were being sold for $50 and vision quests for $150, for example, the Circle of Elders of the Indigenous Nations of North America (the representative body of traditional indigenous leadership on this continent) authorized AIM to "undertake to end the activities of the plastic medicine men." To this end the American Indian Movement (AIM) has disrupted a number of the $500-per-head, weekend-long spiritual retreats conducted by one of the more sophisticated marketeers in Colorado. As Oren Lyons, a traditional Chief of the Onondaga Nation, puts it:

> The bottom line here is that we have more need for intercultural respect today than at any time in human history. And nothing blocks respect and communication faster . . . than delusions by one party about another. We've got real problems today, problems which threaten the survival of the planet. Indians and non-Indians must confront these problems together, and this means we must have honest dialogue, but this dialogue is impossible so long as non-Indians remain deluded about things as basic as Indian spirituality. (Churchill 94)

Indian reburial, as we argue in this essay, is a material demonstration of Native American spirituality that refuses commodification and thus helps expel the consumable representations of Indian existence, be it led by museum experts or by "plastic medicine men." This is an important point. For today, as in the seventies, the most popular representations of Indians depict a fantasmatic, pre-contact people. The inference, of course, is that contemporary Indians aren't really Indians, that only their ancestors were. This is what is so problematic about the popularity of a film like *Dances with Wolves* (1990). One of the main criticisms of this film in the Indian community is that it perpetuates the illusion of a vanishing race (see Dorris). The Plains culture, as it is put at the end of the film, "came to an end thirteen years later in Nebraska." This implies that the Lakota people the movie audience has come to love were indeed exterminated by colonial agents and that "real Indians no longer live and no longer feel the vestiges of frontier policy" (Brunette 7). Thus, even though the very people who are playing the parts of nineteenth-century Lakota on the screen are presently residents of the Pine Ridge reservation in South Dakota, members of the audience can leave the theater having experienced a cathartic bout of guilt that will in no way help them connect the story they have seen with the contemporary situation in South Dakota. In many ways the dominant culture's attraction to nineteenth-century Indians resembles what anthropologist Renato Rosaldo has described as "imperialist nostalgia," a longing for the culture one has destroyed. "Imperialist nostalgia," Rosaldo writes, "uses a pose of innocent yearning both to capture people's imagination and to conceal its complicity with often brutal domination" (69).

Mainstream America's newfound love for "authentic" Indians, or its imperialist nostalgia, can in fact make contemporary Indian politics more difficult. Vine Deloria, Jr., a Lakota lawyer and professor of political science, has argued that the attempts by Indian leaders to be taken seriously by the American public in the seventies were constantly thwarted by the non-Indian public's desire to see their version of "authentic" Indians. Although a small number of books were published on contemporary Indian issues during the early seventies (*The Tortured Americans* by Robert Burnette, for example, and Deloria's *Custer Died for Your Sins*), the public turned overwhelmingly to books on the "real" Indians of yesteryear (Dee Brown's *Bury My Heart at Wounded Knee* and *The Memoirs of Chief Red Fox*—written by a 101-year-old man who claimed to be a Sioux chief although, according to Deloria, nobody from any Sioux reservation seemed to know him). Thus, while the Indian public was busy reading such books as *The New Indians* by Stan Steiner and *The Unjust Society* by Harold Cardinal (books on contemporary Indian problems), the non-Indian public was in a frenzy buying books about Indians of the last century. It is no wonder then that when Indians arrived in Washington in the fall of 1972 (a cross-country pilgrimage to publicize abuses of treaty rights referred to as the Trail of Broken Treaties) and took over and trashed the Bureau of Indian Affairs, the American public watching the event on TV was unable to understand where these Native Americans were coming from. For Deloria, America's refusal to give up its longstanding misconceptions of Indian identity is the greatest barrier to the solution of the problems of the Indians.

At this point it is necessary to recall that in the fifties America's indigenous population was itself rediscovering its religious ceremonies, celebrating them openly for the first time in decades. Ironically, during this same period Indians had to wage an intensive political struggle against the federal government's policy of relocation and termination under which many tribes saw their land—the *sine qua non* of Indian identity and spiritual life—taken away from under their feet. America's Indians also had to fight the newly created Indian Claims Commission (1946) which sought to resolve all Native American land claims with monetary compensation, yet another instance of the inability of the dominant society to understand the uncommodifiable value that native peoples place on their land. The most famous example of the incommensurability of the two systems of value is the claim of the Oglala band of the Sioux on the Black Hills, which was settled in 1974 by the court for $102 million (it has now grown to $250 million); the Sioux, refusing to be paid off for the sale of sacred lands, have not touched the money to this day. The Oglala, living in deep poverty and having exhausted court remedies for return of the land, continue to seek a legislative solution. We mention this example—and there are many others—to demonstrate that for Native Americans, traditional spiritual beliefs and practices are caught in a web of political struggle in this country.

B. Translating Indians into Archeological Resources

One of the first demands of Native American groups in drafting federal reburial legislation was to stop their dead ancestors or sacred objects from being referred to as "archeological resources" (see S 1980 Sec. 4[b]). The use of such terminology was firmly entrenched, having been standard practice since Indian remains were first collected by Thomas Jefferson. Such "scholarly" treatment of Indians, collecting their remains and sacred objects like fossils and botanical specimens, was institutionalized in the Bureau of American Ethnology as well as in the other great natural history museums established in the mid to late 1800s: the Smithsonian, the Peabody, the Chicago Field Museum. By "resourcing" North America's first inhabitants, this branch of science attempted to transform Indian ancestors as *subjects*, whose agential status was still present for their descendants, into *objects*, which were no longer capable of active participation in the world. Donna Haraway, biologist and historian of science, has written brilliantly on how science constantly transforms the world-as-active-subject into the world-as-resource. Such translations, Haraway notes, are precisely what allow science to escape accountability and responsibility. She argues that science must come to terms with the agency of the objects it studies; in other words, science must find a way to grant its objects the status of subjects. In calling for reburial, Native Americans are asking for no less.

The translation of, say, Ojibwe or Lakota burial grounds and sacred objects into the object system of archeology not only "resources" the Native American past for science, it also makes that past a part of the dominant nationalist narrative of the State in the form of a "prehistory" (in celebrating its centennial, North Dakota recently used artifacts of the Lakota past to refer to the "prehistory of North Dakota"). Needless to say, this also works at the national level. Thus is the Indian past appropriated and reshaped to serve the ends of dominant white society in the United States.

It was the Antiquities Law of 1906 that not only "protected" Native American bones, sacred objects, and sites as archeological resources, but also established the national parks system. Most people now know that the creation of these "public" places went hand in hand with the theft of reservation land and the expulsion of indigenous peoples from the parks' borders. This is why the national parks system is today one of the main repositories of Indian bones and sacred sites. Furthermore, the expulsion of Native Americans from these sites in the early twentieth century remains logically consistent with the earlier colonialist (Lockean) philosophy that viewed land in America as *terra vacantis* (empty land), salvageable—that is, convertible to property—only when "improved" by the labor of European farmers (see Cronon 54–82). It is probably no coincidence, then, that in the early twentieth century, imperialist nostalgia was able to "retrieve" those displaced Amerindians not only by inventing narratives of "our prehistory," but also by creating the popular category of the "primitive" in high modernist art.

Archeologists' specific translation of Indian bones into "knowledge" has indeed changed over time. In contrast to British archeology, which from the 1850s onward was engaged in a worldwide project of gathering evidence of humankind's progress and Britain's preeminent role, American archeology began as a predominantly colonialist venture: it engaged in the study of its own subjugated populations, viewing them as static, incapable of change, and thus inferior. With the development in the sixties of the "New Archeology," which was influenced by structuralism, American archeology no longer looked for racial types; its new interest was in discovering universal rules common to "prehistorical" peoples, rules that would be of value to modern society (see Trigger). Today's descendants of the New Archeology are the paleopathologists who claim the *knowledge* they extract from Indian bones is beneficial to all "mankind." From the paleopathologist's perspective, then, the stakes of science outweigh those of the Native American community, which is seen as merely one more minority interest group. Thus, the previously mentioned bill on Indian reburial that recently passed in Congress contains a provision that exempts the return of Indian human remains for reburial when scientific interest is compelling.

Accordingly, paleopathologists are sometimes eager to prove to indigenous peoples as well as others that their work is not only of practical value but potentially of special use to Native Americans. An example of one such attempt is provided by a paper entitled "Study of Old Human Remains: How Does It Help Present People," which was delivered by John G. Gregg, a paleopathologist who lives and works in South Dakota, at the 1989 World Archeological Congress. The theme of that year's global meeting of archeologists was "Archeological Ethics and the Treatment of the Dead"; pointedly, it was held in Vermillion, South Dakota: Indian country. Given the focus and location of the conference, we might assume that Gregg's paper would seize the occasion to present the most persuasive case that paleopathology has to offer the Indian public. Yet this was not the case. We offer the following summary of Gregg's paper to illustrate the racism implicit in such "scientific" arguments.

Gregg compares diseases present in three populations: first, in Indian skeletal remains from an eighteenth-century Arikara burial site in the Upper Missouri River Basin; second, in the present-day South Dakota Indian population (made up of a variety of tribes); and third, in all other races in the United States. In South Dakota's present-day Indian community, Gregg found that cleft-palate deformities occur at a rate two to three times higher than that found in all other races in the United States. While Gregg states that he found this disorder to be rare in the eighteenth-century Indian site (thus implying the "cause" of the deformity must be sought in today's Indian community), he also notes that the eighteenth-century site may not be an adequate indicator of the absence of cleft-palate problems for the Arikara since infants with malformed anatomies may have been "eliminated by natural selection," and their remains would thus not end up in the community cemetery. (Gregg, by the way, never mentions how many bodies were present in the Arikara site—ten, twenty, 100?) Undaunted by the illogical nature of the comparison, not to mention the rather unscientific lack of interest in possible environmental factors, Gregg goes on to suggest that "the reservation system's tight gene pool" might be a factor in the high rate of this disorder in the Native American community and that from the standpoint of preventive medicine this disorder could be alleviated "through sociocultural change," a racist argument for assimilation.[6] But aside from the highly questionable use of "scientific" evidence in Gregg's arguments, one can only wonder why this paleopathologist even needed the bones from the eighteenth-century Arikara site to come to his conclusion about present-day Indian populations.

C. *Religious Features of the "Scientific" Translations of Indian Bones*

While the stockpiling of Indian bones in both American and European museums is typically held up as a scientific activity—something to be distinguished from the "religious" arguments Native Americans give when asserting authority over their ancestors' bones—the secular nature of such scientific bone collecting is actually not all that certain. From a legal point of view it is without sure standing. Common law in Europe generally stipulates that no one can hold property interests in the dead, and yet Indian demands for reburial of dead ancestors provoked many in the scientific and museum communities to file suits claiming that the dead bodies in their possession were indeed their property (this also happened with individuals who "discovered" Indian graves on their private property and then proceeded to varnish the bones for public display and sell off the grave goods on the antiquities market). In fact, the ways in which museums and state historical societies have hoarded dead Indians most closely resembles the use of the relics of saints in the European Middle Ages. In medieval Europe, one could do a good business trafficking in the bones of the saints. To this day altars in Catholic churches are still required to contain a holy relic, a tradition that goes back to the first masses which were said over the dead lying in the catacombs of Rome. Like the state historical societies that cropped up across the Indian-inhabited plains of the past century, the parishes scattered throughout the vulnerable countryside of Carolingian Europe also needed protection for their fragile, new communities. The bones of saints gave these parishes a sense of identity, protection, and economic sustenance in a period before national identity, central government, and fiscal planning. Before the reemergence of political institutions that would in time develop into the modern state, local saints provided a form of social organization (see Geary, *Furta Sacra*).

Something like this also occurred in the frontier states from the 1850s onward. The institutions which hold the majority of Indian bones in the Midwest are the state historical societies, institutions which remain to this day—in contrast to their counterparts on the East Coast—centralized repositories of state history. In Minnesota, for example, the State Historical Society was chartered before the state itself. This explains why, after the bloody Dakota Indian uprising in southern Minnesota in 1862, the mutilated body of Chief Little Crow was held—and at times displayed—in the Minnesota Historical Society until 1971, when Indian activists obtained its release. The body of Little Crow was then buried by his grandson and other family members. Why did the Historical Society find it necessary to display the bones of a conquered Dakota chief? Just as Christianity is filled with stories of relics which intercede on behalf of mortals, the white newcomers to Dakota territory, we would argue, used the bones of Chief Little Crow to send what they understood to be a powerful message to the Indians around them (see Carley). By displaying Little Crow in this way in order to fend off their political adversaries, the first Minnesotans practiced what their feudal counterparts would have called "humiliation" of the relic (see Geary, "L'humiliation"): they would debase a great figure until their aim was attained.[7]

Another similarity between the medieval and modern display of dead "others" is economic. With a nice set of relics, a medieval church could become a hub of economic activity; attracting pilgrims from throughout Christendom meant more income for local business. Likewise Indian burial displays are a source of income in depressed rural areas. In 1990 in rural Illinois, for example, residents put up massive resistance to local Indian demands that the exposed Indian burial site called Dickson Mounds be closed (see Cassel). The open burial site—named after Don Dickson, a popular chiropractor and amateur archeologist who "discovered" the 900-year-old Indian settlement in 1927—exposes 236 Indian dead to an enormous volume of tourists. In January 1990, alone, some 24,000 people from all over the state visited the museum after hearing that it might close due to pressure from local and national Indian groups. A museum survey found that eighty-five percent of its visitors opposed the closing. Illinois Attorney General Neil Hartigan, the leading Democratic candidate for governor, actually promised to keep Dickson Mounds open if elected that November. Dickson Mounds is still a three-story state-owned museum, the county's main tourist attraction which continues to be fondly remembered by generations of local white people who made the pilgrimage there as schoolchildren. (Listening to white opposition to Indian demands that they be allowed to rebury their "old ones," one would think the tribes were calling for the desecration of a holy shrine.) Fortunately many such sites—in Kansas, Alabama, and Nebraska, for example—have recently been closed as a result of Indian opposition.

In debates over Indian reburial, one often hears social scientists complain that Native Americans' demands for repatriation—demands based on the belief that their ancestors held in museum vaults are, in fact, in captivity, unable to complete their spiritual journey—violate the separation of church and state. Given the previous discussion, the scientific community's claim to be trafficking only in the secular domain with regard to Indian bones is patently weak. And for those non-Indians who claim that the afterlife of bones is inconsequential, something the dominant culture has outgrown, it is instructive to recall the emotional investment in and perseverance of the U.S. Government over the return of the bones of POWs from Vietnam. Apparently the dominant culture does know that it perpetuates itself through such symbolic battles. As we know from anthropology, collecting the symbolically powerful objects of another culture can, in fact, destroy that culture.

D. From Collections to Fetishizations: Recalling the Power of the Untranslatable

We can see, then, why state historical societies began collecting Indian dead, but the story of the acquisition of Native American dead by the large East Coast museums such as the Smithsonian is historically different and beyond the scope of this essay. It is important to note, however, that Thomas Jefferson was one of the first to excavate an Indian burial mound and that to this day racial biology experiments have had the blessing of the federal government. In 1868, for example, the Surgeon General issued an order to Army medical doctors to procure as many Indian crania as possible. Under the order 4,000 crania were obtained from the dead bodies of Native Americans. Indian men, women, and children, often those killed on a battlefield or massacre site, were beheaded and their crania taken to the Army Medical Museum. There, doctors measured the crania, using pseudo-scientific assumptions to prove the intellectual and moral inferiority of Indians. These studies were used until the 1920s by federal officials as a measure of racial purity to determine who was and who was not a full-blood Indian. (Mixed-bloods, it should be noted, could legally sell the land they "received" after the Allotment Act of 1887, while full-bloods had to have the permission of federal authorities and were therefore a bit more difficult to swindle.) Tribal enrollment lists from the early twentieth century based on such racist biology continue to be the legal documents used to determine heirs in awarding land claim compensation.[8]

The tradition of collecting objects of Native American material culture pries such objects from the original relations of the production of their meaning. While ostensibly engaged merely in the display of that culture, museums, in fact, suppress the history of their appropriation: for all their fastidious detail in presenting ethnographic displays, curators appear to retain shabby records when it comes to how they procured their objects—the large number of unprovenienced bones uncovered by the reburial controversy is proof of this.[9] Together the activity of Western museums has produced collections in which meaning and value are generated by the relations between the things displayed (the object-system) while other social relations are bracketed. In this respect, the distinction between collection and fetishism begins to blur as the paradigm of classification and display takes on an aspect of accumulation and secrecy (see Clifford 220).

In this light we want to suggest that the retention of such a large number of Native American bones can be usefully theorized around the notion of the fetish. Hegel was the first to theorize the fantasmatic African culture of the fetish as a moment just prior to History. For Hegel, the fetish was precisely that object of the Spirit that failed to participate in the Idea, an object which never experienced a negation and *Aufhebung* (higher synthesis) to a truth beyond its natural materiality. This aspect of the object's untranscended materiality is also at the core of Marxism's theory of the commodity fetish, psychoanalysis's sexual fetish, and modernism's fetish as art object (Pietz 7). Likewise with Indian bones: whether commodified as tourist displays or appropriated as the "prehistory" of either a particular state or the entire United States, they function within the dominant logic of both consumerism and archeology, as if something of their irreducible materiality remained untranscended or untranslated. The success with which Native Americans have been able to close down tourist displays and stop the digging in their ancestors' graves is proof that in the symbolic system of the dominant culture, the bones can be made to signal their residual resistance to commodification.

It may be in the domain of science, however, that an *Aufhebung* will finally take place with respect to these human remains. And yet what is so bizarre is that the scientific community—in particular, physical anthropologists and paleopathologists—actually admits that it does not yet have a way of extracting the information it claims these bones contain (insisting that such methods will become available in a matter of only a few years). If these bones are reburied, it is reasoned, irreplaceable *data* will be lost. The intense, personal, and irrationally confident arguments one hears from paleopathologists and physical anthropologists on this point are clues that we are still in the domain of the fetish.

To show how commodity ideology works, Marx describes a method by which the value system of one type of society is framed in terms of the value system of another society. "The whole mystery of commodities," Marx concludes, "all the magic and necromancy that surrounds the products of labor on the basis of commodity production, vanishes—or here we could say is revealed as fetishism—as soon as we come to other forms of production" (169). The cultural economy of Native Americans that has succeeded in removing their ancestors' bones from the economies of tourism, from the Enlightenment (museum-)defined epistemologies of accumulation, edification, and preservation, and in some cases from the data banks of pseudo-science, does in fact produce, we would argue, a radically uncommodified form of value. Carefully exploiting their ancestors' resistance to commodification, Native Americans retrieve their dead and, in reburying them, release them into another symbolic economy. The bones do not, however, come back unchanged from their sojourn in the symbolic economy of the dominant. They take on the added meaning of a political victory and signify a newfound control over the past which empowers Indians in the present.[10]

E. The Cultural Politics of Indian Reburial: Thinking beyond the Possible

The movement of cultural patrimony we have been tracing is vitally important to postcolonial politics. Whether it takes the form of a postcolonial nation-state like Egypt demanding the return of the Sphinx's beard from the British Museum (Prott) or a stateless nation like the Omaha in Nebraska seeking the release of their Sacred Pole from Harvard's Peabody Museum (Ridington), these "relocation programs" now being scripted by formerly colonized peoples mark the shift from a politics of decolonization to one of self-determination. Our essay has tried to show how imperialist nostalgia and neocolonialist practices masquerading as science thwart the cultural politics of self-determination for Native Americans.

The struggle for self-determination took a particular form for the Indian tribes of North Dakota when they aimed their sites at the necropolis lying below the State's Historical Society. How are the politics of Indian self-determination manifest in this incident? Imagine that the history of a place like North Dakota is somehow present in the land like geological formations. Historians then, we might say, work like geologists: they "read" the land, trying to make sense of the traces left by events and peoples who went before them. In this light, by housing North Dakota's Indian dead in its basement vault, the State Historical Society housed a repressed "reading" of the land underground, while above ground they memorialized a different, (triumphalist) reading: above ground sat the archives and displays that make up the "official" record from which North Dakotan history is produced and below ground lay the boxes of Indian bones which were not slated to be translated into histories or stories but rather into non-narrative, scientific data. In this light, Indian self-determination meant relocating the dead ancestors to a place where they would no longer serve as, literally, the repressed foundation of official state history. Reburied, the dead ancestors might stimulate stories of empowerment for their offspring.

The actions of the Indian Reinterment Committee in fact released a number of such stories, one of which is the story of the journey on which its ancestors had embarked at the time of their death. Telling the story of the ancestors' journey, one must recount how their relatives mournfully bid them farewell at the grave site and how eventually they came to stay in the kingdoms of science and state history where they became not even lowly subjects but rather objects of analysis and imperialist fantasy. To continue the tale of the journey also means telling about the rescue to new burial grounds and how the newly relocated souls began advising the living inhabitants of Indian country.

For centuries Native Americans have been presented as the primitive "Other" in mainstream American history. In our essay we have described how in the last half of the twentieth century North American Indians have resisted being exoticized or transformed into mere objects of knowledge for scientific and popular cultural consumption. Now we would like to suggest that by studying Indian reburial, non-Indians might learn something important—another aspect of what we are calling the cultural politics of Indian reburial. The attention present-day Indians are according to the plight of their dead ancestors is in keeping with many Native Americans' belief that they must live not just for today but for the next seven generations. We believe that this view of life which acknowledges that we live for more than ourselves extends our political thinking in a productive way.

The philosopher Emmanuel Levinas has written about the dominant Western society's need to find new ways of relating to "Others"—those whose cultures differ radically from their own. He finds a model for this in the filial relationship. Our children, he says, are radically different from us and yet they are in some way still us. They are ours without being a possession or a property. Our relation to them is not a relation of knowledge, that is to say, we do not attempt to know them or understand them uniquely through the detached and ahistorical medium of reason. The filial relation, Levinas writes, requires that we think "beyond the possible . . . "

> as if my being, in fecundity—and starting from the children's possibilities— exceeded the possibilities inscribed in the nature of a being. I would like to underline the upheaval—that this signifies—of the ontological condition and also of the logic of substance, on the one hand, and of transcendental subjectivity on the other. . . . The fact of seeing the possibilities of the other as your own possibilities, *of being able to escape the closure of your identity and what is bestowed on you, toward something which is not bestowed on you and which is nevertheless yours*—this is paternity. This future beyond my own being, this dimension constitutive of time, takes on a concrete content in paternity. . . . To consider the Other as a son is precisely to establish with him those relations I call "beyond the possible." (36; our emphasis)

Despite the somewhat unfortunate patriarchal vocabulary, we think Levinas is trying to work out something which parallels Native American experience in the reburial issue. We would furthermore argue that both the Native Americans' and Levinas's sense of "beyond the possible" is quite different from the *utopian* thinking of much revolutionary leftist thought: while a utopia is by definition a visionary system of political or social perfection without a place (*ou* from the Greek, meaning "not" and *topia* from *topos* meaning place), Native American visions of the future, entwined as they are in filial relations, are by contrast always concerned with place. The very "grounded" way in which American Indians seek to move beyond the possible is evident in the call for reburial. May such journeys of Indian self-determination proceed without further interruption!

Notes

This essay is part of a book *Interrupted Journeys: The Cultural Politics of Indian Reburial* forthcoming from the University of Minnesota Press. An earlier version of this essay appeared in *Discourse* 14.1 (Winter 1991–92).

1. The North Dakota Indian Affairs Commission is made up of tribal chairpersons (the offical representatives of thousands of Indian members), council members, and North Dakota state legislators. It is chaired by the Governor.

2. Here Pemina refers to the elders' uncertainty about the legal means to attain their aim.

3. Physical anthropologists generally insist that Indian bones be "analyzed" before they are reburied. This usually entails crushing and grinding the bones to a dust, a procedure many Native Americans, including Pemina, are opposed to (see Yellow Bird 1987).

4. One example of how Indian reburial surfaced in the seventies is the following: in 1971 the Twin Cities Institute for Talented Youth sponsored an excavation project at an Indian burial mound a few hours from Minneapolis—according to the then chair of the anthropology department at the University of Minnesota the brochure described the gravedigging as a "treasure hunt." The American Indian Movement (AIM), however, surprised the teenage archeologists by arriving at the excavation site with television cameras just before the six o'clock news. AIM members burned the excavation notes, seized the shovels, and began filling in the trenches. (It should be noted that AIM offered to compensate the students for property losses.) One tearful youngster remarked to the press, "We were trying to preserve culture, not destroy it." AIM went on to occupy the office of the state archeologist and demanded equal protection for Native American graves. In 1971 the law governing grave sites in Minnesota was the Cemetery Act of 1906 which only covered burials made after 1860; in other words, it protected only the graves of the State's first white settlers. For an account of this incident see Deloria 30–31.

5. A poll taken in the major Minneapolis newspaper a few days after AIM's takeover of the state archeologist's office in 1971 showed that the public was strongly sympathetic to the Indians' position (see *Minneapolis Star and Tribune*). It is noteworthy that the 1971 poll came up again in 1989 during negotiations between the State's Indian leaders and the University of Minnesota, which was holding the remains of some 300 Indians in its anthropology department. The poll was perceived as a reminder to the archeological community that the public was not disposed to its position, and it may be a reason why the university avoided public debate on the issue and quickly complied with the Indians' request to have the bones reburied.

6. Such assimilationist arguments abound in mainstream discourse. Recently an economist in the *Wall Street Journal* argued that the only economic solution for Indian poverty was for Indians to sell their treaty rights and reservation lands (see Velk). Velk is a professor of economics at McGill University in Canada.

7. It was not only the State Historical Society that added the newly killed Dakota to its "collection"; the very night after U.S. cavalry in Mankato hung the 38 Sioux who served as the scapegoats for the 1862 uprising (the largest public hanging in U.S. history), Doctor William Mayo—whose sons would go on to found the famous Mayo Clinic in nearby Rochester, Minnesota—dug up the shallow graves of the condemned Indians and took the body of Cut Nose, which he used in his study of osteology. The incident is also described in *The Doctors Mayo*: recounting the Mankato hanging, Helen Clapesattle writes,

So many *unmourned* dead were a windfall when subjects for dissection were hard to get. In the crowd of spectators were many medical men, including Dr. Mayo, and under cover of darkness the grave was hastily opened and the bodies removed and distributed. To Dr. Mayo's lot fell the body of Cut Nose, a hideously ugly brave . . . his body was dissected by Dr. Mayo . . . and the skeleton was cleaned and articulated for the doctor's permanent use. (37; emphasis added)

8. The White Earth Reservation Land Settlement Act passed by Congress in 1986 is a good example of such practices.

9. "Unprovenienced" means without record of where the bones were found or of the surrounding plant life that would have been part of the Indians' diet—information that is necessary to make claims about bones being records of nutritional intake.

10. It is interesting to note in this regard that in the recent megashow on Mexico by the Metropolitan Museum of Art in New York, many Indian and Hispanic communities were resistant to the state "borrowing" objects which still have enormous symbolic value for them (see Hamill). The attempted removal of a seventeenth-century baptismal font from a local church, for example, caused the citizens of that community to form a human chain when museum curators arrived with federal troops. That baptismal font never traveled to New York. Local communities know that when an object travels in a symbolic economy that is beyond their control, it may not come back the same, if it comes back at all. Such acts of resistance foreground the issue of power at stake.

Works Cited

Brown, Dee. *Bury My Heart at Wounded Knee*. New York: Holt, 1970.

Brunette, Paula. Rev. of "Dances with Wolves." *News from Indian Country*. Hayward, Wisconsin. Dec. 1990: 7.

Burnette, Robert, and Richard Erdoes. *The Tortured Americans*. Englewood Cliffs, NJ: Prentice Hall, 1971.

Cardinal, Harold. *The Unjust Society*. Edmonton: M. G. Hartig, 1969.

Carley, Kenneth. *The Sioux Uprising of 1862*. St. Paul: Minnesota Historical Society, 1976.

Cassel, Andrew. "American Indians Seek Closure of Tourist-Attraction." *St. Paul Pioneer Press Dispatch* 22 Feb. 1990: A1.

Casteneda, Carlos. *Journey to Ixtlan: The Lessons of Don Juan*. New York: Simon and Schuster, 1972.

———. *A Separate Reality: Further Conversations with Don Juan*. New York: Simon and Schuster, 1971.

———. *Teachings of Don Juan: A Yaqui Way of Knowledge*. Berkeley: U of California P, 1968.

Churchill, Ward. "Spiritual Hucksterism." *Zeta* 3 (1990): 94–98.

Clapesattle, Helen. *The Doctors Mayo*. New York: Pocket, 1956.

Clifford, James. "On Collecting Art and Culture." *The Predicament of Culture: Twentieth Century Ethnography, Literature and Art*. Cambridge: Harvard UP, 1988. 215–51.

Cronon, William. *Changes in the Land: Indians, Colonists, and the Ecology of New England*. New York: Hill, 1983.

Deloria, Vine, Jr. *Custer Died for Your Sins: An Indian Manifesto.* New York: Macmillan, 1969.

———. *God is Red.* New York: Grosset, 1973.

Dorris, Michael. "Indians in Aspic." *New York Times* 24 Feb. 1991: E17.

Geary, P. J. *Furta Sacra: Theft of Relics in the Central Middle Ages.* Princeton: Princeton UP, 1978.

———. "L'humiliation des saints." *Annales ESC* 1 (1979): 27–42.

Gregg, John G. "Study of Old Remains: How Does It Help Present People?" World Archeological Congress. 7–10 Aug. 1989. U of South Dakota, Vermillion.

Hamill, Pete. "Here Comes Mexico: The Metropolitan Museum Pulls Off the Greatest Show of Mexican Art Ever." *Connoisseur* Oct. 1990: 93–97.

Haraway, Donna. *Simians, Cyborgs, and Women: The Reinvention of Nature.* New York: Routledge, 1991.

Levinas, Emmanuel. *Ethics and Infinity: Conversations with Philippe Nemo.* Trans. Richard Cohen. Pittsburgh: Duquesne UP, 1985.

Marx, Karl. *Capital.* Trans. Ben Fowkes. Vol. 1. New York: Vintage, 1977.

Minneapolis Star and Tribune. 12 Sept. 1971: B13.

Pietz, William. "The Problem of the Fetish, Part I." *Res* 9 (1985): 5–17.

Preston, Douglas. "Skeletons in Our Museums' Closets." *Harpers* Feb. 1989: 66–76.

Prott, Lyndel V. "Cultural Rights as Peoples' Rights in International Law." *Rights of Peoples.* Ed. James Crawford. Oxford: Clarendon Press, 1988.

Red Fox, Chief. *The Memoirs of Chief Red Fox.* New York: McGraw-Hill, 1971.

Ridington, Robin. "Omaha Survival: A Vanishing Indian Tribe That Would Not Vanish." *The American Indian Quarterly* 11.1 (1987): 37–51.

Rosaldo, Renato. *Culture & Truth: The Remaking of Social Analysis.* New York: Vintage, 1989.

S 1980. "A Bill to Provide for the Repatriation of Native American Groups or Cultural Patrimony." Sponsored by Sen. Daniel Inouye. 101st Congress. 1st Session. Washington: GPO, 1990.

Steiner, Stan. *The New Indians.* New York: Harper and Row, 1968.

Trigger, Bruce. "Alternative Archeologies: Nationalist, Colonialist, Imperialist." *Man* 19.3 (1984): 355–70.

Velk, Tom. "Welfare, Not Cowboys Kills Indians." *Wall Street Journal* 7 Sept. 1990: A14.

Yellow Bird, Pemina. "May the Tribal Spirits Rest in Peace." *Grand Forks Herald* 26 Jul. 1987: C4.

2 | Faceless Tongues

Language and Citizenship in Nineteenth-Century Latin America

Julio Ramos

Commenting on a well-known photograph of Einstein, Peter Sloterdijk states that sticking out one's tongue is an act of aggression, a flight from the unavoidably unequal conditions of a stratified dialogue (140–41). In other traditions, however, sticking out one's tongue means placing oneself under the scrutiny of a doctor's examination. It is thus assumed that the particular inflections of the tongue's colors, its line of flight from health and normality, are read by the examiner as symptoms of a sickness of which the patient, perhaps, is aware, but not knowledgeable. My use of the phrase is closer to this popular *doxa* than to Sloterdijk's philosophy of laughter.

Moreover, *to stick out one's tongue* is also a literal version of *enseñar la lengua*, which could be translated as to *teach the language*. And, adding weight to the slippery thingness of the tongue, the phrase *enseñar la lengua* slides further into a revealing ambiguity, meaning not only to teach the language, but also to show the tongue or *mostrarla*, as when one mocks or shows one's tongue to a medical examiner. This paper deals precisely with this ambiguity, the institutional gap between the discourses of knowledge in the national pedagogical scene, and the popular tongue's lines of flight and resistance.

Not by chance, a story written by Leopoldo Lugones, an Argentine nationalist of the early twentieth century and a defender of language purity, marks our entry into the pedagogical scene. Written in the early 1900s during a period of vast immigration in Buenos Aires, "Izur" is a fiction about an obsessive scientist—an anthropologist with a linguistic vocation, one could say—who buys a monkey in a circus and embarks on the project of teaching the animal how to speak.[1] The hypothesis of this parodic man of the Enlightenment is the following: although monkeys have the physiological means to produce meaningful sounds, they do not speak (or only communicate among themselves in secret and unintelligible ways) because they refuse to *work*. With a shrewd, perverse lucidity, the mad linguist establishes a correlation between language, sociability, and work: to speak, to enter the territory regulated by the law of language, is concomitant with the incorporation of the speaking body into a rationalized working force. By refusing to speak, the monkey evades work.

What, after all, could a monkey learn? Patiently, at first, the linguist attempts to teach the ape some fundamental points of articulation. Considering the monkey to be somewhat like a child, he hopes that by taking his master as a role model the pupil will learn by mimesis. And the monkey does so: he imitates the man's posturing and *sticks out his tongue*. This reinforces another of the linguist's hypotheses: monkeys (like children and other subalterns, he suggests) first learn how to *mock*, later to curse.[2] This second hypothesis apparently confirmed, the pedagogical strategies change, and the education of the monkey is transformed into torture. He is beaten and kept without water and food; but of course, he does not speak.

Nevertheless, the linguist insists on the pedagogical mission. Mocking their obsessed master, his servants reinforce his initial suspicions: they claim that at night the studious monkey escapes his quarters and asks the cooks—in eloquent Spanish—for water and food. In response to the mockery, the master intensifies the disciplinary measures and dehydrates the monkey to death.

Paradoxically, the last scene in the story seems to fulfill the mad linguist's pedagogical dreams. Just before dying the monkey speaks: "Amo, agua. Amo, mi amo." "Master, water. Master, my master." The monkey enters the site of language but not as an autonomous subject: for to speak presupposes for the monkey the prior learning of power's proper names: "Master, my master." More importantly, perhaps, it also requires an internalization of the hierarchy, a strange love for one's master: "Amo, *mi* amo." But such is the case, in "Izur," only if we read the amorous phrase of recognition spoken by the monkey from the perspective of the master. From another perspective the phrase of recognition, articulated precisely at the moment of death, the phrase that seems to fix the monkey's position as subaltern in a predictable dialectic, could well be read as the *fleeing* disciple's last joke on his master; an ironic and impossible recognition played against the grain of the master/slave dialectic.

If it were not written around 1906, perhaps we could read this story—with Borges—as a fantastic tale of horror, closer to Poe than to any specific debates in the Argentine cultural political arena (see Borges). In 1906, however, Argentine pedagogues, social scientists, and many literary people (like Lugones himself) were actively engaged in elaborating discourses on what they often represented, in their own metaphors, as a deep crisis of the Argentine "soul": a crisis manifested in the "contamination" of the national language in the mouths of the millions of working-class immigrants.[3] The monkey in "Izur" would be just that, a marvelous ape, if Lugones himself had not mined his text with indications for an alternative reading: the monkey, says the narrator twice, had anthropomorphic features, resembling those of a *mulatto*.

By the turn of the century there were not many blacks or mulattos in Argentina. The dominant elites, however, were beginning to mark southern European immigrants with the stereotypical metaphor of "blackness." Moreover, Lugones's narrator interprets the ape's silence as an effect of atavism, a key trope in turn-of-the-century anthropology which, as we will see later, was often used to pathologize the immigrants' quotidian practices and "deviations" from dominant culture. Thus "Izur" is not simply a grotesque story about violence to animals, it is also a reflection on the conditions for the incorporation of an ethnically marked other into the rationalized space of the national language. "Izur" is an ironic exploration of the violence—and love— displayed by the actors in the national pedagogical scene.

To approach the issue from a different angle, I would ask: First, when did "language" become an object of reflection in Latin America, that is, when was it constructed as a specific domain, and to what kinds of political problematics did such a reflection respond? And second, what discourses were primarily involved in the representation and control of linguistic heterogeneity in multilingual and multiethnic nineteenth-century Latin America?[4] These questions are part of a more general ongoing work on the roles played by the discourses on linguistic heterogeneity and the representation of subaltern speech throughout the process of nation-building in Latin America. Here I will focus on three such discursive formations: first, grammar as it relates to state-formation and the invention of citizenship in the works of Latin America's major grammarian and nineteenth-century linguist, Andrés Bello; secondly, the representation of ethno-linguistic difference in Cuban abolitionist fiction; and finally, returning to some of the issues raised in our brief reading of Lugones's "Izur," the pathologization of immigrant speech by the emerging discipline of anthropology in turn-of-the-century Argentina.

With these questions in mind, it is useful to recall the first major "national" grammars published by the Venezuelan Bello while he was President of the University of Chile in the 1840s.[5] Articulated simultaneously in poetry, historiography, grammatical discourse, and law, Bello's work is irreducible to twentieth-century categories of specialized intellectual production.[6] Despite the heterogeneity of Bello's work, however, his interventions in different domains usually shared a concern with normativity and law. Driven by the rationalizing, modernizing impulse distinctive of Enlightenment's discourses,[7] Bello's work is a multifarious reflection on the relationship between the local and the universal, particularities and totality, the specificity of action and social law, or, in linguistic terms, between what he deemed the spontaneity of popular speech and the systematization of language produced by writing.

For Bello, grammar was a foundational discourse of the modern state.[8] Given the geographic, ethnic, and linguistic diversity of the continent, Bello invested grammar with the task of establishing a rationalized master-code which he considered an irreducible condition for the implementation of modern law. Moreover, Bello believed that linguistic centralization was necessary in order to maintain the cultural and economic ties between the newly independent nations once the authority of Spain's strict bureaucratic institutions (including the Royal Academy of Language) had been destabilized, if not demolished. It is not coincidental that Bello dedicated his major grammar to his "brothers, the citizens of Spanish America" (*Gramática* 11): his grammatical project meant to establish a communicational network, not simply for Chileans, but for the "brotherhood" of all Spanish-speaking areas on the continent.[9] In its systematizing impulse, Bello's grammar could almost be read today as an instance of science fiction. Our contemporary mistrust of totalizing projects, however, should not allow us to forget the specific institutional effects of such "imaginings." Bello's grammar is still today a canonical text in its genre, a pedagogical classic, and, indeed, one which effectively contributed to the standardization of Spanish throughout the continent, at least at the level of the dominant elites and official culture.

What are the boundaries of the linguistic "brotherhood" imagined in the process of grammatical representation? In Bello, grammatical writing begins as a response to a specific terror: the monstrosity, for the man of the Enlightenment, of dispersion and fragmentation. With great trepidation, he often compares the situation of the Spanish language in postcolonial America with Latin's fragmentation in the declining days of the Empire. Such monstrosity is linked, in Bello's grammar, to the proliferation of dialects, "the multitude of irregular, licentious, barbarous dialects, embryons of future languages that, through a very slow period of elaboration, would reproduce in America what Europe suffered during the tenebrous times of Latin's corruption" (*Gramática* 12). Defined as "inferior, vulgar speech," dialect becomes the *other* of grammatical discourse, as well as its object of representation.[10]

In Bello's normative grammar, to represent the otherness of dialect inscribes a strategy of contention, a way of dominating the chaotic spontaneity and dispersion of popular orality under the dispensation of universal, corrective laws. In that sense, the representation and subordination of the vernacular in grammar is concomitant with the impulse of containment and centralization deployed by the state and modern law, particularly in those early stages of national consolidation. Thus grammar—argued Bello against his younger, romantic critics[11]—was not motivated by a conservative, scholastic vocation; its modernizing and civilizing mission should fulfill a paradigmatic role among the discourses of nation-building. Abstracting its norms from the literary classics, grammar provided the new nations with a rational master-code by means of which society could dominate and productively transform "nature" and "spontaneity" in the "chaotic" American world. Grammar was a sophisticated modern machine which elaborated and purified the laws of meaning—the structures of citizenship—of the "barbarism" of orality and local knowledge. Significantly, Bello believed that literacy, generated by the study of grammar and literature, marked Latin America's participation in the Western legacy, distinguishing its "civilization" from "barbarous" Asia and Africa.[12]

The authority of grammar was grounded in the project of national consolidation in at least three specific ways: at the most obvious level, grammar would generate a standard code for national and international commerce between the distant regions of the continent; this code would facilitate the "execution of the law, administration of the state, [and] national unity" (*Gramática* 12)[13] by substituting the authority of local, consuetudinary conventions with centralized, written law; finally, and perhaps more crucial for us, through literary *exempla*, grammatical education provided the emerging, secular society with the symbolic, moral structures for the constitution of law-abiding citizens. Indeed, in his representation of dialect, Bello's metaphors consistently slide toward the identification of popular, "vulgar" speech with moral "deviations." Popular neologisms, for example, are like a turbulence which "alter the structure of language" by flooding it with "a mass of irregular dialects" which are "corrupt," "barbarous," "repugnant," and, consistently, "vicious" and "licentious." Thus, the boundary of grammatical discourse is not only the linguistic, dialectologically abject, but also the positioning of popular forms of communication outside moral law. In this respect, the normativity provided by grammar did not simply play a circumstantial role in the establishment of the modern market or modern forms of legal contracts.[14] Rather, grammaticality marked the internalization of the law in a complex process of subject-formation which transformed the heterogeneity of bodies into modern, moral, speaking subjects: disciplined bodies that could speak the language of the family, the army, rationalized labor, and other national institutions.[15]

Bello's identification of grammatical with moral "deviations" also conditions his reaction against "modern" poetry, whose relative autonomy from rhetoric and grammar he described accurately, although in negative terms. In several of his critiques of the romantic poets—the Cuban José María Heredia (Bello, "Juicio"), among others—Bello explicitly links poetic detachment from rhetoric and grammar with a deeper kind of "incorrection": erotic excess as a romantic vice. Rephrasing Goethe, Bello claims for poetry—under the surveillance of grammar's law—the task of providing rules for the imagination, a mechanism for the containment of passion and desire. Thus, again, detachment from grammatical correction, in poetry or speech, was construed by Bello as the linguistic marker of a transgression against sociability and moral law.

Bello's fear of poetry's linguistic and erotic excesses indicates a drift in the relationship between Latin American literature and the network of sociability. In the context of a relatively intense division of intellectual labor, toward the last two decades of the nineteenth century, literature's modernizing and civilizing mission was often questioned, both by intellectuals in other fields and also by writers who sought autonomy from the official institutions which had guaranteed the legitimacy of literary interventions in the public sphere. Thus literature (poetic practices at first) began to lose its paradigmatic role in the constitution of the national languages. Indeed, it could be argued that modern literature, in Latin America and probably elsewhere, is constituted as a relatively autonomous field of intellectual activity when it ceases to play an organic role in state-formation. In Latin America, however, this process of literary autonomization is extremely uneven and does not have major institutional effects until the last decades of the nineteenth century, when the state and the discourses of the law develop their own discursive mechanisms and cease to depend on literature for the formalization of political, normative, or legal contents.[16]

Until then, many forms of writing that today we would ascribe to the literary institution—the novel, for example—sustained a public authority embedded in the foundational project of national consolidation. Throughout the nineteenth century, at least, narrative fiction gained legitimacy by exploring, often in utopian ways, the possibility of dialogue and alliances between conflicting forms of communication in the heterogeneous, not yet centralized, postcolonial societies.

In her work on Latin American romance, Doris Sommer shows how seduction and erotic relationships between characters in nineteenth-century novels allegorically project the political negotiations necessary for national consolidation. I would like to suggest that these alliances do not only take place at the level of plot structures. The "imagining" and the *impossibility* of these alliances overdetermine the representation of discourse and the forms of verbal contact and exchange in the novels. This is particularly the case with the construct of black speech in nineteenth-century Cuban abolitionist novels.[17]

Although written in a colonial situation, these abolitionist narratives are fictions on the possibilities of a national state in Cuba and on the conditions necessary for incorporation of the slaves into the symbolic order of a modern nation. They explore the legal, medical, cultural, and linguistic status of slaves and their free descendants, usually from the perspectives of liberals who correctly saw slavery as a major obstacle to the modernization of their society. More significantly, however, beyond the criticism of the Spanish colonial rule and the institution of slavery, these novels display the anxiety of the white, creole elites in a predominantly black and mulatto society just a few miles away from Haiti, where the recently emancipated slaves, just a few decades earlier, had successfully revolted against the white colonial rulers.

Once again, in abolitionist fiction, writing begins as a response to a fear, attempting to fill the gaps in the projected structure of the nation. Narrative fiction provided the white elites with a laboratory of prospective fantasies in which they projected imaginary solutions to the contradictions that impeded the constitution of a national subject. In many ways, abolitionist novels form a very elaborate heterology (see Certeau, *Heterologies*), an archive of discourses about a feared, menacing other, the slave, who thus becomes the key figure of liminality in the emerging rhetorics of national identity. More than alternative histories—as the novelists often preferred to present their works— these texts were closer to ethnological representations of the black, "barbarous" body, gazed at by white, creole intellectuals and inscribed as a major "enigma" yet to be solved by the discourses on nationality. In response to the enigma, these novels are often formalizations of stereotypes which could compensate, perhaps, for the fears that otherwise bonded the white elite together.

At the center of this fictional project we find, again, the question of the other's barbarous and unintelligible language: the question of the black "minor" tongue or "dialect."[18] In the abolitionist novel, the aporias of national consolidation are consistently thematized as the other's silence, as the positioning of a subaltern outside the borders of rational verbal exchange and national language. In Cirilo Villaverde's *Cecilia*, for example, the key value of "civility" is distributed among the non-white characters according to their command of standard (white) Spanish; the narrator tirelessly comments on his characters' orality and, when reporting their speech, vertically detaches his discourse from the "vulgar" speech represented. In the first novel of the series, Suárez y Romero's *Francisco. El ingenio o las delicias del campo*, the author is seemingly less insistent on the linguistic hierarchization. Nevertheless, his novel— which in many ways could be summarized as a text about the silence of the slaves, their lack of institutional representation under slavery—is also a metalinguistic exercise representing the lack of communication among the social groups as a major cause of the final tragedy. In Antonio Zambrana's *El negro Francisco*, we find a slightly revised reflection on the slave's silence, which the author interprets, as Villaverde had, as a sign of barbarism. Zambrana's slave protagonist is introduced in the following terms: "A prisoner of war in his country, Francisco had been sold as a slave when he was twelve years old. . . . [His African traditions] were, as in the case of other slaves, a *mystery*. A slave rarely speaks of his motherland in the presence of white people, first because he does not consider such talk to be prudent, and second because he considers [talking to whites about his tradition] a kind of profanation" (21). The slave's silence is interpreted by the narrator as an act of resistance which could only be deciphered by the privileged hermeneutics of the novelist who figuratively interpellates the slave to tell his story.[19] In Zambrana's novel, even the tragic heroine Camila, a literate mulatta who has been educated in the city by the slave-owning family, is often characterized as a subject dominated by primary physical impulses, almost incapable of participating in the "higher" functions of discourse:

> She had qualities which appealed, not to the soft pleasures of the soul, but to the delirious drunkness of the senses. Her morbid forms, the feline graciousness of her movements, her palpitating breast, her lips—were made for kissing, rather than for words, her voice whose tones hinted at that sweet flexibility which makes ardent the caresses of language. . . . (47)

A similar description of another mulatta protagonist is found in Villaverde's *Cecilia*: "Her mouth was small and her lips full, indicating more voluptuousness than strength of character" (7). The descriptions of the sensual mouth of the mulattas, good only for kissing (or for an "ill intended expression" in the case of Cecilia), underscore the pervasive relationship between morality and the law of language previously noted in Bello. The narrator's gazing at the mulatta's mouth could well be read as a metonymical reference to orality, the expression of the body's passions, according to Bello (see Gelpí). At the border of rational language, the ethnically and (here, at least) gendered other is positioned as a body moved by the dangerous impulses of sexuality. And in these novels the sexuality of the mulatta is a stereotypical condensation of the unmanageable drives which destabilize the social structures projected by the fictional world, generating interracial relationships which "contaminate" the purity of the white families and the ideal hierarchies of the virtual nation.[20]

Since the national enigma is thematized as a silence, a gap in the national language delineated by the speechless black body, one could read the verbal organization of the novels in which slaves are made to speak as formal strategies for the fictional resolution of the enigma. As Bakhtin and Vološinov have insisted, the rhetorical flexibility of the novel makes it a privileged site for the representation of contact between conflicting languages or sociolects in a particular territory. Thus, as Pasolini showed with respect to Italy, the novel's heteroglossia becomes politically significant, especially in moments when the homogeneity of the national language is felt to be problematic.[21] In the case of multiethnic Cuba, we can read the different novelistic forms of reported speech and the progressive elaboration of indirect discourse in the genre, for example, as fictional, dialogical solutions to what the novels themselves represent as the national enigma: the slave's silence. Thus the distribution of represented discourse in abolitionist fiction is not merely a stylistic variable[22]; the inscription of subaltern speech in these novels (and later in the *novela indigenista*[23]) projected models of linguistic subordination and containment for the future nation. By representing subaltern speech and by attempting to establish fictional dialogue between the ethno-linguistic groups in conflict, these novels imaginatively mapped the preconditions for the establishment of a homogeneous national language.

Nevertheless, neither dialogue nor any type of erotic alliance or negotiation completely fulfill the allegorical hypostasis of the nation. The verbal (or erotic) exchanges always manifest the violence of irreducible hierarchies. While exploring the possibilities of national condensation, these novels insistently represent the failure, the inconsistencies of the alliances, the unsurmountable gaps between the conflicting ethno-linguistic groups in the heterogeneous territory of the nation. In that sense, far from achieving dialogue, these novels consistently display the limits of their own postulation. At the border of the genre, we are left with the silence of the other, the speechless slave who, emblematically, in Villaverde's *Cecilia*, chooses to swallow his tongue before entering the overdetermined spaces assigned to him in verbal exchange. The sugar mill nurse, María de Regla, a mulatta who speaks Spanish with "precision and clarity," tells the story of the suicide of Pedro Carabalí, a runaway slave who, expecting mercy from the masters, returns to the plantation but is instead brutally punished. In the infirmary:

> [Pedro] became very furious. In his native tongue [he was a *bozal*, a non-Spanish speaking African slave] he whispered words that I could not understand. He went mad. And then they brought Julián, more dead than alive. . . . Pedro saw him. Julián was Pedro's godson. So Pedro found out that they had captured his fellow runaways. That really made him go crazy. I am sure that if he had been able, he would have broken the mantrap to pieces. . . . I looked out of the window for a second, and then I felt Pedro moving. I turned my face and noticed that he was sticking his fingers in his mouth. I thought nothing of it. But then he made a movement as if he were becoming nauseous. I ran to his side. . . . He was just taking his finger out of his mouth and gritting his teeth and trying to hang on to the bed's frame with both hands. Then he began to convulse. I was horrified, I called the doctor, and not knowing when nor how, I saw him die in my arms. (221–22)

When the plantation doctor arrives, he concludes that Pedro Carabalí had choked to death on his own tongue.

If the abolitionist novel, since Suárez y Romero's *Francisco*, was an allegorical incorporation of the speechless black body into the space regulated by the national discourses, then we can read this scene as the novel's representation of the aporia confronted by such an allegorical agenda, as a figuration of the silent resistance confronted by the novelistic and ethnographic project. Carabalí—which in Cuba meant not only a specific African origin, but also a rebellious slave—chooses to swallow his tongue, his mother tongue, rather than enter the negotiations of verbal exchange. In his silence, the national allegory is stifled.

Indeed, at least throughout the nineteenth century, literature played a fundamental role in the representation and containment of ethno-linguistic diversity in Latin America. Nevertheless, it would be inaccurate to claim that only literary forms were involved in the representation of such linguistic heterogeneity. Toward the turn of the century, for example, the question of the disintegration of the national language in the changing cities of the time became an object of interest and concern not only for specialized philologists and intellectuals of literary background, but also for the first generation of Latin American professional social scientists. Such was the case with the late-nineteenth-century criminal anthropologists in Argentina who, generally obsessed with the "crises" generated by modern urban life, placed the body and language of the new working classes under the therapeutic scrutiny of the ethnographic gaze.[24]

Of course, criminal anthropology was not a Latin American invention. The late-nineteenth-century Argentine anthropologists were avid readers of the theories of Cesare Lombroso, whose *L'uomo delinquente in rapporto all'antropologia, alla giurisprudenza ed alle discipline carcerarie* (1876), translated into the major European languages by the 1880s, had by then become a canonical text in the emerging field of criminology. The key metaphor in Lombroso's discourse on criminality was *atavism,* a concept that criminal anthropology, in its representation of social "disorders," literally translated from the lexicon of mid-nineteenth-century genetic biology. For Gregor Mendel, atavism, a notion that was also crucial to Darwin, is a regression in the natural genetic evolution and progress of organisms, the pathological recurrence of a primitive genetic trait in a developed species. With this notion of atavism as its conceptual matrix, Lombrosian anthropology fabricated an explanation both for racial difference and such social "deviations" as criminality and prostitution. Genetically predisposed to deviance, the "born" criminal is represented by Lombroso as the carrier of an atavistic, regressive gene embodying a sort of flashback in the natural evolution and progress of a healthy social organism.

The racist, paranoid fantasies deployed by this deterministic discourse are fairly obvious. Less so, perhaps, is what James Clifford would call the allegorical narrative structure of Lombrosian anthropology's stories about urban life. As Clifford and Renato Rosaldo have suggested, modern ethnography has inscribed the representation of non-Western cultures into the pastoral allegory of a return to an original, primitive state. In Lombrosian anthropology we notice a significant shift in the symbolic topography traced by ethnographic travel.

Far from the nostalgic vocation of the field worker who travels in time and space to the remote origins of humanity, in Lombroso the anthropologist is more like a detective *flâneur* who, remaining in the city, applies his scientific gaze to the marginal areas of modern life.

For Lombroso, primitive life was not only to be found in non-Western forms of social organization. The growing, industrial cities of nineteenth-century Europe were also rich sites for fieldwork on primitive behavior. Although for the anthropologist urban life represented the highest form of progress and civilization, many of its inhabitants—criminals, prostitutes, anarchists, homosexuals—embodied physical and cultural symptoms of a dangerous regression, analogous to atavistic genes in the evolution of the species. The analysis of the social and political context of Lombrosian discourse in Italy—certainly related to the project of national integration and to the intensification of working-class struggles, particularly after the Paris Commune (see Lombroso, *Gli anarchici*)—is beyond the concern of this essay. Nevertheless, it is important to recall that his laborious taxonomies were not of interest just to his scholarly colleagues. His "science of repression," as the criminal anthropologists used to call their discipline, appealed to law enforcers as well, and had concrete effects upon penitentiary and police methods.

The appropriation of Lombrosian discourse in late-nineteenth-century Argentina is not coincidental.[25] Criminal anthropology provided the new, professional Argentine social scientists with a systematic fiction, a pseudoscientific rhetoric for the representation and classification of growing urban populations. Particularly, Lombrosian anthropology placed the problematics of language—the enigmatic, secret "dialects" of the city—at the center of its concern. And, as suggested earlier in our reading of "Izur," the so-called disintegration of the national language in the mouths of working-class immigrants was a major theme of turn-of-the-century Argentine intellectual debates.

Criminal anthropology gained ground and authority as a discourse of *national* surveillance. Its fieldwork site was Buenos Aires during a period of intense urbanization, massive immigration, and proletarianization. Between 1880 and 1890, more than 1,000,000 immigrants arrived in Argentina; between 1890 and 1900, 800,000; and just between 1900 and 1905, 1,200,000 people immigrated. Thus by 1914, thirty percent of the national population consisted of immigrants who had radically transformed the life-world, the culture and politics of Argentina, and particularly of Buenos Aires. Predictably, for the traditional oligarchy these changes represented a deep crisis of the Argentine "national spirit."[26] And very often for these elites, a key manifestation of the national crisis was the linguistic "sickness" of the immigrant working classes, mostly of Italian origin.

Lombrosian anthropology provided the Argentine social scientists with a means to formalize the particular ideological concerns of these elites. For Lombroso, criminal behavior was intimately linked to language, to the paratactic syntax and metaphoric imagination of criminals. Commenting on the atavistic language of criminals, Lombroso writes in *L'uomo delinquente*: "Criminals speak in a different way because they feel differently; they speak in a savage way because they are savages in the midst of the brilliant European civilization. As savages do, criminals frequently use onomatopoeias, automatism and they personify abstract concepts" (225).

Lombroso and his followers created a hermeneutics which interpreted the "enigmas" of marginal sociolects in terms of some of the notions that nineteenth-century poetics had applied to literature. Their evolutionist representation of metaphor (as a dominant trait of criminal language), for example, is not far from romantic ideas on poetic discourse as a return to an original, primitive language. Like the romantics, Lombroso considered metaphor and figurative language an archaic form of communication. Nevertheless, in his deep mistrust of figurative language, the criminal anthropologist inverted the romantic economy, eliding the romantic idealization of primitive authenticity and implying that such a regression to the poetic language of barbarians represented a dangerous aporia in the course of Western progress and rationality.

In Lombroso, as well as in his Argentine followers, such a positivistic, pseudoscientific view of discourse not only held figurative language in low esteem, but also stigmatized it as the expression of barbarism and intellectual underdevelopment. Positive knowledge could assume the figurative language of the "inferior" races and marginal groups as its object of research. But the authority of its discourse, itself a sign of a higher form of civilization, was supposed to have superseded all vestiges of poetic, primitive thought.

Yet the anthropological stories about urban marginality are also rhetorical constructs structured upon metaphors and other figurative displacements. Among the Argentine social scientists, for example, the key concept of social crisis is a metaphor of medical origins which establishes an analogy between social stability and the healthy status of a "natural" body. Signaling the pervasive biologization of the anthropological imagination throughout the nineteenth century, the metaphor of society as a biological organism finds a corollary in the representation of social and political conflicts as symptoms of sicknesses affecting the national organism. Explaining the proliferation of crime as an effect of immigration, the prominent criminologist Francisco Ramos Mejía writes of the "migratory currents which drag to our coasts so many ill germs [from Europe]" (13). In Eusebio Gómez's *La mala vida en Buenos Aires*, immigrants are also "germs," a social and political "virus" which infects the body of the nation.

What was, then, the national "illness"? Evidently, in the urban anthropologist's rhetoric, criminality is metonymically linked to immigration, and immigration is a synecdoche for the increasingly active working classes of the period. For example, Gómez writes in *La mala vida en Buenos Aires*:

> The fact that there are more than a million inhabitants in the capital city of an immigrant's country necessarily implies the daily and considerable increase of the proletarian army, and consequently, the hardening of the conflicts between capital and labor. . . . In my opinion, the proletarian strategies, hateful and destructive, and ill advised by anarchist sectarianism or by socialist propaganda, cause a decrease in morality and generate a series of vices that contribute to the formation of criminality. (34–35)

Immigrants-workers-anarchists-criminals-homosexuals-prostitutes-madmen: the metonymic chain proliferates among the discourses of the emerging social sciences. Since immigrants were figuratively a virus which infected the body of the nation, in such a rhetoric of pathologization the anthropologist figures as a medical researcher tirelessly collecting and classifying data among the cells of the social organism. Concomitant with the emergence of a paranoid, nationalist subject, anthropological discourse gains legitimacy by providing the institutions of power with a therapeutic and prophylactic gaze on the "dangerous classes." In a sense, the virus operates as a self-constituting other, as the condition which, paradoxically, enables the constitution of the healthy national subject.

For now, let us say that the transformation of urban space was generally conceived by the dominant elites as an unmanageable flux which destabilized the structures of the national organism. The therapeutic gaze of the anthropologist responded to such a crisis by representing and ordering the flow, by imposing strict, classificatory categories on the irregular and heterogeneous urban masses. In the words of another influential criminal anthropologist, Luis María Drago, the aim of such discourse was to produce a "tableau of symptoms that could allow us to identify the delinquent" (36). In the fabrication of the tableau, the researcher abstracts a "morphology" and physiognomy of the criminal body. The other's face becomes the focus of the classifying gaze: "The physiognomic studies on live criminals evidence a great deal of facial asymmetries, the lack or total absence of facial hair, the more or less dark color of the skin, a prominent forehead, the irregular position of the ears . . . curved nose, thick and abundant black hair, and in murderers, a glassy, fixed, penetrating stare" (35). Despite the pseudoscientific language, the ethnic and social markers in the tableau are clear. The description displaces the particularity of a face into abstract, ethnic stereotypes with explicit references to non-white Argentines and southern Mediterranean immigrants. In many ways the tableaux of criminal traits were the "scientific" effect of a sinister hermeneutics which interpreted the physiological traits of ethnic difference as signs of social and moral disorders. In other words, we are dealing with an elaborate machine for the fabrication of stereotypes.[27] It is tempting to read this "scientific" apparatus as yet another instance of science fiction, but we should not forget that these fictions had irreducible institutional effects, in Argentina and elsewhere, among lawmakers and enforcers at the turn of the century.

In responding to the question, How can "we" (the "healthy" citizens of the nation) recognize a dangerous other?, the anthropologist-detective morbidly collects all kinds of physical data. His voyeuristic gaze approaches the other's dead or live body as a complex pathological semiosis—a discrete system of "signs" with a particular "morphology"—which must be masterfully decoded and interpreted before being contained and cured. The most minute and insignificant traits of physical difference—the shape of a nose, forehead, and feet, or the size of a dissected brain—become signs of deviance and degeneration.

In its stubborn interpretative drive, its obsession with discovering the laws governing the signs of otherness, the gaze of the anthropologist often focused on tattoos: inscriptions on the other's body. For Lombroso, tattoos were yet another proof of atavism among criminals who, like their "primitive" and "savage" ancestors, inscribed their bodies (*L'uomo* 256). Drago interprets tattoos as a form of criminal writing, as a "style" which expresses the personality of individual criminals. Tattoos are read by Drago as the other's signature, as "unequivocal signs of the other's identity" (82).[28]

Indeed, in the elaboration of his discourse on marginality, the anthropologist-detective not only collects anatomical signs of social difference, but also sets out to record what Drago calls the "expressive" traits of criminality. Information on the other's use of language becomes a privileged heading in the archive of the anthropologist (see Niceforo). Law professor and member of Buenos Aires' Commission on Prisons and Correctional Centers Antonio Dellepiane explains the relevance of linguistic analysis for criminology:

> In an almost palpable way, argot reveals the distinctive traits of the criminal's soul. All the extreme passions of the criminal, the modalities of his moral being, his taste, his tendencies, and his ideas on the world, the soul or future life are manifested in argot. . . . A faithful expression of the mind which creates and cultivates it, argot permits both, the psychologist and the moralist, to reach the most concealed intimacies of the delinquent's conscience. (18–19)

As an indicator of the importance of linguistic analysis among criminologists of the time, it is interesting to note that in Argentina the term for professional delinquents, *lunfardo*, was also the name of "low-life" slang; criminals were identified by their particular use of language. Most anthropologists studied *lunfardo* as an instance of the dynamics of secrecy that distinguish marginal interaction. Criminals, writes Gómez, invent a secret language for self-defense in their "struggle against the social organism" (107). Interestingly, as in the case of Lugones's monkey, Gómez claims that mockery and irony are major means by which the *lunfardo* speaker resists institutional respectability. But more importantly, for him, the "degenerated" Spanish of delinquents was also an expression of the atavistic, genetically regressive psychology of criminals:

> The delinquent's states of consciousness, especially those of the professional delinquent who masters this language, are very special states which are determined by the influence of the hereditary germ, . . . by diverse forms of degeneration, by irresistible impulses and by the concurrence of external factors which, finding favorable grounds in the anomalies of the criminal soul, alter the normal sentimental process of ideas and desires. In a word, delinquents think and feel differently than normal men, and it is logical that a different form of expression corresponds to this different way of thinking and feeling. (108)

As for Lombroso, for Gómez "atavistic influence plays an important role since argot, plagued by metaphorical expressions and onomatopoeias, reproduces the traits of the language of savages" (109).

It is evident, on the other hand, that what the criminal anthropologists labeled *lunfardo* was often indistinguishable from the particular inflections of the Spanish spoken by immigrants. Gómez explicitly establishes the link: "[The] majority of words that constitute the jargon of our criminals are derived from foreign languages, a fact which is explained by the contingent that immigration has contributed to criminality in Buenos Aires" (110). Being a criminal was thus a way of remaining an alien within the space of the national language. And concurrently, not speaking "well" predisposed the immigrant to a position *under*—down by law—at the margins of citizenship. The registers of the minor tongue, the immigrant's flight from the national intonation, were pathologized and criminalized by the "scientific" discourse on language, reinforcing the pervasive identification of grammar, law, and the state, at least throughout the nineteenth century.

Nevertheless, on reading the proliferating dictionaries of *lunfardo* included in the texts by most criminal anthropologists, one cannot help but notice a marked voyeuristic curiosity, the pleasure displayed by the expert who masters the other's word. It is, in part, the pleasure of the anthropological gaze caught in the act of deciphering the other's secrets. It is the self-fulfilling fantasy of making the other speak—of recording the other's word—as a fundamental aspect of the nation's self-consolidation and surveillance.

To conclude, I will briefly comment on a story by one of Leopoldo Lugones's contemporaries, the Uruguayan Horacio Quiroga, written in Argentina precisely during the period of militancy against immigrants and their "contamination" of Spanish. The story is entitled "La lengua," meaning, in the specific context of the narrative, "The Tongue," but also "Language." It is also a tale about a doctor, a dentist—a mouth specialist—who has problems with a patient. The patient, Felippone, of evident Italian descent, speaks badly—"habla mal" or "maldice"—as the narrator emphasizes several times. In particular, Felippone speaks badly of the dentist's dangerous habits, especially his fixation with blood. The circulation of the bad words predictably leaves the dentist without any patients, who wisely fear the instruments of his obsession. The dentist fantasizes vengeance. He waits for Felippone to have a terrible toothache and generously offers him his free services. Felippone accepts the offer and sits in the dentist's chair. The mouth specialist pulls out the other's tongue and attempts to cut it off with a scalpel (a sharp, cutting *stylet*, perhaps?). After the first incision, obsessed with blood, the mad dentist looks inside the mutilated mouth and finds, to his surprise, that Felippone's severed tongue could multiply itself, with an incredible velocity, in the form of small or minor tongues. The mouth specialist, with the same *stylet* or scalpel, unsuccessfully attempts to cut out these minor tongues which, uprooted from the face of the subject, begin to look like the proliferating mouths of a monstrous polyp. Left with no option—at least not in the story—the paranoid mouth specialist shoots Felippone in the face. Nevertheless, the faceless minor tongues, with an unspeakable speed—beyond grammaticality's control—continue the feast of their proliferation. "Tongues, they multiply, and they all utter my name" (88), concludes the dentist. A nightmare, indeed, for a paranoid oral surgeon.

Notes

My thanks are due to Anna K. Stahl and Pamela Cheek, for their attentive and critical readings of the early versions of this paper, and to my colleagues and friends at the Stanford Humanities Center, where I completed the first draft in the Spring of 1991. I also wish to express my deepest appreciation of Angelika Bammer's lucid and generous input.

1. "Izur" appears in Lugones's first collection of short stories, *Las fuerzas extrañas* (1906), and is reproduced in *El payador*.

2. On Caliban's cursing in the pedagogical scene, see Greenblatt 31. Cursing inscribes Caliban's speech in Prospero's differential economy as an ethnically and linguistically marked body whose otherness supports the constitution of the master's eloquence and humanity. In contrast, Izur's mimicry splits dominant discourse, submitting it to an uncanny duplication which displays the rhetorical and institutionally bound status of the master's claim to originality and authenticity. On the strategic uses of mimicry, see Bhabha.

3. In *Didáctica* (1910), his major essay on education and the national question, Lugones writes: "Given the inferior social condition of cosmopolitan immigrants, they tend to deform our language with pernicious contributions. This is extremely serious since that is

how the disintegration of the fatherland begins. In that respect, the legend of Babel is very significant: the dispersion of men originated with language's anarchy" (*El payador* 285); unless noted otherwise, all translations from Spanish are mine.

4. For an exhaustive historical overview of official responses to linguistic heterogeneity in Mexico, see Heath. On the question of diglossia and the drift between written and oral cultures as a prevailing theme in Latin American literature, see Rosenblat. Angel Rama studies the containment of cultural heterogeneity effected by writing in the organization of Latin American colonial and postcolonial societies in *La ciudad letrada*. On the representation of subaltern speech and the process of subject-formation in nineteenth-century Argentina, see Ludmer.

5. Bello's extensive grammatical and philological writings are included in his *Obras completas*, vols. 4–7. In this paper I particularly refer to his *Gramática* (1847).

6. This was, indeed, not only true for Bello, but for most nineteenth-century Latin American intellectuals whose authority was often grounded in the project of organization and administration of the national states in the decades following the wars of independence from Spain. For a study of the complex relationship between intellectuals and power throughout this formative period, see my *Desencuentros*; chapter two specifically deals with Bello's changing views on intellectuals and the state.

7. See Adorno and Horkheimer, particularly "The Concept of Enlightenment" 3–42; and Reiss. On the linguistic theories of Enlightenment, see Aarsleff.

8. For a classic analysis of linguistic centralization and the establishment of modern institutions in post-revolutionary France, see Balibar and Laporte.

9. In *Imagined Communities*, Benedict Anderson explores the role of writing and the printed word in the process of "imagining" a modern nation. For Anderson, the community of readers brought together particularly by the press share a sense of a *linguistic* belonging that constitutes "the embryo of the nationally-imagined community" (47). In an elaboration and lucid critique of Anderson's notion of community, Mary Louise Pratt states that "this prototype of the modern nation as imagined community is . . . mirrored in linguistics' imagined object of study, the speech community," and moves on to emphasize the drift between the imagined homogeneity of the community and the "fractured reality of linguistic experience in modern stratified societies" (50–51). Indeed, especially in his reflections on language as an all-inclusive sphere, "always open to new speakers, listeners, and readers" (134), Anderson occludes the hegemonic will and violent process of exclusion presupposed by any form of "imagined" homogeneity. On the power relationships that cut through the homogeneity of the centralized, national languages, see also Deleuze and Guattari's work on the "minor" language.

10. On Enlightenment's discourses on *patois* institutionalized by the French Revolution, see Certeau, Julia, and Revel.

11. For example, during his exile in Chile, the Argentinean Domingo F. Sarmiento debated against Bello's grammatical projects: "The people's sovereignty prevails in language; grammarians are like the conservative senate which was created to resist popular offensives in order to protect routines and traditions" (50). Bello responds: "[How] can you allow the people to shape language at their whim, each one having their own, and this resulting in another Babel? In language as in politics, it is indispensable to have a body of learned men who would dictate the laws according to their needs . . . and it would not be any less ludicrous to allow the people to determine those laws. Those who claim in vain a romantic, licentious liberty in the use of language, and who do so for the sake of novelty or to exempt themselves from the labor involved in the study of language, would like to speak and write at their own discretion" ("Ejercicios populares" 438–39).

12. Bello: "What is the source of this progress and civilization, this search for social

improvement and liberty? If we want to know, we should compare Europe and our fortunate America, with the sombrous empires of Asia, in which despotism forces its iron scepter on necks bent in advance by ignorance; or with the African hordes, in which man, barely superior to brutes, is, like them, an object of commerce between his own brothers. Who enlightened the enslaved Europe with the first sparks of civil liberty? Was it not literature?" ("Discurso pronunciado" 5–6).

13. In this respect, it is not coincidental that while working on his grammatical studies Bello was also drafting Chile's *Civil Code*.

14. Such is Balibar and Laporte's argument.

15. Deleuze and Guattari: "Forming grammatically correct sentences is for the normal individual the prerequisite for any submission to social laws. No one is supposed to be ignorant of grammaticality; those who are belong in special institutions. The unity of language is fundamentally political" (101).

16. The process of literature's specialization and autonomy from the state does not imply the circumscription of its authority to an aesthetic sphere. In fact, it could be argued that a fundamental trait of Latin American literature is the irreducible hybridism of its forms and roles in society. This is probably an effect of literature's *uneven* development as an institution whose weak foundations paradoxically have allowed literature to maintain a significant public authority.

17. The first abolitionist narratives are: Juan Francisco Manzano's *Autobiografía* (written in 1835) and Anselmo Suárez y Romero's novel, *Francisco. El ingenio o las delicias del campo* (written in 1838 and published in 1880). They formed part of a portfolio of materials on slavery assembled by a leading Cuban intellectual, Domingo del Monte, for the British abolitionist Richard R. Madden in the late 1830s. The critique of slavery stimulated the writing of three later novels: Cirilo Villaverde's *Cecilia Valdés* (begun in 1839, but not published until 1882 in New York), Gertrudis Gómez de Avelaneda's *Sab* (Madrid, 1841), and Antonio Zambrana's *El negro Francisco* (Santiago del Chile, 1873). In many respects, Alejo Carpentier's first novel, *¡Ecué-Yamba-O!* (1933), is an experimental revision of the major formal and ideological questions raised by the abolitionist narratives. For a comprehensive overview of the theme of slavery and racial conflicts in Cuban literature, see Luis.

18. Significantly, the first Latin American dialectological dictionary, *Diccionario provincial casi-razonado de voces cubanas* (1836) by the Cuban Esteban Pichardo, was contemporary with the first abolitionist fictions. While insisting on the specificity of the Cuban lexicon with respect to Castilian Spanish, Pichardo's classifications devote special attention to the "confused jargon" and "disfigured" Spanish of slaves. For a shrewd analysis of the political and economic roles of lexicography in India, see Amin. A word on creolization is in order: In contrast to the creolization of French in Haiti and the intense process of pidginization in other areas of the British and Dutch Caribbean, slaves and their descendants in the Spanish colonies did not create creole languages. Sidney Mintz discusses this contrast as evidence of Spain's hegemony in her Caribbean colonies. The lack of a creolization does not imply, however, that dominant language actually became a homogeneous, uncontested system in the Spanish colonies. Linguistic contact produced much anxiety among white creole intellectuals. See for example, Bachiller y Morales. Although I cannot develop the argument here, it is important to note that the fear of ethno-linguistic contact conditions the representation of Afro-Cuban speech in the "standard" discourse of narrators in abolitionist fictions. Thus the formal history of the genre—from the initial predominance of indirect discourse and its strict avoidance of the (slave) character's orality in Suárez y Romero's *Francisco*, to the later experimentation with the highly mixed and less subordinative free-indirect discourse in Carpentier's *¡Ecué-Yamba-O!*—is ideologically overdetermined by the changing reflections on the status of ethno-linguistic contact in the national imaginings.

19. For Louis Althusser the "interpellation of individuals as subjects" is the distinctive function of ideology in capitalism. See his "Ideology and Ideological State Apparatuses." Indeed, the abolitionist series was inaugurated by the interpellative demand made on the slave Juan Francisco Manzano who, in response to a request made by Domingo del Monte, a leading creole abolitionist, wrote the only slave autobiography known in Cuba. Emblematically, Manzano, who at the time was a domestic runaway slave, exchanged his narrative for the cost of his manumission. Manzano's interpellated narrative literally guarantees the slave's access to a degree of juridical autonomy. See Manzano. Manzano's narrative was part of the *dossier* on slavery assembled by Del Monte for Richard R. Madden, who then published his translation of the *Autobiografía* in 1840. On subject-formation in Manzano, see Molloy.

20. In that respect, although abolitionist fictions project the incorporation of slaves as *speaking* subjects of a more just, modern Law, they are also phobic fantasies of purity and contamination. Often overdetermining the representations of ethno-linguistic contact in fiction, the rhetoric of purity and "dirt" was nevertheless not a literary invention. The tropes of purity and contamination usually remit to the medical discourses of the time, particularly to the consolidation of hygiene as a national master-discourse after the disastrous cholera epidemic of 1832, precisely during the inaugural decade of the abolitionist series. Significantly, both the novels and hygiene manuals throughout this period devote much attention to black wet nurses—key *figures* of physical and social contact between the castes—who were thought to transmit not only physical diseases, but also psychological and cultural traits to the children of the elite. Since wet nurses usually taught the children of the master how to speak, not surprisingly the discourses on wet nursing symptomatically slide toward the identification of milk and language. On the fundamental role of boundary making and metaphors of purity and contamination in the constitution of cultural identity, see Douglas. On the symbolic power of hygiene, see also Vigarello.

21. For Pasolini, the novel's exploration of the conflicts and possible contact between different language groups since the Risurgimento has served to develop models of linguistic homogenization in Italy, a project only later realized, according to Pasolini, by the mass media.

22. Vološinov: "The conditions of verbal communication, its forms, and its methods of differentiation are dictated by the social and economic prerequisites of a given period. These changing sociolingual conditions are what in fact determines those changes in the forms of reported speech. . . . We would even venture to say that in the forms by which language registers the impressions of received speech and of the speaker, the history of the changing types of socioideological communication stands out in particular bold relief" (123). Of particular importance for the analysis of subjectification in fiction is Ann Banfield's study of direct and indirect discourse.

23. Like the Cuban abolitionist narratives, the indigenist novels of Mexico, Guatemala, and the Andean countries are representations of ethno-linguistic contact in processes of nation-building. See Rama, *Transculturación*; and Cornejo-Polar.

24. Although focusing specifically on the emergence of psychiatry in turn-of-the-century Argentina, Hugo Vezzetti's book on the construction of madness elucidates the social context in which criminal anthropology operates. After the completion of the final draft of this paper, two important articles on Lombroso in Argentina came to my attention (see Salessi; and Molloy 1992).

25. Lombrosian ideas were also very influential in Cuba. For example, the first major book by Fernando Ortiz, founder of Cuban ethnography, was a criminological analysis of African-Cuban culture. In fact, the second edition of Ortiz's *El hampa afrocubana* was introduced by Lombroso.

26. Tulio Halperin Donghi explores the changing views on immigration in "¿Para qué la inmigración?"

27. On stereotypes, see Gilman.
28. On tattoos as inscriptions of difference, see Certeau, "The Scriptural Economy" 139-41.

Works Cited

Aarsleff, Hans. *From Locke to Saussure: Essays on the Study of Language and Intellectual History*. Minneapolis: U of Minnesota P, 1982.

Adorno, Theodor W., and Max Horkheimer. *Dialectic of Enlightenment*. Trans. J. Cumming. New York: Seabury, 1972.

Althusser, Louis. "Ideology and Ideological State Apparatuses." *Essays on Ideology*. London: Verso, 1976. 1-60.

Amin, Shahid. "Editor's Introduction." *A Glossary of North Indian Peasant Life*. William Crook. 1879. Delhi: Oxford UP, 1989. xviii-xlii.

Anderson, Benedict. *Imagined Communities: Reflections on the Origin and Spread of Nationalism*. London: Verso, 1983.

Bachiller y Morales, Antonio. "Desfiguración a que está expuesto el idioma castellano al contacto y mezcla de las razas." Paper read at Anthropological Society of Havana, 1883. *Antología de lingüística cubana*. Ed. G. Alonso and A. L. Fernández. Vol. 1. Havana: Editorial de Ciencias Sociales, 1977. 105-11.

Bakhtin, M. M. "Discourse in the Novel." *The Dialogic Imagination*. Ed. M. Holquist. Trans. C. Emerson and M. Holquist. Austin: U of Texas P, 1981. 259-422.

Balibar, Renée, and Dominique Laporte. *Le français national: Politique et pratiques de la langue nationale sous la Révolution française*. Paris: Hachette, 1974.

Banfield, Ann. *Unspeakable Sentences: Narration and Representation in the Language of Fiction*. London: Routledge, 1982.

Bello, Andrés. "Ejercicios populares de la lengua castellana." *Obras completas* 9: 435-40.

——. "Discurso pronunciado en la instalación de la Universidad de Chile." 1843. *Obras completas* 21: 3-22.

——. *Gramática de la lengua castellana destinada al uso de los americanos*. Vol. 4 of *Obras completas*.

——. "Juicio sobre la poesía de José María Heredia." *Obras completas* 9: 235-50.

——. *Obras completas*. 26 vols. Caracas: La Casa de Bello, 1981.

Bhabha, Homi. "Of Mimicry and Man: The Ambivalence of Colonial Discourse." *October* 28 (1984): 125-33.

Borges, J. L. Prologue. *Izur*. Buenos Aires: Arte Gaglianone, 1982.

Certeau, Michel de. *Heterologies: Discourse on the Other*. Trans. Brian Massumi. Minneapolis: U of Minnesota P, 1986.

——. "The Scriptural Economy." *The Practice of Everyday Life*. Trans. Steven Rendall. Berkeley: U of California P, 1988.

Certeau, Michel de, Dominique Julia, and Jacques Revel. *Une politique de la langue: La Révolution française et les patois*. Paris: Gallimard, 1975.

Clifford, James. "On Ethnographic Allegory." Clifford and Marcus 98-121.

Clifford, James, and G. E. Marcus, eds. *Writing Culture: The Poetics and Politics of Ethnography*. Berkeley: U of California P, 1986.

Cornejo-Polar, Antonio. *Los universos narrativos de José María Arguedas.* Buenos Aires: Editorial Losada, 1973.

Deleuze, Gilles, and Félix Guattari. "November 20, 1923—Postulates of Linguistics." *A Thousand Plateaus: Capitalism and Schizophrenia.* Trans. Brian Massumi. Minneapolis: U of Minnesota P, 1987. 75–110.

Dellepiane, Antonio. *El idioma del delito. Contribución al estudio de la psicología criminal.* Buenos Aires: Arnoldo Moen, 1894.

Donghi, Tulio Halperin. "¿Para qué la inmigración? Ideología y política inmigratoria en la Argentina (1810–1914)." *El espejo de la historia. Problemas argentinos y perspectivas latinoamericanas.* Buenos Aires: Editorial Sudamericana, 1987. 189–238.

Douglas, Mary. *Purity and Danger.* New York: Praeger, 1966.

Drago, Luis María. *Los hombres de presa.* 1888. Buenos Aires: Imprenta La Cultura Argentina, 1921.

Gelpí, Juan G. "El discurso jerárquico en *Cecilia Valdés.*" *Revista de Crítica Literaria Latinoamericana* 34 (1991): 47–61.

Gilman, Sander. *Difference and Pathology: Stereotypes of Sexuality, Race, and Madness.* Ithaca: Cornell UP, 1985.

Gómez, Eusebio. *La mala vida en Buenos Aires.* Buenos Aires: Ediciones Juan Raldán, 1908.

Greenblatt, Stephen J. "Learning to Curse: Aspects of Linguistic Colonialism in the Sixteenth Century." *Learning to Curse: Essays in Early Modern Culture.* New York: Routledge, 1990. 16–39.

Heath, Shirley B. *Telling Tongues: Language Policy in México (From Colony to Nation).* New York: Teachers College P, 1972.

Lombroso, Cesare. *Gli anarchici.* Roma: Napoleone, 1972.

——. *L'uomo delinquente in rapporto all'antropologia, alla giurisprudenza ed alle discipline carcerarie.* 2 vols. Torino: Fratelli Bocca Editori, 1889.

Ludmer, Josefina. *El género gauchesco. Un tratado sobre la patria.* Buenos Aires: Sudamericana, 1988.

Lugones, Leopoldo. "Izur." *El payador y antología de poesía y prosa.* Ed. G. Ara. Caracas: Biblioteca Ayacucho, 1979. 223–30.

Luis, William. *Literary Bondage: Slavery in Cuban Narrative.* Austin: U of Texas P, 1990.

Manzano, Juan Francisco. *Autobiografía, cartas y versos.* Ed. José L. Franco. Havana: Municipio de la Habana, 1937.

——. *Poems by a Slave in the Island of Cuba, Recently Liberated: Translated from the Spanish by R. R. Madden, M. D. with the History of the Early Life of the Negro Poet.* London: Thomas Ward, 1840.

Mintz, Sidney. "The Socio-Historical Background to Pidginization and Creolization." *Pidginization and Creolization of Languages.* Ed. Dell Hymes. Cambridge: Cambridge UP, 1971. 481–96.

Molloy, Sylvia. "From Serf to Self: The Autobiography of Juan Francisco Manzano." *At Face Value: Autobiographical Writing in Spanish America.* Cambridge: Cambridge UP, 1991. 36–54.

——. "To Wilde for Comfort: Desire and Ideology in Fin-de-Siécle Spanish America." *Social Text* 31–2 (1992): 187–201.

Niceforo, Alfredo. *Il jergo nei normali, nei degenerati e nei criminali.* Torino: Fratelli Bocca Editori, 1897.

Ortiz, Fernando. *El hampa afrocubana: Los negros brujos (apuntes para un estudio de la etnología criminal.* Madrid: Librería de Fernando Fe, 1906.

Pasolini, Pier Paolo. "Nuove Questioni Linguistiche." *Empirismo eretic. Saggi.* Roma: Garzanti Editore, 1972. 5–24.

Pratt, Mary Louise. "Linguistic Utopias." *The Linguistics of Writing: Arguments between Language and Literature.* Ed. Nigel Fabb et al. New York: Methuen, 1987. 48–67.

Quiroga, Horacio. "La lengua." *Anaconda. El salvaje. Pasado amor.* Buenos Aires: Sur, 1960. 86–88.

Rama, Angel. *La ciudad letrada.* Hanover: Ediciones del Norte, 1984.

——. *Transculturación narrativa en América Latina.* Mexico: Siglo Veintiuno, 1982.

Ramos, Julio. *Desencuentros de la modernidad en América Latina: Literatura y política en el siglo XIX.* Mexico: Fondo de Cultura Económica, 1989.

Ramos-Mejía, Francisco. Introduction. Drago 1–17.

Reiss, Timothy. *The Discourse of Modernism.* Ithaca: Cornell UP, 1982.

Rosaldo, Renato. *Culture and Truth: The Remaking of Social Analysis.* Boston: Beacon, 1989.

——. "From the Door of His Tent: The Fieldworker and the Inquisitor." Clifford and Marcus 77–97.

Rosenblat, Angel. *Lengua literaria y lengua popular en América.* Caracas: Universidad Central de Venezuela, 1969.

Salessi, Jorge. "Tango, nacionalismo y sexualidad: Buenos Aires, 1880–1914." *Hispamérica* 60 (1991): 33–53.

Sarmiento, Domingo F. "Ejercicios populares de la lengua castellana." 1842. *Sarmiento en el destierro.* Ed. A. Donoso. Buenos Aires: Gleizer, 1927. 49–53.

Sloterdijk, Peter. *Critique of Cynical Reason.* Trans. M. Eldred. Minneapolis: U of Minnesota P, 1987.

Sommer, Doris. *Foundational Fictions: The National Romances of Latin America.* Berkeley: U of California P, 1991.

Suárez y Romero, Anselmo. *Francisco. El ingenio o las delicias del campo.* 1880. Havana: Biblioteca de Autores Cubanos, 1970.

Vezzetti, Hugo. *La locura en la Argentina.* Buenos Aires: Folios Ediciones, 1983.

Vigarello, Georges. *Le propre et le sale. L'hygiène du corps depuis le Moyen Age.* Paris: Seuil, 1985.

Villaverde, Cirilio. *Cecilia Valdés.* 1882. Mexico: Editorial Porrúa, 1979.

Vološinov, V. N. *Marxism and the Philosophy of Language.* Trans. L. Matejka and I. R. Titunik. Cambridge: Harvard UP, 1986.

Zambrana, Antonio. *El negro Francisco.* 1873. Havana: Imprenta P. Fernández, 1948.

3 | The Imam and the Indian

Amitav Ghosh

I MET THE Imam of the village and Khamees the Rat at about the same time. I don't exactly remember now—it happened more than six years ago—but I think I met the Imam first.

But this is not quite accurate. I didn't really "meet" the Imam. I inflicted myself upon him. Perhaps that explains what happened.

Still, there was nothing else I could have done. As the man who led the daily prayers in the mosque, he was a leading figure in the village, and since I, a foreigner, had come to live there, he may well for all I knew have been offended had I neglected to pay him a call. Besides, I wanted to meet him; I was intrigued by what I'd heard about him.

People didn't often talk about the Imam in the village, but when they did, they usually spoke of him somewhat dismissively, but also a little wistfully, as they might of some old, half-forgotten thing, like the annual flooding of the Nile. Listening to my friends speak of him, I had an inkling, long before I actually met him, that he already belonged, in a way, to the village's past. I thought I knew this for certain when I heard that apart from being an Imam he was also, by profession, a barber and a healer. People said he knew a great deal about herbs and poultices and the old kind of medicine. This interested me. This was Tradition: I knew that in rural Egypt Imams and other religious figures are often by custom associated with those two professions.

The trouble was that these accomplishments bought the Imam very little credit in the village. The villagers didn't any longer want an Imam who was also a barber and a healer. The older people wanted someone who had studied at al-Azhar and could quote from Jamal ad-Din Afghani and Mohammad Abduh as fluently as he could from the Hadith, and the younger men wanted a fierce, black-bearded orator, someone whose voice would thunder from the mimbar and reveal to them their destiny. No one had time for old-fashioned Imams who made themselves ridiculous by boiling herbs and cutting hair.

Yet Ustad Ahmed, who taught in the village's secondary school and was as well-read a man as I have ever met, often said—and this was not something he said of many people—that the old Imam read a lot. A lot of what? Politics, theology, even popular science . . . that kind of thing.

47

This made me all the more determined to meet him, and one evening, a few months after I first came to the village, I found my way to his house. He lived in the center of the village, on the edge of the dusty open square which had the mosque in its middle. This was the oldest part of the village: a maze of low mud huts huddled together like confectionery on a tray, each hut crowned with a billowing, tousled head of straw.

When I knocked on the door the Imam opened it himself. He was a big man, with very bright brown eyes, set deep in a wrinkled, weather-beaten face. Like the room behind him, he was distinctly untidy: his blue jallabeyya was mud-stained and unwashed and his turban had been knotted anyhow around his head. But his beard, short and white and neatly trimmed, was everything a barber's beard should be. Age had been harsh on his face, but there was a certain energy in the way he arched his shoulders, in the clarity of his eyes and in the way he fidgeted constantly, was never still: it was plain that he was a vigorous, restive kind of person.

"Welcome," he said, courteous but unsmiling, and stood aside and waved me in. It was a long dark room, with sloping walls and a very low ceiling. There was a bed in it and a couple of mats but little else, apart from a few, scattered books: everything bore that dull patina of grime which speaks of years of neglect. Later, I learned that the Imam had divorced his first wife and his second had left him, so that now he lived quite alone and had his meals with his son's family who lived across the square.

"Welcome," he said again, formally.

"Welcome to you," I said, giving him the formal response, and then we began the long, reassuring litany of Arabic phrases of greeting.

"How are you?"

"How are you?"

"You have brought blessings?"

"May God bless you."

"Welcome."

"Welcome to you."

"You have brought light."

"The light is yours."

"How are you?"

"How are you?"

He was very polite, very proper. In a moment he produced a kerosene stove and began to brew tea. But even in the performance of that little ritual there was something about him that was guarded, watchful.

"You're the *doktor al-Hindi*," he said to me at last, "aren't you? The Indian doctor?"

I nodded, for that was the name the village had given me. Then I told him that I wanted to talk to him about the methods of his system of medicine.

He looked very surprised and for a while he was silent. Then he put his right hand to his heart and began again on the ritual of greetings and responses, but in a markedly different way this time; one that I had learnt to recognize as a means of changing the subject.

"Welcome."

"Welcome to you."

"You have brought light."

"The light is yours."

And so on.

At the end of it I repeated what I had said.

"Why do you want to hear about *my* herbs?" he retorted. "Why don't you go back to your own country and find out about your own?"

"I will," I said. "Soon. But right now . . . "

"No, no," he said restlessly. "Forget all about that; I'm trying to forget about it myself."

And then I knew that he would never talk to me about his craft, not just because he had taken a dislike to me for some reason of his own, but because his medicines were as discredited in his own eyes as they were in his clients'; because he knew as well as anybody else that the people who came to him now did so only because of old habits; because he bitterly regretted his inherited association with these relics of the past.

"Instead," he said, "let me tell you about what I have been learning over the last few years. Then you can go back to your country and tell them about it."

He jumped up, his eyes shining, reached under his bed and brought out a glistening new biscuit tin.

"Here!" he said, opening it. "Look!"

Inside the box was a hypodermic syringe and a couple of glass phials. This is what he had been learning, he told me: the art of mixing and giving injections. And there was a huge market for it too, in the village: everybody wanted injections, for coughs, colds, fevers, whatever. There was a good living in it. He wanted to demonstrate his skill to me right there, on my arm, and when I protested that I wasn't ill, that I didn't need an injection just then, he was offended. "All right," he said curtly, standing up. "I have to go to the mosque right now. Perhaps we can talk about this some other day."

That was the end of my interview. I walked with him to the mosque and there, with an air of calculated finality, he took my hand in his, gave it a perfunctory shake and vanished up the stairs.

Khamees the Rat I met one morning when I was walking through the rice fields that lay behind the village, watching people transplant their seedlings. Everybody I met was cheerful and busy and the flooded rice fields were sparkling in the clear sunlight. If I shut my ears to the language, I thought, and stretch the date palms a bit and give them a few coconuts, I could easily be back somewhere in Bengal.

I was a long way from the village and not quite sure of my bearings, when I spotted a group of people who had finished their work and were sitting on the path, passing around a hookah.

"*Ahlan!*" a man in a brown jallabeyya called out to me. "Hullo! Aren't you the Indian *doktor*?"

"Yes," I called back. "And who're you?"

"He's a rat," someone answered, raising a gale of laughter. "Don't go anywhere near him."

"Tell me *ya doktor*," the Rat said, "if I get on my donkey and ride steadily for thirty days will I make it to India?"

"No," I said. "You wouldn't make it in thirty months."

"Thirty months!" he said. "You must have come a long way."

"Yes."

"As for me," he declared, "I've never even been as far as Alexandria and if I can help it I never will."

I laughed: it did not occur to me to believe him.

When I first came to that quiet corner of the Nile Delta I had expected to find on that most ancient and most settled of soils a settled and restful people. I couldn't have been more wrong.

The men of the village had all the busy restlessness of airline passengers in a transit lounge. Many of them had worked and traveled in the sheikhdoms of the Persian Gulf, others had been in Libya and Jordan and Syria, some had been to the Yemen as soldiers, others to Saudi Arabia as pilgrims, a few had visited Europe: some of them had passports so thick they opened out like inkblackened concertinas. And none of this was new: their grandparents and ancestors and relatives had traveled and migrated too, in much the same way as mine had, in the Indian subcontinent—because of wars, or for money and jobs, or perhaps simply because they got tired of living always in one place. You could read the history of this restlessness in the villagers' surnames: they had names which derived from cities in the Levant, from Turkey, from faraway towns in Nubia; it was as though people had drifted here from every corner of the Middle East. The wanderlust of its founders had been plowed into the soil of the village: it seemed to me sometimes that every man in it was a traveler. Everyone, that is, except Khamees the Rat, and even his surname, as I discovered later, meant "of Sudan."

"Well never mind *ya doktor*," Khamees said to me now, "since you're not going to make it back to your country by sundown anyway, why don't you come and sit with us for a while?"

He smiled and moved up to make room for me.

I liked him at once. He was about my age, in the early twenties, scrawny, with a thin, mobile face deeply scorched by the sun. He had that brightness of eye and the quick, slightly sardonic turn to his mouth that I associated with faces in the coffee-houses of universities in Delhi and Calcutta; he seemed to belong to a world of late-night rehearsals and black coffee and lecture rooms, even though, in fact, unlike most people in the village, he was completely illiterate. Later I learned that he was called the Rat—Khamees the Rat—because he was said to gnaw away at things with his tongue, like a rat did with its teeth. He laughed at everything, people said—at his father, the village's patron saint, the village elders, the Imam, everything.

That day he decided to laugh at me.

"All right *ya doktor*," he said to me as soon as I had seated myself. "Tell me, is it true what they say, that in your country you burn your dead?"

No sooner had he said it than the women of the group clasped their hands to their hearts and muttered in breathless horror: "*Haram! Haram!*"

My heart sank. This was a conversation I usually went through at least once a day and I was desperately tired of it. "Yes," I said, "it's true; some people in my country burn their dead."

"You mean," said Khamees in mock horror, "that you put them on heaps of wood and just light them up?"

"Yes," I said, hoping that he would tire of this sport if I humored him.

"Why?" he said. "Is there a shortage of kindling in your country?"

"No," I said helplessly, "you don't understand." Somewhere in the limitless riches of the Arabic language a word such as "cremate" must exist, but if it does, I never succeeded in finding it. Instead, for lack of any other, I had to use the word "burn." That was unfortunate, for "burn" was the word for what happened to wood and straw and the eternally damned.

Khamees the Rat turned to his spellbound listeners. "I'll tell you why they do it," he said. "They do it so that their bodies can't be punished after the Day of Judgement."

Everybody burst into wonderstruck laughter. "Why, how clever," cried one of the younger girls. "What a good idea! We ought to start doing it ourselves. That way we can do exactly what we like and when we die and the Day of Judgement comes, there'll be nothing there to judge."

Khamees had got his laugh. Now he gestured to them to be quiet again.

"All right then *ya doktor*," he said. "Tell me something else: is it true that you are a Magian? That in your country everybody worships cows? Is it true that the other day when you were walking through the fields you saw a man beating a cow and you were so upset that you burst into tears and ran back to your room?"

"No, it's not true," I said, but without much hope: I had heard this story before and knew that there was nothing I could say which would effectively give it the lie. "You're wrong. In my country people beat their cows all the time; I promise you."

I could see that no one believed me.

"Everything's upside-down in their country," said a dark, aquiline young woman who, I was told later, was Khamees's wife. "Tell us *ya doktor*: in your country, do you have crops and fields and canals like we do?"

"Yes," I said, "we have crops and fields, but we don't always have canals. In some parts of my country they aren't needed because it rains all the year around."

"*Ya salám*," she cried, striking her forehead with the heel of her palm. "Do you hear that, oh you people? Oh, the Protector, oh, the Lord! It rains all the year round in his country."

She had gone pale with amazement. "So tell us then," she demanded, "do you have night and day like we do?"

"Shut up woman," said Khamees. "Of course they don't. It's day all the time over there, didn't you know? They arranged it like that so they wouldn't have to spend any money on lamps."

We all laughed, and then someone pointed to a baby lying in the shade of a tree swaddled in a sheet of cloth. "That's Khamees's baby," I was told. "He was born last month."

"That's wonderful," I said. "Khamees must be very happy."

Khamees gave a cry of delight. "The Indian knows I'm happy because I've had a son," he said to the others. "He understands that people are happy when they have children: he's not as upside-down as we thought."

He slapped me on the knee and lit up the hookah and from that moment we were friends.

One evening, perhaps a month or so after I first met Khamees, he and his brothers and I were walking back to the village from the fields when he spotted the old Imam sitting on the steps that led to the mosque.

"Listen," he said to me, "you know the old Imam, don't you? I saw you talking to him once."

"Yes," I said. "I talked to him once."

"My wife's ill," Khamees said. "I want the Imam to come to my house to give her an injection. He won't come if I ask him, he doesn't like me. You go and ask."

"He doesn't like me either," I said.

"Never mind," Khamees insisted. "He'll come if you ask him—he knows you're a foreigner. He'll listen to you."

While Khamees waited on the edge of the square with his brothers I went across to the Imam. I could tell that he had seen me—and Khamees—from a long way off, that he knew I was crossing the square to talk to him. But he would not look in my direction. Instead, he pretended to be deep in conversation with a man who was sitting beside him, an elderly and pious shopkeeper whom I knew slightly.

When I reached them I said "Good evening" very pointedly to the Imam. He could not ignore me any longer then, but his response was short and curt, and he turned back at once to resume his conversation.

The old shopkeeper was embarrassed now, for he was a courteous, gracious man in the way that seemed to come so naturally to the elders of the village. "Please sit down," he said to me. "Do sit. Shall we get you a chair?"

Then he turned to the Imam and said, slightly puzzled: "You know the Indian *doktor*, don't you? He's come all the way from India to be a student at the University of Alexandria."

"I know him," said the Imam. "He came around to ask me questions. But as for this student business, I don't know. What's *he* going to study? He doesn't even write in Arabic."

"Well," said the shopkeeper judiciously, "that's true; but after all he writes his own languages and he knows English."

"Oh those," said the Imam. "What's the use of *those* languages? They're the easiest languages in the world. Anyone can write those."

He turned to face me for the first time. His eyes were very bright and his mouth was twitching with anger. "Tell me," he said, "why do you worship cows?"

I was so taken aback that I began to stammer. The Imam ignored me. He turned to the old shopkeeper and said: "That's what they do in his country— did you know?—they worship cows."

He shot me a glance from the corner of his eyes. "And shall I tell you what else they do?" he said to the shopkeeper.

He let the question hang for a moment. And then, very loudly, he hissed: "They burn their dead."

The shopkeeper recoiled as though he had been slapped. His hands flew to his mouth. "Oh God!" he muttered. "*Ya Allah.*"

"That's what they do," said the Imam. "They burn their dead."

Then suddenly he turned to me and said, very rapidly: "Why do you allow it? Can't you see that it's a primitive and backward custom? Are you savages that you permit something like that? Look at you: you've had some kind of education; you should know better. How will your country ever progress if you carry on doing these things? You've even been to the West; you've seen how advanced they are. Now tell me: have you ever seen them burning their dead?"

The Imam was shouting now and a circle of young men and boys had gathered around us. Under the pressure of their interested eyes my tongue began to trip, even on syllables I thought I had mastered. I found myself growing angry—as much with my own incompetence as with the Imam.

"Yes, they do burn their dead in the West," I managed to say somehow. I raised my voice too now. "They have special electric furnaces meant just for that."

The Imam could see that he had stung me. He turned away and laughed. "He's lying," he said to the crowd. "They don't burn their dead in the West. They're not an ignorant people. They're advanced, they're educated, they have science, they have guns and tanks and bombs."

"We have them too!" I shouted back at him. I was as confused now as I was angry. "In my country we have all those things too," I said to the crowd. "We have guns and tanks and bombs. And they're better than anything you have—we're way ahead of you."

The Imam could no longer disguise his anger. "I tell you, he's lying," he said. "Our guns and bombs are much better than theirs. Ours are second only to the West's."

"It's you who's lying," I said. "You know nothing about this. Ours are much better. Why, in my country we've even had a nuclear explosion. You won't be able to match that in a hundred years."

So there we were, the Imam and I, delegates from two superseded civilizations vying with each other to lay claim to the violence of the West.

At that moment, despite the vast gap that lay between us, we understood each other perfectly. We were both traveling, he and I: we were traveling in the West. The only difference was that I had actually been there, in person: I could have told him about the ancient English university I had won a scholarship to, about punk dons with safety pins in their mortar-board, about superhighways and sex shops and Picasso. But none of it would have mattered. We would have known, both of us, that all that was mere fluff: at the bottom, for him as for me and millions and millions of people on the landmasses around us, the West meant only this—science and tanks and guns and bombs.

And we recognized too the inescapability of these things, their strength, their power—evident in nothing so much as this: that even for him, a man of God, and for me, a student of the "humane" sciences, they had usurped the place of all other languages of argument. He knew, just as I did, that he could no longer say to me, as Ibn Battuta might have when he traveled to India in the fourteenth century: "You should do this or that because it is right or good or because God wills it so." He could not have said it because that language is dead: those things are no longer sayable; they sound absurd. Instead he had had, of necessity, to use that other language, so universal that it extended equally to him, an old-fashioned village Imam, and great leaders at SALT conferences: he had had to say to me: "You ought not to do this because otherwise you will not have guns and tanks and bombs."

Since he was a man of God his was the greater defeat.

For a moment then I was desperately envious. The Imam would not have said any of these things to me had I been a Westerner. He would not have dared. Whether I wanted it or not, I would have had around me the protective aura of an inherited expertise in the technology of violence. That aura would have surrounded me, I thought, with a sheet of clear glass, like a bulletproof screen; or perhaps it would have worked as a talisman, like a press card, armed with which I could have gone off to what were said to be the most terrible places in the world that month, to gaze and wonder. And then perhaps I too would one day have had enough material for a book which would have had for its epigraph the line, *The horror! The horror!*—for the virtue of a sheet of glass is that it does not require one to look within.

But that still leaves Khamees the Rat waiting on the edge of the square.

In the end it was he and his brothers who led me away from the Imam. They took me home with them, and there, while Khamees's wife cooked dinner for us—she was not so ill after all—Khamees said to me: "Do not be upset, *ya doktor*. Forget about all those guns and things. I'll tell you what: *I'll* come to visit you in your country, even though I've never been anywhere. I'll come all the way."

He slipped a finger under his skull-cap and scratched his head, thinking hard.

Then he added: "But if I die, you must bury me."

Reprinted by permission from *Granta* 20 (Winter 1986) 135–46.

(Re)Locating
"Home" and "Community"

4 | On Language Memoir

Alice Yaeger Kaplan

FOR SEVERAL YEARS I have been working on a memoir which I refer to, in shorthand, as a "memoir about learning French." This phrase, "a memoir about learning French" really says very little about my book, which has challenged me to think about language and identity; to say what happened to my identity when my language changed from English to French; to say what it has meant to me to take on the attributes of French culture, as a student, then as a professor; to imagine what my second identity has to do with myself and my family—how new selves, new families emerge in a second language both as reactions and as mirrors of the first one.[1] Above all, writing about learning French has challenged me to write out of my own love and my experience— rather than as a distant expert.

When I began, I read as many scholarly disquisitions as I could find on second language acquisition—linguistics, sociology, education—and I found methods and statistics and the occasional anecdote, but nothing, really, about what is going on inside the head of the person who suddenly finds herself passionately engaged in new sounds and a new voice, who discovers that "*chat*" is not a cat at all, but a new creature in new surroundings. I wanted to see the "cat," then the "*chat*." I wanted the differences between languages to come alive in a dialogue and characterization. What I was looking for was not theory, but fiction. When I turned to fiction I found, to my delight, that there is an entire genre of twentieth-century autobiographical writing which is in essence about language learning. But it has never been categorized or named as such, either because it is discussed in terms of the history of a specific ethnic or national literature, or because language is understood in these books as mere décor in a drama of upward mobility or exile.

In the genre I am calling "language memoir," the second language is not always a "foreign" language; sometimes it is a new dialect, a language of upward mobility, a language of power or expressivity within the native language. Learning a new language becomes a family drama when the speaker returns to the situation of her or his origins and confronts parents and family in the new tongue. Sometimes the speaker longs for the old language, and sometimes dreads it; more often dread and longing for home coexist across the narrative.

I have always heard it said that people learn languages "in order to communicate" and "out of empathy for others." I never believed it, because it wasn't true of my own experience learning French, and now that I am a French teacher, it isn't true of my students. "Communication" and "empathy"—such positive, altruistic motives—cannot possibly take into account the variety of contexts in which languages are learned, the motivations, the emotional tenor of the new and old languages, the way language functions for each personality. Students learn out of desire and fear and greed and a need to escape as much as out of empathy. Language learning is clearly more interesting, and less innocent, than the truism would indicate.

Once I discovered the language memoir genre, I had companionship in writing my memoir. In the French tradition alone, right off the top, were Sartre, *Les Mots*; Sarraute, *Enfance*; Ernaux, *La Place*; Charef, *Le Thé au Harem d'Archi Ahmed*. As a way of demonstrating how language memoir works its particular magic, I single out two American texts, Richard Rodriguez's *Hunger of Memory*, and Alfred Kazin's *A Walker in the City*, for discussion here. They, in particular, taught me how to take my time with memories of words, and sounds; they helped me to remember situations where I hid in my second language, where I leaped out of myself. They helped me to understand, through the smallest details, the relationship of language to community. Even when I didn't agree with Rodriguez and Kazin—when I hated their political views, rejected their ambitions, disagreed with their vision of the family—I felt we were kindred. We were holding the same magnifying glass up to our language. I didn't always like Kazin and Rodriguez, but I knew them. That's a decent ambition for a memoir writer: to be known, rather than to be liked. A single concrete detail from one of their books—the way someone says hello, holds a pencil, wears a scarf—tells more about race, class, and gender than the dreary litany of categories ("I am a white, female, middle-class heterosexual") that has come to pass in contemporary criticism for "subject positioning."

Public and Private Languages in the Immigrant Novel: Rodriguez and Kazin

Richard Rodriguez's *Hunger of Memory: The Education of Richard Rodriguez* is the story of a Chicano immigrant who understands very early in his life that access to success in the United States has to do with his mastery of American English, and hence with the loss of his family language, Spanish. It is a highly polarized narrative, as Spanish represents the intimate, private family language, and English the language of the public sphere. Rodriguez tells the heartbreaking story of his mother, a clerk typist, whose main chance to rise to the middle class was destroyed by a spelling mistake:

One morning there was a letter to be sent to a Washington cabinet officer. On the dictating tape, a voice referred to urban guerrillas. My mother typed (the wrong word, correctly): "gorillas." The mistake horrified the anti-poverty bureaucrats who shortly after arranged to have her returned to her previous position. She would go no further. So she willed her ambition to her children. (54)

Richard Rodriguez versus Rich-heard Road-ree-guess; the autobiographer learns to hear his own name in English as a series of discrete English words connoting understanding but also the mob (herd/heard); travel but also exile (road); wonder but also confusion (guess). The words contained in his American name sum up the tones he will strike in his story, as he tells of prying himself loose from his humble Sacramento family, his success in school, his graduate-school persona. Eventually he is so successful that he becomes a spokesman for assimilation. *Hunger of Memory* is a compilation of highly personal, passionate speeches that Rodriguez gave in conference rooms and banquet halls around the country during the 1970s, right-wing polemics opposing the affirmative action, bilingual education, and Chicano nationalism of the left, all of which seem to mock his own hard-won success. In spite of his assurance that ethnic identity is a loser's strategy, Rodriguez does not hide the loss he has suffered, and the pain he feels makes his story compelling, even to those readers who would most oppose its message:

Once I learned public language, it would never again be easy for me to hear intimate family voices. More and more of my day was spent hearing words. But that may only be a way of saying that the day I raised my hand in class and spoke loudly to an entire roomful of faces, my childhood started to end. (28)

When Richard Rodriguez talks about the audience for his writing, he states specifically that he is writing "graffiti," that is, writing for a public who does not know him: "As I use words that someone far from home can understand, I create my listener. I imagine her listening" (188). Mysteriously feminine, anonymous, yet also public, Richard Rodriguez's ideal reader shines a beam toward him like the Statue of Liberty. When he tries to return to his family language, Spanish, he stammers.

Alfred Kazin, telling his Depression-era childhood, writing in the melting-pot ambiance of the 1940s, isn't as angry a narrator as Rodriguez; he is a buffoon. Kazin stammers in the public school language, English. He paces the roof of his tenement with pebbles in his mouth. He is sent to a speech clinic "where I sat in a circle of lispers and cleft palates and foreign accents holding a mirror before my lips and rolling difficult sounds over and over" (24). The descriptive climax of *A Walker in the City* comes with this voyage to the speech clinic, where Kazin sees a sign that sums up to him the horror of American conformity and American mechanization: "a great illustrated medical chart headed THE HUMAN FACTORY, which showed the exact course a mouthful of food follows as it falls from chamber to chamber of the body" (24). The chart evokes all the horror of turning his stuttering, accented, Yiddish-born English into "standard English," an English that goes down smooth. As Kazin contemplates the chart, and his battle with standard English, two pieces of salami fall out of his sandwich and slip through a grate onto a hill of dust. I quote the passage at length because no paraphrase can do justice to its "wild passive despair," the despair of wanting and resisting the language of the public sphere:

> I remember how sickeningly vivid an odd thread of hair looked on the salami, as if my lunch were turning stiff with death. . . . I had never known, I knew instantly I would never in my heart again submit to, such wild passive despair as I felt at that moment, sitting on the steps before THE HUMAN FACTORY, where little robots gathered and shoveled the food from chamber to chamber of the body. They had put me out into the streets, I thought to myself; with their mirrors and their everlasting pulling at me to imitate their effortless bright speech and their stupefaction that a boy could stammer and stumble on every other English word he carried in his head, they had put me out into the streets, had left me high and dry on the steps of that drugstore staring at the remains of my lunch turning black and grimy in the dust. (25)

Just as assimilated Jewish intellectuals were beginning to penetrate American intellectual life (Trilling, for example, at Columbia), Kazin reminded them in vivid detail how they had gotten there, and at what cost.

A *Walker in the City* is full of English, but also Yiddish and Hebrew and even French. Hebrew means mechanical memorization in order to be confirmed at the synagogue. The Melamed calls Kazin an idiot, eats peas while teaching him, and slaps him on the hands every time he makes a mistake. French means a blond neighbor, Mrs. Solovey, beaten and abused by her pharmacist husband and longing to share her romantic notions of the world with the neighbor boy. From Mrs. Solovey, Kazin learns the thrill of language as dream and escape: her speech to him on the pleasures of speaking French is one of the most eloquent expressions I have found in literature of the refusal of language that is merely *instrumental*:

> "I suppose you are learning French only to read? The way you do everything! But that is a mistake, I can assure you! It is necessary to speak, to speak! Think how you would be happy to speak French well! To speak a foreign language is to depart from yourself. Do you not think it is tiresome to speak the same language all the time? *Their* language! To feel that you are in a kind of prison, where the words you speak everyday are like the walls of your cell? To know with every word that you are the same, and no other, and

that it is difficult to escape? But when I speak French to you I have the sensation that for a moment I have left, and I am happy." (27)

Mrs. Solovey, this immigrant Emma Bovary, commits suicide, but her fantasy of "departing" from herself in a new language remains with Alfred. Eventually it is through literary language that Alfred Kazin will depart from Brownsville, aided by the vernacular of the forbidden New Testament ("For now we see through a glass, darkly") that he reads in secret on his fire escape and by the Americans—Dickinson, Whitman, and James—also "outsiders," and yet who lead him toward his identity as an American. Kazin learns, from literature, to reject the split between family language and public language, out crowd and in crowd, that haunted him and would haunt Rodriguez in another generation:

> Why were these people *here*, and we *there*? Why had I always to think of insider and outsider, of their belonging and our not belonging, when books had carried me this far, and when, as I could already see, it was myself that would carry me farther—beyond these petty distinctions I had so long made in loneliness. (Kazin 173)

Literature aids in the construction of a self who can travel, and it finally heals the past and present. Only the lonely, fearful self would think of this travel as an escape.

There is no language change without emotional consequences. Principally: loss. That language equals home, that language is a home, as surely as a roof over one's head is a home, and that to be without a language, or to be between languages, is as miserable in its way as to be without bread.

There are languages in which we feel our mother's heart beating; other languages in which we feel distant and safe; other languages—jargon languages in particular—are the language of professional ambition and achievement; others the language of pain. Two great polylingual writers of our century, Nabokov and Canetti, have described strong associational worlds having to do with specific languages. For Canetti, German is the language of maternal discipline; for Nabokov, his chosen language is found in the pun, in the cosmopolitan thrill of *crossing language*, with one language expressing itself as a private joke inside another, but also that loneliness of a secret that few can share. For Eva Hoffman, a Polish immigrant training to be an American intellectual, her American friends in graduate school speak in a jazz riff—the shape and pace of their speech boiled down to that. Ferdinand, the adolescent narrator of Céline's *Mort à crédit*, is sent by his striving Parisian merchant parents to a decrepit boarding school in England, which is named, in the original French text, *Meanwell College*. "Mean" translated back into French, is *vouloir dire*; literally "want to say"—but Ferdinand goes on a language strike at

Meanwell College, refusing to speak a single word of English. The whole episode becomes a vaudeville, as over-enthused English adults circle around Ferdinand, screaming heys and hellos at him, trying to seduce him into slipping into speech.

As I keep writing I remember more and more of these language scenes from my favorite books, until all of literature starts to seem like a "language memoir." I learned in graduate school in the 1970s that language is the subject of every novel, because novels are made out of language and sooner or later—and if you look hard enough—they're going to reflect on their own form. That is not what I mean here. A friend who taught me much of what I know about French, a doctor named Micheline Veaux, once told me that speech is the highest and lowest human function, the *endroit charnière* (the hitch post), between the mechanical grunt of the vocal chords and the poetry of cognition.

Language is the place where our bodies and minds collide, where our groundedness in place and time and our capacity for fantasy and invention must come to terms. That collision, fantasmagoric and social, is the subject of language memoir, including my own:

"Micheline"
from *French Lessons: A Memoir* [2]

I went into the pharmacy near my apartment to ask for medicine for mosquito bites in my best French: "quelque chose contre les *piques* de moustiques" (something against . . .). But since *pique* means *spade*, not bite (bite is *piqûre*), the pharmacist and I were off and running, his hilarity, my blushes, his old man Legion of Honor gallantry, and all the rest. "Please call me Papillon," he said, and he invited me to his family lunch that Saturday. I like to tell the story to students because it is about a French mistake leading to something good.

It was one of those endless meals you read about in language classes—a first course of foie gras and a second course of rabbit and French fries and a salad and cheese course and a fancy store-bought dessert. Bottles of wine with dust still on them from the cave tucked under the pharmacy, the kind with sediment in the bottom and a ten-layered taste you can study. I was seated up at the head of the table, in close range of Papillon who teased me and told stories about his adventures in Chicago, in the twenties. "I am Veaux—veal—you understand?" he kept saying in a Maurice-Chevalier-only-more-so fractured English. He told me what it was like to sit on a park bench in Chicago and watch the girls; he raved about the American girls and how tough they were, like soldiers, with legs like bayonets. His daughter Micheline was there, across the table from me, a cautious smile set on her face. She interrupted Papillon's flights of fancy to question me in a calm pedagogical voice, every word with its beat. Her children were at the table too: Florence was deeply shy; Sylvie and François were kids, François barely out of shorts. The meal was served by a Spanish woman named Carmen, with one eye that twitched and looked askance. The apartment was gilded with extravagant Lalique vases of all sizes and deco furniture, big red club chairs with arms wide enough to hold two tea cups. I walked out of there dazed, onto the street where the sun was setting over Aliénor of Aquitaine's tower, across the street. Five hours had passed.

I went back year after year to see this family from my junior year abroad in 1973–74. I went to Papillon's apartment above the pharmacy, then to Micheline's house, rue de Patay, then back to Papillon's retirement house in Pessac, for the traditional Saturday lunch. I heard many more Papillon stories: how he went to Spain with his medicines, to help the Republicans, and came back disgusted by their violence. I heard about his medals, his stamp collection, his pharmaceutical vases. I heard how he controlled pharmaceutical supplies during the Occupation. I heard about his love for the Maréchal Pétain, "who was betrayed by France." He had a scarf with a drawing of the island where Pétain was exiled, and a motto about France's shame. He tried to lend it to me once to wear on a train trip, he thought I would get cold, but Micheline intervened, gently: "You're not going to send this poor young American girl off to Corsica with a Philippe Pétain label around her neck." The children rolled their eyes and explained later what American children are rarely called upon to explain: the connection between family history, family prejudices, and big history, with a capital H. It would take me ten more years to figure out that if you had been a World War I veteran and not a Jew, Pétain could have been your hero in 1940. No matter how much wrong he did after, the memory of Verdun might have blinded you to it.

I think a lot about that Pétain scarf and the way Papillon wanted me to wrap up in it. I always go back to him for understanding France: the Third Republic, Gaullism, the Spanish Loyalists, French myths about the U.S. For each mystery about France I can think back to Papillon barking out some absurd slogan that would turn out to be soaked in politics, and I remember his bottles and his jars and vases like a stage set.

He was always taking things down off his shelves, as an offering: a stamp, a handkerchief, a pharmaceutical vase. Things, but always things with history. He had enough things, it seemed, to give to all Bordeaux and still there would be more.

Each of the children followed in the family's medical tradition: François became a pharmacist, Sylvie a dentist, Florence a pathologist. Papillon died in 1987; the next year François bought a pharmacy, and Sylvie married Richard.

The family dog, Virginie, a puppy when I was nineteen, was blind and emaciated like a skeleton when I was 34. No one could bear to put her to sleep.

I measured the passing of time by that house, that dog, as our lives mingled and meshed. They became my French family and I their American friend.

From the beginning I loved the fact that Micheline healed people with language troubles. "Dr. Micheline Veaux: Maladies du Langage" [Illnesses of Language] was inscribed on a bronze plaque over her doorbell. Micheline Veaux is a *phoniatre*, a physician who specializes in problems, physical and mental, that show themselves in speech. People recovering from throat operations, stutterers, aphasiacs, immigrants with psychological traumas in their newly acquired tongue. People who, for one reason or another, speak in the wrong pitch—too high or too low—and hurt their voices. She works with them on a keyboard, and helps them find their register. Her work is psychoanalytic; she believes, for example, that it is dangerous to treat a symptom without treating the cause. It is dangerous to cure someone of stuttering if the stuttering fulfills a psychic need that the person hasn't understood. Language is not a machine you can break and fix with the right technique, it is a function of the whole person, an expression of culture, desire, need. Her respect for everything that is alive in speech was profoundly new to me, and it corresponded to my need to wonder about language. Inside our language is our history, personal and political. This is what Micheline showed me.

When you ring the doorbell at Micheline's house, the first sound you hear is Virginie, the dachshund, crying and scraping her nails over the tile floor in the hallway. Micheline's office is to the left of the hallway, and it is decorated in the style favored by French doctors: empire. The furniture is straight-edged and commanding. A desk, glass-cased étagères full of books and toys. An analyst's couch. She is the *chef*, the boss. But not in the style of Napoleon: physically she is big, sitting behind her empire desk, with her warrior's beaked nose, her olive skin and frosted hair. She is from the Auvergne, the Massif Central where her Protestant ancestors are buried—there is a trace in her looks of Vercingétorix, the warrior of Ancient Gaul who held off Caesar in that very region. She wears big swathes of expensive fabric, but she can't be bothered with shoes—hers look squashed. There are tape recorders around, and records, along with the children's toys, and on the wall is a model of a throat and mouth with tongue, tonsils, and teeth.

Micheline gave me one of the psychological tests she gives her patients:
"My father is a tailor," I was supposed to write. "Mon père est tailleur." But many of her patients write instead, "Mon père est ailleurs" ("My father is some-

where else"). French lets you make dramatic puns this way, because of "liaison": a fact of French pronunciation which means that a consonant at the end of one word (the "t" in "est") can hook up with the subsequent word beginning with a vowel ("ailleurs"), creating an ambiguity as to whether the word you are hearing is "ailleurs" or "tailleur." The French psychoanalyst Jacques Lacan would have appreciated Micheline's test sentence. He believed that the child gains access to language only when it perceives the existence of the father, which allows it to break out of infantile dualisms—self and mother, inside and outside. "Somewhere out there, somewhere else, is my father": this, says Lacan, is the child's inauguration into language, the symbolic order, and the law. But it is mothers, traditionally, who teach language, who listen and correct, it is mothers who are the first to hear new words. It is mothers who break or heal a child's tongue.

In spite of her testing, Micheline is not a Lacanian. "Dictation is a police state," she told me, "with grammar as the law. Dictation can ruin a child's relationship to language."

Dictation is one of the permanent rites of French education. You listen to the teacher's voice and you write down every word. For every wrong accent, every wrong verb ending, you lose points; your listening and your knowledge of the transition from voice to writing must be exquisite. Around the time that Micheline was analyzing its dangers, I was learning to give dictation in the French classes I taught. How I must love the law, I thought; how I love getting every word perfect, and now giving them and getting them back. And Micheline's resistance to dictation, the deep seriousness of her critique, made the dull pedagogical exercise seem like a rebellion. She wanted me to relax with my French, to live with it. I wanted to control every word.

I went into her office wanting to work on my French, and she recorded my voice on her tape recorder. I heard my foreign intonation, which she called my "song." "You'll never get rid of that song," she said, "but what does it matter?" I wanted to hire her, pay her thousands of dollars, to rid me of it.

"Speech," Micheline told me, "is the highest and lowest human function, the *endroit charnière* between the mechanical grunt of the vocal cords and the poetry of cognition."

I met her most successful former patient, a Vietnamese boat person named, like the past participle, Vu. He no longer stuttered. He came to New York one spring and looked me up, and we walked down Riverside Drive together to Grant's tomb. It happened to be the tenth anniversary of the fall of Saigon, April 30, 1985, and this made me feel that we ought to be together, on that day. I took him to dinner, Texas barbecue. When I was in Paris he called me. We started to compete. We got annoyed at one another. He wanted to be my

French teacher; I wanted my French to be better than his. He worked for the bureau of standardization and wanted to write novels. We picked at one another—he found every wrong word I uttered—in fact we argued about the meanings of words and their usage. "His is standard," I thought, "merely standard." Micheline was disgusted by my lack of generosity where Vu was concerned. "Perhaps he doesn't have every quality," she told me, "but you have no idea what he has been through, how he has rebuilt his life from nothing. Losing his mother and sister in a boat—we haven't a clue what that was like." I was jealous of his success, his transcendence of the worst odds, his pain conquered. It was a measly feeling.

Every time I went back to Bordeaux they told me whether or not I'd lost my French. "You've still got it." Or, "You're starting to lose it but you'll get it back." "It" seemed to depend on nothing—not whether I'd been teaching, not whether I'd been spending time with French people. Some fluke of memory and forgetting was involved. Sometimes I would call them from the States, after months of silence, and my simplest comments were unfathomable to them.

Micheline helped me study for the GREs in French from a practice book: "Is France sometimes referred to as a pentagon, an octagon, or a hexagon?" This made us laugh, because we had traveled through the entire hexagon, Micheline and the kids and me, and in the car they had instructed me about the shape of France. Micheline's children knew the green Michelin guidebooks so well that they could imitate them effortlessly, and as we drove into the next one-horse town, François would elaborate a parody: "Autin-sur-mer, pearl of the Atlantic. . . . " I learned to swear in traffic jams, listening to Micheline in the driver's seat. My family snapshots from those trips show the Châteaux of the Loire, force-fed geese of the Dordogne, Sylvie, Micheline and me on a bench, looking exactly alike in our posture and pose. Sometimes an American would walk into the restaurant, the hotel, the church where we were, and I felt safe and warm with my French family, protected from myself. I heard the American voices and they were foreign to me.

Not that France didn't change. France became more American every year, even as Americans longed more and more for the traditions they had lost that France still had. That was part of what we wanted in each other, in the beginning: me the ritual of France, Micheline the ease of America.

In the seventies, as the American middle class abandoned their soup cans and frozen food for lengthy recipes à la Julia Child, Micheline was moving in the opposite direction. Around the time that wine became weekly, if not daily, in American middle-class families, it disappeared from Micheline's lunch table altogether. In fact I first learned the world for "daily"—*quotidien*—at lunch when Micheline described a magazine article about "daily alcoholism" in France, the thousands of French people who were alcoholics without really knowing it, merely because of the amount of wine they drank with every meal. Around the time that instant mashed potato flakes and TV dinners became an embarrassment in bourgeois Minneapolis, they appeared in bourgeois Bordeaux. The first action she took the day after her divorce, Micheline told me, was to buy a freezer. This was her freedom.

She took me to the cafeteria at the *hypermarché*, not a super but a hyper market it's so big, on the outskirts of Bordeaux. The food was Woolworth's only worse, frozen veal covered in Cheese Whiz and pizza sauce. I ate with relish, this dish I would have rejected at home but which in France was exotic. The place was decorated American Western style, big painted cowboys with neon lassos. I marveled at the novel décor with my French family.

Usually we didn't go out. There was no hanging around in cafés. And then, when Papillon got too old, even the obligatory Saturday lunch at his house ended. Meals shrank. Sometimes dinner was salmon spread on packaged toast, or a piece of cheese from the glass cheese cage. Often it was only out of respect for the visiting francophiles that tradition was trotted out. Florence made a crusted fish or her endive in béchamel and a tarte; François, with his pharmacist's nose, brought just the right wine from the inexhaustible cellar.

I went back there every summer, every trip, for no reason, as though it were my family. Each time I felt the same mixture of anticipation and annoyance, as though it were my family so I had to go. I expected to be bored there, quiet. I went just to go to the same places: the bus stop at the Barrière de Pessac, the big book store, the street where I shopped for clothes when I was a student. I went because I needed to make sure the places were still there, to make sure I really once lived there and I was really attached to this foreign place.

There in Bordeaux is where my mouth and my eyes and my ears for France started to work. When I was fifteen and had my first conversation all in French, in Switzerland, it was a religious awakening. In Bordeaux it became regular, boring, real. *Quotidien.*

There is more to language learning than the memorization of verbs and the mastery of an accent. Or rather, there is more to the memorization of verbs and the mastery of an accent than our foreign language textbooks let us in on.

Language memoirs are closest in genre to the classic *Bildungsroman*—the novel of education and development. The difference, in language memoir, is that it's not yourself you're growing into, but another self, perceived as better, more powerful, safer. The change in language is the emblem of a *leap* into a new persona.

When I reread "Micheline," I was surprised by the strength of my desire for a new self. I had wanted to trade in my voice, even its timbre, for another one. Micheline—whose life's work was to help people with problems of voice and identity—saw this before I did and encouraged me to relax.

Why didn't I want to relax with my accent and my mistakes? What was at stake?

These were some of the questions I needed to face as I continued my work on *French Lessons*.

Notes

1. *French Lessons: A Memoir.* Chicago: U of Chicago P, 1993.
2. Reprinted courtesy U of Chicago P.

Works Cited

Canetti, Elias. *The Tongue Set Free: Remembrance of a European Childhood.* Trans. Joachim Neugroschel. New York: Seabury, 1979. Trans. of *Die gerettete Zunge: Geschichte einer Jugend.* Munich: Carl Hanser, 1977.

Céline, Louis-Ferdinand. *Death on the Installment Plan.* Trans. Ralph Manheim. New York: New Directions, 1966. Trans. of *Mort à crédit.* Paris: Denoël, 1936.

Charef, Mehdi. *Tea in the Harem.* Trans. Ed Emery. London: Serpent's Tail, 1989. Trans. of *Le Thé au Harem d'Archi Ahmed.* Paris: Mercure de France, 1983.

Ernaux, Annie. *A Man's Place.* Trans. Tanya Leslie. New York: Four Walls Eight Windows, 1992. Trans. of *La Place.* Paris: Gallimard, 1983.

Hoffman, Eva. *Lost in Translation: A Life in a New Language.* New York: Dutton, 1989.

Kazin, Alfred. *A Walker in the City.* 1951. New York: Harvest/Harcourt, 1979.

Nabokov, Vladimir. *Speak, Memory: An Autobiography Revisited.* New York: Putnam's, 1967. Originally published as *Conclusive Evidence: A Memoir.* New York: Harper, 1951 and as *Speak, Memory.* New York: Grosset, 1960.

Rodriguez, Richard. *Hunger of Memory: The Education of Richard Rodriguez.* 1982. New York: Bantam, 1983.

Sarraute, Nathalie. *Childhood.* Trans. Barbara Wright. New York: Braziller, 1984. Trans. of *Enfance.* Paris: Gallimard, 1983.

Sartre, Jean-Paul. *The Words.* Trans. Bernard Frechtman. New York: Vintage, 1964. Trans. of *Les Mots.* Paris: Gallimard, 1964.

5 | Pictures of a Displaced Girlhood

Marianne Hirsch

for Angelika, Marta, and Mona

Displacement is an exile from older certitudes of meaning, a possibly permanent sojourn in the wilderness.

—Mark Krupnik

Borderlands are physically present wherever two or more cultures edge each other . . . Living on borders and in margins, keeping intact one's shifting multiple identity and integrity, is like trying to swim in a new element, an "alien" element . . . not comfortable but home.

—Gloria Anzaldúa

I AM SITTING on an airplane crossing the Atlantic. It is September 1991, a few days before my birthday, and I am returning to the United States from a study trip through Kenya and Tanzania. This is the second leg of a long journey, and I am tired though happy to be going home after visiting so many unfamiliar places and feeling so much like an outsider, a tourist. I spend my time reading: it's what I most enjoy about airplane travel—reading in a state of suspension, a no-place between home and abroad which gives me the possibility of immersing myself entirely in the space of the book I have selected for the occasion. Only this time, I am not prepared for what happens. I am reading Eva Hoffman's *Lost in Translation*, a book I have owned since it was first published in 1989, but which I have put off even though friends have urged me to read it right away. Actually, I was going to get to it on a previous vacation but lost it on the way and had to wait to purchase it again when I came home. Now this trip is almost over, and I have finally settled into Hoffman. I am reaching the end of the first part of Hoffman's narrative, the end of her sea journey from Poland to Canada at age thirteen. *I discern the outlines of massive gray shapes against the cloudy sky,* I read. *Closer still, the shapes resolve into buildings, tall and monolithic to my eyes. Montreal. It actually exists, more powerful than any figment of the imagination. We look at the approaching city wordlessly. The brief* Batory *interlude is over and so is the narrative of my childhood* (95).

But now I can no longer see the page. Tears are flowing down my face, I realize I am sobbing. These sentences have released a loss whose depths I had never, until that moment, allowed myself to feel or remember.

It is July, 1962. I am almost thirteen and I am crossing the Atlantic, from Brussels to New York, on only the second airplane journey I have ever taken. But I am not sitting by the window. I do not want to see the expanse of ocean that will separate me from the familiar world I am leaving behind forever and, indeed, from my childhood. I do not want to see the shapes of the cities, rivers, and mountains that are to be my new home, the spaces of my adolescence and adulthood. Am I reading a book on this trip? I don't remember—all I remember is crying through what feels like the entire flight (14 hours), crying with abandon in public, so that everyone can see that I do not want to go. I take some small pleasure in the tears and the attention they are getting me, especially from the handsome young Lufthansa steward who keeps bringing me snacks and drinks so that I might stop. My parents have given up trying to make this move seem acceptable, they are just letting me cry as they deal with their own excitements and anxieties. But I know I am miserably unhappy, and I am determined to remain so. I continue to cry as we land in New York and as we go through the endless bureaucracies of immigration. I cry on the plane to Providence, Rhode Island, where, from a window seat I see an empty expanse that seems totally unpopulated to the European eye. I cry as we are picked up at the airport by Mrs. Hoffmann (no relative of Eva's I'm sure) from the Jewish Family Service, and I cry as I enter the South Providence flat—the upper floor of a brown wooden house on what looks like a desolate street—she has rented for our adjustment period. My mother waits for Mrs. Hoffmann to leave. And then she too starts to cry.

Eva Hoffman's story is my story and the only lens through which I can read it is a totally unreconstructed form of identification—a response quite unfamiliar to someone who has been studying and teaching literature for twenty-five years and one which makes me uneasy. Yet I recognize so many of the scenes she evokes. Like Hoffman, I too *come from the war*, from that generation of the immediate postwar in Eastern Europe which grew up hearing stories of hiding, persecution, extermination, and miraculous survival every day and dreamt of them every night. *This—the pain of this—is where I come from, and . . . it's useless to try to get away*. I recognize myself in her portrait of *children too overshadowed by our parents' stories, and without enough sympathy for ourselves, for the serious dilemmas of our own lives* (230). Her Cracow is so much like my Bucharest, her parents' urban middle-class respectability and relative material comfort and their simultaneous marginality, and discomfort as Jews, so much like my parents'. Equally similar are our parents' far-reaching ambitions for their children's happiness and success, ambitions which do not offset the attitudes of *modernist nihilism* and deep skepticism with which they raised us. So many details are similar, down to the remedy for colds made from milk, egg yolk, and sugar (only my mother, unlike Eva's, never added chocolate, perhaps because cocoa was only rarely available). I too remember vividly the day of Stalin's death and the somber funerary marches through the city under the enormous images of Lenin and Stalin and "the two grandfathers" (as I called Marx and Engels). I still feel the *cognitive disjunction* in which my friends and I grew up, hearing at home that we are to disregard most of what we might hear at school. Around the same time, in the late fifties, her parents and mine made the enormous decision to get out—to leave the place that was both *home* and *hostile* territory—and at roughly the same age Hoffman and I left behind the only world we knew.

It is with smiling recognition that I read Hoffman's first impressions of Vancouver; I nod through her bafflement at the shaggy bathroom rugs, at the toilet paper that comes in different colors, at her paralysis when it comes to choosing among brands of toothpaste. I recognize her inability to understand American humor, her incompetence at telling a joke. I empathize with the loss she experiences when her name is changed from Ewa to Eva—more slightly than mine, who had to switch from Marianne to a Mary Ann whose "r" I could not pronounce, making it "Mady Ann." *These new appellations which we ourselves can't yet pronounce, are not us. They are identification tags, disembodied signs pointing to objects that happen to be my sister and myself. We walk to our seats, into a roomful of unknown faces, with names that make us strangers to ourselves* (105).

The relentless rhythm of the wheels is like scissors cutting a three-thousand-mile rip through my life. From now on, my life will be divided into two parts with the line drawn by that train (100). The flight across the Atlantic is for me what the train ride through Canada is for Hoffman. That is why it is so hard for me to write about the period of transition—my adolescence. My childhood remained in Rumania. It is in Vienna that I have my first period, my first crush, wear my first stockings, try on lipstick. My first date, my first kiss, my first dances and parties, are all in Providence. That's where I lose my pudginess, grow another two inches (or is it two centimeters?), have my teeth straightened, become a teenager. But which of those changes are due to chronology, which to geography? I have never been able to sort them out. I remember during my year in Vienna being unable to find a single comfortable item of clothing—everything itches and scratches, everything feels wrong against my skin, everything makes me miserable. Is that because I have just turned twelve, gotten my period and am going through puberty, or is it because everything I wear is too childish and totally "square" by Viennese standards and I go through each day feeling wrong, ashamed, out of place? I try to make the transition from ankle socks to nylon stockings, from soap and water to face creams, make-up and cologne, from sandals to heels, from childish freedom to flirting and an obsessive interest in boys in the space of a few weeks, but what is the cost? What gets silenced and censored in the process? And how do I manage, in the space of another few adjustment weeks, to make a second transition to small-town American teenage-hood—another set of rules and standards, for me only another set of faux-pas and embarrassments? Like Hoffman, I feel *less agile and self-confident with every transformation. I hold my head rigidly, so that my precarious bouffant doesn't fall down, and I smile often, the way I see other girls do, though I'm careful not to open my lips too wide or bite them, so my lipstick won't get smudged. . . . In its elaborate packaging, my body is stiff, sulky, wary. When I'm with my peers, who come by crinolines, lipstick, cars, and self-confidence naturally, my gestures show that I'm here provisionally, by their grace, that I don't rightfully belong* (109, 110). Like Hoffman, *I'm a pretend teenager among the real stuff* (118).

But does any girl *come by crinolines, lipstick, cars, and self-confidence naturally?* Was my discomfort and Hoffman's the result of our cultural displacement or was it due to a chronological transition that teenage culture and the demands of adult femininity have made inherently and deeply *unnatural* for even the most comfortably indigenous American girl? In their recent research into female adolescence, Carol Gilligan and her colleagues find that girls use images of violent rupture, death, and drowning when they describe the transition between childhood and adolescence, a transition they locate between the ages of twelve and thirteen. Gilligan's reading of Margaret Atwood's poem "This Is a Photograph of Me" allows her to characterize this transition topographically as a form of displacement. When she moves out of childhood and into adolescence, Atwood's persona simply disappears by drowning. As she describes the lake, the poet locates herself at the center, beneath its surface: "It is difficult to say where/precisely, or to say/how large or small I am/ . . . but if you look long enough,/ eventually/ you will be able to see me." Around the age of thirteen, Gilligan suggests, girls lose their place: without their voice and their certainty, they become "divided from their own knowledge, regularly prefacing their observations by saying 'I don't know' " (*Making Connections* 14). Whatever knowledge they preserve from their earlier selves must go underground; if they want to preserve or to perpetuate it they must "join the resistance." Gilligan describes this underground world as a "remote island," implying that every transition into female adulthood is a process of acculturation to an alien realm or, could one say, an experience of emigration? The lessons of femininity acquired during adolescence, therefore, require a move into a different culture with a different language. Girls must unlearn what they knew as they gain, sometimes through gestures of mimicry and impersonation, new skills and new selves.

But if for American girls, to move into adolescence feels like emigrating to a foreign culture and learning the new language of femininity under patriarchy, what additional pressures confront girls like Hoffman and myself who, in addition to learning the language of patriarchy, literally had to learn English and acclimate to American culture? Reading Gilligan has been an astounding discovery for me who had, like Hoffman, attributed my awkwardness and alienation to my status as a "newcomer" and was therefore unable to perceive the similar discomfort and alienation of my female peers. At my recent 25th high school reunion, classmates confessed their own insecurities but remembered me as completely "together" even as early as tenth grade—only a year after I came. I can only marvel at my own powers of impersonation, but I realize now what I could not see then: that they also had to exercise a form of mimicry in their performances of feminine behavior. Yet unlike theirs, my own and Hoffman's process of unlearning and learning, of resisting and assimilating was a double one which must have been doubly difficult to negotiate. It must have left us doubly displaced and dispossessed, doubly at risk, perhaps doubly resistant to assimilation. If most girls leave their "home" as they move into adolescence, Hoffman and I left two homes—our girlhood and our Europe. But, despite the common structure, the effects of this double displacement were different for me and for Hoffman, as were the strategies of relocation we were able to develop.

On the cover of my paperback edition of *Lost in Translation* there is a picture of a photo album, set at an angle, facing a beautiful pink flower. A small black and white photograph, mounted with old-fashioned black triangles, shows two little girls in a bleak-looking forest or park. It's clearly autumn, the leaves are on the ground and the two little girls in the photo are wearing winter coats and hats. Presumably the older girl (she seems to be six or seven) is Eva and the younger, who must be about four, is her sister Alina. Eva is smiling self-confidently as she protectively puts her arm around her sister in her plaid coat, white tights, and high top boots. Alina looks more tentative, less comfortable. This is Eva (or Ewa) in the Polish surroundings she inhabits with such effortless comfort, the home which in her book is cast as *paradise* and *the safe enclosures of Eden*. Later Hoffman describes another photo, one she obviously rejected as an image for the cover of her book: *About a year after our arrival in Vancouver, someone takes a photograph of my family in their backyard, and looking at it, I reject the image it gives of myself categorically. This clumsy looking creature, with legs oddly turned in their high-heeled pumps, shoulders bent with the strain of resentment and ingratiation, is not myself* (110). A third photograph described toward the end of *Lost in Translation* mediates Hoffman's astonished reunion, in New York, with a childhood friend from Cracow. *In this picture three little girls are standing on a riverbank holding hands and showing off the daisy wreaths on their heads. I remember the day when this picture was taken quite distinctly—the excursion on the Vistula during which we disembarked on a picnic, and how the three of us looked for flowers to weave those wreaths, something little girls in Poland did during those days. But as Zofia and I look back and forth from the photograph to each other, we feel the madeleine's sweet cheat: "Oh my God," Zofia keeps saying in mixed delight and befuddlement. We can't jump over such a large time canyon. The image won't quite come together with this moment* (222). The two women are unable to *recapture their past.* At this point I wonder about Hoffman's obsession with the canyon, with a disjunction that defines her life and her book: I begin to notice the pervasive nostalgia that clings to everything Polish. Suddenly alienated by the way she has constructed her story, I resist identification, start shaking my head in disagreement, resent her for breaking the ease with which I had been making my way through her book.

The three photographs trace Hoffman's journey from *paradise* into *exile* and to *the new world*. In *paradise*, she is at home with herself, smiling self-confidently; in *exile*, she has become not herself, someone she is forced to reject, denegate. *The new world* is defined by the unbridgeable canyon at the center of her life. Eva and Zofia can look at the photo, but they cannot recapture their childhoods. They cannot find themselves—for Eva locates herself more in that childhood image than in her adulthood. An adult in New York, a Harvard Ph.D., an American writer, Eva still describes herself as a newcomer, an immigrant, unable to read her husband's emotions, unable to feel comfortable in English. Her friends are always either *Polish* or *American*; to them she remains throughout her over thirty years on this side of the Atlantic a foreigner, a *silly little Polish person.* When she describes relationships with friends and lovers, it is to point out how differently she sees the world from them, it is to analyze their consensus and her own exclusion. Even when she feels that she is in her world (*I fit, and my surroundings fit me*), her consciousness splits off, and there is *an awareness that there is another place—another point at the base of the triangle, which renders this place relative, which locates me within that relativity itself* (170). This doubleness and relativity I understand, but I cannot identify with Hoffman's nostalgic attempt to overcome it by returning to her Polish childhood. Her discomfort with her present double vision is clearly motivated by her construction of Poland (or is it childhood?) unequivocally as paradise, home of *the first things, the incomparable things, the only things. It's by adhering to the contours of a few childhood objects that the substance of our selves—the molten force we're made of—molds and shapes itself. We are not yet divided* (74). Thinking about my own experience, I want her to see that in Poland, as a child, she was already divided.

As I continue to read, I am more and more bothered by the contradictions between the Edenic construction of Cracow—her smile in the cover photo—and the prehistory of her parents' hiding in a *branch-covered forest bunker during the war*—perhaps the same forest where the two little girls' picture is taken? What repressions are behind the feeling that Cracow is *both home and the universe* when only a few years before all of her parents' relatives had died there, including her aunt who *was among those who had to dig their own graves, and . . . her hair turned gray the day before her death* (7). What does it take for Hoffman to consider this place *paradise*? Why would she want to recapture a childhood that rests on such a legacy? Hoffman's denial is painful to read, yet it is basic to her construction of her narrative and her world, of her self: *this is real*, she says about the eye-witness account of her aunt's death. *But is it? It doesn't have the same palpable reality as the Cracow tramway. Maybe it didn't happen after all, maybe it's only a story, and a story can be told differently, it can be changed.* With her evocation of childhood plenitude, Hoffman has displaced the reality of the war, of the anti-Semitism she admittedly still experiences, but which she simply dismisses by calling it *primitive*. Canada to her own Polish self was *an enormous cold blankness*, but to her parents, in their war-time forest confinement, it spoke *of majestic wilderness, of animals roaming without being pursued, of freedom*. Born of this prison-house imagination, Canada is freedom, but, in spite of so many assurances to the contrary, Hoffman, in what may well be an understandable childish strategy of survival, has displaced her parents' suffering with her own happiness, and Canada is only *exile* for her.

I identify neither with Hoffman's nostalgically Edenic representation of Poland, nor with her utter sense of dispossession later, nor do I share her desperate desire to displace the relativity, the fracturing, the double-consciousness of immigrant experience. For me displacement and bilingualism preceded emigration, they are the conditions into which I was born. Even as a child, in the midst of those first affections so eloquently celebrated in *Lost in Translation*, I was already *divided*. If displacement is indeed an "exile from older certitudes of meaning" as Mark Krupnik suggests in the epigraph to this essay, then I was already born into "the wilderness." As I recognize these differences between us, I see that I can read Hoffman only as a pre-text for my own narrative of cultural displacement.

The legendary place of origin I will never see is Czernowitz, capital of the Bukowina, a province of the Austro-Hungarian Empire which in 1918 was annexed by Rumania and in 1945 by the USSR. This is where my parents, their relatives and friends, everyone I know and respect, came from—the city where they continued to speak German through years of Rumanian and Russian rule, where they studied French and poetry, went to concerts, swam in the Prut river and climbed the Tsetsina mountain, strolled down the Herrengasse on Sundays, ate delicious Torten at each other's houses and cheese dumplings at Friedmann's restaurant. Here my maternal grandfather was a lawyer and my mother grew up in a comfortable apartment with Persian carpets and a set of brown leather furniture in their "Herrenzimmer," a room whose uses I have trouble imagining. My father's family was poor, his mother a widow with four children, but he told other glamorous stories of socialist and Zionist youth movements, of hard work and its rewards, and youthful camaraderie with friends who continued to be important throughout his life. Here also is where my father was beaten up for being a Jew and where my mother could not study medicine because Jews were allowed only into some university faculties. These scenes and objects are more real to me than the scenes of my own childhood, especially when it comes to the narrative of my parents' survival during The War: these moments from my parents' history easily displace my own narrative. When I later learn that "our" Czernowitz is the home of Paul Celan, Aharon Apelfeld, Josef Schmidt, Rose Ausländer, and other well-known "German" artists, I merely nod—this is in fact the image I always had of it. I know many details of the two years of Russian occupation and the two years of the Antonescu collaborationist regime. For years I have located myself in the courage of their survival, of my parents' unique marriage in the ghetto the day before they thought they might be deported, the two times they evaded deportation, the night my father got out of bed to answer a knock by the Gestapo. Their subsequent escape from what had become a Soviet republic to Rumania after the war and the three years preceding my birth—the pain of leaving everything they knew behind, the hardships of their dislocation, my mother's two miscarriages—in my mind displace my own loss and dislocation.

Throughout her thirteen Polish years, Hoffman lives in the same house, sleeps in the same bed, speaks one language. I am born in Timisoara, a city with a sizeable German and Hungarian population, and move to Bucharest before I can remember. Timisoara remains a second home, this is where my grandparents stay, but they moved, and I only see the building where I spent the first two years of my life from the outside. In Bucharest we move again when I am eight. In Timisoara I grow to the age of two speaking only German—my grandmother knows only enough Rumanian to buy eggs and vegetables at the market. In Bucharest I learn Rumanian but I speak it with an accent. I go to a German school and I am more fluent than my classmates, many of whom are Rumanian and speak a strongly accented and grammatically incorrect German. But in third grade my best friend is Marianne Döhring from East Berlin, and I quickly realize that my German, of which I had been quite proud, is literally a Balkanization of the real thing. I learn to mimic Berlinerisch, and I learn to be embarrassed about the way I speak my native language. This gets worse when I move to Vienna and my German is no longer recognized as native—at this point, though I express myself with ease and am proud of my writing, I also don't have a language any more. I thus cannot share Hoffman's shock at her linguistic dislocation: *But mostly, the problem is that the signifier has become severed from the signified. The words I learn now don't stand for things in the same unquestioned way as they did in my native tongue. "River" in Polish was a vital sound, energized by the essence of riverhood, of my rivers, of being immersed in rivers. "River" in English is cold—a word without an aura. I am becoming a living avatar of structuralist wisdom; I cannot help knowing that words are just themselves. But it's a terrible knowledge, without any of the consolations that wisdom usually brings. It is the loss of a living connection* (106, 107). For me, this is a connection I must never have known since I was never located in one language as firmly as was Hoffman.

Like Hoffman, I am conscious of my Jewish identity throughout my childhood in Rumania. We don't ever go to synagogue (after a rabbi refused to marry my parents in the ghetto on a Friday afternoon, my father stays away from rabbis) so being Jewish is the history and the reality of anti-Semitism and persecution, it is the cultural legacy of Czernowitz, it is, same as for Hoffman, a sense of cultural superiority. It is also my difference from my Rumanian friends ("How do you cross yourself, with two fingers or three?" they ask to determine whether I am Catholic or Orthodox. My shameful reply, "I don't cross myself," reveals that I am nothing). And being Jewish is the fear of repetition, the nightly dreams of The War. It is what makes us leave and what allows us to leave. When we get to Vienna my parents decide it might be easier not to be Jewish any longer, and they truthfully put "atheist" on our forms. But it is a lie I have to defend in front of Sabine, the only other Jewish girl in my class. She eventually guesses, of course, and I confess. But when I join the Hashomer Hatzair to which she belongs, I only feel more left out because I don't know any of the songs and stories about Israel, even though my father belonged to the same group thirty years earlier. Jewishness is an ambiguous and complicated location: one in which I both am and am not at home.

For us, Vienna is just a way station on the way to what will be our future home. We consider Israel, Canada, Australia, the United States, and we spend eight months waiting for our American visa. I desperately want to stay in Vienna: in spite of the lie about our Jewishness, in spite of the fact that my German sounds wrong and that I am much more childish than my classmates, in spite of the damp and dark two rooms without kitchen privileges we rent, I begin to feel at home here.

I have a cousin who is three years older and who introduces me to the mysteries of Western consumerism ("there's this drink called Coca Cola and it is so amazing that once you taste it you will never be able to stop drinking it"). I spend the summer at an international camp where I use the little bit of French I learned in Rumania to interpret between the Austrian and the French girls.

By the end of the summer, I can actually speak French. In the neighborhood Gymnasium I attend for the year, I have a best friend, Angelika, who also feels like an outsider—her mother is an actress, her parents don't live together, she has less money than the other children. Through Angelika I want to become Austrian, but when there is a chance to act in a television commercial with her, I am rejected because of my "foreign" accent.

Marianne and Clementine
Vienna, 1962

Looking at pictures from that year I see the sadness and discomfort I displaced by fighting not to emigrate further. In most of the photos I anxiously hold on to Clementine, the brown and white guinea pig I acquire to consolidate my friendship with Angelika who has a black guinea pig named Vladimir—we want them to play together and marry. In the pictures, Clementine and I look rather forlorn—she is the repository of my loneliness and desire for love and acceptance. But I smile in the picture Angelika takes—the guinea pigs bring us closer together. I have often come back to this girlhood fantasy of relocation through a friendship which, by way of the guinea pigs, becomes a fantasy of marriage, home, and lasting togetherness.

It works, because by the end

Angelika and Vladimir
Vienna, 1962

of the year I look happier. My hair is wavy, I am wearing a petticoat, I pose in front of various Viennese monuments, I look a little more like the other girls in the photos: I have to prove that this has become home. I don't want to leave. When I do leave, Angelika keeps "Tinerl" now indeed wedded to Vladimir, but not quite as we had imagined. My history of multiple displacements—linguistic, religious, relational—makes displacement (and relocation) my strategy of survival. When I get to Providence, I don't know English—I have resisted learning it so as to have some control over my fate. I eventually have to learn, but I continue to raid the public library for all the French and German books they have. A girl named Jennifer is the only one who expresses an interest in my story, but even she finds me hard to take on. I know so little, I am younger, I do everything wrong.

In the pictures from our first summer, I wear a sailor dress that is much too small for me, and I look grotesque: a chubby child infantilized by my linguistic paralysis, I look much younger than I do in the Vienna photos taken only a month earlier. I try to repeat the comfort Clementine gave me, but this time I have a hamster who dies two months later. Other hamsters follow but it never works; they are single hamsters, not the instruments of relationship like Clementine. The cages they live in show my distance from them and emblematize my own confinement in this lonely new American, teenage identity I reject.

Providence, 1962

I stop crying when Mona arrives with her family from Egypt. She's a year older but she's in my class. We can speak French. We can try to read the cultural signs together. The French we speak is our own private language: we both roll our r's, and there are many words I don't know, so we mix it with the English we are

Marianne and Mona
Providence, 1963

both acquiring. To her I am not "Mady Ann," but "Marianne" pronounced in French. I become comfortable with the Arabic sounds I hear at her house, and I learn some Arabic words. Her family is also Jewish but it means something totally different to them. I prefer the Middle Eastern dishes they serve to the tuna fish sandwiches on sponge-like white bread I get at American homes. I become involved in her brothers' and parents' adjustment problems. We try to teach her mother enough English to do the shopping, and we explain to her that American girls should be allowed to go out. I'm better in school, but Mona is much better at learning the styles, the songs, the gestures that will make us American—something we both want and do not want to be. She's better at flirting and more attractive to boys, but I join in the talk, I have crushes on the best friends of the boys she has crushes on, we go to dances at the Jewish community center where I have to lie about my age to join, and we have our first boyfriends. Mona is in every picture taken during that time. I am blond, she is brunette; my hair is thin and straight, hers is thick and wavy; yet we have the same outfit, the same posture, the same hairstyle, in every photo. Mona is the mediating figure who allows me both to acculturate and not to. Together we create a space at the border, a space that is neither Rumanian nor Egyptian nor American, with an idiolect that is neither German nor Arabic nor English but some mixture of all of these, translated into the French that is "our" language. When I go to France for a summer and learn a more authentic accent, I cannot use it when speaking with Mona. My pride in my good accent is mixed with regret at losing French as the borderland home I shared with Mona. And when I meet Mona later and we both have children nearly of the age we were then, we speak English and I know we cannot be close in this "foreign" tongue in which we have come to lead our lives, after all.

At the end of ninth grade I know enough English to write a composition about what it is like to lose one's country—to be located nowhere, and have no cultural identity. I so eloquently express the pain and nostalgia of homelessness and so feelingly describe patriotic feelings that have no *patria* to attach themselves to that I am asked to read it at a school assembly. Some people weep and I get much praise, but I am a bit embarrassed by the nostalgia I have been able to evoke and which I cultivate so I can remain on the border. I also want Mona to participate in the glory and help her write her own version of this story; our origins could not be more different, but the feelings of displacement are the same.

They are me, communicated to the whole school in English, but they are also an acting job, an impersonation of what I think it all should sound and feel like. But in our graduation picture from Nathan Bishop Junior High School, Mona and I sit in the front row, our hair is teased just the right amount, we smile just like the other girls and we fold our hands on our laps with just the right modesty: we pass.

Nathan Bishop Junior High School 1963

Only some of the inscriptions on the back give me away. Most are generic: "To Marianne, a great kid whom I'll never forget, Love ya, Nancy Weisman"; "To Marianne, A real sweet kid, AFA, Mary Beth." But some note the difference: "To 'Maddy Ann', a wonderful kid with the cute accente (sic), Karen Powell"; "À Marianne (Mady Ann), The Silent One, It's been great knowing you and since we live so close, I'll see you dans l'avenir, Good luck, ne jamais, Mike Dickens." And Mona, of course, grew up with a different style of dedication: "À ma soeur Marianne, Tombe du 1er étage/ tombe du 2ème étage, Tombe d'où tu veux, Mais ne tombe pas amoureuse, Mona Chamuel," she writes and places an elegant squiggle under her signature. This formulaic verse actually says a great deal about our struggles with adjustment to American teenage girlhood: our sense of falling and the ways in which we caught ourselves and literally held on to each other in our friendship.

After Mona goes to a different high school and we begin to spend less time together, I do not replace her with an American friend but choose Marta, who came to live in Providence from Brazil for several years. This time I can initiate her into the ways of American teenage-hood. Her experience is different from mine for she has already spent one year in the United States and is determined to go back home as soon as she can. Still, we share both a basic alienation and a pervasive cultural relativism through which we observe the practices of our peers. I hear a lot of Portuguese, learn how things are done in Brazil, and my borderland existence continues. I don't have the right "r," but I know how to pronounce the "t" in her name, avoiding the more common "Marda" or even "Martha" she has become. We even speak some French together, and for years people comment on the Eastern European accent Marta acquires in English. In all our pictures, we wear the same outfits and hairstyles, our postures and gestures are identical, and through high school and later college we are inseparable. We need each other to mediate our acculturation, and I identify with Marta's desire to go back home, though I don't have a place to return to. I am homeless and, in a different way, so is she since she has recently lost her mother. We understand each other's pain. We join the group of outcasts in our high school. They all smoke and wear black and act out their rebellion, but for us it is more reasonable to watch and join in the conversations about Dostoevsky as we safely continue our good-girl existence. We cannot afford to alienate our parents quite as much as they can; we have to be more cautious, more measured in our rebellions. Our families, after all, are on the border with us: my mother, especially, is unhappy about everything "American" and needs, demands, protection and support, not adolescent rage and rejection. I get annoyed by her unhappiness, but in retrospect I realize that my own strategies of displacement act out *her* ambivalence about assimilating, that feeling perfectly acculturated would be a betrayal of my connection to her. Again relationship becomes the place of relocation, the substitute for assimilation. Thus cultural displacement requires different negotiations in the process of separation and individuation than those theorized by psychoanalytic models. Marta and I negotiate together the contradictions between sixties adolescent rebellion and the strong familial bonds forged by the experience of emigration.

As it turns out, Marta stays in the states and we both go to Brown, take the same courses and major in comparative literature, the academic counterpart of the borderland. We share emotional and intellectual passion. Our English gets good enough to love T. S. Eliot and Yeats and our French to read Baudelaire. We study for exams together, read each other's papers, share each other's anxieties, and reassure each other. We live with our parents and study together in the snack bar and the reserve room of the library. We provide for each other the peer experience others find in dorms and clubs and sororities. She still sees her high school boyfriend and I quickly find a steady boyfriend in college. We always go out together—both boys are American—and we marry within a week of each other. Eventually we are both divorced.

The late sixties offer many opportunities for group identity, but even as I protest the Vietnam War and become involved in curriculum restructuring, I do so from the margins. The women's movement changes all that. I join a consciousness raising group in 1970 and experience a feeling of group allegiance for the very first time in my life. The perception of commonality, the feelings

Marianne and Marta 1965

of connection and mutual recognition are exhilarating and I become addicted to them. Not only do I see my own experiences validated and mirrored in those of others, but there is a mission in common, a politics based on those experiences. It is the life-sustaining, re-locating friendships with Mona and with Marta but now practiced on what feels like a global scale. Things really come together when I am able to incorporate female/feminist bonding into my work as well as my life. I have recently described my personal and professional "coming-to feminism" as a "story of affiliations and collaborations": "It was through several collaborative writing projects and through repeated dialogic encounters with other feminist critics that I was able to develop a feminist reading practice and a feminist critical voice of my own. To see my ideas mir-

Marianne and Marta
Providence, 1967

rored in those of others, to develop together a politics and a practice of mutual support, was not only to acquire professional confidence but also to experience thinking as powerful and radical. I see now (and I appreciate the irony) that I learned in those years to fear conflict and disagreement. Was it my personal history that made consensus so precious? Or was it that our commonalities were made precarious by institutional pressures?" (Hirsch and Keller 381).

Feminism is an enlarged borderland space for me, one which over the years has changed, reshaped, and transformed itself. At first, ironically, cultural differences seem to fade into the background, suddenly unimportant in the face of female bonding which had replaced culture, become a location. Later, I can begin to look at differences again. From a polar geography dividing the feminine from the masculine world, and studying the specificity of each, I have moved to a multiple topography that sees differences within masculine and feminine locations. Again, my history of multiple displacements has prepared me to conceive of identity as fractured and self-contradictory, as inflected by nationality, ethnicity, class, race, and history. But it has also made me appreciate those moments of commonality which allow for the adoption of a voice on behalf of women and for the commitment to social change. I now understand how my feminist work is inflected by my girlhood adjustments. During adolescence, friendship provided a form of displacement and resistance: to cultural assimilation as well as to femininity. It was a place on the border between cultures, between girlhood and womanhood. Like those early friendships, feminism itself became a space of relation and relocation, a place from which I could think and speak and write, a home on the border.

Everything comes together, everything I love, as in the fantasies of my childhood; I am the sum of my parts (226). Yes there are such moments, but I am suspicious of them. Displacement, or *Verschiebung*, Freud says, is the transfer of psychic energy from one idea to another, one which originally had little intensity but which, in the process, gains centrality and importance. A strategy of defense and survival, it offers a way to appease the censor. As an aesthetic it favors metonymy over metaphor.

As I finish reading Hoffman through the lens of my own experiences, I see the differences between us in terms of displacement. Both of us were culturally displaced. Yet displacement for Hoffman was the removal from one mythic place of origin and plenitude to another space of exile. Except for her passionate involvement with music, which mysteriously disappears in the third part of the book, there was no visible reinvestment of energy, no relief in the Freudian sense of displacement as *Verschiebung*. This direct, unmediated confrontation of cultures accounts for what Hoffman calls her *immigrant rage* and the *trained serenity* with which she has learned to disguise it.

I chose a different strategy, that of the border, which can be seen as a kind of *Verschiebung* in the Freudian sense. In fundamental ways, I remain in this shifting space. Often longing for a more singular and straightforward sense of identity and identification, I nevertheless embrace multiple displacement as a strategy both of assimilation and of resistance. The issue of my name, for example, is never resolved—it's Marianne [Märiäne] in German and Marianne [Märiän] in French, Mariana [Märiänä] in Rumanian, but in English I accept many versions, from Mary Anne to Maryanna [Maryanä] to Mary Anna [Märyänä] to Marian [Marien]. I sometimes find it hard to remember which I am to which friends, and I do wonder what this multiplicity means, but it simply doesn't bother me as much as it does some of my friends who have to get used to using different signifiers when referring to the same person.

Instead of engaging directly the America I was placed in, I came to it through a chain of displacements and attempts at relocation—through Vienna, through my involvement with French, through my friendships with Mona and with Marta. I do not shuttle between the surface control and the internal rage that define the sides of Hoffman's Archimedean triangle. Instead, I invest my psychic energies in a series of (dis) and (re) locations that allow me to live in this "permanent sojourn in the wilderness," this "alien element," which is, and always has been, "not comfortable but home."

Works Cited

Anzaldúa, Gloria. *Borderlands/La Frontera: The New Mestiza.* San Francisco: Spinsters, Aunt Lute, 1987.

Freud, Sigmund. *The Interpretation of Dreams.* 1900. *The Standard Edition of the Complete Psychological Works of Sigmund Freud.* Trans. and ed. James Strachey. 24 Vols. London: Hogarth, 1953–74.

Gilligan, Carol, Nona P. Lyons, and Rudy Hanmer, eds. *Making Connections: The Relational View of Adolescent Girls at Emma Willard School.* Troy, NY: Emma Willard, 1989.

Gilligan, Carol, Annie G. Rogers, and Deborah Tolman. *Women, Girls and Psychotherapy: Reframing Resistance.* Binghamton, NY: Harrington Park, 1991.

Gilligan, Carol, Janie Victoria Ward, and Jill McLean Taylor. *Mapping the Moral Domain: A Contribution of Women's Thinking to Psychological Theory and Education.* Cambridge: Harvard UP, 1988.

Hirsch, Marianne, and Evelyn Fox Keller, eds. *Conflicts in Feminism.* New York: Routledge, 1991.

Hoffman, Eva. *Lost in Translation: A Life in a New Language.* New York: Penguin, 1987.

Krupnik, Mark. *Displacement: Derrida and After.* Bloomington: Indiana UP, 1983.

6 | Mother Tongues and Other Strangers

Writing "Family" across Cultural Divides

Angelika Bammer

La famille n'existe pas
—Simone Weil

"All of them are my family"
—Irena Klepfisz

OF THE ANIMATED films that my children like to watch, one is a particular favorite: *An American Tail*, the story of the little boy mouse, Feivel. It recounts Feivel's adventures from the time that he and his family leave their Russian *shtetl* to escape the constantly threatening pogroms until they make a new home for themselves in America. The narrative begins with a Hanukkah celebration in Moskowitz. The father is the master of ceremonies, as it were, telling stories, answering questions, giving out the Hanukkah gifts. His gift to Feivel, in a gesture that prefigures the film's reassuring and suturing end, is the hat that he takes from his own head to place on the head of his son. The hat is too big for Feivel and slides down over his eyes. But it is his inheritance, as his father's successor, to grow into.

An American Tail is a story of separation and repair, of loss and restoration. It is the story of a family torn from its moorings (forced to leave its native home after a particularly violent pogrom) and in the process itself torn apart as its members are separated on the emigration journey. At the same time, it is the story of a family gathered together again in a new home that re(dis-?)places the old one. At the end, as Feivel is reunited with the family he has been seeking to find ever since they were separated in passage, he again puts on the hat. Now it fits: Feivel is ready to take his place as a man, within the family and as an American.[1] Family, a place to call home, and faith in the permanence of both are triumphantly affirmed. *An American Tail*, in short, is a fantasy, a fantasy of identity (re)constitution within the always again recuperable hold of the dual communities of nation and family. For not only are Feivel and his family Americans now, it is America that makes this family possible.

Traces of this fantasy as it has played itself out can be found in places like the Ellis Island Museum of Immigration where, carefully labeled with the name of the person or family to whom it belonged, there are objects (clothes, pictures, ritual objects, dishes and utensils for the preparation and serving of food) that people bore with them—translated in the most literal sense—from the home they left to the home they came to build elsewhere. The objects they carried were the material link between these two sites around which the family, as lived continuity, could (re)focus. In these objects in glass cases, the fantasy is symbolically marked; at other times, it is dramatically enacted. An example, even if extreme, is a report that appeared in the *New York Times* in 1991 that described the death or maiming on southern California roads of "[h]undreds of illegal immigrants coming north from Mexico." Unfamiliar with American ways, much less with multilane, high-speed megahighways, these "rural people . . . on their way to Los Angeles," we are told, are struck by cars or trucks as, in their attempt to elude immigration patrols, they sometimes run back and forth across as many as sixteen lanes of traffic. As I drive around town on my daily routines, the memory of these people ("The victims range in age from 3 years old to 80" [Mydans A13]) flashes through my body with a visceral shock. In my mind's eye I have an image of a family—a family not unlike my own—holding hands and "dashing . . . hand-in-hand, into the oncoming traffic" (Mydans A1). For I, too, engage in these rituals, enacting, holding on to a continuity of family across cultural divides: I hold in my hands, with much the same marvel that I felt as a child, the crystal glass paperweight that belonged to my grandparents; I tell my children stories in the German language that is my mother tongue, not the language of the country that is our home now.

I am thus haunted and compelled by the image of the human chain, the bond that embodies the promise of protection it is rarely able to sustain. For almost always somewhere on the way—on the boat, across the highway—"the chain gets broken" (A13). It is thus with this image of the human chain that my reflections on family begin: What is its purpose? What are its consequences? Is its breaking inevitable, necessary? What if this chain could somehow remain intact, if we didn't let go, weren't separated in mid-passage? Conversely, what if we never had it at all, nothing to hold us or let go of in the first place? In particular, I wonder how we translate "family" through the experience of cultural displacement?[2] When do these acts of translation become dramatic enactments ("holding hands, forming human chains . . . [as we] try to cross the highway" [Mydans A13]) and when do they, like the objects displayed in the Ellis Island Museum, come to rest as symbolic markers of passage and continuity? How, why do we do it, this carrying with us, this pulling across? At what cost? And what gets "lost in translation"?[3]

This essay is a reflection on family: what we hold onto and of what we need to let go; what we translate ("carry over") through periods of change, at our peril and for our survival. It is a reflection on the ways in which these issues of peril and survival are different for those who, by force or by choice, are divided between different cultures. In the process of reflecting on these questions, basic and contradictory assumptions about family once again come up: that it affords protection, for example, or that it is an ominous place.[4] My particular concern here, again, is what happens to all of these, including the assumption of what "family" is, when the family in question has been uprooted or otherwise displaced from its cultural moorings.

I write in the context of a political atmosphere (the 1992 American presidential campaign) in which the debate over "family values"—a debate at the heart of which are the related questions of what counts as a family and which families count—has acquired national proportions. It is a context in which those of us who are critical of the repressive function of the institution family have learned the danger of ceding its affective power to the forces on the Right. It is a context that also calls on us to become more critically aware of how we ourselves sometimes unwittingly use the term in traditionally normative ways to mean biologically based and patriarchally structured nuclear units.[5] On the most general level, then, this essay aims to remind us once again, from the perspective of all those who have been displaced from the normative ground of authorized tradition, that both within "our own" culture, and certainly beyond, there are many other ways to think and live family.

Art Spiegelman's *Maus*, like *An American Tail*, addresses many of these issues. It, too, is the tale of a family torn apart, not just displaced, but literally dismembered by the Holocaust. *Maus* tells several stories at once: the story of Vladek Spiegelman from his years as a dashing young man ("People always told me I looked just like Rudolph Valentino" [*Maus* 13]) and successful entrepreneur in pre-World War II Poland to the end of his life as an old man in New York City; the story of the Jews in Vladek's old world—the Spiegelmans, the Zylberbergs (the family of Vladek's wife, Anja), their extended family network of relatives and friends—from the mid-1930s through the war and Holocaust to the immediate post-war years; the story, finally, of Art, the son of Vladek and Anja born in America after the war, younger brother to their first child, Richieu, whom Art never knew because Richieu died in the Holocaust.

However, *Maus* does not only tell of a family torn apart. Like *An American Tail*, it also records the struggle of parents and children alike to keep the family together, to re-member, re-connect it again after the violence of its disruption. In this sense, *Maus*, not unlike the objects displayed in the Ellis Island Museum, establishes the "link, through the present, of past and future" that Simone Weil posited as the basis of social community. In the case of the

Spiegelman family, the links are established through stories told in different media and different voices: the mother's diaries, both the ones she kept during the war and the one she began again when Art was a child; the father's oral narrative that Art elicits by his insistent need and desire to know what happened to and in his family; the photographic image of Richieu; and, finally, the comic strip narrative created by Art to gather together as many of the disparate pieces as he can and join them, mosaic-like, into a family (hi)story. Thus, the formal composition of *Maus* creates a structure that bridges, even though it cannot fill in, the spaces of silence created by the people whose stories had remained untold: the mother, killed by suicide in 1968, whose diaries were either lost (in the war) or destroyed (by her husband after her death); the father who has lived for decades with the weight of the history he now recounts because, as he tells Art, "[i]t would take *many* books, my life, and no one wants anyway to hear such stories" (*Maus* 12); the brother, Richieu, who, killed at age five, has no story record to pass on other than the minimal fragment of a childhood photo. *Maus*, in the most literal sense, *re*places the stories of these lives by remembering and (re)inscribing them into a composite family history.

The things (objects, stories, rituals) we take with us from old homes to new represent the link between future and past that Simone Weil maintains is what constitutes "grounding" (*enracinement*): the knowledge that we are part of a social community. "Human beings are grounded through their actual, active, and natural participation in a community," Weil writes, a community that "keeps alive certain treasures of the past and certain visions of the future" (45). It is in this sense of a community that grounds us in history through generations future and past, that, as Weil sees it in the passage from which the first epigraph comes, "family no longer exists" (90). In the world about which Weil is writing—modern Western (European) society—family has become, in her view, a place to which we withdraw, an isolated refuge that no longer links us to anything. The only functional community left (in her sense of community), concluded Weil as she wrote *L'Enracinement* in the winter of 1942/43, is, in the West today, the nation.[6] Her contention, in short, is that the strongest affective bond (that which, in Benedict Anderson's words, we might be willing to die for) has been transferred—or displaced—from the private level of domestic relations ("family" in the literal sense) to the public level of community and national culture ("family" in the symbolic sense).

Eric Hobsbawm argues along similar lines (even though the case he makes is different) in his analysis of the recent rise of new nationalisms and ethnicities. Examining the relationship between nationalism and the politics of ethnicity, Hobsbawm notes that both establish an inclusion/exclusion structure in which those who belong can be distinguished, separated out, from those who are outsiders. In the course of the nineteenth century, it was the nation-state

that became the locus of such "we"/"they" positioning, he observes; more recently, in the period most commonly referred to in terms of "post-" (post-colonial, post-War, post-Cold War, post-communist, and even post-history), the
nation—in a transnational global economy increasingly destabilized and dispersed—is no longer the guarantor of social coherence or cultural authority.
Ethnicity, argues Hobsbawm, steps into the breach to provide a new identifica-
tory locus. In short, the new ethnicities are the fracture lines along which the
nation breaks. Their construction and deployment is a post-national strategy
of sorts for salvaging and recouping a sense of group belonging.

Thus, while Weil maintains that the less family constitutes a locus of historical community, the more nation takes over its affective function, Hobsbawm argues that the less nation provides a stable point of reference and identification, the more other communities—ethnic and familial, say—shift to the
political foreground. What these two positions share is the recognition that
not only are family, community, and nation unstable and mutable concepts,
but also that both the concepts and the communities to which they refer are
inseparably interconnected. When one or the other declines in importance, it
seems, the other(s) rise(s) commensurately.

When "home and country" is no longer a functional equation, the identification with a national culture is also destabilized. Nation, in such contexts,
tends to either disintegrate into a negatively laden set of associations or recede
into the nostalgic distance of myth. Either way, nation as family in the Weilian
or Andersonian sense becomes, as it were, dysfunctional. Under these circumstances—and this is where I take issue with Weil—family, in the more literal
(domestic) or community/clan sense, can gain considerably in importance.

This is the point of departure for the narrative of *Maus*, both on the part
of the son who wants to know his family history ("Start with Mom . . . Tell me
how you met" [*Maus* 12]), and on the part of the father who agrees to tell it.
In the case of Vladek Spiegelman and the Jews whose stories are recounted in
Maus, the national identity they had believed to be a home was no refuge from
persecution: In the eyes of the world (in this case, Nazis and Poles alike) they
were "Jews," not Polish citizens.[7] What is more, during the period of history
in which Vladek's story takes place, the nation to which Vladek and his com-
patriot mice belonged disintegrated beneath them. As the map on the back of
the first volume of *Maus* illustrates, "Poland" effectively ceased to exist: one
part was incorporated into the German Reich; another annexed to Russia; the
remainder (the central part where not only the capital, Warsaw, was, but also
four of the major Nazi death camps) was renamed "General Gouvernement"
by the German occupiers. Vladek's world since then, the home where Art grew
up, is represented by another, smaller map ex-centrically superimposed on the
1940s map of Poland: "Rego Park, N.Y." Between these places that map a life
another has inserted itself, which for Vladek and his family redrew the map of

the world: the work and death camps of Auschwitz and Auschwitz II (Birke-nau).[8] In the face of this remapping of the world—a world in which the concept of nation has been dispersed into the reality of diasporic identity—the question of how and where to reorient and reground oneself takes Art Spiegelman back to the family. Thus, he dedicates the first volume of *Maus* to his mother and the second to his brother and daughter.

Where do we belong when the map of our world has been redrawn; who are our communities; what is the place of family? These are some of the questions that frame the narrative of *Maus*. The prefatory vignette from Art's childhood condenses these questions parabolically. Having fallen down and hurt himself, little Art is hurt even more by his friends who run away laughing. His father's response is not to comfort him but to give him the question that, in *Maus*, is the equivalent of Feivel's hat: Who is my friend? Whom can I trust, and who will betray me?

The assumption, of course (an assumption that *Maus* underscores), is that our "friends"—those with whom we belong—are those most like us: mice go with mice, cats with cats, etc. At the same time, the unstable foundation of this assumption is exposed at the beginning of *Maus II*, as Art and his wife discuss her cartoon depiction. On Art's sketchpad are some of the options: a moose, a dog, a frog. Françoise's position (with which Art, in the end, concurs) is that she should be "[a] *mouse*, of course!" (*Maus II* 11) because she has converted to Judaism. This exchange draws attention to the constructedness of the very categories whose presumed givenness was the foundation of Nazi logic. By thus illustrating the degree to which what we are ("mice," "pigs," "cats," or "frogs") is an identity lived out on the continuum between choice and necessity, *Maus* acknowledges the historical force of these constructs while exposing their artificiality.[9] Art Spiegelman includes himself, as author and protagonist both, in the resulting dilemma (am I my self or the mask I wear?) by depicting himself, at a moment when he is feeling overwhelmed, as a simple human being with a mouse mask (*Maus II* 41–47). Earlier, in *Maus*, (Polish) mice, trying to survive by disguising themselves as "Poles" had been depicted wearing pig masks. However, here—not coincidentally in the central chapter on Auschwitz—the issue of masking suddenly takes a much more startling turn. For the images in this chapter propose that under the circumstantial masks we wear in acts of mimicry or masquerade, there is another layer which is much less often perceived as a mask but which still covers up our underlying common humanness: the cultural identity (mouseness, catness, or pigness, say) by which we are defined and as which we, in turn, define ourselves. Yet, having made this proposal, the text immediately counters it by revealing, piled around the base of the drafting table at which Art (a human with a mouse mask) sits, a veritable mountain of dead mice: "real" mice, not humans with mouse masks.

The question of authenticity—who has more: the humans with mouse masks or the maskless mice?—is suspended in light of the historically more urgent one: the question of exigency.

One of the primary places where issues of national culture and family coherence come together is the question of language. As *Maus* illustrates, the problem is not just whether the family (hi)story will be told, but *how*, that is, in what language: Which/whose language shall the family speak, literally and culturally? The question that *Maus* adds is what happens when the family is itself divided across cultures: pre-war, eastern European, on the one hand; postwar American, on the other? How does family even translate across such a divide when the very meaning of "family" within the family differs? The extended family network within which Vladek and Anja lived before and during the war is not only a different, but virtually a different *kind* of family from the small and fragmented one held together by Art and Vladek. This difference is highlighted by the images of family mealtimes then and now: In the first case, images of the family clan (grandparents, children, and grandchildren, uncles, cousins, and aunts) gathered around a large dinner table fill up to half a page (*Maus* 19, 22, 74–76); in the second case, the truncated family that gathers at mealtime, if then (we never see more than three members of the family eating together at one time), easily fits into half a narrow column (*Maus* 43; *Maus II* 20).

In this light, Art Spiegelman's choice of the comic strip form as his narrative vehicle is also a choice about family. For he has chosen a cultural language that decidedly positions him not only on one side of the divide but also on the side that his father isn't. For Art, growing up as an American boy in the 1950s and 60s, comic books are an ordinary part of the cultural language of everyday life. For Vladek, they are not only foreign ("I don't *ever* read such comics" [*Maus* 133]), but exotic, *extra*ordinary, a means by which to become successful "the American way," rich and famous "like . . . *Walt Disney*" (*Maus* 133). Likewise, the language of Art's and Vladek's Jewishness has changed: Vladek's was shaped in a pre-Holocaust world in which the continuity of tradition was still palpable; Art's has been formed in a post-Holocaust world in which that continuity has been decisively ruptured.[10]

In a footnote to an essay on some of the ways in which language can be a "home" for people who have lost their cultural home physically, Karla Schultz complicates the traditional notion of a "mother tongue" by taking the concept literally. For, she observes, while it is conventionally taken to mean the native language of the mother, in the case of immigrants (or refugees), it "may also be understood as the language the mother learns from (or for) her children. The traditional definition thus is enlarged from being the language *originally* spoken by the mother to include the language *newly* learned by her for the sake of those whom she loves most" (132).[11] The question, then, becomes: Which is the mother tongue in this case: that of the parent(s) or that of the child(ren)? A solution by which to avoid such an either/or choice is to construct the family language multilingually. Such a construct allows for families with more than one native culture or more than one mother tongue to expand into, rather than fragment over, a dialogic space in which "family" can be spoken in a variety of ways and need not be translated to be communicable.[12]

Maus negotiates the space of cultural difference within family in a similar way by also constructing a dialogic narrative. Art asks, tape records, describes, and draws; Vladek answers, narrates, remembers. The negotiations over who is given narrative space, and when, punctuate the narrative: Vladek, for example, wants to talk about the glaucoma in his left eye, while Art wants to hear about the Holocaust. Compromising, they agree to take turns and share narrative authority. Sometimes the tension inherent in the search for common ground across the differences of culture and history erupts in anger or collapses in defeat; at other times it grows into understanding. As they enact it, however, the space of commonality assumed by the term "family" becomes real, a continually (re)negotiated interaction.

To the extent that family can provide a foundation for the groundedness of which Simone Weil spoke, it can provide the sense of coherence that holds an individual in place, particularly in times of external uncertainty. In such times, when the world outside appears a threatening and alien place, the family can seem the bedrock of constancy and security that one must hold onto at all costs. Yet this insistence on holding family together—on not letting go— risks destroying the very bonds it was meant to sustain. On one level, as in the case of the Mexican families torn apart on the California freeways, the destruction can be literal, physical. On another, it can take the form of psychological violence.[13]

Elias Canetti, born into a Sephardic Jewish family in Bulgaria in 1905, tells the story of such violence. His, too, was a family in which there were several mother tongues: the Ladino that the parents spoke with their children, relatives, and friends; the Bulgarian that the child used with neighborhood children and the help; the English that he learned when they moved to Manchester; and, finally, the German that the parents reserved for themselves to create a linguistic space of intimacy. The borders between these different languages were not to be transgressed nor were the territories they staked out to be negotiated; change came only by decree. Canetti recounts how, as an eight-year-old, he learned German as a result of such a decree. After his father's sudden death, his young mother forced her son to fill the place that her husband had, linguistically and affectively, occupied. Abruptly and with the utmost haste, the boy had to learn the very language from which the father's living presence had excluded him. And he did, with his mother as teacher:

She read me a sentence in German and had me repeat it. Since she disliked my pronunciation, I repeated it several times, until she seemed able to bear it. But I only did this a few times, for she mocked my pronunciation and as there was nothing more unbearable to me than her mockery, I made a great effort and soon spoke it right. Only then did she tell me the meaning of the sentence in English. But she never repeated it, I had to remember it once and for all. (83)

"The terror in which I lived," he concludes laconically, "was for her a peda-gogical matter" (84).

The terror that Canetti describes is a response to the violence that some-times lies at the heart of family togetherness. It is a terror that can be insepa-rable from what we call love; for as Canetti himself confirms at the conclusion of his tale, he not only learned German, but this language—his mother tongue in every sense of the word—became, for him and his mother, "the language of our love" (87). This complex nexus of love and terror, played out within the space and in the name of family, is also probed in *Maus*. The adult son is treated as a child over whom the parents have proprietary rights. When Vladek doesn't approve of the coat that Art wears, Vladek simply throws it out and replaces it with another he deems more appropriate (*Maus* 67–69).[14] Because he, Vladek, doesn't want them, he destroys the diaries that Anja had intended for her son (*Maus* 158–59). In rage, Art calls him a "murderer," and on this note the first volume of *Maus* ends.[15] The most extreme example of the cata-strophic consequences of refusing to let go, however, is the story of Richieu. For, as Vladek tells it, the mother's unwillingness to part with her child was, in part, responsible for his death. When, in 1941, as the violence against and deportations of Jews were visibly and alarmingly on the rise, a family friend suggested that their children might be safer if they were temporarily given to Polish families, Anja's response was to hold her child tight and vow that she would "*never* give up my baby. *Never!*" (*Maus* 81). The friend's child was given away and Richieu was kept home; the other child, as Vladek tells it, "re-mained alive; ours did not" (*Maus* 81). The very act that was meant to be life-sustaining proved tragically fatal. The crucial question, we might con-clude, is not whether or not to hold on, but when to let go and how to know when that "when" is.

If there is validity to the psychoanalytic premise that individuation is the result of the successful separation between parent(s) and child, then letting go, in every respect, is necessary.[16] For people and families who have been dis-placed from the places and communities that for them were "home," this proc-ess is necessarily more complicated. In circumstances where the family is vir-tually the only remaining link to the home they have lost, it can be as difficult for children to distance themselves from their parents as for parents to let go of their children. In such cases, severing, or even loosening, the familial bonds—bonds that ground them in community (and, by extension, as Weil suggests, in history)—can be perceived more as a negation than an affirmation of self.

Immigrants, refugees, people living in exile attest to the crises this dilemma represents. For Holocaust survivors and their children, as for other refugee survivors of genocidal acts, this dilemma is immeasurably intensified by the fact that they are not only physically displaced from their communities of origin, but that these communities, including often their families, no longer exist.[17] Thus, *Generations of the Holocaust* begins with the observation that "the very concept of 'family' is highly charged for survivors" (Bergmann 23). To the extent that children of survivors often either try to vicariously live out their parents' disrupted lives or expend much effort rebelling against this expectation, Martin Bergmann, one of the editors, notes, they "do not get to live their own lives" (265). Either way, he concludes, one of the most critical tasks in therapy with children of survivors is helping them to "finish the interrupted work of separation and individuation" (265). This often means unlearning the very skills they had to acquire: learning to let go when holding on seemed the only way to survive, or learning to attach when survival taught them separation. This is what Art and Vladek Spiegelman are also struggling to learn. In this sense, *Maus* plays out the primal family drama: the need of both parents and children to sever their dependency bonds so that attachments can be freely chosen.

The first volume of *Maus* ends with just such an act of separation: Art turns his back on his father and walks away alone; Vladek's last word to his son in this section is "stranger" (*Maus* 159). But if Art has the last word first, he allows Vladek the concluding last word at the end of *Maus II*. The generosity of this act is intensified by the fact that Vladek, exhausted and overwhelmed by the work of memory he has just gone through, addresses Art as "Richieu," and Art does not correct him. Thus, in a final gesture of conciliation, the family is rejoined: both parents and all their children together. As Art stands by his father's bed and the father turns to sleep, the family is reconstituted in an act of remembering that names and forgives.[18] Richieu is invoked as his name is called out; by ceding his brother (t)his place and by allowing his father to claim his first son, Art puts aside his lifelong sibling rivalry. Anja is remembered through the final image of the tombstone that bears her name and dates next to those of her husband; she is laid to rest in the family grave, and so is her son's anger at his mother for having taken her life and left him. It is this family—his family—disrupted and incomplete as it is, that Art Spiegelman in his parting gesture literally and symbolically underwrites as he signs his name under the names of his parents and brother.

To the extent that family is a vital nexus between the outer social world and the inner world of the individual psyche, the relationship of a given family to its social context is critical to the psychological development and well-being of an individual. Another way of putting it is that the social contract is both anchored and mediated narcissistically in what Piera Castoriadis-Aulagnier calls the "narcissistic contract" (182–93). Exploring some of the implications of what radical mental health professionals posit as axiomatic, namely the "inner relationships between consciousness and social context" (Fanon, *Black Skin* 97)—relationships that both traverse and are mediated by the family—Castoriadis-Aulagnier elaborates on two key points that are of particular relevance here. The first is that "[t]he relationship of the parental couple to the child is always marked by the relationship of the couple to the social environment in which they find themselves (the term 'environment,' depending on the particular situation of the couple, referring either to society in the broader sense or to the subgroup whose values the couple shares)." The second point, which addresses the implications of the first on the child's development of a sense of self, is that "[t]he conflict that might exist between the couple and their environment risks confirming the impression on the child's psyche that what is taking place in the outside world and her/his fantasized experience of being rejected by, excluded from, aggressed upon by anyone in power, are, in fact, identical" (183–84). Since the experience of cultural displacement obviously constitutes a significant disturbance in the relationship between a family and its social environment, Castoriadis-Aulagnier's theses open up important paths toward understanding, and responding to, the particular difficulties that families—children and parents alike—encounter in such situations.

For one, this experience can have significant implications for the successful resolution of the Oedipal conflict. In a jointly authored paper, two psychoanalysts, Esperanza de Plá and Elena de la Aldea, propose that cultural displacement is always in some way experienced as expulsion, a form of rejection not just by one's native ("father")land but also, by extension, by one's parents who failed to provide the stability and security of home. "The very fact of being 'foreign,'" they propose, "contains an element of parental rejection" (64). In such a situation, they note, the resolution of the Oedipal conflict can be seriously disturbed, since it is difficult, if not impossible, to *choose* separation when one is already feeling rejected. The condition of being foreign, in other words, complicates the separation between parents and children.

In this process, language plays a complex role, both binding and dividing family members. For not only do parents and children often end up with different native languages, their different relationships to these languages can have notable social consequences. For example, in terms of both intra- and extrafamilial relations, the traditional positions of authority can be confused or even reversed depending on who does—or does not—master a given language. While the relationship of the parents to the language of the country that has become their new home is often, as it is tellingly put, broken, their children typically make the new language their own, learning to speak it fluently, accent-free, and with confidence. The children come to master the very cultural codes (language, modes of dress, forms of social interaction), ignorance of which functionally reduces the parents to children.[19] Eva Hoffman, daughter of Polish Jewish parents who emigrated to Canada in the late 1950s, describes her experience of this process. When the adolescent Eva, eager to assimilate, stops going to synagogue, her parents don't protest. " 'In Poland,' her mother says, 'I would have known how to bring you up.' " "But here," the narrator—her now authorial daughter—points out, "she has lost . . . her authority." At the same time, the daughter, who is "becoming 'English' " while her parents remain Polish, holds on at the very point when, developmentally, she should be letting go. Their intent is the same: to protect the already frayed fabric of family from unraveling completely: "There is only the tiny cluster, the four of us . . . "(145).

Both in theoretical and practical terms, cases like these could add significantly to our understanding of what "family" is, in its complex and variable formations. In particular, they could add to our understanding of the relationship between its internal dynamics and external events, such as the removal, forced or voluntary, from the place that had been "home," the destruction or loss of one's culture or people. This, in turn, would address—and in part perhaps redress—one of the most dogged problems of traditional psychoanalysis, namely the fact that it tends to falter, if not stop, at the very point at which both psyche and self need to be (re)thought in broader social terms, not just in terms of domestic relations.

And yet, at least in the field of psychoanalytic theory, remarkably little attention has been paid to this phenomenon thus far. In their introduction to *Psicoanálisis de la migración y del exilio* (Psychoanalysis of Migration and Exile), one of the few significant works on the subject, León and Rebeca Grinberg note that while human migration and its "historical, demographic, cultural, religious, political, ideological, sociological, economic, etc." effects have been the object of numerous studies in many disciplines, it is only "in recent years that the topic has also begun to interest professionals in the field of mental health" (11). In particular, they point out, it has as yet "hardly been examined at all from the perspective of psychoanalysis"—"despite the fact," they add, "(or perhaps precisely because of the fact) that many of the pioneers in the field suffered this experience personally" (11–12). To date, not much seems to have changed in this regard. As recently as 1991, an article in the *Argentinian Review of Psychopathology* notes that in light of the fact that recent seismic shifts in the global order and the attendant social, economic, and political crises have brought cultural displacement to the attention of both public, political consciousness and private, therapeutic practices, the continuing avoidance of the issue in psychoanalytic literature is striking (see Carlisky and Kijak). The normative concept of family as an (at least, externally) stable unit into which one is born and out of which one grows continues to be assumed, it appears, despite massive and increasing evidence to the contrary. Cases where the stability and coherence of the family is disrupted and destroyed as much by external as by internal forces—as in the case of refugees, (im)migrants, people living in exile or under conditions of colonization, say—are still typically left to sociologists or anthropologists or, in practice, to relief or social workers.

Not only does this prevent us from seeing how much more varied and complex than our conventional model of "family" families really are, it gets in the way of the conceptually and politically crucial next step: the critique of the (Western) family model as the normative paradigm within which human behavior and its pathologies are charted. It was toward this level of critique that Frantz Fanon was pushing when he wrote *Black Skin, White Masks* as a radical intervention into the colonialist politics of psychoanalytic assumptions and psychiatric practices. In so doing, he was probing the limits of the discipline itself by questioning the validity of some of its most basic assumptions, among them the nature and centrality of the family model. The task of psychoanalysis, namely "the understanding of given behavior patterns—within the specific group represented by the family," he notes, works in the European context where "the family represents in effect a certain fashion in which the world presents itself to the child" (*Black Skin* 141). In other contexts, however—notably, in large parts of the non-European "Third" world—other ways of understanding both the world and the self prevail. "[N]eurosis," he boldly concludes, "is not a basic element of human reality" (*Black Skin* 151): for what might be deemed (and termed) neurotic from the perspective of one set of assumptions might, from another, be seen as a legitimate response to oppressive conditions. The last chapter of Fanon's subsequent study, *The Wretched of the Earth*, "Colonial War and Mental Disorders," illustrates this thesis with a series of examples from the colonial war in Algeria. One of these, a case study of *"puerperal psychoses among the refugees,"* notes that among the hundreds of thousands of Algerian women whom the war had made refugees in the wake of the scorched earth policy of the French colonial army, such psychoses were not "abnormal" but the common experience. Moreover, he concludes, given the conditions under which these women live and give birth—"the extreme poverty and precariousness of living conditions . . . [t]he atmosphere of permanent insecurity . . . kept up by frequent invasions of French troops, bombardments from the air, machine-gunning . . . together with the break-up of homes"—make it eminently clear that "the fundamental nature of these [psychoses and mental disorders] is not cleared up by the regression and soothing of the disorders" (*Wretched* 279).

The work of people like Frantz Fanon, León and Rebeca Grinberg, Esperanza de Plá, Elena de la Aldea, and Piera Castoriadis-Aulagnier, as well as the struggle of countless women, men, and children to translate the concept and structure of family across cultures, document the need for a model of family that recognizes cultural displacement as a central factor shaping human development and social reality in our century. To the extent that the family constitutes a critical nexus in the relationship between the realms of the psychological and the social/political, such a model is all the more necessary.

What this calls for, I believe, is a much broader and more differentiated view, one that can learn from and creatively adapt models operative in other cultural contexts, including those "other" cultures within our own. In this respect, we might find the work of social and cultural anthropologists, for whom the comparative study of family and kinship structures has been a focus of critical inquiry for well over a century, particularly useful. For as their work has amply documented, family "in our sense" (biological and nuclear) only applies in very specific contexts, of which modern Western industrial society is but one. My argument is that even here—in our (modern, Western, industrial) society—this model of family is seriously limited and limiting.

The problem with the Oedipal model, for example, is not just its (cultural) narrowness, a problem that could be rectified by expanding it "multiculturally," but the degree to which it is predicated upon a model of selfhood that does not accommodate the needs and traditions of other people of other cultures, including those displaced by and within our own. If the process of individuation were mapped differently, as a process of exchange and interaction, say, instead of a process of separation and substitution, such differences could be recognized as variations on, not deviations from, the theme of selfhood. Within such an other model, individuation—"growing *up*," as we tellingly say—might be thought of less in terms of autonomy (growing out of the family) than in terms of responsibility (growing into social community). Family, then, could be rethought in terms of our bonds to our various communities.

In the normative, Western, psychoanalytic models identity is constructed along a vertical axis in which self is defined in relation to an other/others perceived in hierarchical terms. The significance of horizontally defined relationships—siblings or peer communities—is hardly brought into play.[20] This paradigm is problematic in a number of ways. Even in the context of the particular sociocultural milieus (the Western European bourgeoisie) within which the theories took shape, milieus in which the verticality of power relations was firmly inscribed, horizontal relationships between siblings and peers presumably also played a formative role in an individual's self-formation. Indeed, in the very circles from which Freud's patients, for the most part, came, the family in its nuclear form, as it came to be normatively defined, was more often a principle than a practice. Thus, the model already marginalizes, if not altogether obscures, relationships that do not fit the categorical constraints of "family in our sense." How much more significant, we might ask, might such "other" relationships be in cases where the notions and practices of "family" are different to begin with, cultures and social contexts in which familial communities are structured less around bourgeois, patriarchal, nuclear families than around extended-family, kinship, or peer networks.[21]

Patricia Hill Collins gives an example from the African-American community in which "women-centered networks of community-based child care often extend beyond the boundaries of biologically related individuals and include 'fictive kin' " (120). This structure, she explains, has historical roots, not just in the translation of West African traditions to America by Africans displaced from their native cultures through slavery but also in the functional adaptations of African-American communities to the race and gender oppression they experienced in America. Both African and African-American communities, notes Hill, "recognized that vesting one person with full responsibility for mothering a child may not be wise or possible" (119). Thus, mothering is shared by both "bloodmothers" and "othermothers" in a dynamic, dialectical, and constantly (re)negotiated process that involves "the individual households that make up African-American extended family networks" as well as the black community and its institutions (118). The result is a complex interrelationship of family and community.[22] *Maus*, too, illustrates this interrelationship as both Vladek's and Art's narratives demonstrate the degree to which their family and the Jewish community sustain and support one another. Even *An American Tail*, with its fantasy of a family put together again whole as if nothing had been lost on its journey, acknowledges the degree to which the functional reality of family is broader than that which the term conventionally signifies. Thus, as Feivel's search for his family is finally approaching the happy end, the group that searches for and finds him is not just his biological family but includes those close friends and comrades who have become his familial community.[23]

The centrality of a paradigm in which "family" is assumed to be not only a biological, nuclear family but one in which the formative relationships are those that operate on a vertical axis is called into question by the complex ways in which the experience of cultural displacement (re)configures bonds of loyalty, commitment, and responsibility. As the locus of cultural authority in such families tends to shift, the sites of power and security are often dispersed and multiply situated. In this context, relationships other than those between parent and child (such as between siblings and peers) can be psychologically and socially formative. The question, then, is: Given this displacement of the locus of familial identity and authority, what happens to the notion of family? Does it disintegrate, itself displaced onto a variety of dispersed sites (of which "family in our sense"—nuclear, heterosexual, and patriarchal—is only one)?

Is it affirmed with a reactionary vengeance? Or is it rewritten, recast not in the preset mold of one particular tradition but in the form of a sketch that can be erased and (re)drawn, depending on what—then and there—is called for?

Upon re-reading the *New York Times* article on Mexican (im)migrants with which I began, I realize that my memory has effected a translation of its own, for nowhere in the article is a family or families mentioned. The protagonists of the story are generalized "immigrants" or "illegal aliens." The family association was obviously created in my mind by the accompanying image of one of the new signs posted alongside California highways in border areas: In silhouette form, a man, woman, and child are shown holding hands and running toward the highway. Above the figures, bold capital letters spell "CAUTION." However, as the article points out, the sign is ambiguous, indeed dangerously so. For, if one includes as readers not just the motorists but also those "rural people" by the road looking for a place to cross, it can be read either as a warning *not* to do what the sign shows or, conversely, as an injunction to do it. To a given reader, in a given state of ignorance, confusion, or fear, it can suggest a bewildering set of conflicting options: "Hold on and run," "Let go and stay," "Let go and run," "Hold on and stay." How we define ourselves in relation to family has much to do with our response to these options. What remains is the ambiguity of the caution sign. It is this ambiguity, the pain and freedom of its irresolution, that we must live with.

On the other hand, if we think of family in more broad and generous terms, we might channel this ambivalence toward the equally critical (certainly no less difficult) work of sorting out the nature of our ties to our various communities.[24] For they, too, in the sense of the second epigraph, are our "families." It is the relationship, finally, between these two—the families to whom we are born and the communities to which we are joined by choice, tradition, or force of historical necessity—that shapes our sense not only of who we are but of our location as subjects of/in history.

Notes

I thank Enrique Garcia, Irena Grudzinska-Gross, and Bobby Paul for their various gifts of friendship, insight, and references during my work on this essay. All translations, unless otherwise noted, are my own.

1. Feivel's predestined role as the future man in the family was clearly indicated by the symbolic transfer of the hat. Another, albeit much less foregrounded, clue that he would also surpass his father by acquiring authority in the public realm is the fact that while the parents

never speak anything but heavily accented, Yiddish-inflected English, Feivel and his sister speak perfect American English from the outset.

2. To "translate," from Latin *transferre*, means to bear (or, as the case may be, pull) across.

3. I take this phrase from Hoffman.

4. It is in this latter sense that home—the place where "family," literally and symbolically, resides—is always also *"unhomely"* (*"unheimlich"*): uncanny.

5. In the Freudian model and its derivatives, this is effectively what family means, even though Freud acknowledged the fact of other kinds of families. Indeed, given Freud's own childhood experience, living as he did in an extended family-clan network that included his adult half-brothers, their wives (simultaneously his sisters-in-law and aunts), and their children (simultaneously his nephews and nieces and cousin playmates), to pretend otherwise would have been to ignore his own formative experience. Nevertheless, the degree to which his analytical model posits the biologically based, patrilineal, and patriarchal nuclear unit as normative is evidenced throughout Freud's oeuvre. An example is the discussion of family in "Totem and Taboo." Freud describes a different kind of family unit: the "totem clan" ("The members of a totem clan are brothers and sisters") and even acknowledges the fact that this clan bond "is stronger than the family in our sense." Yet, he goes on to argue, the two— "family in our sense" and "family" in this other sense—"do not coincide, since the totem is . . . inherited through the female line" (484–85). In short, it is only family "in our sense" that, in the end, truly counts as "family."

The degree to which this concept of family has become normative in our (modern, Western, industrial) society is evidenced by the fact that over half a century later and in an entirely different sociocultural context (white, middle-class America as opposed to bourgeois Vienna), the same concept still prevails. As David Schneider put it in his classic study of American kinship, " 'The family' is a cultural unit which contains a husband and a wife who are the mother and father of their child or children. . . . The family, to be a family, must live together" (*American Kinship* 33). In the course of further research and in later editions, Schneider differentiated this concept of family by class, concluding that "the 'family' means something different to the lower class from what it does to the middle class" (Schneider, *American Kinship* 122). Specifically, in light of these class differences, he revised the principle of co-residency that he had previously posited as a necessary dimension of the construct "family."

6. In his discussion of the affective bond between individuals and nation ("why [are] people . . . ready to die for these inventions?" [141]), Benedict Anderson also investigates the affective link between family and nation. Something of the nature of the particular love that nations inspire, he notes, "can be deciphered from the ways in which language describes its object: either in the vocabulary of kinship . . . or that of home." Like family, nation represents "something to which one is naturally tied . . . the domain of disinterested love and solidarity" (143–44).

7. This fact is underscored in *Maus* by the fact that all the cartoon characters are depicted as members of different animal species according to their national identity: the Germans are cats, the Poles pigs, etc. The one exception are those whose Jewishness seems to mark them more powerfully than any presumed national characteristic: for, whatever else they might be (Poles, Germans, or Americans), all the Jews are depicted as mice.

8. This map of Auschwitz is figured on the back of *Maus II*.

9. The complicated and inherently unstable meaning of "alikeness" as a basis of group identity formation can also be put in structural terms: "[S]olidarity is increased when different kinds of bond [sic] replicate each other. Hence the group which raises its food to-

gether, processes it, distributes it, consumes it; the group that is interdependent for its labor; the group which worships its own ancestors and thus is the same 'church'; the group which owns its property as a unit—such a group, with repetitive bonds, each reinforcing the other, is more strongly solidary than is the group which merely shares a single function—say, its name or its emblem. And the degree to which it is solidary is directly proportional to the number of different solidary bonds among its members, and this is inversely proportional to the strength of any particular member's bonds outside that unit" (Schneider, "Some Muddles" 48).

10. The incident of "Parsha's Truma" (*Maus* 57–59) illustrates this rupture. To Vladek's account of one of the most symbolically significant events in his life—the dream prophesy of liberation "on the day of Parsha's Truma"—Art responds uncomprehendingly ("So what's Parsha's Truma?") and skeptically.

11. Schultz's cases in point are T. W. Adorno and Katharina Heunsaker, the protagonist of an immigrant narrative by Hope Williams Sykes, entitled *The Joppa Door* (1937).

12. The rich narrative possibilities opened up by such a concept of family are illustrated by recent literary texts such as Kim Chernin's *In My Mother's House*, an (auto)biographical story of her mother, Rose Chernin, and herself as her mother's daughter, or Amy Tan's *The Joy Luck Club*, the story of four first-generation Chinese immigrant mothers and their second-generation Chinese-American daughters. In both cases, the dialogic narrative structure, in which mothers and daughters take terms occupying the position of narrative authority, structurally replicates the constant process of cultural negotiation within and among families in immigrant communities.

13. Alice Miller's *The Drama of the Gifted Child* gives a compelling account of this process and its effects on the child.

14. The "new" coat that Vladek gives Art is actually Vladek's old one. Like the hat that Feivel inherited from his father in *An American Tail*, the coat that Art gets from his father also doesn't fit. The difference is that Feivel is thrilled with the gift, while Art is dismayed at this act of appropriation.

15. Earlier, Art had directed the same accusation at his mother for her refusal to let go of him emotionally (*Maus* 103).

16. "Separation," should not, of course, be interpreted to mean a state of uncontingent disconnection. Rather, the assumption is that we need to be able to effect the initial individuating move out of the bondedness of family identity in order to become maturely functioning participants within a social community. The debate in psychoanalytic circles over what separation actually means and entails is too far-reaching for me to go into here. However, I see my own work as a contribution to, not deviation from, that discussion.

17. In her essay, "Women without Children/Women without Families/Women Alone," Irena Klepfisz describes this dilemma in terms of her choice not only to live as a lesbian but to "remain childless": "I am an only child, a survivor of World War II. My father was killed during the war, as was his whole family; my mother is the only family I have. Most of her friends are, like us, surviving members of families which were wiped out" (11). To not have children is thus to refuse to comply with the need of the survivors to not only not be forgotten but to continue on by regenerating themselves as and through families.

18. The naming of the dead members of the family—Richieu, Anja, and Vladek (who dies in 1982)—evokes the traditional Jewish ritual of *Yizkor*.

19. Kafka's short story, "The Judgment," illustrates the degree to which this shift in or inversion of authority can be deeply disturbing to both parents and children.

20. "Horizontal" and "vertical" are my terms; in anthropological parlance, the terms are "alliance" and "descent" (see, for example, Schneider, "Some Muddles").

21. One might recall, in this context, the number of creation myths that are based not on the concept of a single god/father creator but on the concept of sibling creation.

22. As an illustration of this interrelationship, Collins points, among other things, to "[t]he use of family language in referring to members of the African-American community" (129). The work of Sylvia Yanagisako on Japanese American immigrants and Roger Rouse on Mexican migrants in the United States are also part of the groundbreaking new work on the ways in which family is reconfigured both internally and in relation to external communities through the experience of cultural displacement.

23. In this light, it is all the more striking that the final closeup focuses in tightly on Feivel, his sister, and parents again, pointedly separating them out from the extended family community.

24. The difficulty of this task is readily imaginable. As Schneider puts it, "if a single person's solidarity is qualified by membership in two or more units *of like order*, then his commitment to, his solidarity with, one of them is qualified by the claims of the other upon him. Conflicting claims . . . on one person have to be adjudicated; one wins, the other wins, or both are qualified and compromised in some way" (Schneider, "Some Muddles" 46).

Works Cited

An American Tail. Dir. Don Bluth. Story David Kirschner, Judy Freudberg, Tony Geiss. Prod. Don Bluth, John Pomeroy, and Gary Goldman. Universal Pictures, 1986.

Anderson, Benedict. *Imagined Communities: Reflections on the Origin and Spread of Nationalism*. Rev. ed. London: Verso, 1991.

Bergmann, Martin S., and Milton E. Jucovy, eds. *Generations of the Holocaust*. New York: Basic, 1982.

Canetti, Elias. *The Tongue Set Free: Remembrance of a European Childhood*. Trans. Joachim Neugroschel. New York: Seabury, 1979. Trans. of *Die gerettete Zunge. Geschichte einer Jugend*. Frankfurt am Main: Fischer, 1979.

Carlisky, Néstor J., and Moisés Kijak. "El impacto de la micración en el campo analítico." *Revista Argentina de Psicopatología* 2.6 (1991): 24–27.

Castoriadis-Aulagnier, Piera. *La violence de l'interpretation: Du pictogramme à l'enoncé*. Paris: PUF, 1975. 182–93.

Chernin, Kim. *In My Mother's House: A Daughter's Story*. New York: Harper, 1983.

Collins, Patricia Hill. *Black Feminist Thought: Knowledge, Consciousness and the Politics of Empowerment*. New York: Routledge, 1991.

de Plá, Esperanza P., and Elena de la Aldea. "L'Etranger et la fonction du père." *Géopsychanalyse: Les souterrains de l'institution. Rencontre franco-latino-américaine*. Ed. René Major. Paris: René Major, 1981. 61–66.

Fanon, Frantz. *Black Skin, White Masks*. Trans. Charles Lam Markmann. New York: Grove, 1967.

———. *The Wretched of the Earth*. Trans. Constance Farrington. New York: Grove, 1968.

Freud, Sigmund. "Totem and Taboo." *The Freud Reader*. Ed. Peter Gay. New York: Norton, 1989. 481–513.

Grinberg, León, and Rebeca Grinberg. *Psicoanálisis de la micración y del exilio*. Madrid: Aljanea Editorial, 1984.

Hobsbawm, Eric. Keynote Address. American Anthropological Association Convention. Chicago, 1991.

Hoffman, Eva. *Lost in Translation: A Life in a New Language*. Harmondworth, England: Penguin, 1989.

Kafka, Franz. "The Judgment" ["Das Urteil"]. *The Penal Colony: Stories and Short Pieces*. Trans. Willa Muir and Edwin Muir. New York: Schocken, 1976.

Klepfisz, Irena. "*Oyf keyver oves*: Poland, 1983." *Dreams of an Insomniac: Jewish Feminist Essays, Speeches and Diatribes*. Portland: Eighth Mountain, 1990. 85–113.

———. "Women without Children/Women without Families/Women Alone." *Dreams of an Insomniac*. 3–14.

Miller, Alice. *The Drama of the Gifted Child*. Trans. Ruth Ward. New York: Basic, 1981.

Mydans, Seth. "One Last Deadly Crossing for Illegal Aliens." *New York Times* 7 Jan. 1991: A1, A13.

Rouse, Roger Christopher. "Mexican Migration to the United States." *Family Relations in the Development of a Transnational Migrant Circuit*. Ph.D. Thesis. Stanford U, 1989.

Schneider, David M. "Some Muddles in the Models: Or, How the System Really Works." *The Relevance of Models for Social Anthropology*. Ed. Michael Banton. A.S.A. Monographs. London: Tavistock, 1965. 25–86.

———. *American Kinship: A Cultural Account*. Second ed. Chicago: U of Chicago P, 1980. First ed. 1968.

Schultz, Karla Lydia. "At Home in the Language: The Cases of an Exile and an Immigrant." *Yearbook of German-American Studies* 20 (1985): 125–32.

Spiegelman, Art. *Maus: A Survivor's Tale*. New York: Pantheon, 1986.

———. *Maus: A Survivor's Tale, II: And Here My Troubles Began*. New York: Pantheon, 1991.

Tan, Amy. *The Joy Luck Club*. New York: Putnam, 1989.

Weil, Simone. *The Need for Roots: Prelude to a Declaration of Duties toward Mankind*. Trans. A. F. Wills. London: Routledge, 1952. Trans. of *L'Enracinement: Prélude à une déclaration des devoirs envers l'être humain*. Paris: Gallimard, 1949.

Yanagisako, Sylvia Junko. *Transforming the Past: Tradition and Kinship among Japanese Americans*. Stanford: Stanford UP, 1985.

7 Double Articulation
A Place in the World
Doreen Massey

IT IS PERHAPS a long time now since easy assumptions were made about the correspondence between community and locality, between community and place. At times, the "community studies" literature of some decades ago encouraged a view that the terms "local" and "community" went naturally together. Communities were local and were formed in place. It may have been that the flowering of these studies reflected what seemed to be the threat to such "local communities." In the United Kingdom, for example, such social formations were being dispersed by migration, as people left to look for jobs or a more "modern" life, or they were being uprooted by policies of decentralization as the urban working class moved to New Towns beyond the metropolis, or they were being weakened by the decline of the industries which had once been their economic core. What was clear, in any case, was that the tight, integral relation between community and local place was becoming increasingly difficult to sustain, both in practice—in the world of the communities themselves—and in theory.

In the end, the loosening of the connection between these terms (except where it has led to the doleful conclusion that we are therefore left with a society entirely devoid of community) has had some liberating effects, at least in debate about theory. Most importantly, it has led to a questioning of the assumed relation between community and place at a more conceptual level. Maybe, it began to be argued, those two terms should always have been held conceptually distinct. For although they may, and do, at times come together there is no necessary reason for them to do so (see Agnew and Duncan).

Most obviously, it was clear that there are many "places" (and their size may range from the small settlement to the continent, with entities such as "Europe" striving to be built) where the internal social relations lack the kind of coherence which is said to underlie that notion of community. From cosmopolitan metropolis, to sprawling suburbs, to areas precisely being contested over which social group should dominate, this is true. Hanif Kureishi, in a pub in Bradford, Yorkshire, surveyed the scene: "there were five or six gay men and two lesbian couples. Three white kids wore black leather jackets and had mohicans: their mauve, red and yellow hair stood up straight for a good twelve inches and curved across their heads like a feather glued on its thin edge to a billiard ball. And there were the Asians. This was not one large solid community with a shared outlook, common beliefs and an established form of life. . . . It was diverse, disparate, strikingly various" (155). Nor is this in fact a new phenomenon, as an examination of the history of many a metropolis and port around the world will show.

Moreover the non-equation holds the other way around as well. "Communities" are not necessarily place-bound. Religious groupings may maintain a notion of community that is international, and political affiliations may likewise engender feelings of commonality, of shared heritage, visions, and commitments, which do not depend upon place.

And yet, in spite of all this, and while the notion of community has been held up to stringent examination, the notion of *place* has been much less rigorously explored. Indeed, in much of the debate today about globalization, about migration and cultural shifts, about the reorganization of time and space, there is often a background motif which is unquestioning about the nature of "places," which holds—probably implicitly—to a notion of essential places. There are a number of aspects to this. It includes the idea that places have essential characteristics, that it is possible somehow to distill their intrinsic nature. Very often, moreover, that intrinsic nature is seen as eternal, unchanging. And even where change is acknowledged, this approach often views the "essence of place" as having evolved through a history which is read as a sequence of events that happened only within the place itself. It is, in that sense, an internal history. Spelled out like that, such a view of place probably seems patently false. And yet it is there, both in the theoretical literature and in many a political discourse. Harvey, for instance, equates the notion of place with stasis and nostalgia, seeing it as almost inevitably "reactionary" in political terms, as associated with (what he sees as) the inertia of Being as opposed to the (potentially progressive) dynamism of Becoming. He writes of the significance of place-identity in what he sees as the horrendous flux and complexity of the postmodern condition. But the way he characterizes place-identity is highly specific. Thus, in writing of the limited spatial reach of many oppositional organizations (oppositional to capitalism, that is), he argues that:

> the capacity of most social movements to command place better than space puts a strong emphasis upon the potential connection between place and social identity. This is manifest in political action. . . . In clinging, often of necessity, to a place-bound identity, however, such oppositional movements become a part of the very fragmentation which a mobile capitalism and flexible accumulation can feed upon. (302–03)

Moreover Harvey claims that these place-identities are constructed, necessarily, in particular ways: "The assertion of any place-bound identity has to rest at some point on the motivational power of tradition" (303). Further, he argues that the forces of globalization and time-space compression have emphasized a need "to construct place and its meanings qualitatively. Capitalist hegemony over space puts the aesthetics of place very much back on the agenda" (303). And aestheticization, too, has irretrievably reactionary implications: "Geographical and aesthetic interventions always seem to imply nationalist, and hence unavoidably reactionary, politics" (283).

Now, there are many elements in that argument (and Harvey is by no means the only one to make it, although he makes it more explicitly than most) which deserve further attention, leaps of logic which ought to be investigated. The necessity of drawing upon tradition—and the unexamined but implied nature of that tradition—is one example. Another is the nature of the counterposition of space and place. Most important of all is the equation, throughout all the passages on place, of place-*based* with place-*bound*. All these will be questioned later in this paper.

Nonetheless, this theorization of the nature of place is indeed, as Harvey argues, reflected in (or maybe drawn from) the world beyond academe. The advertising of places, in the now-innumerable competitions between them—whether it be for mobile capital or the next venue of the Olympic Games—relies heavily on the creation and mobilization of such images of place. The rapidly growing "heritage industry" does much the same thing, freezing moments of the past of a place ("the real Lancashire") to present as its essential essence, or telling a story of the place which, even though it might recognize the comings and goings of trade and migration, still nonetheless keeps its eye firmly focused on the place itself, constructing a history which somehow actually happened only within it. More dangerous still are some elements of the "new nationalisms" that are currently reasserting themselves, perhaps particularly those in Europe: the association of the true nature of an area, and of its boundaries, by reference back to a particular moment in history. Nor is it only from what might once have been characterized as the right hand end of the political spectrum that such formulations come. In the battle of London's Docklands, between "invading" yuppies and "the local working class," while the yuppies (and the investment houses) were busy constructing an image of the place which was forward-looking, arguing for change and for opening out (all the while using selected bits of the past—from street names, to warehouses, to the docks themselves—as bric-a-brac for decoration), the local working class sometimes closed defensively around quite another definition of the area. The *real* Isle of Dogs (for this was the real, local name) was that of a working-class community built around heavy manual labor, around tight streets and frequent poverty, around pubs and football.

In general, "the left" and progressive people supported this struggle of the existing dock-area groups against the newcomers, and I did so, actively, myself. Yet there are aspects of the way the struggle was promoted, and most particularly in relation to the battle over the nature of the place itself and the formulation of the alternatives, which should be confronted. In some of its aspects it did indeed, as Harvey suggests is inevitable, characterize the place in terms uniquely of its past and, moreover, in terms of a static view of that past. Yet the "local community," itself constructed in its initial moments by the dictates of the demands of capital for labor, had in fact only been there for a couple of centuries. Before that, what was the essential nature of the Isle of Dogs? (It has to be said here, and most emphatically, that not all aspects of the working-class rejection of the incoming yuppies could be characterized this way. There was many a forward-looking vision, too, including a *People's Plan for Docklands*, produced by local groups with the support of the Greater London Council, now abolished. This plan did not only look backwards, nor argue for stasis, but tried to design a type of change which would build on and into the existing social fabric.) There were other problems, too, with some (again not all) of the defensive visions of the area's essential nature. In too many cases it was a male interpretation of the past that was delineated, or male haunts and activities which dominated the overall picture: football, pubs, the docks. A woman's view would most likely be very different, both in describing the geography of the place and in the recounted activities and social relations. Just as the present character of the place is being battled over, so there is no one single "past" to point to anyway.[1] And there are other traits which make it difficult in any case to defend that past. As well as the heavily patriarchal organization of economy, household, and social life, there were elements of racism. Indeed, a few decades ago some areas within the larger Docklands region were among the most active in the country in trying to exclude "immigrants" of color. Presumably, part of the basis on which this exclusion was argued was a characterization of the place (as historically "our place," belonging to our kind of people) not unlike that which was used in the 1980s against the encroaching yuppies. But while in the one case the characterization would have crucially included the fact of being "white," in the case of the yuppies such a characterization was unnecessary: the yuppies are white, too.[2]

I have deliberately chosen to focus here on a difficult case; trodden on delicate ground. It would have been far easier just to criticize, say, the heritage industry for its patent falsifications and sentimentalizations. But in fact the issues are more difficult and raw than that. Within a couple of miles from where the incursion of the nouveau riche is being resisted, the local council after much debate and deliberation decided on a housing policy which gives priority in housing allocation to those with roots in the area. This is not a case of defining a middle-class area to protect status, exclusivity, and capital values. The housing is public housing, the people with roots in the area are working class; but they are also predominantly white, while those who might otherwise, were this policy not in operation, be allocated housing include a far higher proportion of people of color, particularly Asian. Two points seem clear. First, and very obviously, the way in which we characterize places is fundamentally political. But second, and far less obviously perhaps, the politics lies not just in the particular characteristics assigned to places (whether they include racist or sexist features, to which social class they are assigned) but in the very way in which the image of place is constructed. Thus the comparison between the various characterizations of the Docklands can be made on two dimensions. The first dimension concerns the empirical grounds of the distinction. In the case where the perceived threat was people of color, the distinction between "us" and "them" was on grounds of ethnicity; in the case against the yuppies, it was on grounds of class. It was this which enabled progressive people to argue against the locals in the first case and with them in the second. But on the second dimension of comparison, the two characterizations of Docklands are the same: they are both essentialist, which here implies exclusivist, visions of the social character (inherent nature) of the place. Yet the argument of this paper is that we should question any characterization of place which is singular, essentialist, and which relies on a view of there having been one past of this place, one story to tell, most particularly where that story is an internalized one of the evolution of that place within its bounds.

However all the examples I have just cited might seem to prove the case, as stated by Harvey, that the whole notion of place is inevitably tied up with backward-looking nostalgia, with stasis, and with reaction. My answer would be that in many cases it is in fact so, but that it is not necessarily so, that another view of place is possible and that—precisely given the predominance of examples such as the foregoing—it is important to argue for an alternative view.

In fact, the construction of any actual place completely belies the kind of characterizations just referred to. For such characterizations of place are all attempts to fix meanings and often to enclose them too: to give places single, fixed identities and to define them as bounded and enclosed, characterized by their own internal history, and through their differentiation from "outside." Yet is anywhere like that today? The Docklands of east London have had their character molded, not just by what has happened within the area we now call Docklands, but also by the long-established and constantly changing relations with the world beyond. There is a real difference between on the one hand telling the history of Docklands as a sequence of things which happened within the area (from fields, to docks, to high-tech offices) and, on the other hand, understanding these changes as inextricably a product of changing interrelations with and roles within a wider context. This is the contrast between "internalized histories," referred to above, and open, extroverted ones. The current local people came here, "originally," from outside, displacing the settlements and lifestyles of an already-established rural existence; the connections to London and to the rest of Britain were always vital, for here was the market for the goods which the economic activities of Docklands imported and sometimes processed; and the goods which were brought here were the products of the whole world, the sign in the nineteenth century of location at the heart of a vast Empire. The "settled," "local" communities of the former dock areas of today's London would not have been there without the existence of an international division of labor. And their characteristics—from street names, to customs, to local knowledges, to the mix of the population—have all been molded by the position to which the area held within that international division of labor. This, then, is the first point about an alternative conceptualization of place: that the characteristics of any place are formed in part through the location and role of that place within a wider structuring of society—the economic aspects of which I have called elsewhere a wider *spatial division of labor* (see *Spatial Divisions*). More generally, the identity of a place is formed out of social interrelations, and a proportion of those interrelations—larger or smaller, depending on the time and on the place—will stretch beyond that "place" itself. In that sense, if social space is conceived of as constructed out of the vast, intricate complexity of social processes and social interactions at all scales from the local to the global, then "a place" is best thought of as a particular part of, a particular moment in, the global network of those social relations and understandings.[3]

Such a re-understanding of the notion of place also challenges the kind of counterposition between space and place referred to earlier and adopted by, among others, Harvey. In Harvey's conceptualization, space is interaction and place is enclosure. In the alternative view, place is thought of, not as an inward-looking enclosure but as simply a subset of the interactions which constitute space, a local articulation within the wider whole.

Second, if that is so, then the identity of a place is also necessarily unfixed. In part, it is unfixed simply because those relations themselves are dynamic. Not only are they not static in their daily, weekly, yearly operation, but also they may undergo major shifts and restructurings. The current contest over London's Docklands takes place precisely around the shift between spatial divisions of labor at national and international levels and the question of what should be the area's role within them. The old international division of labor, in which Britain, along with most of what was to be constructed as "the first world," imported goods and raw materials for consumption, for manufacture, and for re-export is now far less important in the formation of the global economy. And intranationally, the old focus on major urban ports and dockside processing has crumbled too. It is international and national shifts which have undermined the rationale for this part of east London as it was. The proposal from the property developers, and from the Conservative government, and what indeed is well on the way to happening, is that the area should become the focal point in yet another international division of labor, that of the late twentieth century—that this part of Docklands should provide space for the extension of the City of London and its associated activities to enable the maintenance of London as one of the three great "World Cities" of international finance. In that sense what is going on in Docklands is the superimposition of the area's role in one spatial division of labor, and of the local effects of the playing of that role, upon its role in a previous spatial division of labor. The contests which are currently under way, the sniping and occasional eruptions of violence between the social groups, the employment of ex-dockers as builders and security guards, the employment of the women of the area as cleaners and shop assistants in the new developments, and the appropriation of the past in the design of the area . . . all these things are products of the interaction between the social requirements and effects of two international divisions of labor. And this, too, is an element of the specificity of place—nowhere else in the world has experienced just this succession of roles within the wider scheme of things, nor these particular interactions between them. Nor have the populations within them made these particular interpretations, and these lives, out of such developments.

Moreover, and thirdly, what this means in turn is that, because it is not just the present which is characterized by, molded by, interactions with the outside world, but also the history of the place, there is no singular origin either. There is no one essential past about which to get nostalgic. This is true in the sense that there has never been a historical moment untouched by the world beyond; in that sense the global has always been part of the construction of the local. It is true in the sense that historical change has been continuous; to fix on one moment, or one period, by which to characterize the ever-shifting medley of social relations which have taken place in that location (to talk of the true culture of a particular part of the Baltic region, say, by picking on one social formation which happens, since "Europe" was settled, to have been formed in that spot) is to make a claim about a particular moment in time-space as having a verity which others do not. Battles over such claims are in that sense really power struggles over the right to define particular parts of space-time. And finally there is no one essential past to any place simply by virtue of the fact that there will always be differing interpretations even of any one moment in that past.

A fourth and final point which it seems important in this context to make about an alternative understanding of place is that it is (or should be) problematic to characterize any place by counterposition to an other which is outside. If the global really is, as has been argued above, part of the constitution of, and therefore inside, the local, then the definition of the specificity of the local place cannot be made through counterposition *against* what lies outside; rather it must be made precisely through the particularity of the interrelations *with* the outside. It is, if you like, an extroverted notion of the identity of place, an internationalist constitution of the local place and its particularity.

What I am arguing for, then, is a non-essentialism in the way in which we think about place, and it is perhaps strange that given the context of wider arguments about the importance of non-essentialist theorizing, this particular case has been so little examined. For such a view of place is important politically, in the widest sense of that word. It is about constructing a sense of a locality's place in the world (its identity) which has the courage to admit that it's open. This absolutely does not mean a de-prioritizing of, or a lack of recognition and appreciation of, specificity and uniqueness. If anything, it is to allow us to take uniqueness on board more fully, not to see it flattened beneath those approaches which view the worldwide global accumulation of capital as the only valid theme, the only story with any explanatory power. Rather what is at issue is the way we analyze and understand the production of specificity and uniqueness. The argument here is that understanding the specificity of place may best be approached through an analysis, first, of the particularity of the social interactions which intersect at that location and of what people make of them in their interpretations and in their lives and, second, of the fact that the meeting of those social relations at that location in itself produces new effects, new social processes. The meeting of old working class and yuppies on the Isle of Dogs alters the character and trajectories of both, produces new interactions. Moreover, all of this is always in process, as new layers of meetings and understandings and spatial divisions of labor are laid down, one upon the other, and react the one with the other, over time.

There are many connections potentially to be made between this discussion about the identity of place and the debate about personal identity and subjectivity. In this latter debate, Chantal Mouffe has written (and in a way which brings these issues together nicely):

Many communitarians seem to believe that we belong to only one community, defined empirically and even geographically, and that this community could be unified by a single idea of the common good. But we are in fact always multiple and contradictory subjects, inhabitants of a diversity of communities (as many, really, as the social relations in which we participate and the subject-positions they define), constructed by a variety of discourses and precariously and temporarily sutured at the intersection of those positions. (44)

What I have been arguing here is a strategy very similar to that, but applied to our understanding of the identity of place. It is a notion of identity that crucially hinges on the notion of articulation: "a subject constructed at the point of intersection" (Mouffe 35). Moreover, if places are conceptualized in this way and also take account of the construction of the subjects within them, which help in turn to produce the place, then the identity of place is a double articulation.

This way of thinking about place has some interesting political implications even as it raises some thorny political issues.

A first implication is that all places are, and are already, articulations. Thus the migrant moves neither from nor to a "pure" place in the sense laid out at the beginning of this paper. This does not mean that there is no difference between the experience of migration and that, for instance, of living generation after generation in one relatively "undisturbed" locality. What it does mean, however, is that dis*place*ment occurs between contexts which are themselves already complex constructions. It is not only recent migrants, the recently displaced, who are in that sense culturally complex. It is true also of those who have lived in the same place for years—"born and bred here, and my family before me." This is true not only in the obvious sense for the places which are patently culturally mixed, in the differentiated structures of their populations for instance—Kureishi's Bradford, or Kilburn (the part of London where I currently live) with its mix of Irish, Indian, Bangladeshi, and Caribbean inheritances (see Massey, "Power"). It is also true of places which appear to be, or which *are*, more culturally homogeneous. The character of the white working class of the Isle of Dogs, even the small mining villages in deepest Northumberland and Durham, has been partly formed by its wider setting, by its interactions with "outside." Most obviously, what it means to be "British" even for the white *rentier* middle classes of "the home counties" (the name says it all) is deeply constructed out of the fact of Empire, of the UK's long history of global connections. The global is part of the local, not just as an invasion, nor even as a patently evident cultural mix, but as part of the very constitution of its "heartlands." Those who are not displaced should recognize our/their global connections just as do those who have recently migrated.

This view of place points to inevitable contradictions and conflicts "on the ground." It is evident from all the preceding discussion that, whatever the abstract concept of place which people hold, there will always be differences, debates, even struggles, about how places are viewed. There will be differences within the place, and differences between those within (or some of them) and some without. There is no single simple "authenticity"—a unique eternal truth of the place—to be used as reference, either now or in the past. This does not mean not remembering nor does it mean taking no account of something which may be called "tradition." But remembering does not have to take the form of the nostalgic wallowing implied by Harvey. Thus bell hooks talks of "a politicization of memory that distinguishes nostalgia, that longing for something to be as once it was, a kind of useless act, from that remembering that serves to illuminate and transform the present" (147). Nor does "tradition" have to be merely closed and self-serving; it too can recognize a past openness. And anyway there will be multiple memories of those traditions.

Furthermore, it will often be the case that the multiplicity of place-identities, held by different groups, cannot always happily coexist. Patrick Wright points to the real social conflicts (actual or currently latent) inherent in the views of Hackney held by different groups which live within that borough of inner London. Iris Young, in her essay on "the ideal of community and the politics of difference," although starting off from a perhaps dubious assumption of an equivalence between community and spatial propinquity, develops an interesting notion, in many ways related to what is being argued here, of "the unoppressive city . . . as openness to unassimilated otherness" (319). She writes "the appreciation of ethnic foods or professional musicians, for example, consists in the recognition that these transcend the familiar everyday world of my life" and that "[t]his instantiates social relations as difference in the sense of an understanding of groups and cultures that are different, with exchanging and overlapping interactions that do not issue in community, yet which prevent them from being outside of one another" (319). She admits that she is postulating an ideal. But until we reach it, and probably still then, there will be relations of contest and contradiction, of dominance and subordination, between the groups of unassimilated others (of which the reference to some as "ethnic" with the implication that others are not is one index), and these relations will be powerful in determining what becomes the hegemonic view of any particular place. Which meaning of a place will be hegemonic is always being negotiated, and it is in that sense always the subject of power and of politics.

Moreover, the burden of the argument of this paper is that the "political" character of this defining of places exists at two distinct levels. On the one hand are the politics of the empirical characterization of place. At this level we may wish to distinguish politically between, say, the local organization of an area of working-class people resisting disruption by yuppie gentrifiers, and the people of the same area working to resist the arrival of people from ethnic minority backgrounds. The social terms on which such changes-to-place happen, and the political view to be taken of them, draw on wider structures of values which do not in themselves directly relate to the question of the nature of place, but the implications of which have to be evaluated each time, over and again, in each situation and in each place. On the other hand, however, are the politics of conceptualizing the nature of place itself. It is the contention here that all sides in such debates and struggles over what happens in particular places should resist the temptation to appeal to notions of the essence of their area and should refuse the easy option of claiming a truth of a place (whatever that "truth" is claimed to be) in terms which entail ownership and exclusion. The attempt to align "us" and "them" with the geographical concepts of "local" and "global" is always deeply problematical. For in the historical and geographical construction of places, the "other" in general terms is already within. The global is everywhere and already, in one way or another, implicated in the local.

Notes

1. A detailed and fascinating discussion of such differences in another British working-class context, that of Burnley in Lancashire, and of its perpetual representation from a male point of view (including a male view of the women in such continuities) is one thread in Carolyn Steedman's *Landscape for a Good Woman.*

2. In the week before the copy-editing arrived for this article, the racist grouping, the British National Party, won a seat in a local election in this area. A prime issue was housing. This question of the defense of place is one which will not go away.

3. This way of thinking about space is spelled out in more detail in Massey, "Politics and Space/Time."

Works Cited

Agnew, J. A., and J. S. Duncan, eds. *The Power of Place: Bringing Together Geographical and Sociological Imaginations.* Boston: Hyman, 1989.

Harvey, David. *The Condition of Postmodernity.* Oxford: Blackwell, 1989.

hooks, bell. *Yearning: Race, Gender, and Cultural Politics.* London: Turnaround, 1991.

Kureishi, Hanif. "Bradford." *Granta* 20 (1986): 147–70.

Massey, Doreen. "Politics and Space/Time." *New Left Review* 196 (Nov./Dec. 1992): 65–84.

——. "Power Geometry and a Progressive Sense of Place." *Mapping the Futures: Local Cultures Global Change.* Ed. J. Bird, B. Curtis, T. Putnam, G. Robertson, and L. Tickner. London: Routledge, 1993.

———. *Spatial Divisions of Labour: Social Structures and the Geography of Production.* Basingstoke: Macmillan, 1984.

Mouffe, Chantal. "Radical Democracy: Modern or Postmodern?" *Universal Abandon?: The Politics of Postmodernism.* Ed. Andrew Ross. Minneapolis: U of Minnesota P, 1988. 31–45.

Steedman, Carolyn. *Landscape for a Good Woman: A Story of Two Lives.* London: Virago, 1986.

Wright, Patrick. *On Living in an Old Country: The National Past in Contemporary Britain.* London: Verso, 1985.

Young, Iris Marion. "The Ideal of Community and the Politics of Difference." *Feminism/Postmodernism.* Ed. Linda J. Nicholson. London: Routledge, 1990. 300–23.

"Natives," Empires, and
the Contingencies of Race

8 | Where Have All the Natives Gone?

Rey Chow

The Inauthentic Native

A COUPLE OF years ago, I was serving on a faculty search committee at the University of Minnesota. The search was for a specialist in Chinese language and literature. A candidate from the People's Republic of China gave a talk that discussed why we still enjoy reading the eighteenth-century classic, *The Dream of the Red Chamber*. The talk was a theoretical demonstration of how no particular interpretation of this book could exhaust the possibilities of reading. During the search committee's discussion of the various candidates afterwards, one faculty member, an American Marxist, voiced his disparaging view of this particular candidate in the following way: "The talk was not about why we still enjoy reading *The Dream of the Red Chamber*. It was about why she enjoys reading it. She does because she likes capitalism!"

This colleague of mine stunned me with a kind of discrimination that has yet to be given its proper name. The closest designation we currently have for his attitude is racism, that is, a reduction of someone from a particular group to the stereotypes, negative *or* positive, we have of that group. But what is at stake here is not really "race" as much as it is the assumption that a "native" of communist China ought to be faithful to her nation's official political ideology. Instead of "racial" characteristics, communist beliefs became the stereotype with which my colleague was reading this candidate. The fact that she did not speak from such beliefs but instead from an understanding of the text's irreducible plurality (an understanding he equated with "capitalism") greatly disturbed him; his lament was that this candidate had betrayed our expectation of what communist "ethnic specimens" ought to be.

My colleague's disturbance takes us to the familiarly ironic scenarios of anthropology, in which Western anthropologists are uneasy at seeing "natives" who have gone "civilized" or who, like the anthropologists themselves, have taken up the active task of shaping their own culture. Margaret Mead, for instance, found the interest of certain Arapesh Indians (in Highland New Guinea) in cultural influences other than their own "annoying" since, as James Clifford puts it, "*Their* culture collecting complicated hers" (232). Similarly,

Claude Lévi-Strauss, doing his "fieldwork" in New York on American ethnology, was troubled by the sight, in the New York Public Library reading room where he was doing research for his *Elementary Structures of Kinship*, of a feathered Indian with a Parker pen. As Clifford comments:

> For Lévi-Strauss the Indian is primarily associated with the past, the "extinct" societies recorded in the precious Bureau of American Ethnology *Annual Reports*. The anthropologist feels himself "going back in time." . . . In modern New York an Indian can appear only as a survival or a kind of incongruous parody. (245)

My colleague shares the predicament of Mead and Lévi-Strauss insofar as the stereotypical "native" is receding from view. What confronts the Western scholar is the discomforting fact that the natives are no longer staying in their frames. In the case of the faculty search at Minnesota, what I heard was not the usual desire to *archaize* the modern Chinese person,[1] but rather a valorizing, on the part of the Western critic, of the official political and cultural difference of the People's Republic of China as the designator of the candidate's supposed "authenticity." If a native from the People's Republic of China espouses capitalism, then she has already been corrupted. An ethnic specimen that was not pure was not of use to him.

The Native As Image

In the politics of identifying "authentic" natives, several strands of the word "identification" are at stake: How do we identify the native? How do we identify with her? How do we construct the native's "identity"? What processes of identification are involved? We cannot approach this politics without being critical of a particular relation to *images* that is in question.

In his volume of essays exploring film culture, Fredric Jameson writes that "The visual is *essentially* pornographic. . . . Pornographic films are . . . only the potentiation of films in general, which ask us to stare at the world as though it were a naked body" (1).[2] This straightforward definition of the visual image sums up many of the problems we encounter in cultural criticism today, whether or not the topic in question is film. The activity of watching is linked by projection to physical nakedness. Watching is theoretically defined as the primary agency of violence, an act that pierces the other, who inhabits the place of the passive victim on display. The image, then, is an aggressive sight that reveals itself in the other; it is the site of the aggressed. Moreover, the image is what has been devastated, left bare, and left behind by aggression—hence Jameson's view that it is naked and pornographic.

For many, the image is also the site of possible change. In many critical discourses, the image is implicitly the place where battles are fought and strategies of resistance negotiated. Such discourses try to inhabit this image-site by providing alternative sights, alternative ways of watching *that would change the image.* Thus one of the most important enterprises nowadays is that of investigating the "subjectivity" of the other-as-oppressed-victim. "Subjectivity" becomes a way to change the defiled image, the stripped image, the image-reduced-to-nakedness, by showing the truth behind/beneath/around it. The problem with the reinvention of subjectivity as such is that it tries to combat the politics of the image, a politics that is conducted on surfaces, by a politics of depths, hidden truths, and inner voices. The most important aspect of the image—its power precisely as image and nothing else—is thus bypassed and left untouched.[3] It is in this problematic of *the image as the bad thing to be replaced* that I lodge the following arguments about the "native."

The question in which I am primarily interested is: Is there a way of "finding" the native without simply ignoring the image, or substituting a "correct" image of the ethnic specimen for an "incorrect" one, or giving the native a "true" voice "behind" her "false" image? How could we deal with the native in an age when there is no possibility of avoiding the reduction/abstraction of the native as image? How can we write about the native by not ignoring the defiled, degraded image that is an inerasable part of her status—that is, by not resorting to the idealist belief that everything would be all right if the inner truth of the native were restored because the inner truth would lead to the "correct" image? I want to highlight the native—nowadays often a synonym for the oppressed, the marginalized, the wronged—because I think that the space occupied by the native in postcolonial discourses is also the space of error, illusion, deception, and filth. How would we write this space in such a way as to refuse the facile turn of sanctifying the defiled image with pieties and thus enriching ourselves precisely with what can be called the surplus value of the oppressed, a surplus value that results from *exchanging* the defiled image for something more noble?

The Native As Silent Object

The production of the native is in part the production of our postcolonial modernity. Before elaborating on the relation between "native" and "modernity," however, I want to examine how current theoretical discussions of the native problematize the space of the native in the form of a symptom of the white man. Following Lacan, I use "symptom" not in the derogatory sense of a dispensable shadow but in the sense of something that gives the subject its ontological consistency and its fundamental structure. Slavoj Žižek explains the non-pejorative sense of "symptom" this way:

If, however, we conceive the symptom as Lacan did in his last writings and seminars, namely as a particular signifying formation which confers on the subject its very ontological consistency, enabling it to structure its basic, constitutive relationship towards enjoyment (*jouissance*), then the entire relationship [between subject and symptom] is reversed, for if the symptom is dissolved, the subject itself disintegrates. In this sense, "Woman is a symptom of man" means that man himself exists only through woman qua his symptom: his very ontological consistency depends on, is "externalized" in, his symptom. ("Rossellini" 21)

As the white man's symptom, as that which is externalized in relation to the white-man-as-subject, the space occupied by the native is essentially objective, the space of the object.

Because of the symptomatic way non-white peoples are constructed in postcoloniality, and because "symptom" is conventionally regarded in a secondary, derivative sense, many critics of colonialism attempt to write about these peoples in such a way as to wrest them away from their status as symptom or object. The result is a certain inevitable subjectivizing, and here the anti-imperialist project runs a parallel course with the type of feminist project that seeks to restore the truth to women's distorted and violated identities by theorizing female subjectivity. We see this in Frantz Fanon's formulation of the native. Like Freud's construction of woman (which, though criticized, is repeated by many feminists), Fanon's construction of the native is Oedipal. Freud's question was "What does woman want?" Fanon, elaborating on the necessity of violence in the native's formation, asks, "What does the black man want?"[4] The native (the black man) is thus imagined to be an angry son who wants to displace the white man, the father. While Freud would go on to represent woman as lack, Fanon's argument is that the native is someone from whom something has been stolen. The native, then, is also lack.

This Oedipal structure of thinking—a structure of thinking that theorizes subjectivity as compensation for a presumed lack—characterizes discourses on the non-West in a pervasive manner, including, occasionally, the discourse of those who are otherwise critical of its patriarchal overtones. In her reading of Julia Kristeva's *About Chinese Women*, for instance, Gayatri Spivak criticizes Kristeva's ethnocentric sense of "alienation" at the sight of some Chinese women in Huxian Square. Kristeva's passage goes as follows:

An enormous crowd is sitting in the sun: they wait for us wordlessly, perfectly still. Calm eyes, not even curious, but slightly amused or anxious: in any case, piercing, and certain of belonging to a community with which we will never have anything to do. (11)

Citing this passage, which is followed a few pages later by the question, "Who is speaking, then, before the stare of the peasants at Huxian?" (15), Spivak charges Kristeva for being primarily interested in her own identity rather than in these other women's. While I agree with this observation, I find Spivak's formulation of these other women's identity in terms of "envy" troubling:

> Who is speaking here? An effort to answer that question might have revealed more about the mute women of Huxian Square, *looking with qualified envy* at the "incursion of the West." ("French Feminism" 141; my emphasis)

Doesn't the word "envy" here remind us of that condition ascribed to women by Freud, against which feminists revolt—namely, "penis envy"? "Envy" is the other side of the "violence" of which Fanon speaks as the fundamental part of the native's formation. But both affects—the one of wanting to *have* what the other has; the other, of destroying the other so that one can *be* in his place—are affects produced by a patriarchal ideology that assumes that the other at the low side of the hierarchy of self/other is "lacking" (in the pejorative, undesirable sense). Such an ideology, while acknowledging that a lack cannot be filled, also concentrates on how it might be filled (by the same thing), even if imperfectly. The fate of the native is then like that of Freud's woman: Even though she will never have a penis, she will for the rest of her life be trapped within the longing for it and its substitutes.

What we see in the accounts by Kristeva and Spivak is a battle for demonstrating the *unspeaking* truth of the native. While Spivak shows how the articulation of the Western critic is itself already a sign of her privileged identity, for Kristeva it is the limits of Western articulation and articulation itself that have to be recognized in the presence of the silent Chinese women. Throughout Kristeva's encounter with these women, therefore, we find descriptions of the others' looking—their "calm eyes," their "indefinable stare" (13), and so on—that try to capture their undisturbed presence. If these others have been turned into objects, it is because these objects' gaze makes the Western "subject" feel alienated from her own familiar (familial) humanity:

> They don't distinguish among us man or woman, blonde or brunette, this or that feature of face or body. As though they were discovering some weird and peculiar animals, harmless but insane. (11)

> I don't feel like a foreigner, the way I do in Baghdad or New York. I feel like an ape, a martian, an *other*. (12)

Between a critical desire to subjectivize them with envy and a "humble" gesture to revere them as silent objects, is there any alternative for these "natives"?

Kristeva's way of "giving in" to the strangeness of the other is a philosophical and semiotic gesture that characterizes many European intellectuals, whose discourse becomes self-accusatory and, *pace* Rousseau, confessional when confronted by the other.[5] When that other is Asia and the "Far East," it always seems as if the European intellectual must speak in absolute terms, making this other an utterly incomprehensible, terrifying, and fascinating spectacle. For example, after visiting Japan, Alexandre Kojève, who had asserted that history had come to an end (he was convinced of this in the United States, where he thought he found the "classless society" predicted by Marx as the goal of human history), wrote a long footnote to the effect that his experience with the Japanese had radically changed his opinion about history. For Kojève in 1959, like Roland Barthes about a decade later, the formalized rituals of Japanese society suggested that the Japanese had arrived at the end of history three centuries earlier. As Barthes would say, semiologically, that Japanese culture is made up of empty signs, Kojève writes:

> all Japanese without exception are currently in a position to live according to totally *formalized* values—that is, values completely empty of all "human" content in the "historical" sense. Thus, in the extreme, every Japanese is in principle capable of committing, from pure snobbery, a perfectly "gratuitous" *suicide.* . . . (162)[6]

Michel Serres, on the other hand, also finds "the end of history" when he goes east, but it is in agricultural China that he finds the absolute totality of the other. Confronted with the Chinese who have to make use of every bit of land for cultivation, Serres comments with statements like the following in an essay called "China Loam":

> Farming has covered over everything like a tidal wave.
> It is the totality.
> This positiveness is so complete, so compact, that it can only be expressed negatively. There is no margin, no gap, no passes, no omission, no waste, no vestiges. The fringe, the fuzzy area, the refuse, the wasteland, the open-space have all disappeared: no surplus, no vacuum, no history, no time. (5)

> Here the utmost limit of what we call history had already been reached a thousand years ago. (6)

To the extent that it is our own limit that we encounter when we encounter another, all these intellectuals can do is to render the other as the negative of what they are and what they do. As Serres puts it, the spectacle of China's total rationality is so "positive, so rational, so well-adapted that one can only speak of it in negative terms" (5). As such, the "native" is turned into an absolute entity in the form of an image (the "empty" Japanese ritual or "China loam"), whose silence becomes the occasion for *our* speech.[7] The gaze of the Western scholar is "pornographic" and the native becomes a mere "naked body" in the sense described by Jameson. Whether positive or negative, the construction of the native remains at the level of image-identification, a process in which "our" own identity is measured in terms of the degrees to which we resemble her and to which she resembles us. Is there a way of conceiving of the native beyond imagistic resemblance?

This question is what prompts Spivak's bold and provocative statement, "The subaltern cannot speak."[8] Because it seems to cast the native permanently in the form of a silent object, Spivak's statement foreseeably gives rise to pious defenses of the native as a voiced subject and leads many to jump on the bandwagon of declaring solidarity with "subalterns" of different kinds. Speaking sincerely of the multiple voices of the native woman thus, Benita Parry criticizes Spivak for assigning an absolute power to the imperialist discourse:

> Since the native woman is constructed within multiple social relationships and positioned as the product of different class, caste and cultural specificities, it should be possible to locate traces and testimony of women's voice on those sites where women inscribed themselves as healers, ascetics, singers of sacred songs, artisans and artists, and by this to modify Spivak's model of the silent subaltern. (35)

In contrast to Spivak, Parry supports Homi Bhabha's argument that since a discursive system is inevitably split in enunciation, the colonist's text itself already contains a native voice—ambivalently. The colonial text's "hybridity," to use Bhabha's word, means that the subaltern has spoken (39–43).[9] But what kind of an argument is it to say that the subaltern's "voice" can be found in the *ambivalence* of the imperialist's speech? It is an argument which ultimately makes it unnecessary to come to terms with the subaltern since she has already "spoken," as it were, in the system's gaps. All we would need to do would be to continue to study—to deconstruct—the rich and ambivalent language of the imperialist! What Bhabha's word "hybridity" revives, in the masquerade of deconstruction, anti-imperialism, and "difficult" theory, is an old functionalist notion of what a dominant culture permits in the interest of maintaining its own equilibrium. Such functionalism informs the investigatory methods of classical anthropology and sociology as much as it does the colonial policies of the British Empire. The kind of subject constitution it allows, a subject constitution firmly inscribed in Anglo-American liberal humanism, is the other side of the process of image-identification, in which we try to make the native more like us by giving her a "voice."

The charge of Spivak's essay, on the other hand, is a protest against the *two* sides of image-identification, the *two* types of freedom the subaltern has been allowed—object formation and subject constitution—which would result either in the subaltern's protection (as object) from her own kind or her achievement as a voice assimilable to the project of imperialism. That is why Spivak concludes by challenging precisely the optimistic view that the subaltern has already spoken: "The subaltern cannot speak. There is no virtue in global laundry lists with 'woman' as a pious item" ("Subaltern" 308).

Instead, a radical alternative can be conceived only when we recognize the essential *untranslatability* from the subaltern discourse to imperialist discourse. Using Jean-François Lyotard's notion of the *différend*, which Spivak explains as "the inaccessibility of, or untranslatability from, one mode of discourse in a dispute to another" ("Subaltern" 300), she argues the impossibility of the subaltern's constitution *in life*.[10] The subaltern cannot speak, not because there are not activities in which we can locate a subaltern mode of life/culture/subjectivity, but because, as is indicated by the critique of thought and articulation given to us by Western intellectuals such as Lacan, Foucault, Barthes, Kristeva, and Derrida (Spivak's most important reference), "speaking" itself belongs to an already well-defined structure and history of domination. As Spivak says in an interview: "If the subaltern can speak then, thank God, the subaltern is not a subaltern any more" ("New Historicism" 158).

It is only when we acknowledge the fact that the subaltern cannot speak that we can begin to plot a different kind of process of identification for the native. It follows that, within Spivak's argument, it is a *silent* gesture on the part of a young Hindu woman, Bhuvaneswari Bhaduri, who committed suicide during her menstruation so that the suicide could not be interpreted as a case of illicit pregnancy, that becomes a telling instance of subaltern writing, a writing whose message is only understood retrospectively ("Subaltern" 307–08). As such, the "identity" of the native is inimitable, beyond the resemblance of the image. The type of identification offered by her silent space is what may be called symbolic identification. In the words of Slavoj Žižek:

> in imaginary identification we imitate the other at the level of resemblance— we identify ourselves with the image of the other inasmuch as we are 'like him,' while in symbolic identification we identify ourselves with the other precisely at a point at which he is inimitable, at the point which eludes resemblance. (*Sublime Object* 109)

Local Resurrections, New Histories

As an issue of postcoloniality, the problem of the native is also the problem of modernity and modernity's relation to "endangered authenticities" (Clifford 5). The question to ask is not whether we can return the native to her authentic origin, but what our fascination with the native means in terms of the irreversibility of modernity.

There are many commendable accounts of how the native in the non-Western world has been used by the West as a means to promote and develop its own intellectual contours.[11] According to these accounts, modernism, especially the modernism that we associate with the art of Modigliani, Picasso, Gauguin, the novels of Gustave Flaubert, Marcel Proust, D. H. Lawrence, James Joyce, Henry Miller, and so forth, was possible only because these "first world" artists with famous names incorporated into their "creativity" the culture and art work of the peoples of the non-West. But while Western artists continue to receive attention specifically categorized in time, place, and name, the treatment of the works of non-Western peoples continues to partake of systemic patterns of exploitation and distortion.

Apart from the general attribution of "anonymity" to native artists, "native works" have been bifurcated either as timeless (in which case they would go into art museums) or as historical (in which case they would go into ethnographic museums). While most cultural critics today are alert to the pitfalls of the "timeless art" argument, many are still mired in efforts to invoke "history," "contexts," and "specificities" as ways to resurrect the native. In doing so, are they restoring to the native what has been stolen from her? Or are they in fact avoiding the genuine problem of the native's status as object by providing *something* that is more manageable and comforting—namely, a phantom history in which natives appear as our equals and our images, in our shapes and our forms? Nancy Armstrong summarizes our predicament this way:

> The new wave of culture criticism still assumes that we must either be a subject who partakes in the power of gazing or else be an object that is by implication the object of a pornographic gaze. The strategy of identifying people according to "subject positions" in a vast and intricate differential system of interests and needs is perhaps the most effective way we now have of avoiding the problem incurred whenever we classify political interests by means of bodies inscribed with signs of race, class, and gender. But even the "subject" of the critical term "subject position" tends to dissolve too readily back into a popular and sentimental version of the bourgeois self. By definition, this self grants priority to an embodied subject over the body as an object. To insist on being "subjects" as opposed to "objects" is to assume that we must have certain powers of observation, classification, and definition in order to exist; these powers make "us" human. According to the logic governing such thinking as it was formulated in the nineteenth century, only certain kinds of subjects are really subjects; to be human, anyone must be one of "us." (33)

As we challenge a dominant discourse by "resurrecting" the victimized voice/self of the native with our readings—and such is the impulse behind many "new historical" accounts—we step, far too quickly, into the otherwise silent and invisible place of the native and turn ourselves into living agents/witnesses for her. This process, in which *we* become visible, also neutralizes the untranslatability of the native's experience and the history of that untranslatability. The hasty supply of original "contexts" and "specificities" easily becomes complicitous with the dominant discourse, which achieves hegemony precisely by its capacity to convert, recode, make transparent, and thus represent even those experiences that resist it with a stubborn opacity. The danger of historical contextualization turning into cultural corporations is what leads Clifford to say:

> I do not argue, as some critics have, that non-Western objects are properly understood only with reference to their original milieux. Ethnographic contextualizations are as problematic as aesthetic ones, as susceptible to purified, ahistorical treatment. (12)

The problem of modernity, then, is not simply an "amalgamating" of "disparate experience"[12] but rather the confrontation between what are now called the "first" and "third" worlds in the form of the *différend*, that is, the untranslatability of "third world" experiences into the "first world." This is because, in order for her experience to become translatable, the "native" cannot simply "speak" but must also provide the justice/justification for her speech, a justice/justification that has been destroyed in the encounter with the imperialist.[13] The native's victimization consists in the fact that the active evidence—the original witness—of her victimization may no longer exist in any intelligible, coherent shape. Rather than saying that the native has already spoken because the dominant hegemonic discourse is split/hybrid/different from itself, and rather than restoring her to her "authentic" context, we should argue that it is the native's silence which is the most important clue to her displacement. That silence is at once the *evidence* of imperialist oppression (the naked body, the defiled image) and what, in the absence of the original witness to that oppression, must act in its place by *performing* or *feigning* as the pre-imperialist gaze.

A Brown Man's Eye for a White Man's Eye

As part of my argument, I read an anti-imperialist text whose intentions are both anti-pornographic (anti-the-bad-"image"-thing) and restorative. Despite such intentions, this text is, I believe, an example of how cultural criticism can further engender exploitation of the native, who is crossed out not once (by the imperialist forces of domination), nor twice (by the cultural processes of subjection), but three times—the third time by the anti-imperialist critic himself.

In his book, *The Colonial Harem*, Malek Alloula focuses on picture postcards of Algerian women produced and sent home by the French during the early decades of the twentieth century. Alloula's point is a simple one, namely, that these native women have been used as a means to represent a European phantasm of the Oriental female. The mundane postcard therefore supports, through its pornographic gaze at the female native, the larger French colonial project in Algeria. Alloula describes his own undertaking as an attempt "to return this immense postcard to its sender" (5).

There is no return to any origin which is not already a construction and therefore a kind of writing. Here Alloula writes by explicitly identifying with the naked or half-naked women: "What I read on these cards does not leave me indifferent. It demonstrates to me, were that still necessary, the desolate poverty of *a gaze that I myself,* as an Algerian, *must have been the object of* at some moment in my personal history" (5; my emphasis). This claim of identification with the women as image and as object notwithstanding, the male critic remains invisible himself. If the picture postcards are the kind of *evidence-and-witness* of the oppression of the native that I have been talking about, then what happens in Alloula's text is an attempt to fill in the space left open by the silent women by a self-appointed gesture of witnessing, which turns into a second gaze at the "images" of French colonialism. The Algerian women are exhibited as objects not only by the French but also by Alloula's discourse. Even though the male critic sympathizes with the natives, his status as invisible writing subject is essentially *different from,* not identical with, the status of the pictures in front of us.

The anti-imperialist charge of Alloula's discourse would have us believe that the French gaze at these women is pornographic while his is not. This is so because he distinguishes between erotism and pornography, calling the picture postcards a "suberotism" (which is the book title in French and the title of the last chapter). In her introduction to the book, Barbara Harlow supports the point of Alloula's project by citing Spivak's statement, "brown women saved by white men from brown men" (xviii).[14] In effect, however, because Alloula is intent on captivating the essence of the colonizer's discourse as a way to retaliate against his enemy, his own discourse coincides much more closely with the enemy's than with the women's. What emerges finally is not an identification between the critic and the images of the women as he wishes, but an identification between the critic and the gaze of the colonialist-photographer *over the images of the women,* which become bearers of multiple exploitations. Because Alloula's identification is with the gaze of the colonialist-photographer, the women remain frozen in their poses.[15] The real question raised by Alloula's text is therefore not, Can brown women be saved from brown men by white men, but, Can brown women be saved from white men by brown men?

Alloula writes: "A reading of the sort that I propose to undertake would be entirely superfluous if there existed photographic traces of the gaze of the colonized upon the colonizer" (5). The problem of a statement like this lies in the way it hierarchizes the possibilities of native discourse: had there been photographs that reciprocate in a symmetrical fashion the exploitative gaze of the colonizer, he says, he would not have to write his book. His book is second best. The desire for revenge—to do to the enemy *exactly* what the enemy did to him, so that colonizer and colonized would meet eye to eye—is the fantasy of envy and violence that has been running throughout masculinist anti-imperialist discourse since Fanon. This fantasy, as I have already suggested, is Oedipal in structure.

To make his project what he intended it to be—a *symbolic* identification, as defined by Žižek, with the native women not only as images but also as oppressed victims with their own stories—Alloula would need to follow either one of two alternatives. The first of these would require, in a manner characteristic of the poststructuralist distrust of anything that seems "spontaneous" or "self-evident," a careful reading of the materiality of the images.[16] Such a reading would show that what is assumed to be pornographic is not necessarily so, but is more often a projection, onto the images, of the photographer's (or viewer's) own repression.[17] As it stands, however, Alloula's "reading" only understands the images in terms of *content* rather than as a signifying process which bears alternative clues of reading that may well undo its supposed messages. Alloula bases his reading on very traditional assumptions of the visual as the naked, by equating photography with a "scopic desire" to unveil what is "inside" the women's clothes, etc. Thus he not only confirms Jameson's notion that "the visual is essentially pornographic," but unwittingly provides a demonstration of how this is so in his own anti-pornographic writing.

On the other hand, if the problem with poststructuralist analysis is that it too happily dissolves the pornographic obviousness of the images and thus misses their abusive structuration, then a second alternative would have been for Alloula to exclude images from his book. Alloula's entire message could have been delivered verbally. Instead, the images of the Algerian women are exposed a second time and made to stand as a transparent medium, a homoerotic link connecting the brown man to the white man, connecting "third world" nationalism to "first world" imperialism. What results is neither a dissembling of the pornographic apparatus of imperialist domination nor a restoration of the native to her "authentic" history, but a perfect symmetry between the imperialist and anti-imperialist gazes, which cross over the images of native women as silent objects.

The Native in the Age of Discursive Reproduction

Modernity is ambivalent in its very origin. In trying to become "new" and "novel"—a kind of primary moment—it must incessantly deal with its connection with what *precedes* it—what was primary to it—in the form of a destruction. As Paul de Man writes, "modernity exists in the form of a desire to wipe out whatever came earlier, in the hope of reaching at last a point that could be called a true present, a point of origin that marks a new departure" (148). If the impetus of modernity is a criticism of the past, then much of our cultural criticism is still modernist.

Many accounts of modernity view the world retrospectively, in sadness. The world is thought of as a vast collection, a museum of lives which has been more or less stabilized for/by our gaze. To an anthropologist like Lévi-Strauss in the 1940s, a city like New York "anticipates humanity's entropic future and gathers up its diverse pasts in decontextualized, collectible forms" (Clifford 244). The cosmopolitanizing of humanity also signals the vanishing of human diversity, an event the modern anthropologist laments. Isn't there much similarity between the nostalgic culture-collecting of a Lévi-Strauss and what is being undertaken in the name of "new historicism," which always argues for preserving the "specifics" of particular cultures? Despite the liberalist political outlook of many of its practitioners, the new historical enterprise often strikes one as being in agreement with Francis Fukuyama's pronouncement about "the end of history":

> In the post-historical period there will be neither art nor philosophy, just the perpetual caretaking of the museum of human history. I can feel in myself, and see in others around me, a powerful nostalgia for the time when history existed. (18)

Why are we so fascinated with "history" and with the "native" in "modern" times? What do we gain from our labor on these "endangered authenticities" which are presumed to be from a different time and a different place? What can be said about the juxtaposition of "us" (our discourse) and "them"? What kind of *surplus value* is derived from this juxtaposition?

These questions are also questions about the irreversibility of modernity. In the absence of that original witness of the native's destruction, and in the untranslatability of the native's discourse into imperialist discourse, natives, like commodities, become knowable only through routes that diverge from their original "homes." Judging from the interest invested by contemporary cultural studies in the "displaced native," we may say that the native is precisely caught up in the twin process of what Arjun Appadurai calls "commoditization by diversion" and "the aesthetics of decontextualization," a process in which

> value . . . is accelerated or enhanced by placing objects and things in unlikely contexts. . . . Such diversion is . . . an instrument . . . of the (potential) intensification of commoditization by the enhancement of value attendant upon its diversion. This enhancement of value through the diversion of commodities from their customary circuits underlies the plunder of enemy valuables

in warfare, the purchase and display of "primitive" utilitarian objects, the framing of "found" objects, the making of collections of any sort. In all these examples, diversions of things combine the aesthetic impulse, the entrepreneurial link, and the touch of the morally shocking. (28)

Appadurai, whose intention is to argue that "commodities, like persons, have social lives" (3), refrains from including human beings in his account of commodities. By centering the politics of commoditization on *things* in exchange, he anthropomorphizes things but avoids blurring the line between things and people, and thus preserves the safe boundaries of an old, respectable humanism. However, the most critical implication of his theory begins precisely where he stops. Where Appadurai would not go on, we must, and say that *persons, like things, have commodified lives*: The commoditization of "ethnic specimens" is *already* part of the conceptualization of "the social life of things" indicated in the title of his volume. The forces of commoditization, as part and parcel of the "process" of modernity, do not distinguish between things and people.

To elaborate this, let us turn for a moment to the texts of that great modernist, Walter Benjamin. I have in mind "Eduard Fuchs: Collector and Historian," "The Work of Art in the Age of Mechanical Reproduction," and "Theses on the Philosophy of History." Together these texts offer a writing of the native that has yet to be fully recognized.

Benjamin was himself a passionate collector of books, art, and other objects.[18] As an allegorist, Benjamin's writing is often remarkable for the way it juxtaposes dissimilar things, allowing them to illuminate one another suddenly and unexpectedly. Such is the way he reads the "modernity" of the collector and the making of literature by a poet like Baudelaire. Like the process of "commoditization by diversion" described by Appadurai, Baudelaire's poetry specializes in wresting things from their original contexts. Following Benjamin's allegorical method, I juxtapose his description of Baudelaire with anthropologist Sally Price's description of modernist art collecting:

> Tearing things out of the context of their usual interrelations—which is quite normal where commodities are being exhibited—is a procedure very characteristic of Baudelaire. (Benjamin, "Central Park" 41)

> Once rescued from their homes among the termites and the elements, the objects come into the protective custody of Western owners, something like orphans from a Third-World war, where they are kept cool, dry, and dusted, and where they are loved and appreciated. (Price 76)

Such a juxtaposition makes way for a reading of Benjamin's theses of *history* against the background of primitive art in civilized places (to allude to the title of Price's book). What emerges in this reading is not so much the violence of Benjamin's messianism as the affinity and comparableness between that vio-

lence and the violence of modernist collecting. Think, for instance, of the notion of "a fight for the history of the oppressed." If we refuse, for the time
being, the common moralistic reading of this notion (a reading which emphasizes the salvational aspect of Benjamin's writings and which dominates Benjamin scholarship) and instead insert "the oppressed" into the collection of
things that fascinate Benjamin, we see that "the oppressed" shares a similar
status with a host of other cultural objects—books, antiques, art, toys, and
prostitutes. The language of fighting, plundering, stealing, and abducting is
uniformly the language of "wresting objects from native settings" (Price 74).
The violent concept that is often quoted by Benjamin lovers as a way to read
against "progress"—the concept of blasting open the continuum of history[19]—is as much a precise description of imperialism's relentless destruction
of local cultures as it is a "politically correct" metaphor for redeeming the history of "the oppressed."

By underlining the mutual implication of Benjamin's discourse and the discourse of imperialism, my aim is not that of attacking the "ambiguous" or
"problematic" moral stance of Benjamin the writer. Rather, it is to point out
the ever-changing but ever-present complicity between our critical articulation
and the political environment at which that articulation is directed. Because of
this, whenever the oppressed, the native, the subaltern, and so forth are used
to represent the point of "authenticity" for our critical discourse, they become
at the same time the place of myth-making and an escape from the impure
nature of political realities. In the same way that "native imprints" suggest
"primitivism" in modernist art, we turn, increasingly with fascination, to the
oppressed to locate a "genuine" critical origin.

Consider now Benjamin's argument in the essay with which we are all familiar, "The Work of Art in the Age of Mechanical Reproduction." The usual
understanding of this essay is that Benjamin is describing a process in which
the technology of mechanical reproduction has accelerated to such a degree
that it is no longer relevant to think of the "original" of any art work. The age
of mechanical reproduction is an age in which the aura of art—its ties to a
particular place, culture, or ritual—is in decline. Benjamin is at once nostalgic
about the aura and enchanted by its loss. While the aura represents art's close
relation with the community that generates it, the loss of the aura is the sign
of art's emancipation into mass culture, a new collective culture of "collect-
ibles."

For our present purposes, we can rethink the aura of an art object as that
"historical specificity" which makes it unique to a particular place at a particular time. The vast machines of modernist production and reproduction now
make this "historical specificity" a thing of the past and a concept in demise.
Instead of the authentic, mysterious work with its irreproducible aura, we have
technologically reproduced "copies" which need not have the original as a ref-

erent in the market of mass culture. The original, marked by some unique difference that sets it apart from the mass-produced copies, becomes now a special prize of collectors with exquisite but old-fashioned "taste."

Benjamin's notion of the aura and its decline partakes of the contradictions inherent to modernist processes of displacement and identification. The displaced object is both a sign of violence and of "progress." Purloined aggressively from its original place, this displaced object becomes infinitely reproducible in the cosmopolitan space. Displacement constitutes identity, but as such it is the identity of the ever-shifting. Benjamin shows how the new reproductive technology such as film brings the object within close proximity to the viewer and at the same time allows the viewer to experiment with different viewing positions. From the perspective of the 1990s, the irony of Benjamin's 1936 essay is that while he associated the new perceptive possibilities brought by mechanical reproduction with communist cultural production, he was actually describing the modes of receptivity that have become standard fare for audiences in the capitalist world.[20]

Such contradictions help in some way to explain the double-edged process in which we find ourselves whenever we try to resuscitate the "ethnic specimen" or "native cultures." Once again, we need to extend Benjamin's conceptualization, a conceptualization that is ostensibly only about objects—works of art and their mechanical reproduction—to human beings. Once we do that, we see that in our fascination with the "authentic native," we are actually engaged in a search for the equivalent of the aura even while our search processes themselves take us farther and farther away from that "original" point of identification. Although we act like good communists who dream of finding and serving the "real people," we actually live and work like dirty capitalists accustomed to switching channels constantly. As we keep switching channels and browsing through different "local" cultures, we produce an infinite number of "natives," all with predictably automaton-like features that do not so much de-universalize Western hegemony as they confirm its protean capacity for infinite displacement. The "authentic" native, like the aura in a kind of *mise en abîme*, keeps receding from our grasp. Meanwhile our machinery churns out inauthentic and imperfect natives who are always already copies. The most radical message offered to us by Benjamin's texts is that the commodified aspects of mass reproduction, often described with existentialist angst as alienated labor, are actually a displacement *structural to* the modernist handling of history, in which the problematic of the authentic native now returns with a vengeance. We could rewrite the title of Benjamin's essay as "The Native in the Age of Discursive Reproduction."

In his lecture at the Annual Conference of the Semiotic Society of America in the fall of 1990, J. Hillis Miller returns to Benjamin's remarkable essay as part of a discussion about cultural studies in the age of digital reproduction.[21] One of the scandalous points Miller makes is that Benjamin's formulation of communism and fascism in terms of the "politicization of art" and the "aestheticization of politics" is actually a reversible one.[22] Therein lies its danger. What Miller means is that what begins as a mobilization for political change based on an interest in/respect for the cultural difference of our others (the politicization of art) can easily grow into its ugly opposite. That is to say, the promotion of a type of politics that is based on the need to distinguish between "differences" may consequently lead, as in the case of the Nazis, to an oppression that springs from the transformation of "difference" into "superiority." Any pride that "we" are stronger, healthier, and more beautiful can become, in effect, the aestheticization of politics.

Accordingly, it is ironic that in much of the work we do in cultural studies today, we resort to cultural/ethnic/local "difference" not as an open-ended process but as a preordained fact. The irony is that such a valorization of cultural difference occurs at a time when difference-as-aura-of-the-original has long been problematized by the very availability—and increasing indispensability—of our reproductive apparatuses. Following the drift of Benjamin's argument, Miller writes:

> this celebration of cultural specificity has occurred at a time when that specificity is being drastically altered by technological and other changes that are leading to internationalization of art and of culture generally. The work of cultural studies inevitably participates in that uprooting. . . . [A]rchival work . . . is another form of the digital reproduction that puts everything on the same plane of instant availability. . . . By a paradox familiar to anthropologists, the effort of understanding, preservation, and celebration participates in the drastic alteration of the cultures it would preserve. The more cultural studies try to save and empower local cultures the more they may endanger them. (18)

For Miller, to hang onto the "local" as the absolutely different—that is, absolutely identical with itself—means to attempt to hang onto a rigid stratification of the world in the age of digital reproduction:

> if the politicizing of art is only the specular image of the aestheticizing of politics, can the former as exemplified in cultural studies be exempt from the terrible possibilities of the aestheticizing of politics? . . . [T]he more cultural studies works for the celebration, preservation, and empowerment of subordinated cultures the more it may aid in the replication of just those political orders it would contest. . . . Are not cultural studies caught in a form of the penchant of all national aestheticisms and aesthetic nationalisms toward war? (19–20)

The Native as other and Other

So far my argument has demonstrated a few things. I present the place of the native as that of the image and the silent object, which is often equated with a kind of "lack" in a pejorative sense. After Fanon, we tend to fill this lack with a type of discourse that posits envy and violence as the necessary structure of the native's subjectivity. Corresponding to this is the wave of "new history" which wants to resurrect the native by restoring her to her original context. But new historicism, as a modernist collecting of culture specimens, inevitably comes up against its own aporia, namely, that the possibility of *gathering* "endangered authenticities" is also the possibility of dispensing with the authentic altogether. This is indicated by the collage of Benjamin's critical items—history, collecting, and the mechanical reproduction of art—in which the aura is experienced only in ruin. We are left with the question of how cultural difference can be imagined without being collapsed into the neutrality of a globalist technocracy (as the possibilities of mechanical reproduction imply) and without being frozen into the lifeless "image" of the other that we encounter in Alloula's book.

Alloula's book is disturbing because its use of the image, albeit a problematic one, nonetheless confronts us with the reality of a *relation* which is neither innocuous nor avoidable. This is the relation between technological reproduction and cultural displacement. If technological reproduction is inevitable, is not cultural displacement also? If cultural displacement is conceived derogatorily, must technological reproduction be condemned moralistically then? Does the necessity of the first make the second a necessary virtue, or does the problematic nature of the second render the first equally problematic? This nexus of questions becomes most poignant when the representation of the "native" is not only in the form of a visual other, but explicitly in the form of a pornographic image produced by the technology of photography. Should the criticism of this kind of image lead to 1) the criticism of the visual image itself (if, as Jameson says, the visual is essentially pornographic); 2) an alternative form of conceiving of "otherness" that is completely free of the image; and 3) a subsequent construction of the "native" as "truth" rather than "falsehood"?

While we have no simple answer to these questions, we know that "false" images are going to remain with us whether or not we like it. That is not simply because they are willfully planted there by individuals desiring to corrupt the world; rather it is because the image itself is traditionally always regarded with suspicion, as a site of duplicity if not of direct degeneration. Is there a way in which we can re-imagine our relation to the "pornographic" image of the native?

Ever since Jean-Jacques Rousseau, the native has been imagined as a kind of total other—a utopian image whose imaginary self-sufficiency is used as a stage for the incomplete (or "antagonistic")[23] nature of human society. Rousseau's savage is "self-sufficient" because he possesses *nothing* and is in that sense indifferent and independent. The true difference between the savage and civil man is that man is completable only through others; that is, his identity is always obtained through otherness:

> the savage lives within himself; social man lives always outside himself; he knows how to live only in the opinion of others, it is, so to speak, from their judgment alone that he derives the sense of his own experience. (136)

Rousseau's formulation of the native is interesting not simply because of its idealism. To be sure, this idealism continues to be picked up by other intellectuals such as Kristeva, Barthes, Serres, and others, who (mis)apply it to *specific other cultures*. In doing so, they limit and thus demolish the most important aspect of Rousseau's text, which is that the idealized native is, literally, topographically *nowhere*. No cruise ship ever takes us to see a self-sufficient "native," nor are the remains of any such person to be found at any archeological site.

Rousseau's savage is, then, not simply a cultural "other," but, in Lacanian language, the Other (big Other) that exists before "separation," before the emergence of the *objet petit a,* the name for those subjectivized, privatized, and missing parts of the whole.[24] Why is this important? Because it enables us to imagine the native in a way that has been foreclosed by the Manichaean aesthetics[25] in which she is always already cast—as the white man's other, as the degraded and falsified image, as the subject constituted solely by her envy and violence, *and* as the "identity" that can never free itself of any of this "pornography." My invocation of the big Other is hence not an attempt to depoliticize the realities of displaced identities in the postimperialist world; rather, it is an attempt to broaden that politics to include more *general* questions of exploitation, resistance, and survival by using the historical experience of the "native" as its shifting ground.

A moment in Homi Bhabha's reading of Fanon suggests a similar attempt at a more extended politics when he points out how Fanon, writing in times of political urgency, has limited it to the colonial situation:

> At times Fanon attempts too close a correspondence between the *mise-en-scène* of unconscious fantasy and the phantoms of racist fear and hate that stalk the colonial scene; he turns too hastily from the ambivalences of identification to the antagonistic identities of political alienation and cultural discrimination; he is too quick to name the Other, to personalize its presence in the language of colonial racism— "the real Other for the white man is and will continue to be the black man. And conversely." These attempts, in Fanon's words, to restore the dream to its proper political time and cultural

space can, at times, blunt the edge of Fanon's brilliant illustrations of the complexity of psychic projections in the pathological colonial relation. (" 'What Does the Black Man Want?' " 121)

While not giving up the politically urgent sense in which Fanon wrote, Bhabha indicates that the criticism of the history of colonialism via the problematic of the native's (the black man's) identification can in fact lead to an understanding of the larger problems of otherness that do not necessarily emerge exclusively in anticolonial discourse. This openness, which is not as expediently committed to a particular "position" as most self-declared political discourses are, is to be differentiated from the kind of idealization of another *culture* in the form of a totality that is absolutely different (and indifferent) to our own. This openness is not an attempt to recuperate an originary, primordial space before the sign. Rather, it is a total sign, the Other, the *entire* function of which is to contest the limits of the conventional (arbitrary) sign itself.[26] We may call this big Other the big Difference.

How does the big Other work? It works by combatting the construction of the native as the straightforward or direct "other" of the colonizer. Instead, it adds to this "image" of the native the ability to look, so that the native is "gaze" as well. But this is not the gaze of the native-as-subject, nor the gaze of the anti-imperialist critic like Alloula; rather it is a simulation of the gaze that witnessed the native's oppression prior to her becoming image. (For instance, it is the video camera that records policemen beating their black victim, Rodney King, with clubs in Los Angeles, as he "resists arrest" by pleading for his life.) The big Other thus functions to supplement the identification of the native-as-image in the form of *evidence-cum-witness* that I have been talking about.[27]

In other words, the agency of the native cannot simply be imagined in terms of a resistance against the image—that is, *after* the image has been formed—nor in terms of a subjectivity that existed *before*, beneath, inside, or outside the image. It needs to be rethought as that which bears witness to its own demolition—in a form that is at once image and gaze, but a gaze that exceeds the moment of colonization.

What I am suggesting is a mode of understanding the native in which the native's existence—that is, an existence before becoming "native"—precedes the arrival of the colonizer. Contrary to the model of Western hegemony in which the colonizer is seen as a primary, active "gaze" subjugating the native as passive "object," I want to argue that it is actually the colonizer who feels looked at by the native's gaze. This gaze, which is neither a threat nor a retaliation, makes the colonizer "conscious" of himself, leading to his need to turn this gaze around and look at himself, henceforth "reflected" in the native-object. It is the self-reflection of the colonizer that produces the colonizer as subject (potent gaze, source of meaning and action) and the native as his image, with all the pejorative meanings of "lack" attached to the word "image." Hegel's story of human "self-consciousness" is then not what he supposed it to be—a story about Western Man's highest achievement—but a story about the disturbing effect of Western Man's encounter with those others that Hegel considered primitive. Western Man henceforth became "self-conscious," that is, uneasy and uncomfortable, in his "own" environment.

Because this "originary" *witnessing* is, temporally speaking, lost forever, the native's defiled image must *act* both as "image" (history of her degradation) and as that witnessing gaze. In the silence of the native-as-object—a silence not immediately distinguishable from her ascribed silence/passivity—the indifference of the "originary" witness appears again—in simulation. Like the silent picture postcards reproduced by Alloula, this simulated gaze is *between* the image and the gaze of the colonizer. Where the colonizer undresses her, the native's nakedness stares back at him both as the defiled image of his creation *and* as the indifferent gaze that says, there was nothing—no secret—to be unveiled underneath my clothes. That secret is your fantasm.

The Native Is Not the Non-Duped

I conclude by returning to the issue with which I began, the issue of authenticity. As anthropologist Brian Spooner writes:

> In seeking authenticity people are able to use commodities to express themselves and fix points of security and order in an amorphous modern society. But the evolving relationship between the search for personal authenticity inside and the search for authenticity in carefully selected things outside has received relatively little attention. (226)

My argument *for* the native's status as an indifferent defiled image is really an attempt to get at the root of the problem of the image, in which our cultural studies is deeply involved whenever it deals with "the other." Because the image, in which the other is often cast, is always distrusted as illusion, deception, and falsehood, attempts to salvage the other often turn into attempts to uphold the other as the non-duped—the site of authenticity and true knowledge. Critics who do this can also imply that, having absorbed the primal wisdoms, they are the non-duped themselves.

In a recent essay, "How the Non-Duped Err," Žižek describes the paradox of deception. Žižek, as Jonathan Elmer writes, "concurs with Lacan that '*les non-dupes errent*,' that those who think they are undeceived are the fools" (122). In his work, Žižek often refers to the classic topos in Lacan, the topos that only human beings can "deceive by feigning to deceive," or deceive by telling the truth (3).[28] That this can happen depends on the fact that we all assume that there is always something else under the mask. One deep-rooted example is that under the mask of civilization we are "savages": the savage/primitive/native is then the "truth" that is outside/under the symbolic order. The cultural critic who holds on to such a notion of the native is, by analogy, a psychotic subject:

> the psychotic subject's distrust of the big Other, his *idée fixe* that the big Other (embodied in his intersubjective community) is trying to deceive him, is always and necessarily supported by an unshakable belief in a consistent Other, an Other without gaps, an "Other of the Other" . . . a non-deceived agent holding the reins. His mistake does not consist in his radical disbelief, in his conviction that there is a universal deception—here he is quite right, the symbolic order is ultimately the order of a fundamental deception—his mistake lies on the contrary in his being too easy of belief and supposing the existence of a hidden agency manipulating this deception, trying to dupe him. . . . (Žižek 12)

For us working in anti-imperialist discourse, this "hidden agency manipulating . . . deception" would be precisely "imperialism," "colonialism," "capitalism," and so forth. According to Žižek, our identification with the native in the form of a radical *disbelief* in the defiled images produced by these symbolic orders would not be wrong. What is problematic is our attempt to point to them as if they were one consistent manipulator that is trying to fool us consistently. Our fascination with the native, the oppressed, the savage, and all such figures is therefore a desire to hold onto an unchanging certainty somewhere outside our own "fake" experience. It is a desire for being "non-duped," which is a not-too-innocent desire to seize control.

To insist on the native as an indifferent, defiled image is then to return to the native a capacity for distrusting and resisting the symbolic orders that "fool" her, while not letting go of the "illusion" that has structured her survival. To imagine the coexistence of defilement and indifference *in* the native-object is not to neutralize the massive destructions committed under such orders as imperialism and capitalism. Rather, it is to invent a dimension beyond the deadlock between native and colonizer in which the native can only be the colonizer's defiled image and the anti-imperialist critic can only be psychotic. My argument is: Yes, "natives" are represented as defiled images—that is the fact of our history. But must we represent them a second time by turning history "upside down," this time giving them the sanctified status of the "non-duped"? Defilement and sanctification belong to the same symbolic order.

So where have all the "natives" gone? They have gone . . . between the defiled image and the indifferent gaze. The native is not the defiled image and not not the defiled image. And she stares indifferently, mocking our imprisonment within imagistic resemblance and our self-deception as the non-duped.

Notes

1. I discuss this in the first chapter of *Woman and Chinese Modernity*. One criticism that Sinologists deeply invested in the culture of ancient China often make about contemporary Chinese people is that they are too "Westernized."

2. Jameson's notion of pornography owes its origins, in part at least, to fictional explorations of the relations between sexual images and technology such as J. G. Ballard's *Crash* (first published by Farrar, Straus & Giroux, Inc. in 1973), described by its author as "the first pornographic novel based on technology." See Ballard, "Introduction to the French Edition" (first published in French in 1974 and in English in 1975), p. 6. I am grateful to Chris Andre of Duke University for pointing this out to me.

3. Jean Baudrillard's theory of "seduction" offers a strong critique of modern theory's tendency to go toward depths, thus ignoring the subversive potential of the superficial. See his *Seduction*.

4. See Homi Bhabha, " 'What Does the Black Man Want?' " Bhabha's argument is that "the black man wants the objectifying confrontation with otherness" (120). This essay is based on Bhabha's introduction to Frantz Fanon's *Black Skin, White Masks*.

5. As Jacques Derrida writes of Lévi-Strauss: "the critique of ethnocentrism, a theme so dear to the author of *Tristes Tropiques*, has most often the sole function of constituting the other as a model of original and natural goodness, of accusing and humiliating oneself, of exhibiting its being-unacceptable in an anti-ethnocentric mirror" (114).

6. Barthes's reading of Japan is found in his *Empire of Signs*. For a discussion of Kojève's conception of Japan's "post-historic" condition, see Miyoshi and Harootunian, Introduction, "Postmodernism and Japan." In his *Suicidal Narrative in Modern Japan*, Alan Wolfe offers an astute reading of Kojève's problematic pronouncement and its Orientalist assumptions against the complex background of modern Japanese literature and culture. See especially pp. 216–17 and pp. 220–22 of Wolfe's book.

7. "However impeccably the content of an 'other' culture may be known, however anti-ethnocentrically it is represented, it is its location as the 'closure' of grand theories, the demand that, in analytic terms, it be always the 'good' object of knowledge, the docile body of difference, that reproduces a relation of domination and is the most serious indictment of the institutional powers of critical theory" (Bhabha, "The Commitment to Theory" 124).

8. See "Can the Subaltern Speak?" 308. The Spivak of this essay is very different from the one who speaks of "envy" on behalf of the silent Chinese women in "French Feminism in an International Frame," precisely because she does not read the subaltern in Oedipalized terms.

9. Bhabha's view is expressed in many of his essays. See, for instance, "The Other Question"; "Of Mimicry and Man"; "Signs Taken for Wonders." See also "DissemiNation."

10. Jean-François Lyotard:

I would like to call a *differend* [*différend*] the case where the plaintiff is divested of the means to argue and becomes for that reason a victim. . . . A case of differend between two parties takes place when the 'regulation' of the conflict that opposes them is done in the idiom of one of the parties while the wrong suffered by the other is not signified in that idiom (9).

11. See, for instance, Sally Price; Marianna Torgovnick; the many essays in Clifford and Marcus; and Marcus and Fischer.

12. This is T. S. Eliot's view of the poet's mind when it is "perfectly equipped for its

work" (64). This well-known discussion of the metaphysical poets' relevance to modernity was in part a criticism of Samuel Johnson's remark of them that "the most heterogeneous ideas are yoked by violence together" (Eliot 60).

13. See Lyotard's definition of the *différend*, cited in note 10.

14. Spivak's statement, "White men are saving brown women from brown men," is found in "Subaltern" (296-97). She is describing the British intervention in *sati* (widow sacrifice) in British India, whereby the colonizer attempted to coopt native women under the pretext of freeing them from oppression by their own men.

15. See a similar criticism made by Winifred Woodhull. Because Alloula never really addresses the question of women's interests, Woodhull argues, he ultimately "repeats the gesture of the colonizer by making of the veiled woman the screen on which he projects *his* fantasy . . . of an Algerian nation untroubled by questions of women's oppression" (126). See also Mieke Bal for an argument about the complicity between the critic of colonial visual practice and colonial exploitation itself. Alloula's book is one of several Bal shows as lacking in a careful critique of the critic's own sexist and colonizing position.

16. Deconstructionist anti-colonial critics such as Bhabha have, for instance, elaborated on the "ambivalence" of the image in the following terms:

> the image—as point of identification—marks the site of an ambivalence. Its representation is always spatially split—it makes *present* something that is *absent*—and temporally deferred—it is the representation of a time that is always elsewhere, a repetition. The image is only ever an *appurtenance* to authority and identity; it must never be read mimetically as the 'appearance' of a 'reality.' The access to the image of identity is only ever possible in the *negation* of any sense of originality or plenitude, through the principle of displacement and differentiation (absence/presence; representation/repetition) that always renders it a liminal reality. (" 'What Does the Black Man Want?' " 120)

17. For an example of a poststructuralist analysis of how pornography is in the eye of the beholder, see Judith Butler.

18. In the brief introduction to "Eduard Fuchs," the editors of *The Essential Frankfurt School Reader* write: "the presentation of Fuchs, the collector and often crude materialist, must also be read as one of Benjamin's self-presentations, and even as an *apologia pro vita sua* in the face of criticism" (Arato and Gebhardt 225).

19. "History is the subject of a structure whose site is not homogeneous, empty time, but time filled by the presence of the now [*Jetztzeit*]. Thus, to Robespierre ancient Rome was a past charged with the time of the now which he blasted out of the continuum of history." "The awareness that they are about to make the continuum of history explode is characteristic of the revolutionary classes at the moment of their action" (Benjamin, "Theses" 261).

20. See also Benjamin's similar argument in "The Author as Producer."

21. Miller's reading of "aura" is poststructuralist.

The fact that the modern work of art is reproducible casts its shadow back not just to remove the aura from traditional works but to reveal that aura was always an ideological formation. That is what Benjamin means by saying film in itself, as a means of mechanical reproduction, is revolutionary criticism of traditional concepts of art. As the technological changes Benjamin describes have proceeded apace, the opposition between traditional man or woman and the masses disappears and with it the pertinence of the idea of a people with a specific culture. We are all to some degree members of what Benjamin invidiously calls the 'masses.' We are members of a transnational, multilinguistic, worldwide technological culture that makes the pieties of nationalism seem more and more outdated, nostalgic, perhaps even dangerously reactionary. (10)

A substantially modified version of Miller's essay is found in his book *Illustrations*, many of the views of which I do not share. My present discussion, however, is based entirely on the earlier lecture.

22. "The problem with all Benjamin's symmetrical oppositions is that they tend to dissolve through the effort of thinking they facilitate" (Miller 10).

23. The notion of a radical "antagonism" that structures sociality by making it incapable of self-identification or closure is argued by Laclau and Mouffe. See especially chapter three, "Beyond the Positivity of the Social: Antagonisms and Hegemony."

24. Gilles Deleuze and Félix Guattari make a comparable point when they, criticizing Freudian psychoanalysis as an anthropomorphic representation of sex, equate Lacan's "big Other" with what they call "nonhuman sex" (see 295; 308–10). Deleuze and Guattari's notion of "part objects" or "partial objects" is, of course, very different. They are not "part" of any "whole," but molecular machinic flows and breaks.

25. I take this phrase from Abdul R. JanMohamed.

26. In Saussure, the linguistic sign (made up of a relationship between signifier and signified) is arbitrary because it is conventional—in the sense that it works only within a coherent system of differences.

27. This essay was completed in mid-1991. The subsequent verdict on the King beating in 1992 demonstrated once again the dominant culture's ability to manipulate images to its own advantage by sabotaging the witnessing function crucial to any evidence of abuse. Once it succeeds in divorcing the act of witnessing from the image, the dominant culture can appoint itself as the "true" witness whose observation and interpretation of the image is held as the most accurate one. The Rodney King video and the racial riots that followed the verdict thus became "evidence" not for the historical white discrimination against blacks, but for how necessary that discrimination is!

28. Žižek quotes the Freudian joke about Polish Jews often mentioned by Lacan: "one of them asks the other in an offended tone: 'Why are you telling me that you are going to Lemberg, when you are really going to Lemberg?' " ("How the Non-Duped Err" 3; see also *Sublime Object* 197).

Works Cited

Alloula, Malek. *The Colonial Harem.* Trans. Myrna Godzich and Wlad Godzich. Minneapolis: U of Minnesota P, 1986.

Appadurai, Arjun. "Introduction: Commodities and the Politics of Value." *The Social Life of Things: Commodities in Cultural Perspective.* Ed. Arjun Appadurai. Cambridge: Cambridge UP, 1986. 3–63.

Arato, Andrew, and Eike Gebhardt, eds. *The Essential Frankfurt School Reader.* New York: Urizen, 1978.

Armstrong, Nancy. "The Occidental Alice." *differences* 2.2 (1990): 3–40.

Bal, Mieke. "The Politics of Citation." *Diacritics* 21.1 (1991): 25–45.

Ballard, J. G. *Crash.* First Vintage Books Edition, 1985.

Barthes, Roland. *Empire of Signs.* Trans. Richard Howard. New York: Hill, 1982.

Baudrillard, Jean. *Seduction.* Trans. Brian Singer. New York: St. Martin's, 1990.

Benjamin, Walter. "The Author as Producer." Trans. Edmund Jephcott. Arato and Gebhardt 254–69.

———. "Central Park." Trans. Lloyd Spencer (with the help of Mark Harrington). *New German Critique* 34 (1985): 32–58.

———. "Edward Fuchs: Collector and Historian." Trans. Knut Tarnowski. Arato and Gebhardt 225–53.

———. *Illuminations.* Ed. Hannah Arendt. Trans. Harry Zohn. New York: Schocken, 1969.

———. "Theses on the Philosophy of History." *Illuminations* 253–64.

———. "The Work of Art in the Age of Mechanical Production." *Illuminations* 217–51.

Bhabha, Homi K. "The Commitment to Theory." *Questions of Third Cinema.* Ed. Jim Pines and Paul Willemen. London: British Film Inst., 1989.

———. "DissemiNation: Time, Narrative, and the Margins of the Modern Nation." *Nation and Narration.* Ed. Homi K. Bhabha. London: Routledge, 1990. 291–322.

———. "Of Mimicry and Man: The Ambivalence of Colonial Discourse." *October* 28 (1984): 125–33.

———. "The Other Question—the Stereotype and Colonial Discourse." *Screen* 24.6 (1983): 18–36.

———. "Signs Taken for Wonders: Questions of Ambivalence and Authority under a Tree Outside Delhi, May 1817." *Critical Inquiry* 12.1 (1985): 144–65. Rpt. in *"Race," Writing, and Difference.* Ed. Henry Louis Gates, Jr. Chicago: U of Chicago P, 1985. 163–84.

———. " 'What Does the Black Man Want?' " *New Formations* 1 (1987): 118–24.

Butler, Judith. "The Force of Fantasy: Feminism, Mapplethorpe, and Discursive Excess." *differences* 2.2 (1990): 105–25.

Chow, Rey. *Woman and Chinese Modernity: The Politics of Reading between West and East.* Minneapolis: U of Minnesota P, 1991.

Clifford, James. *The Predicament of Culture: Twentieth-Century Ethnography, Literature, and Art.* Cambridge: Harvard UP, 1988.

Clifford, James, and George E. Marcus, eds. *Writing Culture: The Poetics and Politics of Ethnography.* Berkeley: U of California P, 1986.

Deleuze, Gilles, and Félix Guattari. *Anti-Oedipus: Capitalism and Schizophrenia.* Preface Michel Foucault. Trans. Robert Hurley, Mark Seem, and Helen R. Lane. Minneapolis: U of Minnesota P, 1983.

de Man, Paul. *Blindness and Insight: Essays in the Rhetoric of Contemporary Criticism.* Minneapolis: U of Minnesota P, 1983.

Derrida, Jacques. *Of Grammatology.* Trans. Gayatri Chakravorty Spivak. Baltimore: Johns Hopkins UP, 1976.

Eliot, T. S. "The Metaphysical Poets." *Selected Prose of T. S. Eliot.* Ed. Frank Kermode. New York: Harcourt; Farrar, 1975.

Elmer, Jonathan. Review of Slavoj Žižek's *The Sublime Object of Ideology. Qui Parle* 4.1 (1990): 117–23.

Fanon, Frantz. *Black Skin, White Masks.* London: Pluto, 1986.

Fukuyama, Francis. "The End of History?" *The National Interest* 16 (1989): 3–18.

Harlow, Barbara. Introduction. Alloula ix–xxii.

Jameson, Fredric. *Signatures of the Visible.* New York: Routledge, 1990.

JanMohamed, Abdul R. *Manichean Aesthetics: The Politics of Literature in Colonial Africa.* Amherst: U of Massachusetts P, 1983.

Kojève, Alexandre. *Introduction to the Reading of Hegel: Lectures on the Phenomenology of Spirit.* Assembled by Raymond Queneau. Ed. Allan Bloom. Trans. James H. Nichols, Jr. Ithaca: Cornell UP, 1989.

Kristeva, Julia. *About Chinese Women.* Trans. Anita Barrows. New York: Marion Boyars, 1977, 1986.

Laclau, Ernesto, and Chantal Mouffe. *Hegemony and Socialist Strategy: Towards a Radical Democratic Politics.* Trans. Winston Moore and Paul Cammack. London: Verso, 1985.

Lyotard, Jean-François. *The Differend: Phrases in Dispute.* Trans. Georges Van Den Abbeele. Minneapolis: U of Minnesota P, 1988.

Marcus, George E., and Michael M. J. Fischer, eds. *Anthropology as Cultural Critique: An Experimental Moment in the Human Sciences.* Chicago: U of Chicago P, 1986.

Miller, J. Hillis. *Illustration.* Cambridge: Harvard UP, 1992.

———. "The Work of Cultural Criticism in the Age of Digital Reproduction." Annual Conference of the Semiotic Society of America. Manuscript. 1990.

Miyoshi, Masao, and H. D. Harootunian. Introduction. "Postmodernism and Japan." *The South Atlantic Quarterly* 87.3 (1988): 392–94. Rpt. as *Postmodernism and Japan.* Ed. Masao Miyoshi and H. D. Harootunian. Durham: Duke UP, 1989.

Parry, Benita. "Problems in Current Theories of Colonial Discourse." *Oxford Literary Review* 9.1–2 (1987): 27–58.

Price, Sally. *Primitive Art in Civilized Places.* Chicago: U of Chicago P, 1989.

Rousseau, Jean-Jacques. *A Discourse on Inequality.* Trans. Maurice Cranston. London: Penguin, 1984.

Saussure, Ferdinand de. *Course in General Linguistics.* Trans. Wade Baskin. Ed. Charles Bally et al. Glasgow: Fontana/Collins, 1974.

Serres, Michel. *Detachment.* Trans. Genevieve James and Raymond Federman. Athens: Ohio UP, 1989.

Spivak, Gayatri Chakravorty. "Can the Subaltern Speak? *Marxism and the Interpretation of Culture.* Ed. Cary Nelson and Lawrence Grossberg. Urbana: U of Illinois P, 1988. 271–313.

———. "French Feminism in an International Frame." *In Other Worlds: Essays in Cultural Politics.* London: Methuen, 1987. 134–53.

———. "The New Historicism: Political Commitment and the Postmodern Critic." *Post-Colonial Critic: Interviews, Strategies, Dialogues.* Ed. Sarah Harasym. London: Routledge, 1990. 152–68.

Spooner, Brian. "Weavers and Dealers: The Authenticity of an Oriental Carpet." *The Social Life of Things: Commodities in Cultural Perspective.* Ed. Arjun Appadurai. Cambridge: Cambridge UP, 1986. 195–235.

Torgovnick, Marianna. *Gone Primitive: Savage Intellects, Modern Lives.* Chicago: U of Chicago P, 1990.

Wolfe, Alan. *Suicidal Narrative in Modern Japan: The Case of Dazai Osamu.* Princeton: Princeton UP, 1990.

Woodhull, Winifred. "Unveiling Algeria." *Genders* 10 (1991): 121–26.

Žižek, Slavoj. "How the Non-Duped Err." *Qui Parle* 4.1 (1990): 1–20.

———. "Rossellini: Woman As Symptom of Man." *October* 54 (1990): 18–44.

———. *The Sublime Object of Ideology.* New York: Verso, 1989.

9 | Year of the Ram
Honolulu, Feb. 2, 1991
James Clifford

" . . . A PICTURE OF the animal. 'What you see is horns in the front and then the backbone and then the legs on both sides and the tail going out beyond the legs,' she said."

The new Chinatown atrium. Available cuisines:

Chinese
Japanese
Thai
Korean
Hawaiian
Italian
Mexican
Filipino
Singapore
Lulu International
U.S.

Night in the crowded streets: smoke from food stands, running young men and women from a martial arts club, a dragon, University of Hawaii jazz ensemble, all Asian saxophone section.

The beautiful Hawaiian capes made of feathers were worn in battle. Nearby, a high school band finishes its recital with the Looneytunes theme, immediately followed by "The Star-Spangled Banner." We all stand solemnly.

In a desert the tank is hit and sends up a plume of black smoke.

Heavy flowers around our necks.

"Each day at sunrise the light was radiant in my hut. The gold of Tehamana's face illuminates everything around it, and the two of us go to refresh ourselves in a nearby stream, naturally, simply, as in Paradise."

152

The Hilton Hawaiian Village (2,200 rooms): black football players (Pro Bowl weekend) loom in elevators over white art museum directors (A.A.M.D. annual meeting).

Leisure attire, exposed skin, beaches . . .

In a desert the tank is hit, explodes inside, sears the men's faces, and sends up a plume of black smoke.

"The goat is more earthy, the ram more scholarly."

Football players signing autographs. Museum directors debating multiculturalism.

In the art collector's beautiful home, one wall is entirely composed of video screens. Making and unmaking collages.

"A woman soldier is reported missing in action." Maps. "This will not be another Vietnam." Bombsight footage. Talking general (African-American).

Man (apparently Anglo) in California: "We should go all the way this time, do it right, just get rid of those people."

In slow motion the building implodes.

A museum's dark garden overlooks the million city lights, as if seen from an incoming plane or missile. The performance artist in his mariachi suit and Indian war bonnet says, "It is very strange being here, in the beginning of the third world war."

"Ram or ewe? 'That's anybody's guess,' she said."

In a desert the tank is hit, explodes inside, sears the men's faces, tears sharp pieces of metal into their bodies, and sends up a plume of black smoke.

This garden, this city: "Montezuma entertaining Cortez." Smell of flowers and blood. A writhing dragon. Meat cooking. These streets. Different bodies mingle.

"This will not be another Vietnam."

A Hawaiian man plays with three children on the beach. He seems to be their father. In bathing suits, each one appears distinct, as if from a separate painting. The man is young and muscular. The four build something in the sand. When the youngest begins to cry the father quickly takes him on his lap.

"First we will cut it off, then we will kill it."

And just beneath a white, floating platform, the battleship Arizona still holds her 1,100 drowned men.

"There is no confirmation that women and children were killed in the raid."

Art museum directors discuss the problem of aesthetic universals. The football crowd whoops it up in the bar.

Heavy flowers around our necks.

"The China Daily, the only English-language newspaper published in Beijing, is calling it the Year of the Sheep. But the China Institute of America in Manhattan, which bills itself as this country's oldest bicultural institution concentrating on China, decided that this was the Year of the Ram by taking a vote among its staff."

Tonight, as the year 4688 gets underway, I rub ointment on my sleeping three-year-old son's chapped lips.

In a desert, the tank is hit, explodes inside, sears the men's faces, tears pieces of sharp metal into their bodies, suffocates them, ignites their uniforms, and sends up a plume of black smoke.

This will not be Vietnam.
This will not be America.

Where do we come from?

In a desert,

What are we?

the tank is hit,

Where are we going?

explodes inside . . .

Quotations

New York Times, article on the Chinese Year of the Ram (or Sheep), early February 1991.
Paul Gauguin, *Noa Noa*.
Gulf War media coverage.
Guillermo Gomez-Peña, Honolulu, 1 February 1991.
President George Bush.
General Colin Powell.

10 | Memories of Empire

Bill Schwarz

IT IS STRIKING, in Britain, when we come to view the *movements* in theoretical work to see how the decentered sons and daughters of the black diaspora—or if we extend this as we should, how the offspring of Britain's colonial history—have become centered in the debates about identity. This is a relatively recent occurrence, its origins probably lying in the events of 1981–82 when dispossessed black Britons forced themselves into the field of vision of an essentially myopic public consciousness, long-formed by the historic imperatives of white ethnicity. In contrast to the United States, where the civil rights movement functioned as a vehicle by which Afro-America could confront the public sphere of white America and dramatically proclaim its existential right "to be," this same shift in Britain occurred relatively late in the *longue durée* of colonial emancipation. Yet at the same time—the comparative lateness of this black insurgence perhaps working to overdetermine its influence—the impact on theory, though uneven, has been swift and far-reaching. In Britain, it is the politics of the diaspora which has generated the urgency in current theoretical debate about identity.

More particularly the Caribbean possesses a significant hold on these discussions. Not only does the passage from the West Indies to the cold realities of actually existing England fashion its own perceptions, but the deeper history of the Caribbean as a peculiar distillation of America, Europe, and Africa resonates with contemporaneity. For those with the eyes to see, the tangled iconography of the Ethiopian royal house transported to the dreary high-roads of the metropolitan inner cities does indeed attest to a history made visible. Yet while observable in the present, it is a history full of complexity, not easily conforming to the lived expectation of *roots*. Indeed, the contending, dissonant historical times which have gone into the making of Caribbean identities in the moment of modernity compel us to think in terms of "heteroglossia" and hybridity—of the collision of distinct histories producing new forms.

Yet the theoretical strategies which have proved so effective in creating the poetics of the black diaspora in Britain—in cinema preeminently—have quickly become generalized, applicable it seems not only to understanding the displaced cultures of West Indians in Britain, but the very structures of identity itself. In a number of key documents the "migrant" voices of black Britain came to be *centered* at the cutting edge of theoretical transformation (see especially *ICA Documents 6, ICA Documents 7*, and Rutherford).

I don't mean to suggest that these shifts had no theoretical precedents. Theorizations of sexual politics had been critical, one variant of which introduced the language of psychoanalysis into the arguments, drawing ever more inventively from Lacan. From this perspective—the oxymoron notwithstanding—identity comes to be *essentially* multiple and labile, "more careless, more irrational, more forgetful and more incomplete" (Freud 650).[1] This is a persuasive argument, freeing us from overly rationalistic or cognitive theorizations. It allows, I think, a more profound historicization to emerge.

Even though the most interesting, acute theoretical work on this issue may have cohered most recently around the question of black identities, there is no reason why similar approaches should not throw light on the mechanisms of white ethnicity as well. Yet there is a paradox here. White English identity, cast in the history of Empire, is itself intensely centered. Clearly, it functions through a process of multiple displacements: It is never possible to abstract Englishness, to uncover its deep structure and point to it—"There it is!" Its meanings are precisely, continuously, and necessarily deferred, its constituent symbols dissolving one into another. Yet we know it when we see it. It is powerfully present even in its own denials, and powerfully present too in its subaltern Others. In what ways, then, can we say that white England is "hybrid" or "dissonant" when it can lay claim to a history defined so emphatically by strategies of exclusion? Where do the fault lines fall?

There is—perhaps we don't need to be reminded—a theoretical literature devoted to this, exploring the means by which the Cartesian subject produces its Others. Much of this is as suggestive as it is abstract. Here I intend to follow a different tack—to tell a relatively simple story of a single individual in an attempt to ground some of the abstractions in common currency. The figure I discuss is Paul Scott, a white Englishman and author of a series of novels which took the collective title *The Raj Quartet*. The novels, in recounting the final years of British rule in India, explicitly question the coordinates of postcolonial memory, and in so doing they have been the object of significant public contention.

"Identity," according to one of the most impressive of contemporary theorists, "is formed at the unstable point where the 'unspeakable' stories of subjectivity meet the narratives of history, of a culture" (Stuart Hall 44). The story that follows is an attempt to think through the "unstable" intersections of subjective identity—of public and private, black and white—in which the (literally) "unspeakable" elements of Paul Scott's life occupy a determinate role.

The larger historical narrative, in this instance, articulates the practices of England and its Empire, most of all—given Scott's biography and concerns—by thinking England in terms of India.

The centrality of India to this essay makes necessary one final introductory remark, for while much recent debate on these matters has been framed with reference to Afro-American identities, this has not been exclusively so. Indeed, in the past decade perhaps the single most prominent voice in articulating the need for the invention of new—"British"—ethnicities is an erstwhile citizen, not of Kingston nor Port of Spain, but of Bombay. I refer to Salman Rushdie. Both in his fiction and in his journalism he has single-mindedly attempted to deconstruct the polarity of Britain and its Others. As I have suggested elsewhere, his novels deploy a perception of history in which the work of memory collapses time, restages the past, and rearranges possible futures. Subjective, fractured perceptions organized in memory; the irresolvable interplay between memory and the official history of the public nation; stories which perpetually reinvent—from afar, in exile—the imaginary homeland; those who possess history . . . and those who are stripped of it, blasted out of history, stripped bare, their bodies and spirits scorched and scarred, a humanity stripped down it its racial essence: these themes predominate and organize his writing (Schwarz).

In February 1989, with a cataclysmic shock of unimaginable force, all these themes—which Rushdie had long insisted were deadly serious—turned in on the author and became a matter, immediately, of life or death: the *fatwa* imposed on Rushdie transformed the sense of the possible. Central to the intractable debates which followed was the issue of identity in the postcolonial epoch. On the first anniversary of his "exile" Rushdie proclaimed his allegiance to the *impurity* of identity:

> *The Satanic Verses* celebrates hybridity, impurity, intermingling, the transformation that comes of new and unexpected combinations of human beings, cultures, ideas, politics, movies, songs. It rejoices in mongrelisation and fears the absolutism of the Pure. Melange, hotch-potch, a bit of this and a bit of that is *how newness enters the world*. It is the great possibility that mass migration gives the world, and I have tried to embrace it. *The Satanic Verses* is for change-by-fusion, change-by-conjoining. It is a love-song to our mongrel selves.
>
> Throughout human history, the apostles of purity, those who have claimed to possess a total explanation, have wrought havoc among mere mixed-up human beings. Like millions of people, I am a bastard child of history. ("In Good Faith")

Perhaps, in this larger sense, we are all bastard children of the various empires which produced us, colonizers and colonized alike. But to say this is not to conflate the distinct histories of black and white, colonized and colonizers. It is merely to insist that in order to know "white" we have to learn about the historical formations of both black and white. There is, in other words, an urgency now for the children of the white empires to know where they came from.

We can in fact open the discussion of Paul Scott with Rushdie. In 1984 Scott's *Raj Quartet* was broadcast on television as *The Jewel in the Crown*. Initially, it appeared that the burning historical question was that of verisimilitude—more particularly, whether the producers had accurately reproduced the military uniforms of the period, a matter, it seems, of enduring passion for the British. One sharp, literate, and well-publicized intervention effectively turned the terms of the controversy: that of Salman Rushdie. Rushdie, drawing freely and creatively from Edward Said, denounced the television series as titillating rubbish, peddling a dangerously ethnocentric view of history which (and here Scott's novels equally were condemned) in its very form perpetrated less a settling of accounts with the legacy of the colonial past than its continuation. Writing in a moment still closely overshadowed by the war with Argentina, Rushdie believed "the Raj revisionism," exemplified not only by the televising of Scott's *Quartet*, but also by Richard Attenborough's deplorable *Gandhi* and David Lean's truly ignorant appropriation of *A Passage to India*, functioned as "the artistic counterpart to the rise of conservative ideologies in modern Britain," by which he meant, in a word, Thatcherism ("Outside the Whale" 130).[2]

Rushdie's was a characteristically bold polemic, driven I think by an edge of desperation, wondering what on earth would ever force the English to free themselves from the nightmare of their history. The responses, however, did not fall neatly into the given dispositions of politics or ethnicity. By and large Rushdie's fulminations accorded with those of Ferdinand Mount, something of a self-styled, highbrow, upper-class Englishman, whose views on the virtues of family life propelled him for a while into the claque of Thatcher's policymakers, and who more recently has been installed at the *Times Literary Supplement* (Moore 2). On the other hand Tariq Ali and Christopher Hitchens (*Prepared for the Worst*), sympathetic though they are to Rushdie's politics, believe his view to be profoundly wrong, suggesting *The Raj Quartet* marks precisely the beginnings of a historical understanding of the centrality of India to contemporary English culture which Rushdie himself calls for (Moore 5–6, 138–39, 163, and 165–66). Indeed earlier Tariq Ali had presented Scott as "the main forebear" of Rushdie's own *Midnight's Children* ("*Midnight's Children*" 88).

This cannot be the place to resolve this controversy, a job which would require close and lengthy textual exegesis. My purpose is of a different order, reflecting more on the subjective transformation of Scott himself. Even so, a few key points are relevant. At a formal level, at the highest point of abstraction, Rushdie is obviously right: no account of the destruction of the Raj which dwells in such obsessional detail on the emotional complexities of the white elite—first pulling the white protagonists this way, then that—can possibly serve as an adequate historical explanation of this momentous event. And when Rushdie insists that the form of the novel itself militates against the deconstruction of ethnocentrism he may, again formally, be half right—and we have the evidence of Rushdie's own novels as a powerful alternative. But if the project is more modest—not a full-scale explanation of this epochal historical transformation, but a critical, at times angered, exploration of the mental world of white imperial England—then there is every reason to engage with Scott. In any case, there may be need to elaborate a historical take on this, which would require asking not whether Scott was right or wrong but what possibilities existed within English culture for there to be generated—from within itself—a public critique of its own ethnocentrism.[3]

In fact, the narrative construction of the novels—albeit not the television program—is extraordinarily complex, giving range to a plurality of different voices. If there is a privileging of white over black on the level of structure and form, it is not without ambivalence. Nor are the colonized unrepresented. The articulation of a colonized voice, clearly, is deeply problematic and an issue of contention. But to take one example, the emphasis placed by Scott in the structure of his narrative on Subhas Chandra Bose, whose determination to expel the British led him to create an army to fight alongside the Imperial Japanese forces, highlighted a dimension of the anticolonial movement which—within the official mind of the Raj—remained all but unspeakable.

The core of the novel lies in the figure of Daphne Manners who—in the midst of the August 1942 Quit India campaign—first falls in love with a young Indian man and subsequently is raped in the ominously named Bibighar Gardens. The reverberations from these events, interweaving public and private, run through the sequence of novels. However, in narrative form the various reconstructions of these initiating events dominate the succeeding architecture of the *Quartet*, in which conflicting personal viewpoints, official documents, letters and diaries, and retrospective memories all serve to highlight not only differing perceptions of the white mentality—from diehard to anticolonial— but more importantly, begin to undercut the certainties of the white vision: the narrative opens the possibilities for the relativization of "white" itself.

More particularly, in his fiction Scott possessed an unusually acute sense of the imperatives of white masculinity, or rather of that form of white masculinity which has coalesced in imperial history in the intoxicating figure of "the white man." The elevation of white ethnicity, as essentially a superior form, coupled to an unambivalently forceful conception of active manhood, appears to have cohered as a distinctive, historically specific system of masculine identity in the 1850s and 1860s: this is the evidence in Britain at any rate.[4] Of course there now exists an entire theoretical literature which, though less concerned with conjunctural change, in its investigations of the phallocentric structuring of European rationalism confirms the essentials of such an approach. Scott, I believe, is particularly skilled at uncovering the understated, apparently effortless and benign practices of the masterful, masculine authority of the white elite and in showing the micro-relations of power to be, not contingent, but functioning as a complex system.[5] Many of the dominant voices in the narrative are feminine and—*pace* Rushdie—in form and structure these feminine perceptions of the Raj are at one remove from the conventional masculine representations of the public sphere of administration and politics, allowing an unusual perspective to emerge.[6] The voices most deeply hostile to racial contempt and to the whole cultural apparatus of the Raj are generally female, drawing especially from those women who as spinsters or widows were excluded from the inner culture of the white power elite: it is a view of the colonizers, but of those who within the ruling institutions were effectively powerless. Scott's frequent use of the internal monologue—the inchoate ramblings of the everyday, the fantasized confessions to imagined interlocutors and so on—works to disrupt the highly rationalized masculine identities constructed for public authority; and there are moments of increasing crisis in the sequence of novels when strategic female characters dramatize this antagonism, irrupting into open conflict with the public codes of rational conduct and convention. This is not to suggest that Scott's women protagonists, by virtue of their femininity, possess an instinctive critique of the imperial project.[7] It simply points to the centrality of the discourse of femininity in deconstructing the given codes of the white Englishman, remembering, however—as Scott himself did—the part played by women "in the Englishman's image of himself" (Moore 158).

There is too—necessarily—the question of history. As I see it, Scott was far removed from the quartermaster conception of history, exulting in the iconography of the military, and had no time for cashing in on the nostalgia for the Raj; on the contrary, he was alive to the complexity of relations between past and present, and to the combination of historical times constituting any specific conjuncture. He himself had arrived in India as a junior officer in February 1943, with no knowledge of India and little curiosity, and finally left when his military service came to an end in June 1946. In other words he had no experience of the Raj except in its final moments of disintegration, the implosion of the Quit India campaign, and the imminence of the Japanese invasion having already signaled the end of British rule. More significantly he didn't embark upon the tetralogy until the early sixties, the first volume appearing in 1966. Indeed at the height of the public controversy about Scott there was virtually no recognition of the fact that the novels themselves were largely set in 1964, an unnamed traveler or narrator endeavoring to uncover the events of 1942 and their various repercussions. Thus not only is it the case that Scott's only personal engagement with the Raj was at the moment of its collapse; it should also be remembered that Scott was writing the novels in the aftermath of decolonization. Dien Bien Phu, Bandung, civil rights, Algeria, the Congo—all had already forced their way into the imagination of the declining colonial powers. And in the domestic frame, the reenactment of the primal colonial encounter—in this instance, however, within the white homeland of the metropolis itself—had already advanced, effectively producing a new, radical Right which was to break into the open during that "other 68" of Enoch Powell.

In this reading, *The Raj Quartet* appears not as another installment of a bankrupt attempt to retrieve the imperatives of Englishness, desperate to concoct an antidote to the end of Empire, but as precisely the reverse: an early, faltering, uneven, and contradictory bid to think through historically the enormity of these epochal changes. There is a case for viewing Scott as white England's first novelist of decolonization.

Patently, this is not an unambiguous formulation, for it goes back to the question of the capacities of white England to create such a narrative and to decolonize its own national culture. In this, for Scott, the issue of Powellism was not a contingent political factor but perhaps the central dynamic confronting him, and this clearly registers in the novels themselves. In this sense the novels are about the cultural and psychic interplay of buried historical times and the emerging structures of white racial fear: 1857 (the "Mutiny"), 1919 (the Amritsar massacre), and 1942 (the anticolonial Quit India campaign) are all present for Scott as more or less active historical determinants in the making of the metropolitan radical Right and of the intensely re-racialized idea of England which cohered in Powell's 1968.[8] In his preliminary notes for the second volume Scott referred to the "ghost of transference to the days of the Mutiny" (Moore 75). The scene of Daphne Manners's rape—the Bibighar Gardens—explicitly references the Bibighar massacre of white women and children at Cawnpore in 1857, while Daphne Manners herself is a clear reconfiguration of Marcella Sherwood, the Englishwoman assaulted at Amritsar in 1919. The echoes of this attack at Amritsar, dominated by the memory of the slaughter at Jallianwallah Bargh, also required Scott, effectively, to rewrite Forster's *A Passage to India*—the structural links between Daphne Manners and Adela Quested are evident—for his own times.

On the one hand Scott himself despaired at the ignorance and lack of interest of the English about their own history and about the histories of those they had colonized, and he never wavered from the belief that it was in India that "the British came to the end of themselves" (*Day* 3; *Appointment* 48). A recuperation and redeployment of the appropriate history would serve to lift this national amnesia and free the culture from the incubus of its past. On the other hand there may be evidence that he was wary of the rationalist underpinnings of such a strategy. In the earliest moments of drafting the *Quartet* he talked of a "dangerous racial memory" released by the defeat of colonialism; by the time the project was completed, in 1975, he was citing racism as the dominating force in the contemporary world (*Appointment* 31, 145). However, the image which first produced the idea for the book—a young woman fleeing through the night—came to him "in the dark of a restless, sleepless night" (*Appointment* 60), just as in the novels themselves the memory of Amritsar is most forceful in the person of Mabel Layton, though locked in her unconscious and only ever half-articulated in the disturbed murmurings of her sleep.[9] Without pushing the point too far, Scott seems to have been aware that the processes inscribed in the "repairing" of social memory require a historical reconstruction which is both complex in the grasp of the active if repressed functioning of the past in the present and which is sufficiently alert to the coming of a crisis or emergency. Benjamin's sixth thesis on his *Philosophy of History* comes to mind: "To articulate the past historically . . . means to seize hold of a memory as it flashes up at a moment of danger" (257). As Scott himself implied, the "memory" was the repressed memory of English colonialism, the "moment of danger" the recoding of postcolonial England as belligerently white.

Quite simply, however, the paradox for Scott was that, as he saw it at least, there was no language available through which this past could be articulated, save that which had already been discredited by its complicity with the colonial project. He understood well enough that he was caught in the "crisis of liberal humanism," a system of thought, he suggested, which had dominated Europe from the Renaissance to the moment of decolonization, but which had—whatever other virtues it might boast—functioned as an impetus and justification for Empire and racial subjugation. So profound was this intellectual crisis, he believed, that "[w]e're no longer certain what a human being is" (*Appointment* 48-49). *Aficionados* of cultural theory won't need the connection to be made: in an intuitive, empirical idiom, Scott prefigured here—with perhaps a telling reluctance—a defining theme in contemporary critiques of Eurocentrism.

To say this, however, is not to play a game of vindicating Scott on grounds of superior political correctness: as we shall see, this could not be done. What is more interesting is to try to understand how he himself remained a prisoner of his own past—this issue, after all, lies at the core of his novels—caught by an inability to think his way out of his own historical predicament.

To do this it is necessary to return to Powell. There is a character in *The Raj Quartet*, a policeman by the name of Merrick, who is—to use, for a moment, the vernacular—an evil bastard. At the moment of the uprising in August 1942 it is he who most fully represents the urge to wreak vengeance on the colonized, apportioning systematic humiliation in the desire to reconfirm, in the psyche of the white rulers, racial superiority. He is, in 1942, the continuation of the white psychopathology of 1857 and 1919. While the bulk of the other leading white Englishmen are politically passive, caught in a state of mental paralysis, Merrick assumes the mantle of the colonial white man, and is commensurately active. He despises those colonials around him, identifying both an essential loss of masculinity and a loss of the will to rule. According to Scott, the character "believes there aren't many real white men left" (Spurling 364). The conditions for Merrick's intransigent commitment to the imperial codes of the white man derive, above all else, from class: his origins do not lie in the families of the traditional colonial elite but in the dispossessed lower-middle class of provincial England. The irony, of course, is that he takes it upon himself to save the ruins of colonial England even if this demands the destruction of old upper-class England itself: if the nation has abdicated its will to govern, he must take over in the name of the nation, even if his mere presence destroys the idealized civilization of the past (see Scott, *Day* 409 and *Division* 209). The connection between this fictional character and Powell is all too clear—Powell's radical conservatism, desperate to destroy in order to conserve; his determination to "save India," while the traditional elite languished, tossed from one crisis to the next;[10] and above all, his invocation of the white soul of the nation: all have their fictional counterparts in Merrick.[11]

Although Scott attempted to construct Merrick in as human a manner as possible, there is little doubt that he is the villain. There is little doubt also that Scott's own embattled liberal sentiments find fullest expression in the appropriately feminine character of Sarah Layton and the gentle, skeptical historian Guy Perron. Extra-textual corroboration is not hard to find. He made his own view of the Conservative party clear enough, for example, in a letter written during the general election of 1964, insisting that "behind Toryism is the old dream of master-race stuff" (Moore 72). Yet the limitations of reading the novels in this way are readily apparent, for the fictionalized character of Merrick was also necessarily a product of Scott's fantasies, and to some degree, consciously or unconsciously, must have functioned as a projection of his own interior anxieties. Indeed, in recognizing the less conveniently articulated, demoniac drive of European liberal civilization and appreciating too his own ethnic history, Scott was more aware than some of his critics of the symmetry between his own identity as a "white man"—I mean this in its discursive register—and his own fictionalized creation of the barbaric Merrick.

But this is where the issue gets complicated. The founding image for the novels, the young woman running through the darkness, became linked, in Scott's mind, to the case of Marcella Sherwood and to the racialized fear of the colonized. But given the customary overloading of the construct of white womanhood in the imperial imagination—always prey to assault by subjugated blacks—this is far from an innocent historical image and, as Rushdie insisted, the rape of a white woman can hardly serve as a way of understanding the essentials of the colonial relation. The grounds for Scott making this link, however, derived from a catastrophic personal episode in which he not only experienced himself with extraordinary intensity as white but felt compelled to retreat into his white persona, fully appreciating the racist consequences of his actions. The event occurred on Scott's second visit to India, early in 1964, when he traveled to an isolated village in Andhra Pradesh in order to stay with a wartime companion from the army, an Indian and a subordinate. He subsequently related how this trip of 1964 "sparked off a story set in 1942"—the narrative of *The Raj Quartet* (Moore 72). He recounted the details of the 1964 experience on a number of occasions, once—significantly—in a talk on Powell in which, interwoven with a denunciation of all Powell stood for, Scott stated with unnerving candor: "India always did, still does and probably always will bring out the Enoch in me" (*Appointment* 95).

His own account of the 1964 experience communicates a process of intense, psychic dislocation. He entered a culture in which his metropolitan bearings had no place and yet where he was positioned as the historic *sahib*: he was offered all the material privileges the village could muster (which, to him, were precious few) and expected to organize a tour of inspection. However, this very process of interpellation also triggered the dialectics of colonialism, in which excessive deference and mimicry served to unsettle his authority, inflicting on him, he felt, successive humiliations and instilling in him a fierce, irrational brew of fear, hate, and contempt. The relentless vigilance under which he was placed—always watched, even, to his horror, when his bowels were exploding with dysentery—forced him, as he saw it, to become the ill-tempered colonial, metaphorically transmogrifying into Merrick. Just as the ambivalence of Orwell's white authority impelled him to enact his superiority in the ridiculous but deadly serious pantomime of shooting an elephant, so Scott felt himself both authoritative and a prisoner, his whiteness both the cause of his indignity and his only refuge. His collapse was complete, a fetishistic obsession with his suitcase his only hold on his erstwhile reality. "I longed to see another white face, and to get back into my own white skin" (*Appointment* 102).[12] Amid a plethora of childishly unconvincing excuses he made a desperate escape, returning ashamed to the known terrain of Hyderabad and its dull compulsion of the familiar. In retrospect Scott could not come to terms with "my ridiculous irrational fears, my utter dependence upon the amenities of my own kind of civilization." The whole experience proved "a severe strain on my civilized liberal instincts," leading him better to appreciate "the physical and emotional impulses that had always prompted the British in India to sequester themselves in clubs and messes and forts, to preserve, sometimes to the point of absurdity, their own English middle-class way of life" (*Appointment* 103).

There are a number of plausible readings of this event. One can legitimately take offense at Scott's identification with Powellism, at his coy, knowing familiarity with "Enoch," and conclude that from such a perspective no deconstruction of "white" is conceivable. With this reading we would be back with Rushdie and the case would be closed. Undoubtedly this interpretation possesses a truth, and there are moments when it carries an irrefutable conviction. But in the end I am not convinced. To concentrate only on the *sahib* complex without taking into account the shame and subjective disturbance, to discount the bewilderment with which Scott sees himself come to mirror all he despises in racial arrogance, is to tell only part of the story. A more productive approach would be to locate Scott not simply as the continuator of a colonial recidivism but as representative of a different, more intangible, and complex history: whiteness in crisis.

Perhaps this is too grandiloquent a claim: certainly, it cannot be substantiated fully here. But I think it the only way to explain Scott's deliberate if uneasy exploration of the category white: he takes white as neither given nor an unambivalent signifier of civilization. It is, precisely, a problem. Here the contrast with Forster, for example, is marked. Paul Scott became predictably irritated every time he was compared to Forster, for the comparison often rested on an unthinkingly simple perception of content and hardly at all on aesthetic strategy or form. But while Forster, in the aftermath of Amritsar, was skeptical of the civilizing mission of the Empire, his imagination stopped short of a critique of white ethnicity: indeed for all his debunking of the colonial English, the certitudes of white subjectivity remained in place. In *The Raj Quartet*, on the other hand—especially in the third volume, *The Towers of Silence*, in which the Japanese threaten Imphal and the crisis of the Raj quickens page by page—not only is the narrative constituted by the irruption of the feminine/private, breaking into and disrupting the masculine public sphere, but also leading white protagonists themselves become unhinged. Teddy Bingham, for example, brings about his own destruction simply because he lacks the wits to question the protocols of Old England while his wife, Susan Layton, enters protracted, painful mental decline. Trapped in their own history, they have nowhere to turn.

But to talk of a crisis in white ethnicity is, in historical terms, probably to say nothing more than that the colonial epoch was drawing to its dreadful finale. This would comprise the Bandung version of history, for it was at the Bandung Conference of 1955 that the newly emergent Third World would adopt the "official" viewpoint that the civilization of the white man was coming to an end. In this respect the centrality of Powellism and of kindred racial discourses are once more of significance, for they too can be seen as one white resolution to the global crisis of white authority. Indeed, the parallel experiences of Powell and Scott in India—their periods of military duties virtually overlapping, their shared exclusion from the culture of the traditional colonial elite, their common love for India—may, despite their divergent political trajectories, prove to be relevant, providing each with a peculiarly intense conception of what it was to be a white Englishman. Powell, possessed by a recharged conception of white England, was instrumental in constructing the myth of the exclusive homeland. Scott, caught at the very center of his being by contending strategies for white ethnicity, cautiously endeavored to settle accounts with history and peer nervously into the future.

But it can't quite be left there. A slight turn in angle is necessary, shifting the focus away from ethnicity to gender and sexuality, from the contentions about colonial India to the domestic imperatives of suburban London, and from the public world of politics and literary reputation to the private sphere of home. Above all we need to get an idea of the extraordinary *isolation* Scott inflicted upon himself, and to see that if his whiteness proved at times perplexing, for most of his adult life his sense of his own masculinity—running on a constant current of high-voltage imperiousness—provided him with a desperate, ultimately destructive grip on his own destiny.

Home, for Scott as a young boy, was a respectable suburb of North London, his house a small, semi-detached red brick villa with white-painted bow windows, a fancy porch, and a minute front garden complete with crazy-paving path. It was a cultural world steeped in the unspoken hierarchies of social distinction, yet it was only by seeing the Raj at work that Scott was able to understand the politely bigoted niceties of England. "When I lived in Southgate I knew nothing of India. Returning, I see images of India everywhere . . . the maidan, the club, the cantonment, the governor's residence. Only the names were different." To this degree, he claimed, "India was *never* a surprise to me" (Spurling 3–4). As an adolescent and young man he departed from the social conventions pressing in on him by appropriating the essentials of a Wildean masquerade, spinning a glamorous identity as poet and aesthete.[13] It seems very likely that during this period he had a number of homosexual encounters. At the same time he gravitated to a more starkly conventional existence, at least during the weekday, as an accountant. When war came, eventually he was called up and posted to a training camp in Devonshire. While there he clearly underwent some kind of emotional and sexual crisis which he only referred to later in the most cryptic of terms. His biographer, drawing from private letters and discussions with those who knew him, concludes that the most probable explanation is that Scott's homosexuality was discovered by a colleague or senior officer, and he was threatened with blackmail. Whatever the truth of the matter, his provocatively camp pastiche of a feminized masculinity never reappeared: what did emerge in its place was a ruthlessly instrumental conception of the writer, in which the playfulness of masquerade came to be subsumed by a much more conventional, authoritative masculinity.

On returning from India after the war he set up home with his new wife—whom he had met while posted in Devon—in a suburb of North London close to where he had grown up. Two daughters were born. He returned to accountancy, in the middle fifties became a literary agent, and then eventually dedicated himself full-time to writing. He gained a reputation for being unfailingly gentlemanly in his professional life and for exceptional charm, courtesy, and solicitousness among friends. He had a little family salon and, for the girls, some cats.

The domestic realities, however, belie these images of family harmony. Unknown to even his closest friends, for all his writing life Scott was given to ferociously serious drinking—a couple of bottles of gin or vodka by the early part of the day—accompanied by an intake of nicotine which by no stretch of the imagination could be accounted modest. As the pages of his manuscript for the *Quartet* amassed, his isolation and withdrawal from his family grew to be all but total. His wife, although receiving little social recognition as a writer, produced novels in the kitchen while acting as Scott's paid secretary—until the moment he embarked upon *The Raj Quartet*, when her capacities dwindled. In the midst of her husband's literary project, when the domestic crisis grew manic and apparently inescapable, she suffered a terrifying succession of serious domestic accidents. Gradually Paul, his wife, Penny, and their younger daughter, Sally, were caught in a grotesque, destructive symbiosis—"like a dance of death between the three of us," as Sally Scott imagined it (Spurling 350). Paul and Sally alternated suicide attempts, summoning a grisly nighttime succession of ambulances and police cars. For twelve years his wife kept a bag packed, ready for her departure: when the moment came she fled without it, heading straight for Erin Pizzey's women's refuge at Chiswick. At the same time Sally was in therapy with R. D. Laing. When eventually Paul Scott was to read his wife's affidavit he did so with horror and disbelief, commenting to his daughter: "But if this is true, I must have been a monster" (Spurling 350).

Clearly, emotionally and physically, Scott self-destructed and came close to destroying those around him. If his literary work does mark one of white England's earliest epics of decolonization, then the domestic conditions of its production deserve consideration, for his critique of the colonial order was predicated on an understanding of the centrality of gendered identities to the mission of Empire. The masculine codes of authority underpinning the power of the colonial white man were, as Scott presented it in his fiction, inseparable from the colonial order itself—just as terror in the home exemplified a different facet of assertive manhood. No symmetry is at work here, with the public and the private, the colonial and the gendered, neatly falling into place. Without doubt the self-destructive drive of Scott's life as a writer possessed a multitude of causes which now are unknowable. Even so, in trying to make sense of it, there would be reason to take into account his denial of a more emotionally accommodating masculinity and the complex, contradictory effects of recognizing white as historical construct rather than transcendent signifier. To suggest that recourse to the most elemental imperatives of masculinity was a function of a crisis in his own ethnic identity would be too reductive a conclusion. But there is a sense in which Scott's extreme isolation resulted from a recognition of the degree to which he had become trapped by his own history, able in his imagination to explore the issues of race and nation, class and gender, but incapable of resolving them in his own life. From discussion of the emotional and psychic experiences of this one individual, no general theoretical conclusions can emerge. But the image remains: the lonely Englishman, who glimpsed the enormity of the history which produced him, and brought his own private world tumbling down.

Notes

This is a revised version of an article which originally appeared in *New Formations* 17 (1992) under the title "An Englishman Abroad . . . and at Home: The Case of Paul Scott." This version is more explicitly concerned with the question of identities. I am grateful to Angelika Bammer for her encouragement.

1. An important theoretical precursor to this work on identity can be found in Rose.

2. See also a different version of this essay in the *Observer* 8 May 1984. See too Rushdie's "New Empire." On Lean's *A Passage to India*, a far too indulgent view can be found in Annan.

3. On the historical reconstruction of British discourses of India, old but commendable is *Delusions and Discoveries* by Benita Parry, whom I admire and Scott despised (see Moore 130); and representative of the post-Said/Spivak boom, sustained in its argumentation, Suleri.

4. For suggestive explorations, emphasizing the centrality of Carlyle in fashioning this new organization of imperial manhood, see especially Catherine Hall; and Clarke.

5. A sympathetic feminist reading of Scott appears in Cocks 232.

6. However a fine involution of the conventional voice of public authority is represented in Carritt.

7. Such a notion does have contemporary adherents: see, for example, Brownfoot.

8. In his notebook of 19 June 1968 Scott made the historical link between Powell and Amritsar (Spurling 343).

9. For the linking of the novel's founding image to Jallianwallah Bargh, see *Appointment* 56–57 and 64.

10. Unimpeachable confirmation of this in the historiography can be found in Owen.

11. Tariq Ali was, I think, the first and the most convincing proponent of this position ("English Novels and India"); see Moore 139.

12. In *Staying On*, Scott projects this craving onto Lucy Tusker who perceives an urgent need to return "into my own white skin which . . . I have felt to be increasingly incapa-

ble of containing me, let alone acting as defensive armour" (111). There are predictable but significant echoes of Conrad here: "Things out east were made easy for white men. That was all right. The difficulty was to go on keeping white . . . " (*Shadow Line* 219).

13. For a wonderful approach, see Horne.

Works Cited

Ali, Tariq. "English Novels and India." History workshop seminar. London, June 1984.
———. "*Midnight's Children.*" *New Left Review* 136 (1982): 87–95.
Annan, Noel. "The Unmysterious East." *New York Review of Books* 17 Jan. 1985.
Benjamin, Walter. "Theses on the Philosophy of History." *Illuminations*. Trans. Harry Zohn. London: Fontana, 1973. 255–66.
Brownfoot, Janice. "Sisters under the Skin: Imperialism and the Emancipation of Women in Malaya, 1891–1941." *Making Imperial Mentalities: Socialization and British Imperialism*. Ed. J. A. Mangan. Manchester: Manchester UP, 1990. 46–73.
Carritt, Michael. *A Mole in the Crown*. Hove: Michael Carritt, 1985.
Clarke, Norma. "Strenuous Idleness: Thomas Carlyle and the Man of Letters as Hero." *Manful Assertions: Masculinities in Britain since 1800*. Ed. Michael Roper and John Tosh. London: Routledge, 1991. 25–43.
Cocks, Joan. *The Oppositional Imagination: Feminism, Critique and Political Theory*. London: Routledge, 1989.
Conrad, Joseph. *The Shadow Line. The Nigger of the "Narcissus," Typhoon and the Shadow Line*. London: Everyman, 1967.
Freud, Sigmund. *The Interpretation of Dreams*. Trans. James Strachey. Harmondsworth: Penguin, 1984.
Hall, Catherine. "The Economy of Intellectual Prestige: Thomas Carlyle, John Stuart Mill and the Case of Governor Eyre." *Cultural Critique* 12 (1989): 87–101.
Hall, Stuart. "Minimal Selves." *ICA Documents 6*. London: ICA, 1987. 44–48.
Hitchens, Christopher. "A Sense of Mission: *The Raj Quartet*." *Prepared for the Worst: Selected Essays and Minority Reports*. London: Chatto, 1989. 185–97.
Horne, Peter. "The Gay Bricoleur: The Aesthetics of Masquerade." *England and Modernity*. Ed. Mica Nava and Alan O'Shea. London: Routledge, forthcoming.
ICA Documents 6: Identity. London: ICA, 1987.
ICA Documents 7: Black Film, British Cinema. London: ICA, 1988.
Moore, Robin. *Paul Scott's Raj*. London: Heinemann, 1990.
Owen, Nicholas. " 'Responsibility without Power': The Attlee Government and the End of British Rule in India." *The Attlee Years*. Ed. Nick Tiratsoo. London: Pinter, 1991. 167–89.
Parry, Benita. *Delusions and Discoveries: Studies in the British Imagination, 1880–1930*. London: Lane, 1972.
Rose, Jaqueline. "Femininity and Its Discontents." *Sexuality in the Field of Vision*. London: Verso, 1986. 134–60.
Rushdie, Salman. "In Good Faith." *Independent on Sunday* 4 Feb. 1990.
———. "The New Empire within Britain." *New Society* 9 Dec. 1982.
———. "Outside the Whale." *Granta* 11 (1984).

Rutherford, Jonathan, ed. *Identity: Community, Culture, Difference.* London: Lawrence, 1990.

Schwarz, Bill. "Travelling Stars." *New Formations* 3 (1987): 96–106.

Scott, Paul. *Day of the Scorpion.* St. Albans: Granada, 1982.

———. *A Division of the Spoils.* London: Granada, 1983.

———. *My Appointment with the Muse: Essays, 1961–75.* London: Heinemann, 1986.

———. *Staying On.* London: Pan, 1989.

Spurling, Hilary. *Paul Scott: A Life.* Hutchinson, 1990.

Suleri, Sara. *The Rhetoric of English India.* Chicago: U of Chicago P, 1992.

11 | An Incomplete Replacing
The White South African Expatriate
Sheila Roberts

SOME YEARS AGO in East Lansing, Michigan, I was standing in line with my teenage son to buy tickets for the film *Under the Volcano*. When it was my turn at the box-office, the clerk, hearing my accent, asked me where I was from. As soon as I said, "South Africa," my son walked away, ashamed as always at any reference to our country. The young woman looked at me with cold curiosity. As she handed me the tickets, she announced that "we" should nuke "that place." Then she used a catch-phrase from the Vietnam war, though she was too young to know where it came from. She said we should turn it into a parking lot.

I took my change. "You want to kill the good people with the bad people?" I asked stupidly.

"Yes."

I experienced then a peculiar low-grade horror: low-grade, because the woman, young and therefore still with the thoughtless ferocity of youth, was irrelevant; horror, because I immediately projected on my inner-eye documentary images of the aftermath of nuclear blasts. The horror floated in me during the opening scenes of the movie in which a dance of skeletons is depicted on the Day of the Dead in Cuernavaca, Mexico. And my son was sitting with his shoulder turned away from me.

My son had been eight years old when we emigrated to the United States in 1977. By the time he was twelve and able to understand the full infamy of South African racism, he grew so ashamed of his South African heritage that he not only began inventing a different past for himself but he expected me not to tell people I was from South Africa. Rather, I should say I was from Britain: my accent would carry the lie. At times I went along with his request if he was with me, particularly if there was not much opportunity for a following conversation in which I would have to fabricate an intricate and unlikely past. Other times I would resist. I didn't like the lie. I was disgusted by the institutionalized racism of the National Party Regime, but I was not disgusted with myself. In my youth and as a university student, I had rebelled against the structures and strictures of apartheid. I had not been racist and had finally left the country in order not to be perforce part of the white hegemonic group. Yet, even as I gave myself these comforts, the niggling thought remained that no one who had been born and raised under apartheid could escape all racist taint. From a certain perspective I was as guilty as the next white South African. All the same, vestiges of guilt were not my immediate problem.

What muddied my peace of mind were the bipartisan responses to a place I was experiencing some months after our arrival. The first rush of excitement at being out of South Africa, and the joyous, almost giddy expansiveness in a new personal and political freedom were followed by a darker mood of self-questioning and a vague fearfulness that a desperate remorse might overtake me. "What have you done?" I would ask myself. But the question could not and still cannot be answered fully. On the one hand, I, a widow, had managed to start a new life for myself and my children away from a country that, in the wake of the Soweto Revolution of 1976, was in a state of unprecedented civil turmoil and violence. I had created safety. I had opened up a future for us of multiple possibilities in this country of vital, flourishing arts, well-established democratic systems, and the space they allocated for dissent. There would be the exploration of new landscapes, the easy access of England and Europe, and, in time, a proudful new identity free of the colonial blight.

Yet I had wrenched us out of established lives in a pleasant house of open, outdoor design under blue skies that seemed to be sunny three hundred days a year. We had left an extended family and a set of friends who were interesting, supportive people and political dissidents like myself. It would take months before I would come to understand the full extent of the self-engineered deprivation, a deprivation that has never fully lessened over the years. My children still speak of missing their favorite aunts and their cousins, of wanting to have grandparents in the flesh and not in dulling memories. We would all, in time, long for the sights, sounds, and smells of the South African landscape. We have all got into the habit of comparing each new piece by its resemblance to parts of South Africa: the play of light and the color of the sand in parts of Spain help clarify memories of the Karroo; the Napa Valley outside San Francisco is so like the wine-growing area of the Cape that we are reduced to sighs and whispers of wonderment. When we saw the Peter Weil movie, "Breaker Morant," we huddled together, telling one another, "That must be outside Pretoria," only to discover that the movie had been filmed in Southern Australia. We all experienced depression in the long winter months. What had I done?

My children had easily acquired American accents but I could not change my speech. When I tried I sounded in my own ears too studied, too mocking. The transformation would have to take place naturally or not at all. And it never did happen. So, even if I had been able to acquire an American sense of self, I would not have been so perceived by others: I would see my foreignness in their eyes in perpetuity. And a small, unrealistic, dreamlike part of me would repeatedly suggest that the move here was merely temporary. We were

all going back some day. I needed to retain a mental and idiomatic prepared-
ness for that re-move.

The idea of returning stayed with me as a consoling, if impossible, escape
through the hard years of my children's teens. I hated the schools they went to,
where disorder seemed normal and the life of the mind the refuge of those who
were unpopular. I hated the violence the other kids inflicted on mine and the
fact that the teachers provided no protection. Nothing could have prepared me
for the widespread, seemingly ineradicable racism of the Midwest; for the
enormous cost (in more ways than one) of living; the tardiness and indifference
of doctors, dentists, and policemen; the aggressive rudeness of some of my own
students; and the factionalism of English departments. Of course trifles loom
large when one is away from home. And these discomforts did bring home to
me what a protected, pseudo-British, middle-class "white" milieu we had en-
joyed in our leafy suburb in South Africa.

From the beginning I was seen by American friends and colleagues as not
only an authority on South Africa but also a representative of the "opposition." I resisted that positioning, partly because it was not exact but also because I wanted to enjoy the lightheadedness of freedom: I wanted to dispel the
sound of political argument, speculation, and indignation that had agitated my
waking and dreaming head since young adulthood. I wanted a truly fresh re-
rebirth. Yet I could not help working against my own desire for the pristine. I
searched each daily paper for news of South Africa first. I ordered and read
more books from South Africa than I had done when I lived there. I was anxious not to miss some crucial information, whether presented factually or in
literature. I could not bear the thought of a final amputation of the last connecting strands. Unbeknown to me the strands were frazzling in any case.

Before leaving South Africa I had published a collection of short stories,
and a novel which had been immediately banned by the Censorboard, a banning that had played a part in my decision to leave South Africa. Almost illogi-
cally, however, that banning infused me with a determination to be read by my
compatriots. Therefore, I continued to send manuscripts to my South African
publisher and short fiction to South African journals. South Africa was still my
subject, my obsession, what other immigrants from repressive regimes have
called "the monkey on the back." When my thoughts did turn to creating an
American setting for my fiction, I rejected the idea largely because of my belief
that the work would not ring true. I also had not incorporated that American
experience deeply imaginatively enough to need to write about it.

During the eighties I published two further novels and another collection
of short stories in South Africa. Then in 1987, my publisher, Adriaan Donker,
told me that he was going to branch out into textbook publishing to survive
the boycotts and sanctions and that he did not believe he could consider a further manuscript from me. It was too difficult to market a book when the

author was out of the country and not available for readings and book-signing events.

What was called for was a re-sighting of literary preoccupation and site. At a conference on South African literature that I attended at Northwestern in October 1987, this need became palpably clear. Several South Africans were invited, some direct from South Africa. During the discussions I became aware that I was finally an outsider. People spoke of trends, movements, and rumors of which I knew nothing. They mentioned books and journals I had not seen publicized and they tossed about names of new writers doing exciting things. I listened, not able to contribute much and feeling strangely uncomfortable with my accent, as if I no longer had the right to sound like a South African. I realized that on my next visit Home, I would be a visitor indeed and not an errant "daughter" as in the past.

Out of the pain and humiliation of this unexpected re-displacement, I asked again that question: what had I done? I could answer it more fully now, though not completely, and was thus led to the second question: why, really, had I done it? These questions sent me into a reexamination of memory as I attempted to retrace my steps to a decision that was clearly going to affect me and my children for the rest of our lives. And within eighteen months my backwards quest was given a new coloration of complex grief and elation by the release of Nelson Mandela and the government's empowerment of the African National Congress. Memories of the combative past decades, years of repression and terror for the black population and ones of fearful political engagement, personal alienation and, paradoxically, self-indulgence for dissident whites returned to me with new definition.

As a graduate student in South Africa in the late sixties, I was involved in anti-apartheid student groups, fringe theatre projects, and multi-ethnic writers' guilds. In alternating states of fear and arrogance, we students availed ourselves of the circumscribed action available to us. Except that we did not realize the full extent of its circumscription. Nor, I realize now, did many of us understand our own pacifism for what it was. And some of us, myself included, did not possess the kind of class analysis that would have inspirited us to situate our behavior within a wider, of necessity volatile, revolutionary praxis. When, in the early seventies, the strategies of black resistance were redefined, we were left isolated and confused. The sense of abandonment, of irrelevance, was the first push I and others felt toward a full, voluntary exile.

But to backtrack: at age fifteen, in high school, I went through what Nadine Gordimer has described as a second birth, the discovery that my ethnicity, my skin color, and my membership of the white hegemonic group was not the natural order of the universe but a cluster of constructs inscribed by language and enforced by lawgivers. I am now putting an intellectual inscription on what was a harsher, more visceral awareness: that we whites were cruel and unjust. But it was a shocking coming-of-age, and South African literature is full of sad and humorous accounts of similar rebirths. For instance, the protagonist, Anna Rousseau, in Menan du Plessis's *A State of Fear* is infused with the sudden belief that she is "the first person ever to recognize the iniquity of apartheid." She goes around "for months with a constant shimmer of indignation inside" her (44). Rian Malan in *My Traitor's Heart* writes comically of his own youthful decision to support "the struggle of the people against the tyranny of the . . . bloody Dutchmen" (39). This included growing his hair long; painting on a concrete embankment the words from a James Brown song "Say It Out Loud, I'm Black and I'm Proud"; buying marijuana from Africans and smoking it with them; and declaring himself a Socialist. He and some friends even made a pilgrimage to Red China's embassy in Botswana, hoping to be recruited, but, as he writes, they were not even invited in for tea (50).

But, more seriously, my own resituation against apartheid and politically to the left-of-center eroded what harmony formerly existed in my interaction as a teenager with my parents, and I know that my experience was not in any way unique. My parents saw dissidence as treachery and interpreted Liberalism as the antechamber to Communism. What we young dissidents found unconscionable were our parents' below-the-belt attacks, attacks that reduced our political preoccupations to an interest in black people that was sexual and perverse. Our resentment at these imputations was stiffened by the conflictual nature of some of our own feelings, feelings derived from how we were conditioned as children. Malan speaks for himself but speaks for me too:

> It was quite clear, even to a little boy, that blacks were violent, and inscrutable, and yet I loved them. It was also clear that they were capable, kind, and generous, and yet I was afraid of them. The paradox was a given in my life, part of the natural order of things. It was only later, when I was old enough to be aware of what was happening around me that the paradox started eating at me. I'd been born into an agony of polarization and I felt I had to commit myself one way or the other. I couldn't just stand there, paralysed by the paradox. (73)

So, rebounding from the paradox, and in tense and heightened states, we would go to clandestine meetings; parties in semi-dark rooms with the curtains drawn; poetry readings at the Christian Institute before it was banned; and home movie showings of proscribed films, always with blacks who had the hardihood and the transport to leave the townships. They had to have passes to break the 10:00 p.m. curfew or they could be arrested. We were safer and being safer were guiltily happy to have this connection, not fully aware of its existential anomalies, and desperate for acceptance as true subversives.

Because from its inception the ANC had advocated multiracialism in its membership, in contradistinction to the Pan African Congress's separatist Africanism, we were encouraged to join it. There was the belief, comforting to us whites, that an all-encompassing movement of protest could be instituted, one transcending race and color-consciousness. We were not wrong: we were merely naive and unwittingly premature in our thinking.

From recent publications such as Julie Frederikse's *The Unbreakable Thread: Non-Racialism in South Africa* and Harold Wolpe's *Race, Class and the Apartheid State* I understand more clearly now that the leadership of the ANC, black and white, were actively interrogating the idea of multiracialism as one that in embryo contained a recognition of the relationship of class to revolution. Texts incorporating such political analyses were not freely available in South Africa in the censored intellectual climate of the sixties. The ANC leadership posited that multiracialism had the potential to supplant various narrow nationalisms in a flexible Socialist alternative. As Robert Fatton points out:

> . . . the nonexclusive character of multiracialism represents a minor term of a dialectical process whereby the simultaneous consciousness of race and the acceptance of interracial unity are the elements negating white supremacy. It is an insufficient element, however, as the full unfolding of the dialectics requires the creation of a society without races and without classes. Accordingly, multiracialism is a transitory means to an ultimate end; it is the vehicle of the potential transformation of African nationalism into genuine socialism. (4)

When the ANC moved to press for the socialist conclusion to this dialectic, there was an outcry from the government and various opposition parties against the ANC for being "communists." Even the then Liberal Party took fright, and we young rank-and-file were put doubly on the defensive against our institutions, our families, and our churches. All we could do was hotly reiterate that we were not Communists; that we advocated peaceful change; and that we believed in the processes of law, parliament, and Western civilization. Our very protests and slogans revealed how trapped we were in the impasse experienced by the *colonisateur refusé* so inimitably explicated by Albert Memmi (22). We refused colonialism yet lived in the smoke-screen of its discourse, and remained in our "camp."

I know that close friendships and associations were formed in the cultural gatherings we organized, but the whites who had the best chance of connecting with blacks at a deeper personal level were those who spoke one of the vernaculars. I am not saying that language was always a barrier to relaxed debate, and the blacks (whether African, Indian, or so-called Colored) all spoke English. Many knew Afrikaans, but few chose to speak it. But what was palpable at almost every mixed gathering was the change of tone, pace, and mood when Africans turned to their own and plunged into an unselfconscious, inflected, cadenced vernacular, their faces reflecting the play of feeling the words occasioned.

Obviously, few of us could have learned "tsotsi-taal," the street argot combining English, Afrikaans, vernaculars, and neologisms, and the means to a bantering, humorous, tough exchange. So those of us who knew no vernacular had to rely on our South African brand of English, an "english" that had already undergone remolding over the decades to bear the burden of Afrikaner Nationalism. However, a peripheral remolding was slowly taking place. Government jargon, words like "Homelands," "Bantustans," "Separate Development," "Relocation," "Détente," were being jeered out of existence. "Tribal" was recognized as derogatory and the generic term "Bantu" as laughable. By the late sixties "African" lost currency for the new political-identificatory term "Black," comprehending all who were not white but excluding government collaborators and stooges who had to retain the insulting term "non-white."

We were learning a lesson as important as the earlier one we had learned as teenagers—that apartheid was not the natural order of the universe—and this was that language was not transparent. Moreover, we learned that language could not be divorced from ideology and myth. (And here I enjoy an engaging if unrealistic thought: that maybe under the new dispensation South Africa might in time modify and expand its "english" into a rich polyglossic mélange able to embody the experience of all ethnicities. What a dialect that would be!)

The Rivonia Trial of the mid-sixties, following police discovery of a large cache of weapons and leading in 1964 to Nelson Mandela being sentenced to life imprisonment, had the effect of disempowering the ANC leadership, black and white. In particular, Mandela's imprisonment left a sense of vacuum and a mood of helplessness among black people and anti-government activists. Previously, the Pan African Congress had been critical of the whites among the ANC leaders, accusing them of formulating effete political strategies and shackling the revolutionary struggle. Yet, in an absurd contradiction, during the Rivonia Trial when information about *Omkhonto we Siswe* (the ANC plan for armed resistance) became public, that very white leadership was seen by the authorities as undisputed instigators of violence. Whites were accused of leading gullible and well-meaning blacks into a disastrous campaign that they would not otherwise have been tempted into. Out of the loss of the ANC leadership and its attendant sense of defeat for the black population, the Black Consciousness movement arose, reaching its full strength in the mid-seventies.

What happened then to the student groups was in miniature as contradictory, it seemed, as what had happened to the white ANC leaders. Although up till then we had been harassed by the police, castigated by the press, and rejected by our families—in other words, partly taken seriously—by the end of the sixties our full irrelevance was brought home to us. We were informed by fellow black students that no further contact between us would be permitted, that if we wanted to talk (and talk is what we wanted, more than action perhaps), we should go and talk to other whites. The pretense of the value of dialogue between black and white had, in this interregnum, come to an end.

I believe that many of us had not till then perceived the paradox of our situation, one even larger than our own mixed feelings. As whites we were inextricably part of the very system we challenged and in intricate ways were protected by. To throw in our lot with black revolutionary groups was to work against the very structures that gave us education and the leisure to indulge in dissension and debate. We *were* prepared to give up that status and privilege, we asserted. But because most of us could not commit ourselves to strategies of violence, we showed that we were, finally, not capable of action commensurate with our goals. Our timidity and squeamishness laid us open to charges of imposturing.

Then in the seventies, student groups which had ceased to be taken seriously by blacks were suddenly taken absurdly seriously by the police, as under the perceived threat of the Black Consciousness Movement, Prime Minister John Vorster moved to excoriate all demonstrators. New existential anomalies were brought clearly before us when peaceful demonstrators from the universities of the Witwatersrand and Cape Town were badly beaten by police in a baton charge in 1973. Formerly, police had merely questioned, watched, or followed white students, or planted spies on the campuses. Now they were attacking openly. Many students were severely injured. But there was no recourse to law, no recompense, only governmental approval of police action, press amusement, and black indifference. In Cape Town, students fleeing from a police charge sought sanctuary in the Anglican Cathedral, only to be followed by officers and beaten in the aisles, the transept, and the sanctuary. Ironies were redoubling upon themselves.

I was not among those beaten by police. By then, discouraged, I had retreated from politics, got married, and was starting a family. I recall the feelings of shock and fear I felt when readings about the attack in the dissident English-language newspaper, followed by that sickly sense of personal relief that I had escaped. I subsequently wondered whether the experience of being bashed on the head and shoulders by a police baton and then dragged by the hair (there were such photographs) into a police wagon would have altered my political perceptions. Would such an experience have hardened me into a stubborn *engagement* and a *je m'en foutiste* indifference to paradoxes, large and small? Of course I shall never know the answer. Some of my friends and acquaintances were hardened; some gave up.

But obviously it had become very difficult for most of us to negotiate the contradictions. Those with Marxist leanings had rejected the idea that the struggle was one of race, and now the very government seemed to be validating that rejection. Yet what we understood Steve Biko and the Black Consciousness Movement to be advocating was the total transformation of the existing system into a black creation with no place for whites. At that time it would have taken more political sophistication than most of us possessed to see that the ultimate aim of a movement such as Black Consciousness must be its own abolition. The logical conclusion of its goals had to be nothing less than a colorblind and classless society. With the achievement of that society, Black Consciousness would annul itself. Probably most of us could not grasp this for the same reasons that many blacks also did not during the brutal and polarized years before the Soweto Revolution, when only hatred was in the air.

So, in those dead-seventies before Soweto exploded into action in 1974, some of us were forced back into the white "laager" where we attempted an uneasy imposturing within the economy while subsisting on the periphery of oppositional political debate. Others withdrew into an American-style countercultural indulgence; some, like me, left the country, while the stubbornly *engagés*, today envied by many of those who left, decided to wait out events.

In the eighties I heard that the Black Consciousness Movement had lost ground to the resurgence of ANC support, and I hear now that large numbers of South African expatriates and exiles are returning Home, or trying to return, some perhaps for the kind of personal reason Rian Malan offers in this address to a putative reader:

> It might be hard for you to understand this, being an outsider, but South Africa holds the souls of its sons and daughters in an almost inescapable grasp. History cast all of us in a strange and gripping drama, but I had deserted the stage. I had no idea what my role was, and felt I would never be whole unless I found out. I would live and die in LA and be buried under a tombstone that read, "He Ran Away." People would ask, who was Malan? Ah, a South African. And what did he stand for? He never really knew. (80–81)

Not really knowing what one stood for is perhaps the lot of many South African *colonisateurs refusés* and willing exiles, and hoping finally to know is the major impulse behind this writing. What I stood for was half-informed and inadequate, an inadequacy that made it possible for me to leave in confusion and then to comfort myself that I had voted "with my feet." Now what I stand for is a sense of loss, and an unending longing. But a decision was made in 1977 that now cannot be unmade. When I do mentally project a full return and not merely a visit to South Africa, I am brought quickly back to a recent complication, which is that my grown children have no intention of re-displacing themselves. When we meet for lunches and dinners and start talking, in our usual way, about the "world," it's the one on the North American continent and not the one at the southern tip of Africa.

What is staring me in the face now is a choice—which is finally, no choice—to resituate myself with no backward glances except those of established memories in this American country. Its multiple political problems should begin to interest me and its varied patterns of life should increasingly form the substance of my dreams and my own fiction and, if I can manage it, my re-invention of myself.

Works Cited

Du Plessis, Menan. *A State of Fear*. Cape Town: David Philip, 1983.

Fatton, Robert, Jr. *Black Consciousness in South Africa*. New York: SUNY P, 1986.

Frederikse, Julie. *The Unbreakable Thread: Non-Racialism in South Africa*. Bloomington: Indiana UP, 1990.

Malan, Rian. *My Traitor's Heart*. London: Bodley Head, 1990.

Memmi, Albert. *The Colonized and the Colonizer*. Boston: Beacon, 1967.

Wolpe, Harold. *Race, Class and the Apartheid State*. London: James Curry, 1988.

12 | Écriture judaïque
Where Are the Jews in Western Discourse?

Susan E. Shapiro

"Figuring Out" the Jews in the West

IN THE DOMINANT discourse(s) of the Christian/West[1] the Jew has been located in a place that defines and fixes "his"[2] identity stereotypically.[3] Both in
explicitly Christian discourse and in discourses derived from and influenced by
it, the Jew has been figured in negative terms as that which lacks legitimacy or
value.[4] This negative figure (the Jew as the "Other" of the Christian/West) has
been embodied in the trope of "the Jew," and it is through this tropic lens that
actual Jews have been seen. For example, the figure of the wandering Jew represented the punishment of the Jew exiled from home, condemned to diasporic
suffering until the second coming (see Anderson; and Dundes and Hasan-
Rokem). The perceived carnality of the "Old Testament" corresponded to the
view of the Jew as overly or deviantly sexual.[5] Taking circumcision as a sign
of exclusivity, Jews were seen as intransigent, stubbornly particular, and particularistic.[6] For continuing to identify and live as Jews, they[7] were represented
as refusing to embrace the "universal" spirituality of Christianity. By extension, this meant failing to become fully assimilated to the universal citizenry
of Man in allegiance to the Nation.[8]

Confined to this trope of "the Jew" as to a ghetto, the ongoing and diverse
histories of Jews and Judaism(s) (not only) in the West have been effaced.[9] This
absence or invisibility has been operative not only in the writing of religious
or "world" history, but in other discourses and disciplines, such as literature
and philosophy, as well. In poststructuralist or postmodern theory, the figure
of the Jew appears in numerous guises. Indeed, as compared, say, to the rather
notable absence of Jews as subjects in postcolonial writing,[10] postmodern discourses would initially seem to better or more adequately provide resources for
articulating Jewish (post-Holocaust) identities.[11]

Postmodern discourse has been read as occasioned by, and as identical
with, post-Holocaust writing. Its form of ruptured and displaced writing has
been regarded as representing, or as being a consequence of, the Shoah and its

shattering of the telos and coherence of the Western subject.[12] While this "disaster" is interpreted as an effect of the Shoah, the Shoah is interpreted as a symptom of a disaster within writing [*écriture*] itself (Blanchot; Jabès). In this way, the subject(s) of postmodernism and post-Holocaust writing are identified and the Holocaust is subsumed under the discourse of postmodernism.[13] The question of the identity of the Jew after the Holocaust, thus, figures consistently in postmodern discourses.

There is yet another way in which Jewish and deconstructive writing have been associated. The undecidability of discourse as evidenced in postmodern writing has been interpreted as midrashic in character (see Handleman; and Hartman and Budick) and Midrash, in turn, has been interpreted through the resources of postmodern theories (see Daniel Boyarin, *Intertextuality*). The term "Midrash" has become a trope that, emptied of its historical and cultural specificity, has come to represent the undecidability of meaning itself.[14] Midrash, thus, has been taken as exemplifying, indeed as identical with, deconstruction, while postmodern discourse has been considered a form of what I here term *écriture judaïque*. The displaced, exiled, catastrophic writing of postmodernism is troped by the Jews as other and vice versa; writing and Jew(daism) have become metonyms of one another.

A third point of contact between Jewish and postmodern discourses is occasioned by the association of post-Holocaust writing and *écriture judaïque*. If the previous two affiliations are considered positive, this last one has often been read negatively. As Sander Gilman has demonstrated, the "damaged" language of the Jews has been troped as evidence of their diseased, pathological nature (*Jewish Self-Hatred* 309–92; *Jew's Body* 10–37). Similarly, the critique of deconstructive writing within the academy has increasingly been framed in terms of health and disease: it is seen as dangerous to the hygiene of Western discourse. While in the early stages of its reception deconstruction was often read as culturally Jewish (by both its adherents and critics), after the de Man and Heidegger controversies, the purported "Jewishness" of this writing has been further complicated and put in question.[15]

While there are several thinkers whose writings bear on this inquiry into contemporary critical resources for articulating Jewish identity/ies, I will focus primarily on the work of Jean-François Lyotard, especially his *Heidegger and "the jews."* Framed in the context of historical anti-Judaism in the West, it is an attempt to write against it. Moreover, written specifically in the context of the controversy over Heidegger's Nazism, Lyotard's work asks how to read (and not read) Heidegger in light of the question of how to represent Jews.[16] Lyotard introduces something new and important into this debate. For he calls attention not only to the fate of actual Jews, but to the tropological construction of "the jews" within the rhetoric and logic of Western discourse(s). According to Lyotard, the problem of "the jews" is the problem of originary or primary repression: the desire of the West to forget the unforgettable, or what he calls the "immemorial."[17]

"Primary repression" refers to the belief that all that is present(ed) to both the unconscious and the conscious mind is already pre-encoded. This means that there is an epistemological limit to what can be known of the self. Because what cannot be known, by definition, can be neither represented nor forgotten, there is also that which cannot be remembered because it cannot, in this sense, be forgotten. It can only be "remembered" as the immemorial, or (as it is also sometimes termed in Lyotard's text, so as to signify its difference from the known/forgotten) the "Forgotten."

Secondary repression is the process by which the forgotten past (however indirectly) is re-presented, for example, in dreams. It makes use of two strategies: effacing and representing. The first—effacing—is an attempt to hide or disguise the particulars of a case; it is not a forgetting. Representing, on the other hand, does not hide or disguise, but puts forth an assertion as fact. In so doing, it "forgets" that this "fact" is both partial and constructed. The denial of this amnesia within representation does not allow for anamnesis, for a "re-membering" of the Forgotten. Primary repression is, thus, forgotten in representation, and it is this lack of memory, this silence, of which Lyotard seeks to remind us in the name of "the jews" and Heidegger, both of whom are taken as differently witnessing the immemorial (see Lyotard, *Heidegger* 11–12, 15, 17–20).

In remembering the Forgotten, then, Lyotard must especially be wary of the dangers of amnesia lurking in every representation. He can do so by an *écriture* that writes against representation, a writing that questions representation by a perpetual dismantling and displacing of its subject. Such a writing is evident in the figure of the *différend*, a shifting term Lyotard treats more extensively in his text of that title.[18] In *Heidegger and "the jews,"* the shifting term, the displaced *écriture*, is "the jews."[19] "The jews" in this text, like primary repression, are figured in terms of an "unsettling strangeness" (13) a "stranger in the house" (17). They are, thus, figured as the *unheimlich*, the "uncanny," the "un-homey."[20]

> *"The jews" are the irremissible in the West's movement of remission and pardon. They are what cannot be domesticated in the obsession to dominate, in the compulsion to control domain, in the passion for empire, recurrent ever since Hellenistic Greece and Christian Rome. "The jews," never at home wherever they are, cannot be integrated, converted, or expelled. They are also always away from home when they are at home, in their so-called own tradition, because it includes exodus as its beginning, excision, impropriety, and respect for the forgotten. . . . (22; emphasis mine)*

The anti-Semitism of the Occident should not be confused with its xenophobia; rather, anti-Semitism is one of the means of the apparatus of its culture to bind and represent as much as possible—to protect against—the originary terror, actively to forget it. It is the defensive side of its attack mechanisms—Greek science, Roman law and politics, Christian spirituality, and the Enlightenment, the "underside" of Knowledge, of having, of wanting, of hope. One converts the Jews in the Middle Ages, they resist by mental restriction. One expels them during the classical age, they return. One integrates them in the modern era, they persist in their difference. One exterminates them in the twentieth century. (23)

What is most real about real Jews is that Europe, in any case, does not know what to do with them. . . . "The jews" are the object of a dismissal with which Jews, in particular, are afflicted in reality. (3)[21]

"The jews" are "never at home wherever they are. . . . [T]hey are also always away from home when they are at home." They are the *unheimlich*, the trope or figuration of otherness, of primary repression.[22] Thus, the slippage in the text between the two terms, "the jews" and the *real Jews*,[23] marks the movement for Lyotard between primary and secondary repression, between the immemorial and the representation (and thus forgetting) of the Forgotten.

How can we account for this double negation of Jews in Lyotard's text? Is the European writer necessarily an agent of primary repression in which the *unheimlich* Other is made to disappear? Is the attempt not to forget forgetting always doomed to be figured through repression, that is, forgotten in the end? If so, is it not of some consequence how primary repression is figured?

The Rhetorics and Politics of Identification

One way of approaching the question of who are "the jews" and the *real Jews* in Lyotard's text is to trace out its rhetorics of identification. For the question of identification *is* the "Jewish Question."

A figuring of "the jews" frames *Heidegger and "the jews."* Its opening paragraphs establish "the jews" as a construct. It is a construct, however, that is first defined negatively, in terms of what it is not. The quotation marks signify and secure the borders between the rhetorical trope of "the jews" and the historically marked *real Jews*. However, as Lyotard emphasizes, it is *real Jews* who are "afflicted in reality" with the "dismissal" to which "the jews" are subject (3).

In order to further address this "Jewish" question, consider first what Lyotard says in the end-frame of his text, a final meditation on forgetting and its consequences:

Granel reintroduces today, half a century after the Holocaust, the forgetting of what has tried to forget itself through it. He thus seriously misses the debt that is *our* only lot—the lot of forgetting neither that there is the Forgotten nor what horror the spirit is capable of in its headlong madness to make us forget that fact. "Our" lot? Whose lot? It is the lot of this nonpeople of survivors, Jews and non-Jews, called here "the jews," whose Being-together depends not on the authenticity of any primary roots but on that singular debt of interminable anamnesis. . . . The West is thinkable under the order of *mimesis* only if one forgets that a "people" survives within that is not a nation (a nature). Amorphous, indignant, clumsy, involuntary, this people tries to listen to the Forgotten. (94)

It is with this shifting, displaced trope of "the jews" that Lyotard identifies. He throws in his lot with "the jews," this "nonpeople of survivors, Jews and non-Jews." He refers to their lot as "our lot." This is the point in his text where Lyotard's own identification is most in evidence. "The jews" are a "people" (albeit "an amorphous nonpeople") within the West, "not a nation (a nature)."[24]

Lyotard's identification of/with "the jews" becomes evident in his rhetorics of identification, in his shifting use of "us," "they," "we," "them," "I," and "one." *Heidegger and "the jews"* opens with an "I" that defines Lyotard's use of "the jews." They, like the *real Jews*, are referred to as "they" and "them" in the opening paragraphs and chapters.

A telling use of "us" is introduced as well in the first chapter: "How could this [Heidegger's] thought forget and ignore 'the jews' to the point of suppressing and foreclosing to the very end the horrifying (and inane) attempt at exterminating, at making *us* forget forever what, in Europe, reminds *us*, ever since the beginning, that 'there is' the Forgotten?" (4; emphasis mine).

Who is this "us"? It is the European (Christian/Western) subject: the one who must be reminded of the Other, the Forgotten, that which the West would forget, that which has resisted empire "ever since the beginning." This "us" initially is not "the jews," although through the work of anamnesis, the "us" may throw in their lot with "the jews." It may then become "our lot." The "they" and "them" of "the jews" in the beginning of the text may become "our lot" in the end through the work of remembering the immemorial.

Who, then, is the "one" in this text that we find in sentences like: "Here, to fight against forgetting means to fight to remember that *one* forgets as soon as *one* believes, draws conclusions, and holds for certain"? (10; emphasis mine). "One" marks an ambiguous and distanced form of identification. It is a "them/they" that does not become "ours," that will have to be resisted by the "us," that is, Europeans who increasingly remember the Forgotten and, thus, increasingly identify with/as "the jews."

Écriture judaïque and the Writing of Empire

In this rhetoric of identification, where are the actual Jews? They/we[25] cannot be found, although the "conversion" of Europeans to "the jews" can be traced. It finally becomes clear that it is the putting in place of the European, Western subject (Lyotard's "us") as it remembers the immemorial that is the subject of *Heidegger and "the jews."* The terms of identification differently (differingly?) name the split European subject: split between the "one" that forgets the Forgotten and the "us" that remembers it. It is the imperial subject that is Lyotard's subject. "The jews" are European.

But, as I have already suggested, "the jews" are still subject to, as well as subjects of, the West. In some ways, the double or split European subject of "the jews" seems to resemble what Homi Bhabha terms "the 'splitting' of the national subject."[26] However, in contrast to Bhabha's national subject, the category of "the jews" is not a site of resistance, of a "mimicry" that unmasks the imperial subject of the West from *within* its own terms. Bhabha's observation that the national subject refers not only to the "master" but also to the "slave," making the dialectics of power not a matter of reversal, but of hybridity, is an important shift. The participation of the "slave" in the construction of the "master" gives agency to the colonized and oppressed. But in the case of "the jews," there is another masquerade being performed, another form of mimicry and reversal.

The West produces "the jews" as the other side of empire: They are figured as that which is (those who are) outside, even if physically inside, the West. "The jews" thus metonymically refers to all the Others the West created in its multiple acts of making and building empire. As such, the figure of "the jews" seems ready-to-hand for figuring the colonial and postcolonial subject. But at a cost.

> I write "the jews" this way neither out of prudence nor lack of something better. I use lower case to indicate that I am not thinking of a nation. I make it plural to signify that it is neither a figure nor a political (Zionism), religious (Judaism), or philosophical (Jewish philosophy) subject that I put forward under this name. I use quotation marks to avoid confusing these "jews" with real Jews. What is most real about real Jews is that Europe, in any case, does not know what to do with them; Christians demand their conversion; monarchs expel them; republics assimilate them; Nazis exterminate them. "The jews" are the object of a dismissal with which Jews, in particular, are afflicted in reality. (Lyotard, *Heidegger* 3)[27]

In order for the figure of "the jews" to be useful for Lyotard, it must first be purged of its Jewish "particularity." The category of "the jews" need not necessarily contain Jews.[28] Indeed, the nonintrinsically Jewish character of the category of "the jews" is essential for Lyotard (and not only for him).[29] For the symbol or mark of particularity, of exclusivity, in the West has been predominantly the Jews.[30] Displacing Jewish identity, thus, becomes a way of deconstructing particularity as such.

What should be clear from this polarity between "the jews" and the *real Jews* is that in neither case are the lives, experiences, beliefs, and discourses of Jews themselves expressed. So, for Jews, there is no difference in identifying with either "the jews" or the *real Jews*. Not only are the images of, descriptions of, and attitudes toward "the jews" drawn from the situation of the Jew in (and from the perspective of) the European, Christian/West, but the prevailing understanding of the *real Jews* is informed by these same, negatively defined, images, descriptions, and attitudes.

The problem here is twofold. First, by excluding as particularistic the *real Jews* from the term, "the jews," Lyotard represses and effaces an important aspect of the trope of the Jew(s) in the West that has figured them as stubbornly Other and inassimilable. Second, by representing the *real Jews* as particular(istic) and excluding them from the category of "the jews," Lyotard is purifying that category and, in so doing, ironically and terribly repeating the gesture with which the Jews have historically been separated from the West: marginalized, oppressed, excluded. He is forgetting the Forgotten (through effacement and representation) as he claims Heidegger did in maintaining silence about the Jews and the Shoah, even after 1945. As in the dialectics of emancipation in France after 1778 and in Germany in the nineteenth century where the Jews could be citizens only as "men" but not as Jews, so too in Lyotard's text they could be accepted into the category of "the jews" only on the condition that no traces of their particularity as Jews (as opposed to as "jews") remain:

> And the Jews (without quotation marks) are not less, but rather more exposed than others (they are "stiff necked") to forgetting the unnameable. Every Jew is a bad "jew," a bad witness to what cannot be represented, just like all texts fail to reinscribe what has not been inscribed. (81)

The *real Jew* is here figured as the opposite of "the jew," a "bad witness to what cannot be represented." The Jews, in other words, themselves forget "the jews"; they are "stiff necked" and, thus, "more exposed than others . . . to forgetting the unnameable." This splitting between good "jews" and bad "jews" (that is, *real Jews*) perniciously repeats the negative tropology of Jews in the West. In Lyotard's categories, Jews are the worst representations and representatives of "the jews," just as the stiff-necked Jews of the Old Testament, in their literalistic, carnal hermeneutics, were not the truest interpreters of the book they had inherited. Instead, the Jews, in Christian tropology and political practices, were superseded and replaced by the new chosen people, the Christians, who could interpret the spirit of the Hebrew Bible, the Torah, properly as the "Old Testament." "Christians" (like "the jews") are nonparticularistic, defined as such by their putative "universal" inclusiveness.

This universalism, however, may be regarded as a manifestation of empire. Indeed, the very category of "the jews," instead of including the marginal(ized), constructs its categories by repeating a very ancient dialectic of empire in the West. For the Jews (like Lyotard's *real Jews*) are precisely those who must be excluded from the "new covenant" of Christianity and the "social contract" of emancipation. Thus, Jews (like *real Jews*) bear the negative weight of the West's imperial repression of "the particular," whereas "the jews" (predicated upon the exclusion of the "particularistic") represents the putatively "inclusive" category of the Others of the West.

Thus, while Lyotard's project seems to be an unmasking of the dialectics of empire in the troping of "the jews" as the Other of/in the West, it in fact continues the negative process of forgetting and silencing the Jews through the double strategies of effacement/representation. In Lyotard's text, the work of empire continues. Certain negative situations and experiences of the Jews in the West—diaspora, marginalization, oppression, exclusion, nonrepresentation—are attached to "the jews" and valorized. However, these newly positive figurations are then dialectically opposed in Lyotard's text to many of the old negative stereotypes of the *real Jews*: stiff-necked, particularistic, exclusivistic, badly representing the unrepresentable.

The Jewish question, the "problem" of the situation of the Jews in the West, thus, is reinstated in *Heidegger and "the jews"* through the splitting between "the jews" and *real Jews*. The trope of "the jews" takes the place of the universal Christian, the latest incarnation of the regulative (if not legislative) subject of the West. For it is not the Jew who writes *écriture judaïque* in Lyotard's text but, rather, the European subject who writes this form of post-identity as "the jews."

Who Speaks for/as the Jews?

Bhabha suggests that "that boundary that secures the *cohesive* limits of the western nation may imperceptibly turn into a contentious *internal* liminality that provides a place from which to speak both of, and as, the minority, the exilic, the marginal, and the emergent."[31] He is not, however, suggesting that the European subject is the one who not only "speak(s) both of, and as" (DissemiNation 300), but also *for* the minority; rather, he proposes it is the exilic, the marginal, the minority, and the emergent who find through this internal liminality a place from which to speak *within* the West in a (post)colonial situation. Within Lyotard's text, there is no place for Jews to speak. The "location" of the Jews in his dialectic of "the jews"/*real Jews* is neither to be found in either one of the terms, nor on the boundary between them. The Jews' absence (an old story, indeed) is a necessary condition of Lyotard's very construction of "the jews" as a category. Indeed, as Bhabha notes,

> What does need to be questioned, however, is the *mode of representation of otherness*, which depends crucially on *how* the "west" is deployed within these discourses. . . . Paradoxically, then, cultural otherness functions as the moment of *presence* in a theory of *difference*. The "destiny of non-satisfaction" is fulfilled in the recognition of otherness as a *symbol* (not sign) of the presence of *significance* or *difference*. . . . What is denied is any knowledge of cultural otherness as a differential *sign*, implicated in specific historical and discursive conditions, requiring construction in different practices of reading. The place of otherness is fixed in the west as a subversion of western metaphysics and is finally appropriated by the west as its limit-text, anti-west [in a] . . . process by which forms of racial/cultural/historical otherness have been marginalized in theoretical texts committed to the articulation of *différance, significance*. . . . ("Other" 72–73)

"The jews" becomes a way for the European subject both to critique the (logo)center and identify with/as the margins of the West without changing its terms. It maintains the logic of the West by reducing otherness to a symbol of the limits of the West, its limit-text. As a trope of otherness, "the jews," like exilic figures of diaspora, ironically *contains* the rupturing of Western discourse. This form of writing the Other, *écriture judaïque*, does not signify difference but *différance* within a system opened endlessly (nomadically) internally. It is not ruptured from within or without, opening it to another, an outside; indeed such differences are deferred, erased, effaced. While such strategies of *différance* may certainly be performed in a tone of humility, of epistemological finitude, this *écriture* is also susceptible to a borderless expansion that looks much like another version of empire.

While it is clear that "the jews" is a constructed trope, the constructedness of the category of the *real Jews* is effaced or forgotten. In Lyotard's text, the *real Jews* stand for (re-present) the "real." "The jews" now provides the basis for specifically *European* identification with the margin(al) in the West inasmuch as traditionally negative stereotypes of, for example, the wandering, exiled, diasporic (Jew) are now valorized.

The forgetting in this representation of *real Jews*, Lyotard's failure to place this term as well in quotes, is no mere strategy of marginalization or displacement. Between the positive figuration of "the jews" and the negative figuration of *real Jews* (except insofar as they become "jews," that is, "convert" or assimilate), there is no space left in the West for the intervention of actual Jews in their multiple and conflicting identities. That these are specifically Christian and Western ways of representing Jews, creating "the Jewish problem" or "the question of the Jews," is always/already effaced. The European is never represented to him/herself as specific, located; specificity is only represented as the sign of the parochialism of the *real Jews*.

While Lyotard, certainly, attempts always to deconstruct and displace identity in such a way as to undo the rule of "master narratives" and the oppositional dialectics of identity and difference in the West, he ironically repeats this very dialectic (and one of the West's primary and foundational master narratives) in his rhetoric of identification of/with "the jews." It is always the Jews, as "particularistic," in the dialectics of Christian/Western identity who must be split (Old Testament/New Testament, Old Chosen people/New Chosen people) in the construction of specifically Christian/Western identity. Had Lyotard better been able not to "forget" the historical construction of the Jew(s) in and by the West, he would not, perhaps, have repeated its tropology.

It seems at first that this recognition of the cultural construction of the Jew(s) in the West is precisely what Lyotard is writing. But, instead, he seeks to write his own *écriture judaïque*, his own (re)use of the trope of the Jew as "the jews," now plural, lower case and in quotes. It is a Jewish writing without Jews, much like *écriture feminine* is a writing without women.[32] These strategies of *différance*, however, do not shatter the dialectics of identity in the West or even help us to remember what is forgotten. The Jews are always already "Forgotten." They disappear in, and between, the terms of "the jews"/*real Jews*. The saving grace of "the other within" is an anthem sung by a chorus of post-identity theorists.[33] While there are people relegated to and regulated at the margins of the West, and while there are those who suffer exile and displacement, this European "confession" of *différance* is not adequate; in some ways, it perpetuates and is part of the problem. As Edward Said notes in discussing the massive exiles of this century,

> [A]t most the literature about exile objectifies an anguish and a predicament most people rarely experience at first hand; but to think of the exile informing the literature as beneficially humanistic is to banalize its mutilations, the losses it inflicts on those who suffer them, the muteness with which it responds to any attempt to understand it as "good for us." Is it not true that the views of exile in literature and, moreover, in religion obscure what is truly horrendous: that exile is irredeemably secular and unbearably historical; that it is produced by human beings for other human beings; and that, like death but without death's ultimate mercy, it has torn millions of people from the nourishment of tradition, family and geography? ("Reflections" 357–58)

What, then, are the implications of the treatment of the Jew(s) as the "selected" site of exile and of split, displaced identity in the Christian/West and, more specifically, in Lyotard's postmodern text? What is being "forgotten" here? Is it not the pain, the violence, the irredeemable loss that are effaced in the construction of the category of "the jews"? Who must suffer the dialectics of Christian/Western identity so that it may become "universal" or, in its most recent incarnation, inclusively "post-identified"? Is there a time or space for Jewish identity/ies in this Western tropology of "the jews"/*real Jews*? Lyotard's postmodern discourse may, thus, preserve the ancient economy of identity/difference of the West, now in a more sophisticated form, but with a strangely familiar result: the disappearance, the "forgetting" of the Jews.

When the Jews' exile is taken as a trope—the "wandering Jew" functions as a sign of unredemption and "the jews" as an *unheimlich* symbol of displaced Western identity—a kind of amnesia, a forgetting of pain and violence is "accomplished." A discourse which preserves the always exilic figure of the diasporic Jew in the West further anesthetizes both discourse and memory.[34] The *real Jews*, always already frozen in past time as "Old Testamental" (in Christian time marked as either "B.C." or "A.D."), are treated as fossils or relics. "The jews," however, like "the Other," do not exist in the West and will not, as such, suffer history. The Christian/West has repeatedly made the (for Jews) fatal misidentification of the figure of the Old Testament Jew and actual Jews (obscuring, in the process, the fact that "the Jew" is a specifically *Christian* trope). In this case, too, the West has literalized its tropes of the Jew, whether capitalized,[35] lower cased, pluralized, or put in quotes. Lyotard would do better to deconstruct these terms in their historical specificity than to create again an amorphous, catch-all category on the bodies of dead Jews. For it is the figure of the dead or, at least, persecuted Jew(s) with which Lyotard (and Europe) is most comfortable. One can piously mourn and "remember" dead Jews as the unrepresentable, the immemorial. But actual, living Jews in their/our[36] complex and contradictory identities *as Jews*, still have no place in the Europe of Lyotard's text.

The "Jewish Question" cannot be "solved" until we realize that what is in question is *not* the Jews and never has been. In question and at stake is the power of empire and the imperial subject as Christian/Western. The category of "the jews" as a "solution" to the Jewish Question (which is itself a particularistic way of naming the question of *Western* identity) is an effacing of its true subject: the European Christian. Jews are not *in* these discourses of the West, despite their figurative inclusion.

Indeed, Jew(s) are no more present in Lyotard's *Heidegger and "the jews"* than they/we are in Augustine's hermeneutics of the "Old Testament." "The jews" in Lyotard's text is a mirage. It distracts us from attending to the actual differences of/among Jews within/outside the West and it effaces, as well, the actual history of cultural, religious, and so-called "racial" differences of others.

To get *beyond* the disappearance (indeed, the absence) of the Jews in the discourse(s) of Western identity requires more than a new (and improved?) category of "the jews." These Western discourses must be ruptured by the voices of those who have been made invisible through their/our erasure and objectification.[37] Jews must speak for them/ourselves—and be heard—in/outside of Western discourses. But a discourse, such as Lyotard's, that purports to remember the Jews as "the jews" does not allow a time[38] or space for such speaking or hearing.

Notes

1. I use the term "Christian/West" to signal the intrinsic connection between these identities. The West has been understood as shaped by the "Judeo-Christian tradition," a term which already constitutes a displacement/appropriation of both Judaism and the Torah. When I use the term "Western subject," therefore, I am referring to this Christian, imperial construction of the West, even in its secularized forms.

2. The Jew is figured as male, even if feminized, in the history of Western anti-Judaism. In my treatment of this trope, I maintain this male gendering to make clear that it is a trope and not Jews or Jewish identities that is at issue. This male gendering even informs postmodern discussions of Jews such as Jean-François Lyotard's *Heidegger and "the jews,"* which is the focus of my essay.

3. See Gilman, *Difference and Pathology*:

Stereotypes are a crude set of mental representations of the world. They are palimpsests on which the initial bipolar representations are still vaguely legible. They perpetuate a needed sense of difference between the "self" and the "object," which becomes the "Other." Because there is no real line between self and the Other, an imaginary line must be drawn; and so that the illusion of an absolute difference between self and Other is never troubled, this line is as dynamic in its ability to alter itself as is the self. . . . The most negative stereotype always has an overtly positive counterweight. As any image is shifted, all stereotypes shift. Thus stereotypes are inherently protean rather than rigid. (18)

4. In this brief exposition, I can only allude to the typologies, stereotypes, and dynamics of the history of anti-Judaism in the West. I mention instances and figures of this projection of otherness as/onto Jews to set the scene for the later reappearance of some of these tropes within recent critical theory.

5. In this light, male Jews were also demasculinized, carnally feminized. See Gilman, *Difference and Pathology* chapter 9, 191–216; and also Gilman, *The Jew's Body*.

6. For an explication of Paul's views on circumcision, see Daniel Boyarin, " 'This We Know to Be the Carnal Israel' "; see also Gilman, *The Jew's Body* 91–95; Eilberg-Schwartz 141–76; and Josef Stern.

7. I use the term "they" to refer to these constructions of Jewish identity as the Other. Part of the burden of my argument here is that the tropology of the Jew and Judaism in/outside of the West is not to be literalized or entitized, but rather recognized precisely as figurative.

8. This slippage between Christianity and Nation can be traced throughout the purportedly secular discourse of the late eighteenth/early nineteenth-century period of Emancipation/Enlightenment. For a discussion of the Napoleonic code and its history of effects, see

Chazan and Raphael; and Hyman. That entrance into the liberal social contract was offered to Jewish men only, and then only as individual members of society, not as Jews, is important to note here. As Clermont-Tonnure remarked at the National Assembly in 1789, "To the Jews as individuals—everything; to the Jews as a group—nothing. They must constitute neither a body politic nor an order; they must be citizens individually" (Hyman 5). For a consideration of the impact of this gendered character of liberalism on Jewish women's identities, see Levitt chapter 2. I am indebted to Laura Levitt for the critical use of the term "identity/ies." For the modernization of the Jew in Germany, see Meyer.

9. Again, it is important to differentiate the trope of the Jew from the multiple, complex, even conflicting identities of Jews. The failure to see Jews is fundamentally related to their confusion with the trope of the Jew. As James E. Young suggests in his treatment of John Berryman's "The Imaginary Jew,"

> [A]s becomes painfully clear to [Berryman], it is precisely the point at which a figurative Jew is reified that the danger begins. For as he concludes, it is always only the figurative Jew that antisemites hate—i.e., the imaginary Jew of their minds—but once acted upon, the figure is reified, and real blood flows. (115–16)

10. In " 'Race,' Writing and Culture," Tzvetan Todorov notes the absence of any discussion of Jewish history and the Shoah in Gates, "Race," Writing, and Difference, the volume to which this letter is a response:

> I [Todorov] was surprised, not to say shocked, by the lack of any reference to one of the most odious forms of racism: anti-Semitism. Given the fact that the Nazis' "final solution" to the "Jewish problem" led to the greatest racial massacre in the history of humankind, its absence from the volume suggests that the authors chose to "actively ignore" it, to borrow an expression used by Hazel V. Carby in a different context. ... (377)

His implied question, however, was not addressed in the editor's response. Indeed, "Jews" only appear in the text (as even a glance at its index will indicate) as first-world Zionist oppressors of third-world Palestinians. The most troubling reference, however, appears in Houston Baker's critique of Edward Said's binary opposition between Israelis and Palestinians:

> Said presents a case for the Palestinians by summoning all the texts of Jewish defense, apology, invective, and disparagement. It is difficult to hear a Palestinian voice separate from the world of Jewish discourse. (Of course, Jews are not likely to feel this way, and will probably call for Said's head on a platter. But that is the necessary reaction of well-financed client states.) (388–89)

Not only does Baker confuse Israelis with Jews, using these terms interchangeably, but the association of Jewish Israelis with money, as "well-financed" by the first-world, not only repeats a Christian anti-Jewish trope but constructs all Israelis as first-world, ignoring the fact that many Jewish Israelis are either from Palestine or originate from Arab countries.

This "identification" of Jews and Israelis with whiteness, Europe, and the first-world marks postcolonial feminism as well. Consider, for example, the absence of any writings by Israeli or Mizrahi Jewish women in an anthology as important as Third World Women and the Politics of Feminism. Jewish women, on the other hand, are also often considered white in first-world feminism and are assimilated into the "Judeo-Christian" West. Despite the light skin of some Jewish women (which in our racist society offers privilege), our specific ethnicities and histories both "in" and "out" of the West make Jewish women's experiences more like those of women of color than those of white, first-world women. Like postcolonial writing more generally, however, recent feminist discourse is beginning to make some more inclusive gestures toward Jews. While Audre Lorde, for example, still refers to Jews as part of the white community (and it is the case that some Jews can "pass" and become part of this community), she makes the point that Jews, like blacks, share in histories of racist oppression that affect gender-relations within our particular (Jewish or black) communities (284). Recently, as well, Henry Louis Gates importantly addressed the problem of black anti-Semitism in "Black Demagogues and Pseudo-Scholars" (15).

11. It is precisely these initial presumptions that will be examined and questioned here. (Indeed, postcolonial writings will be found, in the body of this paper, to offer many important resources for the critique of postmodern discourses.) While I distinguish postmodern and postcolonial theories, I recognize that some postcolonial theorists draw upon and reinterpret postmodern theories. I also find persuasive Edward W. Said's argument in "Representing the Colonized" that the crises of postmodern discourse and theory are significantly occasioned by the emergence of postcoloniality. Thus, while there are important differences of positionality between postmodern and postcolonial discourses, I do not seek to mark this difference as a simple either/or. Nor do I wish to elide them under a single "post." To this problematic, I also raise the question of the status of post-Holocaust writing between these two other "posts" —postmodernism and postcolonialism.

12. I alternate between the two terms, "Holocaust" and "Shoah," because different individuals and communities name and, thus, interpret the event differently and because, juxtaposed, each term may call attention to the problems and limits of the other. There are, of course, other terms that have been used to name this event(s): for example, *Churban* and *Tremendum.*

13. See my "Failing Speech." In this essay, I was also concerned with a certain aestheticization and abstraction of the Shoah in postmodern discourse, a concern that is expressed as well by Santner. See, in this regard, note 28 below.

14. This has occurred more through its reception by a general audience not acquainted with specific midrashim than because the writers (cited in the note above) have juxtaposed these interpretive resources. See David Stern, "Midrash and Indeterminacy"; and his *Parables in Midrash.*

15. In an attempt to disavow the Jewishness of deconstruction, David Hirsch goes to the extreme of identifying it with Nazism.

16. I will not attend to the details of the Heidegger controversy here as I am, rather, focusing on the question of the construction of Jewish identity/ies in Lyotard's text.

17. The immemorial is

that which can neither be remembered (represented to consciousness) nor forgotten (consigned to oblivion). It is that which returns, uncannily [*unheimlich*]. As such, the immemorial acts as a kind of *figure* for consciousness and its attempts at representing itself historically. The prime example is Auschwitz [and "the jews"], which obliges us to speak so that this event remains an event, so that its *singularity* is not lost in historical representation, so that it does not become something that happened, among other things. The task of not forgetting, of anamnesis, is the task of the avant-garde, which struggles to keep events from sinking into the oblivion of either representation (voice) or silence. (Readings xxxii)

In the paragraphs that follow, I interpret Lyotard's use of the terms "originary [or primary] repression" and "secondary repression."

18. See Lyotard, *The Differend.* This text is, in my opinion, more nuanced than *Heideg-*

ger and "the jews." Much depends on how one interprets the term, "differend": through a logic that undercuts all metanarrative grounding or through a rhetoric that identifies with, and speaks from, the position of the excluded. Is injustice an abstract and necessary character of the system of reason or is it something that can be ameliorated through a utopic identification with, and listening to, that which cannot be expressed? Both strands seem to be present in Lyotard's text. It is the second, rhetorical attitude of attentiveness to the differend that I find both helpful and important. The logical insight about metanarratives (while accurate) risks the abstract thinking that Eric Santner critiques. See note 28 below.

19. This writing that I am calling *"écriture judaïque"* has been treated in different ways by Edmond Jabès and Jacques Derrida (see, for example, notes 29 and 30 below).

The suggestion was made that instead of writing "the jews" I should write "the lower case" so as to feature this character(istic) and to minimize the confusion between what I and Lyotard refer to as Jews. (I thank Laura Levitt for this suggestion and for reading an earlier draft of this essay.) While I didn't in the end follow this suggestion, it remains an intriguing one. Keeping these terms clearly distinct will require of readers close attention to diacritical marks.

20. I use the term "un-homey" instead of the more usual translation of *unheimlich*, "un-homely," because its connotations seem less problematic.

21. While anti-Semitism is a matter of primary repression, xenophobia pertains, rather, to secondary repression. In understanding Jewishness as a function of anti-Semitism, Lyotard's views seem to be in the "tradition" of Sartre.

22. For a similar description of the Jews in the West, see Pinsker:

> The World saw in this people [the Jews] the uncanny form of one of the dead walking among the living. The ghostlike apparition of a living corpse, of a people without unity or organization, without land or other bonds of unity, no longer alive, and yet walking among the living—this spectral form without precedence in history, unlike anything that preceded or followed it, could but strangely affect the imagination of the nations. (163)

Compare this description with that of the "incarnation," the terrible literalizing of this figure of the *unheimlich*, living dead in the concentration camps:

> Their life is short, but their number is endless; they, the *Muselmänner*, the drowned, form the backbone of the camp, an anonymous mass, continually renewed and always identical, of non-men who march and labour in silence, the divine spark dead within them, already too empty to really suffer. One hesitates to call them living: one hesitates to call their death death, in the face of which they have no fear, as they are too tired to understand. (Levi 82).

23. I have italicized the term *real Jews* to make note of its constructedness despite its lack of diacritical markings in Lyotard's text.

24. The figuration of "the jews" as a "people" (lower case and in quotes to signify that the term does not refer to a historical people), signals the unwelcoming of the Jews (as *unheimlich*) in the West. Lyotard's discourse resonates with the Zionist Leo Pinsker's diagnosis of the situation of the Jew in the West: "[The Jews are at] home everywhere, but are nowhere at home. The nations have *never* to deal with a Jewish nation but always with mere *Jews*. The Jews are not a nation . . . the Jews seem rather to have lost all remembrance of their former home" (162).

In his essay *"Heidegger and 'the jews'*: A Conference in Vienna and Freiberg (1989),"* Lyotard further refines some of the terms he employs in the book of that title. He amends his use of the terms "nation" and "people," only to a certain extent ameliorating their problematic usage in the book. (See, especially, p. 143 of his essay.) However, Lyotard's qualifying commentary, while clarifying and making more explicit some of the terms of his book—for example, the figuration of "the jews" in terms of primary repression (as explicated on pp. 141-143)—does not erase the troubling inscription of his thought within the very dynamics and discourses of the West which he criticizes. In his essay, for example, Lyotard clearly states the problem of representing "the Jewish condition" in the West: "it alone is the impossible witness, always improper (there are only bad jews), to this unconscious affect" (p. 143); yet, as I delineate below, Lyotard appears irresistibly to repeat this problematic equation of the *real Jew* and "bad jews."

25. The dilemma of how to refer to actual Jews, as opposed to Lyotard's "the jews" or *real Jews*, informs and resonates throughout my entire text. I mark this problem of reference here as "they/we" to draw attention to the difference between this question of identification and that referred to in note 7 above. In the pages that follow, however, I do not further mark this difference until the last few paragraphs of this essay.

26. See Bhabha:

> How do we conceive of the "splitting" of the national subject? How do we articulate cultural differences within this vacillation of ideology in which the national discourse also participates, sliding ambivalently from one enunciatory position to another? . . . What might be the cultural and political effects of the liminality of the nation, the margins of modernity, which cannot be signified without the narrative temporalities of splitting, ambivalence and vacillation? ("DissemiNation" 298)

27. While, as I have suggested (in note 21), Lyotard's figuration of "the jews"/*real Jews* (as *unheimlich* others of the West) seems to repeat Sartre's views, Sartre seems to resemble Bhabha when Sartre writes:

> [The democrat] has no eyes for the concrete syntheses with which history confronts him. He recognizes neither Jew, nor Arab, nor Negro, nor bourgeois, nor worker, but only man. . . . He resolves all collectivities into individual elements. . . . This means that he wants to separate the Jew from his religion, from his family, from his ethnic community, in order to plunge him into the democratic crucible whence he will emerge naked and alone, an individual and solitary particle like all the other particles. . . . [The democrat is thus] hostile to the Jew to the extent that the latter thinks of himself as a Jew. (55-57)

28. It may well be that it is the very figuration of "the jews"/*real Jews* as primary repression that is integral to their invisibility, even for Lyotard: 1) They are the products of Western identity and are necessarily, always already, silence(d); 2) With such an identification of Jews/"the jews" and primary repression, a mourning, a "working through," or an undoing of its repetition/return in anti-Semitism would seem impossible. My concerns here resonate with those of Santner (8-30). Like Santner, I am exploring the possibilities of thinking "the 'postwar' under the double sign of the postmodern and the post-Holocaust" (8). As Santner notes,

> To return to Lyotard's remark regarding the relation between amnesia with respect to Auschwitz and the repression of the failures of European modernity more generally to deal with difference, one must wonder whether the elaboration of those failures, which is an essential aspect of so much postmodern critical practice, can also be understood as a gesture of genuine anamnesis and mourning toward the Holocaust and its victims. Insofar as deconstruction as practiced by de Man and others privileges a

heroism of an abstract mode of bereavement—let me call it a heroism of the elegiac loop—it cannot be considered an adequate response to an earlier complicity, however "abstract" it may have been, in German fascism's hegemony over Europe and all that that entailed. . . . The more difficult labour would have been, of course, openly and explicitly to *sediment* these tasks of mourning to explore the ways in which they might, in the long run, mutually enlighten one another. (13-30)

29. In a way, Lyotard's distinction between "the jews" and *real Jews* resembles Derrida's characterization of Edmond Jabès as "more and less Jewish than the Jew" (75). As Derrida goes on to remark,

[T]he Jew's identification with himself [note the male gendering] does not exist. The Jew is split, and split first of all between the two dimensions of the letter: allegory and literality. His history would be but one empirical history among others if he established or nationalized himself within difference and literality. He would have no history at all if he let himself be attenuated within the algebra of an abstract universalism. ("Edmond Jabès" 75)

The split in the identity of the Jew is written by Derrida as a difference between two modes of interpretation: the rabbi and the poet (67). I refer to other forms of splitting (Jewish) identity below.

30. Derrida also treats the question of marks of identity and the displacement of exclusivity in his reflections on circumcision [note again the male figuration of the Jew and Jewish membership] in "Shibboleth." Of course, women, like Jews, are also marked and marginalized as particular, although not necessarily as particularistic.

31. This internal liminality is figured by Bhabha in terms of the *unheimlich*:

I am attempting to discover the uncanny moment of cultural difference. . . . At this point I must give way to the *vox populi*: to . . . [the] wandering peoples who will not be contained within the *Heim* of the national culture . . . but are themselves marks of the shifting boundary that alienates the frontiers of the modern nation. ("DissemiNation" 312, 315)

The use of the uncanny to question national culture, not to re-present it (as in Lyotard's use of "the jews"), offers an epistemological/political reading of the *unheimlich* that differs significantly from its use by Lyotard criticized here.

32. See Tania Modleski, *Feminism without Men*; and "Feminism and the Power of Interpretation." *Écriture judaïque* resembles *écriture feminine* in that, just as the latter is not necessarily produced by women (and, indeed, the category of "woman/women" is contingent), so the former does not require (and in some cases, does not allow) Jews.

33. For example, in a section entitled, "The Stranger within Us" in *Strangers to Ourselves* (169-92), Julia Kristeva writes:

Freud teaches us how to detect foreignness in ourselves. . . . Freud brings us the courage to call ourselves disintegrated in order not to integrate foreigners and even less so to hunt them down, but rather to welcome them to that *uncanny strangeness*, which is as much theirs as it is ours. (191-92; emphasis mine)

Notice the domestication of the *unheimlich* as already (as it were, uncannily) present in the term *heimlich*. Freud's gesture in this regard may be read as his attempt to read the *unheim-*

lich Jews (and, thus, himself) into the universal (and, thus, *heimlich*) condition of humankind itself.

34. The problem is that in signifying certain results of the practices of empire as positive, even if in elegiac terms, some postmodern discourses (including that of Lyotard in *Heidegger and "the jews"*) repeat, rather than get beyond, these practices. Under the guise of identifying with the exiled, the *unheimlich* others, then, these practices are further institutionalized, rather than critiqued.

35. See Derrida, *The Other Heading* 16–28:

> Perhaps identification in general . . . always has a capital form, the figurehead . . . of the advanced point, and of capitalizing reserve. . . . By selection, I will deduce the form of all my propositions from a grammar and syntax of the heading, of the *cap*, from a difference in kind and gender [*genre*], that is, from *capital* and *capitale*. (26–27, 16)

36. Because the subject here is explicitly about Jewish identity, I use the term "their/our" (and, in the paragraphs that follow, the terms "they/we" and "them/ourselves" as well) to further dramatize the dilemma of reference referred to in note 25. As this text is about to go to press in December 1992, I must register my outrage and disgust at Europe's "failure" again to find a safe place within its borders for its *unheimlich* others: once again, "foreigners" and refugees (for example, Africans, Asians, Arabs), gypsies, the handicapped, and Jews among them.

37. This would include the speaking of those Jews that Lyotard excludes from the category of "the jews": the figure of "the political (Zionism), religious (Judaism), or philosophical (Jewish philosophy)" identity/ies of Jews (*Heidegger* 3).

38. For a consideration of Jewish habitation of time instead of space, see Jonathan Boyarin. See also Horowitz for consideration of the situation of Jewish Studies in the "New Academy." I thank Sara Horowitz for her generous reading of an earlier version of this essay.

Works Cited

Anderson, George K. *The Legend of the Wandering Jew.* Hanover: UP of New England, 1966, 1991.

Baker, Houston. "Caliban's Triple Play." Gates, *"Race," Writing, and Difference* 381–95.

Berryman, John. "The Imaginary Jew." *The Kenyon Review* 7 (1945): 529–39.

Bhabha, Homi. "DissemiNation." *Nation and Narration.* Ed. Homi Bhabha. London: Routledge, 1990. 291–322.

———. "The Other Question: Difference, Discrimination and the Discourse of Colonialism." Ferguson 71–87.

Blanchot, Maurice. *The Writing of the Disaster.* Trans. Ann Smock. Lincoln: U of Nebraska P, 1986.

Boyarin, Daniel. *Intertextuality and the Reading of Midrash.* Bloomington: Indiana UP, 1990.

———. " 'This We Know to Be the Carnal Israel': Circumcision and the Erotic Life of God and Israel." *Critical Inquiry* 18.3 (1992): 474–505.

Boyarin, Jonathan. *Storm from Paradise: the Politics of Jewish Memory*. Minneapolis: U of Minnesota P, 1992.

Chazan, Robert, and Marc L. Raphael, eds. *Modern Jewish History: A Source Book*. New York: Schocken, 1969.

Derrida, Jacques. "Edmond Jabès and the Question of the Book." *Writing and Difference*. Trans. Alan Bass. Chicago: U of Chicago P, 1978. 64–78.

———. *The Other Heading: Reflections on Today's Europe*. Trans. Pascale-Anne Brault and Michael B. Naas. Bloomington: Indiana UP, 1992.

———. "Shibboleth." *Midrash and Literature*. Hartman and Budick 340–47.

Dundes, Alan, and Galit Hasan-Rokem, eds. *The Wandering Jew: Essays in the Interpretation of a Christian Legend*. Bloomington: Indiana UP, 1986.

Eilberg-Schwartz, Howard. *The Savage in Judaism: Anthropology of Israelite Religion and Ancient Judaism*. Bloomington: Indiana UP, 1990.

Ferguson, Russell et al., eds. *Out There: Marginalization and Contemporary Cultures*. Cambridge: MIT P, 1990.

Gates, Henry Louis, Jr. "Black Demagogues and Pseudo-Scholars." *New York Times* 20 Jul. 1992: A15.

———, ed. *"Race," Writing, and Difference*. Chicago: U of Chicago P, 1985.

Gilman, Sander L. *Difference and Pathology: Stereotypes of Sexuality, Race, and Madness*. Ithaca: Cornell UP, 1985.

———. *Jewish Self-Hatred: Anti-Semitism and the Hidden Language of the Jews*. Baltimore: Johns Hopkins UP, 1986.

———. *The Jew's Body*. New York: Routledge, 1991.

Handleman, Susan. *Slayers of Moses: The Emergence of Rabbinic Interpretation in Modern Literary Theory*. Albany: SUNY P, 1982.

Hartman, Geoffrey H., and Sanford Budick, eds. *Midrash and Literature*. New Haven: Yale UP, 1986.

Hirsch, David H. *The Deconstruction of Literature: Criticism after Auschwitz*. Hanover: Brown UP, 1991.

Horowitz, Sara. "Jewish Studies as Oppositional? or Gettin' Mighty Lonely Out Here." *Styles of Cultural Activism: From Theory and Pedagogy to Women, Indians, and Communism*. Ed. Philip Goldstein. Newark: U of Delaware P, 1994.

Hyman, Paula. *From Dreyfus to Vichy: The Remaking of French Jewry, 1906–1939*. New York: Columbia UP, 1979.

Jabès, Edmond. *The Book of Questions*. Trans. Rosmarie Waldrop. Middlebury: Wesleyan UP, 1972. Trans. of *Le Livre des Questions*. Paris: Gallimard, 1963.

Kristeva, Julia. *Strangers to Ourselves*. New York: Columbia UP, 1991.

Levi, Primo. *Survival in Auschwitz*. New York: Macmillan, 1961.

Levitt, Laura. *Reconfiguring Home: Jewish Feminist Identity/ies*. Emory University, Ph.D. dissertation, 1993.

Lorde, Audre. "Age, Race, Class, and Sex: Women Redefining Difference." Ferguson 281–88.

Lyotard, Jean-François. *The Differend: Phrases in Dispute*. Trans. Georges Van Den Abbeele. Minneapolis: U of Minnesota P, 1988.

———. *Heidegger and "the jews."* Trans. Andreas Michel and Mark Roberts. Minneapolis: U of Minnesota P, 1990. Trans. of *Heidegger et "le juifs."* Paris: Galilée, 1988.

———. *"Heidegger and 'the jews': A Conference in Vienna and Freiberg (1989)."* Trans. Bill Readings and Kevin Paul Geiman. Minneapolis: U of Minnesota P, 1993.

Meyer, Michael A. *The Origins of the Modern Jew: Jewish Identity and European Culture in Germany, 1749–1824*. Detroit: Wayne State UP, 1979.

Modleski, Tania. "Feminism and the Power of Interpretation: Some Critical Readings." *Feminist Studies/Critical Studies*. Ed. Teresa de Lauretis. Bloomington: Indiana UP, 1986. 121–38.

——. *Feminism without Men: Culture and Criticism in a "Postfeminist" Age*. New York: Routledge, 1991.

Pinsker, Leo. "Auto-Emancipation: An Appeal to His People by a Russian Jew." Chazan and Raphael 161–74.

Readings, Bill. *Introducing Lyotard: Art and Politics*. London: Routledge, 1991.

Said, Edward. "Reflections on Exile." Ferguson 357–66.

——. "Representing the Colonized: Anthropology's Interlocutors." *Critical Inquiry* 15.2 (1989): 205–26.

Santner, Eric. *Stranded Objects: Mourning, Memory, and Film in Postwar Germany*. Ithaca: Cornell UP, 1990.

Sartre, Jean-Paul. *Anti-Semite and Jew*. New York: Schocken, 1948.

Shapiro, Susan. "Failing Speech: Post-Holocaust Writing and the Discourse of Postmodernism." *Semeia* 40 (1987): 65–91.

Stern, David. "Midrash and Indeterminacy." *Critical Inquiry* 14.1 (1988): 133–61.

——. *Parables in Midrash: Narrative and Exegesis in Rabbinic Literature*. Cambridge: Harvard UP, 1991.

Stern, Josef. "Maimonides' Parable of Circumcision." *S'vara: A Journal of Philosophy, Law, and Judaism* 2.2 (1991): 35–48.

Third World Women and the Politics of Feminism. Ed. Chandra Talpade Mohanty, Ann Russo, and Lourdes Torres. Bloomington: Indiana UP, 1991.

Todorov, Tzvetan. " 'Race,' Writing and Culture." Gates, *"Race, Writing, and Difference* 370–80.

Young, James E. *Writing and Rewriting the Holocaust: Narrative and the Consequences of Interpretation*. Bloomington: Indiana UP, 1990.

Options and Exigencies

13 | A "*Mischling*" Attempts to Fight for His Rights

H. G. Adler
Translated by Jamie Owen Daniel

Translator's Introduction

The following text is taken from H. G. Adler's comprehensive 1974 study, *Der verwaltete Mensch: Studien zur Deportation der Juden aus Deutschland* (*The Administered Human Being: A Study of the Deportation of the Jews from Germany*). The volume is "monumental" in both senses of the term: compiled by Adler after some 15 years of meticulous archival research, it is a massive (more than 1,000 pages) account and analysis of the administrative framework that was put in place to implement National Socialist racial policies. It is also a *Trauerarbeit*, a labor of mourning undertaken as a testament to both the millions who were murdered and to Adler's own experience—the book is dedicated to the memory of his parents, Emil Alfred Adler and Alice Adler-Fraenkel, who died in concentration camps in 1942. Adler himself was a survivor of the camp at Theresienstadt, and he notes in his introduction to *Der verwaltete Mensch* that he had written an earlier work, *Theresienstadt 1941–1945* (1955), in order to locate his own experiences of the camp within a broader historical configuration in such a way that, as he puts it, he himself "could continue living" (xvii).

The book maintains this double movement between broader context and personalized detail by including hundreds of individual "case" examples that serve not only to illustrate the everyday repercussions of the administrative decisions and actions Adler documents, but also to counteract the depersonalizing logic that was a key component in their implementation. Adler's account of the apparent demise of Ernst Brüll is but one of many examples of how individuals and families became entrapped within the labyrinthine networks of bureaucracy and legislation that were gradually established for the specific purpose of facilitating and "legitimating" the anti-Semitic agenda of the National Socialist administration.

The circumstances in which Brüll found himself once Germany had invaded and occupied Poland were precarious. Like many others among the "ethnic German" minority (the so-called *Volksdeutsche*) whose families had emigrated from Germany and Austria in previous centuries, Brüll had consistently supported German-language cultural activities in his community, and had always spoken German at home and in the everyday operation of his business. In so doing, he was exercising a legal right that had been guaranteed to European ethnic minority populations after World War I. The Treaty of Versailles had stipulated that ethnic minority citizens were to be considered legally equal before the law; they were also to be allowed to use their own language in dealings with governmental and other authorities, and to establish their own religious, educational, and other cultural institutions in which this language could be used exclusively.[1] Brüll had continued to exercise these rights despite considerable pressure by local Polish authorities to conduct his business affairs in Polish; likewise, he had rejected their demands that he replace the German-speaking employees at his family's textile firm with employees who spoke Polish. This harassment by Polish authorities was hardly unusual, especially in Upper Silesia, where tensions between the German-speaking minority and the majority Polish-speaking population ran high. The situation was not helped when ethnic Germans were perceived to be receiving support from their "patron nation"—for example, German-speaking minors in Upper Silesia received *Winterhilfe*, or winter hardship assistance, from Germany, but their Polish majority counterparts received no such help from the Polish government. By 1939, tensions had accelerated to such a degree that many German schools and churches were forced to shut down, and ethnic Germans were occasionally attacked and even killed in mob violence by majority Poles. Of course, the Nazis were quick to use such incidents as justification for invading Poland and other Eastern European countries on the pretext of "liberating" the ethnic Germans, whether or not these groups welcomed the occupation or had ever expressed support for the National Socialist Agenda.[2]

Once the local anti-German Polish administration had been replaced by a Nazi administration, Brüll would therefore have seemed an exemplary candidate for the status he sought of "citizen of the Reich," a status that was often "awarded" to members of ethnic German populations in Nazi-occupied countries. Brüll was denied this status, however, because of the "Reich Citizenship Law" that had been implemented on November 14, 1935. One of the Nuremberg Laws that were drawn up to "legalize" Nazi racial policies, the Reich Citizenship Law was the first law to establish clear-cut guidelines for determining who would be legally considered a Jew. As Raul Hilberg has pointed out, "while heretofore the population had been divided only into 'Aryans' and 'non-Aryans,' there were now two kinds of non-Aryans: Jews and so-called *Mischlinge*" (18). The term *Mischling* has been left untranslated in the following because of its complex resonance; a neutral translation would be simply "a person of mixed race." But it can also be the equivalent of "hybrid," "mongrel" or "half-breed." This latter meaning was surely that intended by the Nazi legislators who drew up the law.

In addition to defining two kinds of "non-Aryan," the Reich Citizenship Law also defined two kinds of *Mischling*. Regardless of whether they had ever self-identified as Jews, persons who had one Jewish parent or two Jewish grandparents ("half-Jews"), weren't affiliated with a synagogue, or weren't married to a Jewish person as of September 15, 1925, were classified as *Mischlinge* of the first degree.[3] Anyone with one Jewish grandparent was classified as a *Mischling* of the second degree. According to Article 2 of the law, persons legally defined as Jews (those with at least three Jewish grandparents) or as *Mischlinge* were to be denied Reich citizenship except under special circumstances. This meant not only that they could not take part in political life by voting or holding public office, but also that they could not be employed as civil servants in any capacity. The law would later be amended to include the revocation of their right to own property or businesses. The Reich Citizenship Law was thus an important link in the chain of legal decisions that would culminate in the implementation of the "Final Solution" in January of 1942, the policy of racial annihilation that would redefine these people as not only noncitizens, but nonhumans.

⌖

The battle waged by Ernst Brüll—the co-proprietor of the Plutzar & Brüll textile manufacturing company from Nikelsdorf near Bielitz who, as a half-Jew, steadfastly demanded that he be recognized as a German citizen—came to a bitter end. His case merits description in some detail.[4]

Numerous files on Brüll were assembled in Schweiklberg near Vilshofen in Lower Bavaria, where the Regensburg state police authorities had turned over a monastery building to the RFdV[5] on January 1, 1942.[6] In 1941, Ernst Brüll and his German wife Mathilde had filled out questionnaires distributed by the district magistrate in Bielitz on behalf of the local branch office of the German National Registry (*Deutsche Volksliste*). These forms were intended to determine whether or not they could claim German national status. Brüll filled in the following: born on February 15, 1916; Catholic; married since February 5, 1939; presently employed as a "private administrator"; prior to September 1, 1939, "executive officer and coproprietor of a textile manufacturing company." To the question, "Which of your parents or grandparents were of Jewish extraction," he responded, "My father is a Jew (his family has resided here for 180 years). My mother, née Schreinzer, descends from one of the oldest German-Aryan families in Silesia. My parents' marriage was recognized by both the civil authorities and the Church." The response of the local section leader and mayor to the questionnaire was favorable.

Nonetheless, the local branch decided on November 7, 1941, to refuse to register him in the German National Registry. On December 23, Brüll appealed to the administrative head of the district branch of the Registry. He again referred to the fact that his family, which he claimed had always "demonstrated its German attitude under any circumstances" and belonged to many German organizations, had left Vienna 180 years earlier to settle in Bielitz. Three close relatives of his father had "faced the enemy as imperial German soldiers."

> I bring these matters to your attention because I am guided by the apprehension that, in regard to adjudication of the civil citizenship laws, I cannot be

assigned a lesser value than the legal status of a *Mischling* of the first degree as provided for by the Nuremberg Laws. . . . I have never been a member of a Polish organization. My record-keeping, correspondence, and everyday conversations at work have always been conducted in German.

The letter concluded with "Heil Hitler!" as was commonplace in correspondence with public officials, even when those writing were members of the German resistance.

On February 10, 1942, the Bielitz branch office of the German National Registry turned to the local headquarters of the NSDAP[7] with Brüll's appeal. The response, dated March 9, read as follows:

> The half-Jew Ernst Brüll has not shown himself to be an active supporter, willing to sacrifice himself for the German cause. In addition, he has always opposed National Socialism. It is correct that, under the former Polish administration, [he] represented the interests of the firm's German staff . . . against the Polish authorities. The reason for this involvement was the specialized knowledge and efficiency of the German employees, which Ernst Brüll did not want to lose.
>
> Therefore, the local headquarters of the NSDAP must uphold the refusal to include him . . . in the German National Registry.

On March 17, the branch office of the German National Registry forwarded Brüll's appeal to the administrative president of the district office in Kattowitz with the request that a conclusive decision be handed down. From here, the file was sent on March 30 to the NSDAP regional headquarters in Upper Silesia with the request that it be reviewed. There, letters expressing strong support for Brüll were added to the file, among them a letter from SS Officer Rudolf Wiesner,[8] another from the local party section headquarters in Nikelsdorf, as well as one from a gentleman who had been employed by the firm of Plutzar & Brüll for 40 years, 25 of these as general manager. In appending this letter, organizational leader Ditze of the regional party headquarters wrote to the district office of the German National Registry:

> [Even if] Brüll was only a member of insignificant German organizations, his intervention on behalf of German interests indicates that he cannot be rejected on grounds of not having shown the requisite willingness to intervene. It is incontestably clear that he consistently intervened energetically on behalf of the interests and well-being of his predominantly German staff in his capacity as an executive-level employee at the textile firm of his father, the full-Jew Walter Brüll, even when negotiating with the Polish authorities. In addition, the Brüll family has always assisted ethnic Germans who were in financial trouble in an exemplary fashion by providing material support. The Brüll family has also proven its worthiness through its support of German cultural events and social institutions in Bielitz. This assessment is supported by the fully credible testimony of notable and trustworthy ethnic Germans.

Brüll's appeal was nonetheless denied by the administrative president of the district office for the German National Registry on May 20, 1942. This decision was made by a committee composed of Administrative President Springorium (who presided as the committee chair), the head of the presidential department for questions of nationality, one representative each from the RFdV and the Secret Service, the chief of the Secret Police, two members of the group "former ethnic Germans in Poland," and a stenotypist. The decision, which acknowledged everything that had been submitted in favor of Brüll, states that "further appeals will be forwarded to the Central Office [of the German National Registry] because of the critical significance of the case." The text also states the following:

> A number of impoverished German families were offered generous financial support by the Brüll firm. Likewise, the Brüll firm provided ongoing support for German organizations as well as noteworthy donations toward the maintenance of German schools and the German theater in Bielitz.
>
> In spite of the evidence provided of an attitude that is pro-German in and of itself, the district office is of the opinion that there has not been active intervention on the part of the petitioner that would indicate special sacrifices for the German cause in the sense outlined by the Reich's Ministry of the Interior. As exemplary as his intervention on behalf of his German employees may have been . . . what is at issue here are activities that pertain more to the sphere of his business, whereby it is possible that his intervention on behalf of the German employees was made ultimately in the interest of this business. This opinion is supported by the fact that the petitioner has not belonged to any German political associations. Therefore, in the opinion of the district office, there is no evidence provided here that there has been any active intervention requiring special sacrifices towards the German cause.

In response to this decision, Brüll submitted an appeal to the Central Office of the German National Registry on July 5, 1942, through its executive president in Kattowitz. He cited the testimony of many witnesses, among them once again SS Officer Wiesner as well as the Nikelsdorf local party section leader. He also included a number of testimonial appendices, including letters from the Kattowitz Chamber of Commerce and Trade from May of 1939, inquiring as to why the firm used German stationery and handled its correspondence in German. There were 47 signatures on one of the appended documents, in which people who had been employed by the firm for as long as 40 years attested to the truth of the following statement:

> When he was the co-proprietor of our firm, we maintained a consistently cordial and friendly relationship with Mr. Ernst Brüll; he always intervened extensively on behalf of the Germans in our company, and he was always unequivocally pro-German. In spite of the pressure he was under to replace

German administrators and workers with Poles, not a single member of the staff was ever let go because of their ethnic German background. This was entirely owing to the personal intervention of Mr. Ernst Brüll, who handled all communication with the Polish authorities at the time. We were aware that his policy of refusing to acquiesce to strict mandates for dismissals put him in immediate personal danger.

Whenever possible, individual supporters spoke even more emphatically in support of Brüll. The firm's foreman, a weaver, cited Brüll's frequent interventions in 1939 against "strict mandates for dismissal" on the part of the Polish authorities. "My position in particular was threatened, because I am not in command of the Polish language and have always sent my children to German schools." The firm had "promised him financial support" in the event of a compulsory dismissal. German employees who weren't Polish citizens credited Brüll with providing them special protection in cases of "various summons and legal proceedings" as well as against "penalties and firings." In his appeal, Brüll mentioned that his mother, his wife along with their two children, as well as his mother's parents had all been registered in the National Registry; he again enumerated everything that he perceived as his meritorious performance on behalf of the German cause, and also mentioned, in the long document which again ended with "Heil Hitler!": "All of these circumstances, my continuous interventions with the authorities on behalf of Germans, and probably also my 1939 marriage to a German schoolteacher contributed to the fact that I was threatened with *deportation to Bereza-Kartuska.*"

The appeal went through official channels, ultimately to Administrative President Springorium. He declared that "the appeal had been submitted promptly, it is admissible, but nonetheless unfounded." Citing his previous decision, he requested that the higher office "deny the appeal." The executive president of the Province of Upper Silesia, Central Office of the German National Registry, did not come to a decision, but instead, on November 24, 1942, forwarded the case to the SS Reich's Command Headquarters, RFdV, "Superior Court of Appeals for Questions of Nationality," once again explaining the circumstances. According to a memorandum from the headquarters of the RFdV office in question, "the Superior Court of Appeals should come to a conclusive decision in the question of German-Jewish mixed marriages, whereby *Mischlinge* of the first degree can no longer be registered in the German National Registry." The executive president who had previously requested a test case because of the "critical significance of these questions," had not received any "instructions." Additional documentation was concerned with theoretical deliberations, concluding with the following:

In accordance with previous rulings of the Superior Court of Appeals, half-Jews cannot as a general principle be registered in the German National Registry. A rejection raises the question of whether a certificate should be issued to Ernst Brüll confirming that he is not to be considered an ethnic Pole because of his intervention on behalf of German interests during the previous Polish administration. It remains to be determined whether the wife can be registered in Section 2 [of the National Registry] because of her marriage to a half-Jew in 1939.

For a long period after this there is nothing added to the file on Ernst Brüll, for whom things in the meantime had taken a turn for the worse. On December 21, 1943, SS Commander Dr. Wirsich wrote from the staff headquarters of the RFdV in Schweiklberg to unit leader Dr. Ehlich, head of the group "Nationality III B" at the RSHA:[9]

The matter of the Ernst Brüll family was taken up at the 4th session of the Superior Court of Appeals held at the Field Command Offices on December 10, 1943. The SS Command decided that the child Christine Brüll will be registered in Section 2 of the German National Registry. However, a decision as to the acceptance or classification of Ernst and Mathilde Brüll will be postponed until the marriage has either been ended by divorce or proof has been provided to confirm that Ernst Brüll has been sterilized.[10] If the matter . . . has been cleared up either through divorce or the sterilization of the husband, Mathilde B. should be registered in Section 2. In addition, the question of possible espionage on the part of Ernst Brüll should first be clarified. In this matter, SS Section Command Kaltenbrünner referred during the meeting to the fact that Ernst B. has apparently been taken into custody because of an incident of espionage.

Since it seems unwarranted under these circumstances to make public the decision that has already been made regarding the classification of the two-year-old child, I consider it proper to clarify the matter, initially through an investigation on your part. I ask that you . . . extend your investigation not only to include the incident of espionage, but also a clarification of whether Mrs. Mathilde Brüll *knew* that her husband was a half-Jew when she married him in early 1939. In addition, I gather from a letter from the Upper Silesian District Command dated April 29, 1942, that the Brülls already have two children, while only one child—Christine Brüll, born on September 28, 1940—is mentioned in the questionnaire.

Regarding the condition that a divorce or sterilization would have to be carried out before a final decision can be made in this matter, SS Command was motivated by the fact that, unlike the other cases of half-Jews on the agenda, Ernst Brüll is still a young man (he is 28) and his pure German wife (27) makes an extremely favorable racial impression. I consider it proper that the relevant decisions be communicated in the appropriate manner to Mr. and Mrs. Brüll by the state police or by the Security Police Section Command in Kattowitz.

I ask that I be informed of the results of these steps at a specified point in time so that we can then move forward with the National Registry issue. I will authorize nothing in this matter in the meantime. At this point I ask you to inform me as to whether I may send the executive president of the province of Upper Silesia—Central Office of the German National Registry—a copy of this memorandum to serve as a provisional decision, or whether the status of the investigation into the question of espionage makes this inappropriate at this time.

After Wirsich had pressed for an answer to the questions posed in his letter, RSHA III B 4 responded on April 28, 1944:

> The Secret Service section leader in Kattowitz has reported the following: No accusation of espionage has been made against Ernst *Brüll* by the Gestapo in Kattowitz. However, Brüll was taken into custody on July 22, 1943, by the Gestapo Field Service Headquarters in Bielitz. He was then sent to the concentration camp at Auschwitz. Protective custody was ordered on September 6, 1943, for the following reason: as a Jewish *Mischling* of the first degree, Brüll has spread stories of atrocities, and is strongly suspected of having forged travel documents from Switzerland. On January 3, 1944, Brüll was transferred to the concentration camp at Buchenwald-Thüringen, where he is still being held.
>
> There is nothing to suggest that the executive president of the province of Upper Silesia—Central Office of the German National Registry—should not be confidentially informed of the present state of affairs. I will inform you in a timely manner of further findings in our investigation.

Wirsich notified the executive president in Kattowitz of this letter. From here, the Secret Service Command Office forwarded a longer statement by Mathilde Brüll to the RSHA on June 3, 1944. The copy of the text that was sent to Schweiklberg read as follows:

> I met my husband in 1931. He was still a student at the university at the time, and I was attending the teacher's training school. We became engaged in 1935. At that time I knew that my present husband was a German student and a Catholic and that is why I became involved with him. I was still a young girl then and didn't give a second thought to the racial policy laws. But I was aware throughout the entire period of our engagement that my husband is a half-Jew. He was for me the only man whom I had ever known and loved up to that point in my life. But had he been a Jew, I never would have become involved with him. It is difficult for me to explain in retrospect why I married him; in any event he was for me the man that I was, as it were, destined to marry. During the time we were becoming acquainted my husband never had any contact with Jewish circles, and I also never had any contact with these circles.

On November 29, 1944, Mrs. Brüll signed a petition that she submitted to the Secret Service Command Office, asking that it be forwarded to the Superior Court of Appeals.

> Registration in the German National registry was promised to me and my husband by the Superior Court of Appeals on the following conditions:

1) I must sue for a divorce (I am Aryan, my husband is a *Mischling* of the first degree);

2) my husband must be sterilized, which would result in his being reclassified as a privileged alien.

I would like to comment as follows on these two conditions:

Since December 20, 1941, I have been in possession of the blue pass that is issued by the German National Registry.

My husband has, with my consent, refused to be sterilized with the justification that never before has a similar case been brought before the district command in Upper Silesia, and he wants to wait until a general ruling on the treatment of *Mischlinge* of the first degree has been handed down from a possibly revised post-war perspective.

As regards the divorce requested in Point 1, I must ask permission to approach you with the request that this divorce be delayed until there has been a general ruling on marriages between German Aryans and *Mischlinge* of the first degree; I offer the following justification for making this request:

a) To my knowledge, this would be the first case within the jurisdiction of Upper Silesia in which [such] a marriage . . . was brought to an end for reasons of nationality. Conversely, I know of a great number of cases in which marriages between Germans and Jews have been allowed to continue.

b) My husband . . . has been in custody since July 22, 1943, and according to information given me by the Gestapo in Kattowitz, he will not return home before the war is over. Therefore, there will be no conjugal relations between us during the period for which I am requesting a postponement of the divorce proceedings. Thus there can be no possibility of this marriage producing any more children.

c) Two children were previously born of this marriage; Christine, born on September 28, 1940, and Johanna, born on February 11, 1942.

I would like to point out that my daughters take after the Aryan side completely, both with respect to their physical appearance and their development and temperament, and I would ask in this context that the children be subjected to a racial examination if need be.[11]

I would find it extremely trying emotionally as well as morally reprehensible to allow myself to be divorced from my husband at precisely this difficult point in time and thereby deny both of us one another's support and our children their father.

In conclusion, Mrs. Brüll requested that prompt attention be paid to her petition and that the divorce be postponed. The Secret Service Command Office in Kattowitz sent the petition to RSHA III B along with a cover letter dated December 12, 1944; a second letter dated January 12, 1945, was forwarded to the staff headquarters in Schweiklberg "for further action." The Secret Service commented that, according to information received from Buchenwald, Brüll had refused to be sterilized, although he still preferred sterilization to a divorce. Mrs. Brüll expressed the same opinion. She appeared

of her own accord at the local offices and explained her conviction that it would be impossible for her to be separated from her husband. It became clear that the Brülls had married for love and that her feelings for her husband had not diminished. She believes that the fact that her husband is presently in custody makes it morally imperative that she not abandon him. She asked that she be spared this conflict of conscience. . . . It became obvious on the occasion of her visit that she hopes that, after a victorious end to the war, there will be a certain relaxation of the strict regulations against mixed marriages. She hopes, among other things, that some mixed couples will perhaps be permitted to emigrate overseas.

We ask that an immediate answer be provided to the attached petition. If this is not possible, an appropriate answer should be forwarded to local headquarters for the purpose of a verbal transmission.

This answer was never given, and we do not know whether this case came to a tragic or a conciliatory end. When Wirsich responded from Schweiklberg to the RSHA III B 4 report on January 21, 1945, there was no longer a Secret Service Command Office in Kattowitz. Auschwitz had been evacuated, Bielitz was in the hands of the Russians, and yet Ernst Brüll was still awaiting the outcome in Buchenwald. Wirsich didn't have much to say; he left the matter open:

Since the husband Brüll is in a concentration camp and probably won't be released until the end of the war, we can assume that there will be no additional undesired offspring. Thus I don't consider it necessary at this point to further pursue the issues of divorce or sterilization, and I am in favor of postponing any further action in this case.

I would like to request that the Secret Service Command Office make a decision in this matter.

Notes

"Ein 'Mischling' will sein Recht erkämpfen" from Adler 310–16.

1. The complicated status of ethnic German populations in Europe between the World Wars is detailed in Komjathy and Stockwell, on which I rely here. See also Burleigh.

2. As Komjathy and Stockwell point out, until 1934, ethnic Germans in other countries had always been referred to simply as *Auslandsdeutsche*, or "foreign Germans." After 1934, they began to be referred to as *Volksdeutsche*, a nazified term that obviously made it easier for party ideologues to link them to their cause. The term *Auslandsdeutsche* was used only to describe German citizens living abroad. For a more detailed discussion of the appropriation of the ethnic German "cause" by the Third Reich, see Komjathy and Stockwell 6–15.

3. At the same time, many ethnic Germans who did identify as Jews also strongly self-identified as Germans and supported German-language cultural life: "Before the Nazi takeover, and even after it, many Jews regarded themselves as Germans of the Jewish religious

faith . . . and many of them played an eminent role in ethnic German organizations" (Komjathy and Stockwell xi).

4. The events described in the following coincide with the implementation of the socalled Final Solution alluded to in the translator's introduction, the official policy of annihilating the Jews of Europe that was formalized at the Wannsee Conference convened in Berlin on January 20, 1942 (at which Adolf Eichmann took the minutes). Although the Reich Citizenship Law had defined the official legal status of *Mischlinge* in 1935, a policy for how they were to be treated was not clearly defined until the Wannsee Conference. —Trans.

5. The *Reichskommissar für die Festigung deutscher Volksliste* (RFdV) or "Reich Commission on the Establishment of the German National Registry." —Trans.

6. According to microfilm documentation at the Institut für Zeitgeschichte in Munich, file 126/6.

7. The *National-Sozialistische Deutsche Arbeiterpartei* or "National Socialist German Workers' Party," the official name of the Nazi Party. —Trans.

8. Rudolf Wiesner from Bielitz had been president of the pro-German *Jungdeutsche Partei* (*Young German Party*) and represented the ethnic German minority in the Polish Senate from 1935 to 1937. —Trans.

9. The *Reichssicherheitshauptamt* or "Reich Security Headquarters." —Trans.

10. The Conference Protocol from the Wannsee Conference explains the policy that accounts for the radical worsening of Brüll's situation. The Protocol states that, as far as the newly adopted policy of total annihilation was concerned, *Mischlinge* of the first degree were to be "placed into the same position as Jews" (that is, "evacuated," a euphemism for "murdered") unless the person in question was a) married to a German and the marriage had produced children, and/or b) an exception could be made on the basis of meritorious conduct. In either case, the exemption would be allowed only if the person seeking the exemption agreed to be sterilized: "To avoid any progeny and to clean up the *Mischling* problem once and for all, the *Mischlinge* of the first degree who are to be exempted from evacuation must be sterilized" (Hilberg 96–97). —Trans.

11. Mrs. Brüll seems to be aware of the policy finalized at the Wannsee Conference, according to which *Mischlinge* of the second degree were to be treated as Germans except in cases in which the appearance of the person in question was found to be "racially exceptionally poor . . . so that for external reasons alone he has to be considered a Jew" (Hilberg 97). —Trans.

Works Cited

Adler, H. G. *Der verwaltete Mensch: Studien zur Deportation der Juden aus Deutschland.* Tübingen: Mohr, 1974.

Burleigh, Michael. *Germany Turns Eastwards: A Study of Ostforschung in the Third Reich.* New York: Cambridge UP, 1988.

Hilberg, Raul. *Documents of Destruction: Germany and Jewry 1933–1945.* Chicago: Quadrangle, 1971.

Komjathy, Anthony, and Rebecca Stockwell. *German Minorities and the Third Reich: Ethnic Germans of East Central Europe between the Wars.* New York: Holmes, 1980.

Sheltering Battered Bodies
in Language

Imprisonment Once More?

Karen Remmler

> We had the chance to observe how the word became flesh and how this
> incarnated word finally led to heaps of cadavers.
>
> —Jean Améry

IN HIS COLLECTION of essays, *At the Mind's Limits,* Jean Améry speculates on
the consequences of the physical torture and the melding of "word" and
"flesh" that he experienced firsthand as a prisoner of the Gestapo and inmate
in Auschwitz. His insight into the precarious relationship between language
and material reality during the Third Reich raises difficult questions about the
adequacy of linguistic representation to express the pain inflicted upon him
and other survivors of the Holocaust. Although he acknowledges the apparent
ineffability of the pain and the subsequent impulse to remain silent, Améry, at
the same time, warns against a transformation of the suffering into a "mere
memory" (xi). He rebels against a "present that places the incomprehensible
in the cold storage of history and thus falsifies it in a revolting way" (xi). Similarly, Mali Fritz—a Holocaust survivor, who, like Améry, was arrested for her
political activity before being deported by the Gestapo—resists a remembering
that would once more efface the bodies of the dead already made invisible by
Nazi administrative discourse and policies. In her autobiographical account of
her interrogation by the Gestapo and subsequent deportation to Auschwitz-
Birkenau, *Essig gegen den Durst* (Vinegar against the Thirst), Fritz writes
about the difficulty of describing her memories of pain in the language of the
perpetrators. Whereas Améry chose to write in French—the language he
adopted in exile—Fritz writes in her mother tongue, German. In their struggle
to remember the bodies of the dead by expressing the painful recollections of
their own tortured bodies in words they repeatedly found inadequate, Améry
and Fritz experience the "crisis of witnessing" faced by other Holocaust survivors.

Shoshana Felman and Dori Laub argue in *Testimony: Crises of Witnessing
in Literature, Psychoanalysis, and History* that a "crisis of witnessing" is experienced by Holocaust survivors, who attempt to describe their remembrance

of an event that virtually eliminated all its witnesses (xvii). In her analysis of Claude Lanzmann's *Shoah*, Felman shows how the film dramatizes the *"impossibility of testimony"* while, at the same time, affirming the *"necessity of testimony"* and the "historical impossibility of *escaping* the predicament of being—and of having to become—a witness" (224). The heaps of cadavers and the "incarnated" words of Nazism that Améry alludes to are what the Nazis called "Figuren" (210). According to Felman, *Shoah* illustrates the "Nazi scheme" to render the Jews invisible by "reducing even the materiality of the dead bodies to smoke and ashes" (209–10). But not only the corpses are destroyed. Even "the linguistic referentiality and literality of the *word* 'corpse' " is reduced "to the transparency of a pure form and to the pure rhetorical metaphoricity of a mere *figure*" (210). Accordingly, Améry and Fritz, as witnesses to an event seemingly beyond words, are confronted with the need to find a language with which to embody the physical experience of the Holocaust without once more displacing real bodies into "Figuren" that erase not only the corpses of concentration camp prisoners, but also the memories of their existence.

I would like to suggest that Améry and Fritz reinstate the missing body by embodying the pain experienced through torture and imprisonment in metaphors that defy the breakdown between language and material reality. Faced with a "crisis of witnessing" and the ethical dilemma of relying on metaphor to communicate pain, how do Améry and Fritz find a language to recall the connection between word and flesh? Furthermore, how do we read their texts in light of postmodernist theoretical discourses that claim the impossibility of representing a reality in which this connection exists?[1] In order to address these questions about the struggle to express the pain of torture in words, and the precarious role of the scholar who interprets the metaphors of pain in testimonials, I focus on two texts: "Torture" by Jean Améry, and *Essig gegen den Durst* by Mali Fritz.[2] I have chosen to concentrate on these two texts in light of the dilemma of representation that is itself central to debates about the way history is—or is not—represented in both documentary and artistic images of the Holocaust. Jean Améry and Mali Fritz remember the physical pain inflicted on them in Gestapo interrogation cells and German concentration camps in order to regain a semblance of historical identity, an identity grounded in the reality of their scarred bodies. Aware that pain defies language, they nevertheless depend on metaphor to re-member the dismemberment of their bodies and psyches through physical and psychological deprivation. It is the contextualization of the metaphor in their texts, however, that remembers the presence of the body through the word instead of detaching it from material referentiality. In the act of reading, we are confronted with the contradiction that pain—itself unspeakable—becomes the most powerful expression of a historical event that seems to defy words.

I. The Displaced Body

Within the context of the growing gap between language and material reality manifested in the increasing textualizing of the human body in postmodern discourse, Améry's warning against a language that conflates word and flesh takes on new meaning.[3] Whereas Améry's linguistic representations of the body give voice to the bodies destroyed in German concentration camps, the representation of the body in postmodern discourses often implies that the gap between words and body remains unbridgeable.[4]

In ongoing discussions about the relationship between material reality (flesh) and discourse (word) many scholars, questioning the comparatively static biological, physiological, and anatomical models that have traditionally explained the human body, see it as discursively produced, an at once social and cultural construct that is always in process (see Adelson). The body, as an object of study, has been displaced into metaphors, signs, and images.[5] Simultaneously, a distrust of referential representation places the existence of a "real" body in question by drawing attention to the ideological significance of metaphorical structures and narrative forms that construct images of the body.

The emphasis of postmodern theoretical discourses on the ever-changing, cultural-historical construction of the body coincides with technological developments in the fields of medicine, computer science, and communications in which "real" bodies are mapped out or simulated through electronic images.[6] Accordingly, as the body is technologically simulated and transformed into a virtual image by the media, it disappears into a metaphorical discourse that removes real bodies from sight and displaces them into textual surfaces.

> If, today, there can be such an intense fascination with the fate of the body, might this not be because the body no longer exists? For we live under the dark sign of Foucault's prophecy that the bourgeois body is a descent into the empty site of a dissociated ego, a "volume in disintegration," traced by language, lacerated by ideology, and invaded by the relational circuitry of the field of postmodern power. (Kroker and Kroker 20)

The image of the body as a "lacerated" and "disintegrated" sign coincides in part with the awareness of the destructive capabilities of an electronic warfare to reduce, starve, and mutilate bodies without coming into contact with them.[7] The prevalence of metonymical references to displaced bodies, body parts, and conditions in postmodern theoretical discourse emerges, in part, no doubt, out of an increasing capacity for technological destruction and transformation of the body. At the same time, it emerges out of a significant increase in the number of displaced persons across political, cultural, and economic borders since

World War II.[8] In a historical period of physical upheaval and displacement, it is perhaps no coincidence that those who write on the body tend to stress its diseased, wounded, and pained state while at the same time noting the diminishing potential of the body to experience pleasure.[9]

One could argue that the body has often been represented through metaphor, and thus has always, in a sense, been estranged from its living, material reality. Yet, what are the consequences of assuming a lack of referentiality between the lived body and metaphor when words have been used to mediate and obscure the killing of people, as in the case of the Holocaust? Although the problematizing of representation in postmodern theoretical discourses invites us to question the discursive constructions of power relations—including those prevalent during the Holocaust—do they enable us to see the bodies behind the metaphor? When we look at texts that describe extreme bodily sensations, such as the physical pain inflicted by one human being upon another through torture, these questions pose themselves with particular urgency.[10]

Although I do not claim to have definitive answers to these questions, they foreground my discussion of "body displacement" as it is portrayed by Holocaust survivors. I use "body displacement" to signify both the process by which a "real" body is displaced into a site of pain in torture and, conversely, the process by which it is remembered by the tortured individual through representation. The difference between the initial displacement and the secondary replacement is that the first aims to destroy the body, while the second attempts to resituate it in the world. Thus, torture is an extreme form of body displacement because it exposes the illusion of a social contract based on consent (see Scarry, "Consent"). Having been initially displaced physically as one's body is forcibly removed from a relatively safe place to one of danger, the tortured individual undergoes a further displacement as he or she is stripped of the right to mutually acceptable human contact and finds him or herself reduced to victim.

Within the context of postmodern theoretical discourses about the body, Elaine Scarry's work, in particular *The Body in Pain: The Making and the Unmaking of the World*, provides a starting point for analyzing forms of body displacement in written accounts by torture victims. In her analysis of the relations between the body and discourse in torture, Scarry investigates the interaction between metaphors alluding to violated bodies and the physical experience of violation by the tortured individual. Scarry's work, as well as that of Améry and Fritz, suggests that torture exposes the fictionality and fragility of trust between human beings (and the illusion of its existence in the first place): all trust in the world and universally accepted human rights are destroyed. The perception of the body as a social place of orientation, of desire, and of communication radically disintegrates as the body's space is violated in torture. The physical transgression is, at the same time, a violation of the mind and spirit that transforms the body of the tortured individual into a place of pain, thereby exposing the illusion that one has authority over the boundaries and autonomy of one's own body (see Scarry, "Consent").

Scarry's work has been instrumental in alerting scholars to the consequences of relying too heavily on discourse as the definer of experience. It is the real body in pain that we must keep in mind when we interpret accounts of torture. And we must differentiate between the pain experienced by the tortured individual and its figurative appropriation.[11] Given the political consequences of torture, the dilemma underlying Scarry's analysis of the relationship between language and the body in pain is how to express the inexpressible (pain) in order to prevent it (*The Body in Pain* 11). Scarry meticulously explicates the interactions between language and the body in torture in order to maintain the presence of the body despite the inadequacy of words to embody physical pain. The body in pain does not disappear once it is represented in language.[12] As one reviewer puts it, Scarry sees the body as "the determining ground of the symbolic; through the infliction of pain on human bodies, realities are made and unmade, ideas are legitimated and de-legitimated" (McGee 71). Rather than seeing the body as a figurative construction of language, Scarry's deconstruction of torture thus reconstitutes the body as the primary source of metaphor:

> Physical pain . . . is language-destroying. Torture inflicts bodily pain that is itself language-destroying, but torture also mimes . . . this language-destroying capacity in its interrogation, the purpose of which is not to elicit needed information but visibly to deconstruct the prisoner's voice. The word "deconstruct" rather than "destroy" is used in the previous sentence because to say the interrogation "visibly destroys" the prisoner's voice only implies that the *outcome* of the event is the shattering of the person's voice. . . . The prolonged interrogation, however, also graphically objectifies the step-by-step backward movement along the path by which language comes into being and which is here being reversed or uncreated or deconstructed. (19–20)

By inducing pain the torturer reduces the bodies of his victims to pain, thereby making the bodies of the tortured individuals into vehicles and agents of pain (47). Whereas the destruction of the body in pain transforms it into the most immediate site of identity—the tortured body becomes excruciatingly present—the voice is made absent as the tortured are reduced to screaming, moaning, and finally, in death, silent flesh (49).[13] The displaced voice of the tortured becomes the property of the torturer as the powerlessness of the tortured body becomes the powerfulness of the torturer. Thus, "it is in part the obsessive display of agency that permits one person's body to be translated into another person's voice, that allows real human pain to be converted into a regime's fiction of power" (Scarry, *The Body in Pain* 18). At the same moment the torturer commands the tortured individual to speak, he or she destroys the physical capabilities of speech.

Whereas Scarry concentrates on the interaction between words and bodies during torture, my reading of the texts by Améry and Fritz focuses on the remembering process of the individual who survives torture. By exploring how Améry and Fritz write about bodies in pain without once again replicating the extreme displacement experienced in pain into a detached metaphor, I will show how the choice of metaphors translates the language-destroying experience of torture into words that embody the experience. Despite the difficulty of communicating their experience, Améry and Fritz struggle against the silencing of their own physical dislocation through torture and imprisonment by relocating their bodies textually. As they remember their pain through words, the physical experience of torture is displaced from the body into metaphorical images of pain. Language serves to construct the significance and the meaning of the pain for the rememberer rather than be the conveyor of the "fiction of power" for the torturer.

II. The Re-Membered Body

Before turning to Améry and Fritz, I want to outline briefly the ethical concerns shared by many Holocaust scholars about the dilemma of interpreting survivor testimonials with words that could potentially elide the very voices struggling to express the inconceivable horror of the concentration camps.[14] Not surprisingly, this concern is also shared by Holocaust survivors, such as Améry or Fritz, who not only write about the brutality of the Nazi Reich they experienced firsthand, but also question the possibility of communicating this experience in language. Incorporating metaphors of pain, they refuse to capitulate to the postmodern crisis of representation.

This "crisis of representation" is perhaps nowhere rendered as controversial as in current debates about the moral ramifications of remembering the Holocaust not only through documentary testimonials, but also through fictionalized renditions. These debates are part of a larger crisis in postmodern theory about the consequences of shifting attention from the historical to the discursive and from forms of intervention to forms of representation. Scholars engaged in Holocaust studies, such as James Young, Geoffrey H. Hartman, Alan Rosenberg, Shoshana Felman, and Saul Friedlander have written insightfully about this dilemma of representation and testimonial.[15] One of the major aspects of this dilemma is the disjuncture between the apparent ineffability of the pain and suffering experienced by Holocaust survivors and the moral imperative to give testimony to an audience temporally removed from the event.[16]

Whereas Holocaust survivors attempt to bridge the gap between reality and language in their texts, readers of Holocaust literature and testimonials address the need to develop workable guidelines for interpreting the authenticity of experience in testimonial, documentary, and fictionalized descriptions of pain. What value judgments do we make in deeming one description of pain more authentic than another? Has pain been adequately expressed if a writer finds the "right" metaphor? How can the body in pain be present in a text that turns it into a figurative sign?

Scholars who reflect on these questions in their work often point out the tenuous definitions of what constitutes reality, history, and memory. In her essay on Cavani's film *The Night Porter*, Jutta Brückner, for example, draws attention to the relation between the historical remembering of the Holocaust and its representation through metaphor:

> The film, like every B-movie, does not reflect what it does—it simply says something. This transition from historical truth to metaphor is, naturally, extremely problematic at a time when our historical memory is still enough awake to distill the horror and indignation from the terror associated with the original images. The images are, therefore, still imbued with the authentic experience from which they draw their emotional intensity, but are no longer attached to the rigor of historical reflection in which they were, up to now, preserved in their own truth. (353)

The emotional impact of the images associated with the event of the Holocaust remains embedded in metaphors that become estranged from the historical context. Similarly, Young notes in his book *Writing and Rewriting the Holocaust* that developments in literary theory have influenced the means and methods of interpreting representations of the experience of the Holocaust. Young voices the anxiety felt by some Holocaust scholars when texts about the suffering of Jews and others during the Holocaust become objects of a literary inquiry that emphasizes the methods of the interpreter over the remembrance of the events re-presented in the texts: "To concentrate on the poetics of a witness's testimony . . . over the substance of testimony seems to risk displacing the events under discussion altogether" (3). Young calls for an interchange between interpretation and historical context because "the significance and meaning of the events created in these texts often reflect the kind of understanding of events by victims at the time: and as these 'mere' interpretations led to their responses, the interpreted versions of the Holocaust in its texts now lead us to our actions in the world in light of the Holocaust" (3). Thus, the reality of the Holocaust and the materiality of the bodies effaced by it are perceived within the temporal and spatial context of the rememberer, thereby returning historical specificity to the different experiences of pain during the Holocaust.

Yet, the dilemma of expressing the unsayable remains, even in the most concrete representations of the body in pain. Jean Améry's discussion of his tortured body exemplifies this dilemma. Any attempt to metaphorize the pain inflicted upon him during his interrogation by the Gestapo is, to him, "totally senseless" (33). Comparisons of the pain of torture with the sensation of "a red-hot iron in [his] shoulders" or "a dull wooden stake that had been driven into the back of [his] head" would only lead to a "hopeless merry-go-round of figurative speech" (33). His own experience of torture defies language, yet Améry attempts to approximate the consequences of the pain upon his body: "Frail in the face of violence, yelling out in pain, awaiting no help, capable of no resistance, the tortured person is only a body, and nothing else beside that" (33).

Améry describes his own torture by the Gestapo and the SS in a prison at Breendonk, Belgium, in 1943 in order to examine the limits of language in communicating this experience to others. Jean Améry underwent a series of displacements in his lifetime that are common to many forced into exile by totalitarian regimes. He was born in Austria in 1912 as Hans Mayer. After 1945, Mayer changed his name to Jean Améry in protest against the abuse of the German language by the Nazis. As what racialist categories termed a "half-Jew" (his father was Jewish, as was his wife), Améry, from the early thirties on, found himself increasingly at risk in the climate of growing Austrian anti-Semitism. In 1938, after the *Anschluß* (annexation) of Austria to the German Reich, he and his wife fled Austria for Belgium. Thus Améry became physically displaced from his beloved Austrian landscape and his mother tongue. In 1940, after the invasion of Belgium by Germany, Améry was deported to a French holding camp, then transferred to the German-run camp at Gurs. He escaped from Gurs, returned to Belgium, and worked with the Belgian resistance movement until his capture in 1943. His internment at Fort Breendonk, subsequent torture by the Gestapo and SS, and deportation to Auschwitz is the subject of his essays in *At the Mind's Limits*.[17]

In his account of torture and imprisonment in Auschwitz, Améry puts into words what abstracted terms such as "deportation" or "displacement" can only approximate. His torture was the culmination of years of exile. He was already a displaced person, forced into exile by the German Nazis and their Austrian accomplices in 1938. He describes the impact of his forced displacement and deportation as the shock of the interrogator's fist making contact with his skin. This previously unfathomable violation of his body reduces Améry from man to animal:

> But in the world of torture man exists only by ruining the other person who stands before him. A slight pressure by the tool-wielding hand is enough to turn the other—along with his head, in which are perhaps stored Kant and Hegel, and all nine symphonies, and the World as Will and Representation—into a shrilly squealing piglet at slaughter. (35)

The image of a "squealing piglet at slaughter" graphically represents the degree of extreme vulnerability of the "body in pain" denied any semblance of agency. Yet, the remembering of the tortured body reinstates an agency that does not deny the experience of victimization, but recognizes the possibility of resistance against becoming a victim *only*. By reclaiming his body in words, Améry also recognizes the continuation of torture and its lasting effect on his sense of self. Thus, he is only a temporary survivor and his suicide in 1978 is perhaps the final outcome of the pain inflicted upon him during his interrogation by the Gestapo.

In addition to describing the violation of his body at the hands of another human being, Améry describes the loss of trust; not only in the world, but also in the "certainty that by reason of written or unwritten social contracts the other person will spare [him] . . . that he will respect [his] physical, and . . . metaphysical, being" (28). Améry wishes to know "the others, who pulled [him] up by [his] dislocated arms and punished [his] dangling body with the horsewhip" (34). For him the torturers are not "merely brutalized petty bourgeois and subordinate bureaucrats of torture" (34). Drawing from Georges Bataille's discussion of sadism in the work of the Marquis de Sade, Améry arrives at the same conclusions as Scarry about the act of torture as the "unmaking of the world." Understanding sadism as the "radical negation of the other, [and] as the denial of the social principle as well as the reality principle," Améry attributes the behavior of his torturers to their desire to maintain total control over the "flesh and spirit" of another human being in order to achieve a form of "murderous self-realization" (35-36). The tortured becomes the other for the torturer (34).[18] Even after Améry has been transformed into the "total reality" of flesh, the identity of his torturer remains an object of speculation:

> When it [the first blow] has happened and the torturer has expanded into the body of his fellow man and extinguished what was his spirit, he himself can then smoke a cigarette or sit down to breakfast or, if he has the desire, have a look in at the World as Will and Representation. (34)

The blow to the head destroys the world represented by the knowledge stored in the mind. It is destroyed as the violated body loses access to the symbolic realm and its voice is reduced to a physical scream of pain. And yet Améry conjoins word and body by illustrating the etymological origin of "torture" as the Latin "torquere." The bodily sensation of twisting ("torquere") reminds the reader of the corporeality of the word:

> If I finally want to get to the analysis of torture, then unfortunately I cannot spare the reader the objective description of what now took place. . . . In the bunker there hung from the vaulted ceiling a chain that above ran into a roll.

At its bottom end it bore a heavy, broadly curved iron hook. I was led to the instrument. The hook gripped into the shackle that held my hands together behind my back. Then I was raised with the chain until I hung about a meter over the floor. . . . All your life is gathered in a single, limited area of the body, the shoulder joints, and it does not react; for it exhausts itself completely in the expenditure of energy. . . . And now there was a crackling and splintering in my shoulders that my body has not forgotten until this hour. The balls sprang from their sockets. . . . I fell into a void and now hung by my dislocated arms, which had been torn high from behind and were now twisted over my head . . . torture . . . What visual instruction in etymology. (32–33)

Améry's body dangles, no ground under its feet. Dis-located, it becomes all flesh, felt in the sensation of hanging with arms pulled out of their sockets. The displaced arms sway from the chain, no longer connected to the body that is no longer perceived to be whole, no longer felt to belong in one piece to a person named Améry. The word becomes body and the pain need not be represented in metaphorical terms to be communicated.

In contrast to Améry, who refuses to incorporate the language of the torturer into his own text, Mali Fritz, in her autobiographical account of her internment in Auschwitz-Birkenau, *Essig gegen den Durst* (Vinegar against the Thirst), incorporates the words of her interrogators and incarcerators into her own language of anger and despair. Instead of analyzing language abstractly, Fritz places the language of perpetrators and victims side by side, physically displacing their semantic proximity by way of quotation marks. A guard is not a guard but an "escort."

Like Améry, Fritz fled from Austria in 1938 for political reasons, first, and because of her Jewish background, second. An avowed communist who had joined the fight against fascism in the Spanish Civil War, Fritz fled to France. She was arrested in 1941 after being denounced by a former resistance fighter, Josef Pasternak, who became an informant for the French collaborators and later the Gestapo. Fritz escaped from the "reception" camp in Brens, only to be recognized and handed over to the Gestapo by Pasternak in Paris in 1942. Deported to Vienna, she was imprisoned and interrogated for nine months in the notorious "Liesl" prison. After refusing to give the Gestapo information about the whereabouts of other Austrian anti-fascists, Fritz was deported to Auschwitz-Birkenau in 1943. Her survival and the effects of the utter physical and psychological depravation and humiliation in the concentration camp are the subject of *Essig gegen den Durst*.[19]

Moving between past and present tenses in her recounting of total dehumanization, Fritz counters historical approaches to the Holocaust that deny its impact on the present. Fritz's account of her imprisonment depicts the calculated practices of the concentration camp commanders and their subordinates to disorient, degrade, and finally, kill their victims. Seeing the destruction of the powerless inmates as an integral part of the total war waged by the Nazis against other nations and peoples, Fritz describes the unsanitary conditions and intentional neglect in the camps that reduce her body and the bodies of her fellow inmates into pus-ridden, emaciated "living corpses." Fritz's skin becomes covered with the sewage expelled by violated, humiliated, and incarcerated bodies. Exposed to depravation and close to death, Fritz develops a heightened sensitivity toward her body even as her faculties of self-perception are diminished. The outer world—time, space, names and dates—become submerged in the stinking mire that she is forced to wade through as she shovels excrement on work detail.

Infected with typhus, Fritz is transferred to the sick bay that masquerades as a hospital but is actually the last station before death. Her body becomes an item destined to be consumed by ovens. Plagued with burning sores and fever, Fritz disengages herself from her body in hallucinations, only to find her way back to it when touching the boils that are physical remnants of her disease.[20] Years after the Holocaust, it is the lump left in her skin by the boil long healed that reminds Fritz of her displaced existence. The lump serves as a catalyst for remembering her suffering and acts of defiance within the context of the concentration camp where survival was not so much calculated resistance as lucky coincidence or the momentary mercy of a guard. At the same time that the scar left by the once-infected boil revives her memory of the concentration camp, it also establishes her presence as a survivor:

> I don't know anyone here, not even myself. When the fever calms down, I search for and find a place in my face that throbs in a peculiar way: at the bottom of my face to the left, just above the lower jaw, yes, there it is, a small abscess, perhaps a boil, yes, then I know who I am. In the meantime I have lost myself and by touching this infected, throbbing lump, I touch myself, a pain of recognition. (89)

Tellingly, the small, raised blemish embodies the concrete evidence of Fritz's suffering as much as it represents a part of her identity that has not succumbed to the pain. By touching the bump Fritz feels confirmed in her task of remembering her pain. For the bump is a marker of a past not readily recognized or acknowledged in postwar Austria because it is a concrete reminder of the atrocities committed by the Nazis and their Austrian collaborators, who are unwilling to confront their complicity. In the social context of Austria after 1945, her physical presence is shunned because it causes discomfort among those who would rather forget. She defies the displacement of her body into forgetfulness by speaking in public about her experiences. Thus, Fritz reclaims her body by inscribing it with meaning she herself has created.

Yet Fritz's body does not only represent a self-created identity. Upon entering the concentration camp her body also became the physical site upon which the power of the Nazi state was and remains violently engraved. After hearing a doctor, whom she sees after the war, remark that Auschwitz "couldn't have been that bad, otherwise you wouldn't be here" (136), Fritz has the identification number tattooed on her wrist surgically removed, for it textualizes her body as the property of the Nazis. Having erased the Nazi text, she re-inscribes her body in her own words by transferring it from her flesh to the page. She removes the stigma from the body of the victim by transforming it into a text that names the victimizer.

After many years of silence, Mali Fritz was impelled to write about her experiences by her disgust with the election in Austria of Kurt Waldheim to the presidency (despite his alleged participation in wartime atrocities), with promoters of the so-called Auschwitz Lie, and with a growing disregard for the marginalized in Austrian society. By writing about her experiences and by focusing on the body, Fritz refuses to allow her body to be a monument to pain, inscribed with the grotesque euphemisms of the Nazis. She writes her body as it is, scarred, but not defeated. The scars and boils left by the experience of dehumanization in the concentration camp absorb the memories, thus transforming her body into a catalyst both for remembering the pain and for overcoming the pain through writing.

Even as they acknowledge the inexpressibility of pain, Améry and Fritz nevertheless demonstrate the necessity of contextualizing the source of the pain. By concentrating on the material reality of their pain and the agents responsible for it, Améry and Fritz recover their bodies as extensions of their own voices. In refusing to remain silent and in insisting upon giving testimony to the crimes committed against them and others, Améry and Fritz contextualize their pain in metaphors that return their bodies to the text without once again effacing them. It is the pain inflicted upon their bodies by other human beings that recalls the process by which the body in pain was first inscribed onto the page. Like the sharp script etched into the bloody and grooved skin of the condemned in Kafka's "The Penal Colony," the words written by Améry and Fritz remind the reader of the pain attached to and embedded in language.[21] The re-membering in these texts is not the gesture of putting the dismembered body parts back together again nor of giving the displaced bodies reprieve from homelessness.[22] The damage is done and cannot be undone. Despite the inadequacy of language to communicate the experience of torture, Améry's essay and Fritz's account evoke physical sensations of discomfort, revulsion, and anger in the reader. The word is no longer detached from the body in pain from which it is derived. But how do metaphors of pain reincarnate the materiality of language? What is the cost to the writer attempting to describe the inexpressible in terms of his or her own tortured body? By writing about their torture and imprisonment in a language that can only border on the territory of experience, Améry and Fritz regain a semblance of voice in a time when the authenticity of the subject is both philosophically and socially tenuous.

Notes

I would like to thank Angelika Bammer for her rigorous and thoughtful comments on different drafts of this essay. Leslie Adelson and Alberto Sandoval also made valuable suggestions on earlier versions.

1. Saul Friedlander's collection *Probing the Limits of Representation* explores the effect upon Holocaust studies of "postmodern thought's rejection of the possibility of identifying some stable reality or truth beyond the constant polysemy and self-referentiality of linguistic constructs" (4). The contributions raise issues about the applicability of postmodernist perspectives in discussions of both documentary and artistic representations of the Holocaust.

2. These texts should by no means be taken to be representative of accounts of torture by Holocaust survivors. Moreover, they themselves differ considerably both thematically and structurally. "Torture" is from Jean Améry's *At the Mind's Limits* 21–40. Translations from *Essig gegen den Durst* are my own.

3. Elaine Scarry attributes the present concern with the body to a renewed interest in the referentiality of language to the material world. The body has become the most obvious site of investigation since the "live body" is the "most extreme locus of materialization," and, thus, the place from which to explore the turn to the relations between language and history (Introduction xx–xxi). See also Smith-Rosenberg 101–21; Feher; Suleiman; Gallop; and Foucault, *History of Sexuality*.

4. I do not contend that the metaphorization of the body in postmodern discourse is comparable to the effacement of the body into "Figuren" by Nazi word and deed. The two are historically discrete phenomena. The latter was fatally devastating; the former is a body of theoretical constructs that attempt to interpret the perceptual mechanisms that obscure and/or construct the possible referentiality that exists between word and body.

5. Some of the works that address the means and consequences of metaphorical representations of the body in the "postmodern scene" include: Haraway; Hutcheon; Connor; Harvey; Huyssen; Perloff; and Shapiro.

6. In their collection of essays on the body in postmodern culture, Arthur and Marilouise Kroker offer a number of theses on the "disappearing body in the hyper-modern condition" that imply that bodies are more sign than matter:

> In technological society, the body has achieved a purely *rhetorical* existence . . . it is finally free to be emancipated as the rhetorical centre of the lost subject of desire after desire: the *body as metaphor* for a culture where power itself is always fictional. Indeed, why the concern over the body today if not to emphasize the fact that the (natural) body in the postmodern condition has *already* disappeared, and what we experience as the body is only a fantastic simulacra of body rhetorics? (21–22)

7. A number of scholars have traced the relationship between developments in the technologies of war, media, and medicine and the social constructions and perceptions of human bodies. See Jardine; and Probyn.

8. In his book on postwar Germany, *Stranded Objects: Mourning, Memory, and Film in Postwar Germany*, Eric Santner investigates the historical underpinnings of postmodernist discourses that deal with the representation and construction of bodies under conditions of global political upheaval and displacement. He attributes the emphasis on displacement in a metaphorical sense to historical experiences of displacement such as "the redistribution of power and alliances within Europe . . . a general destabilization of European hegemony in the world; the ascendancy of the United States as a world power; [and] the decolonization of the Third World." Additional factors, he goes on, are "the passage into a computer and information-based rather than industrial economy" and "the availability . . . of technologies capable of eliminating life on the planet" (164).

9. In addition to Santner, others, perhaps most notably, feminist scholars, rely on a mingling of semiotics and social theory to gain insight into the correlation between discourse and the human body (Adelson 15). As Susan Rubin Suleiman points out, a hybridizing of postmodernist and feminist discourses "must confront the specific questions and challenges posed to it from within the feminist movement, notably as concerns the political status of the 'decentered subject' " (190). Other scholars have analyzed the semiotic and symbolic structures of meaning that signify bodies in fashion, advertising, film, and art within the context of postcolonial political and social transformations affecting the conception of the body. See Nicholson; Spivak; Treichler; and Waugh.

10. When I use the word torture I refer to acts of violence committed against one person by another under the auspices of a state-sanctioned process of obtaining information *and* maintaining legitimacy through an atmosphere of terror. Edward Peters's *Torture* traces the semantic history of torture in Western Europe from antiquity to the present day. He distinguishes between "judicial torture" and "moral-sentimental" torture, yet argues that judicial torture is "the *only* kind of torture, whether administered by an official judiciary or by other instruments of the state." By contrast, "moral-sentimental" torture, criticized by Peters for being an inflationary use of the term torture, includes the infliction of pain by others not under the jurisdiction of a state power (7).

11. Discussions about the culture, semantics, and meaning of torture abound, ranging from literary treatments such as Franz Kafka's "The Penal Colony" or J. M. Coetzee's *Waiting for the Barbarians* to testimonials written by victims of torture themselves.

12. Leslie Adelson gives a careful and insightful reading of the thin line between representation and reality in Scarry's work, reminding us that "the discursive representation of the body must not be mistaken for the body of experience, however intricately imbricated the two may be" (20).

13. See Adelson's reading of the concept of "double agency" in terms of Scarry's analysis of the "complex construction and experience of the body as subject and/or object" (21).

14. See, in particular, Friedlander; Felman and Laub; Young; Rosenfeld; and Rosenberg and Myers.

15. Friedlander's edition is perhaps the most comprehensive survey of the different approaches to this dilemma. Compare Young's interpretive study of the discursive and filmic images of the Holocaust.

16. Felman and Laub call for a *"textualization of the context"* in order to analyze the "ways in which our cultural frames of reference and our preexisting categories which delimit and determine our perception of reality have failed, essentially, both to contain, and to account for, the scale of what has happened in contemporary history" (xv).

17. For further biographical information, see Friedrich Pfäfflin.

18. Améry's desire to understand the motives and the inclinations of his torturer raises questions about the relationship between the torturer and the tortured. If the individual being tortured loses a sense of identity and of voice, is she or he without agency? Does the agency of the torturer depend on obliterating the agency of another human being considered to be his or her other? Further issues to explore, but which go beyond the scope of this essay, include the interaction between the body in pain and the perception of otherness, and the consequences of placing the victim/torturer relation outside of the absolute categories of victim and victimizer in order to take into account the multiple structures and degrees of victimization or perpetration in different contexts. Any differentiation of the two categories must take the context and the process of torture into account.

19. *Essig gegen den Durst* is only indirectly a reference to the hardships experienced by Christ during his crucifixion; most immediately, it is a reference to a remark made to Fritz by her interrogator preceding her deportation to Auschwitz. In a last attempt to force her to name other anti-fascists he tells Fritz that she will be sent to a place where she will be given vinegar for her thirst and her body thrown to the dogs (5).

20. Other concentration camp survivors describe similar sensations of separation between self and body. The "self conceived as disembodied represents a kind of temporary haven for the victims of camp brutality" (Adelson 22).

21. Kafka's description of the writing/torture machine in "The Penal Colony" (written 1915/16) is perhaps the most vivid example of the complicity between violence and language. As the officer of the penal camp himself demonstrates to the visitor, accused prisoners were strapped belly-down beneath an elaborately designed and mechanized writing instrument and slowly realized the nature of their "guilt" as their crime was carved into their back. The knowledge of the crime literally entered the prisoners through the bloody grooves of inscribed skin. Once the inscription becomes "legible" to the victim, he stops screaming and silently accepts the punishment: death. The unspeakable horror of having one's body serve as a writing tablet is also a reminder of the material relation between the (human) body and writing. Parchment was, after all, skin and guts.

22. Améry described his "homelessness" as the consequence of torture: "Whoever has succumbed to torture can no longer feel at home in the world" (40). See also Levi 132.

Works Cited

Adelson, Leslie. *Making Bodies, Making History: Feminism & German Identity*. Lincoln: U of Nebraska P, 1993.

Améry, Jean. *At the Mind's Limits: Contemplations by a Survivor on Auschwitz and its Realities*. Trans. Sidney Rosenfeld and Stella P. Rosenfeld. Bloomington: Indiana UP, 1980. Trans. of *Jenseits von Schuld und Sühne. Bewältigungsversuche eines Überwältigten*. Munich: Szczesny, 1966.

Brückner, Jutta. "Bilder des Bösen." *Die Inszenierung der Macht: Ästhetische Faszination im Faschismus*. Ed. Klaus Behnken and Frank Wagner. Gesellschaft für bildende Künste, 1987. 345–53.

Coetzee, J. M. *Waiting for the Barbarians*. New York: Penguin, 1982.

Connor, Steven. *Postmodernist Culture: An Introduction to the Theories of the Contemporary.* Oxford: Blackwell, 1989.

Feher, Michel, ed. *Fragments for a History of the Human Body.* 3 vols. New York: Zone, 1989.

Felman, Shoshana, and Laub, Dori, ed. *Testimony: Crises of Witnessing in Literature, Psychoanalysis, and History.* New York: Routledge, 1992.

Foucault, Michel. *Discipline and Punish: The Birth of the Prison.* Trans. Alan Sheridan. New York: Pantheon, 1977.

———. *The History of Sexuality.* Trans. Robert Hurley. 3 vols. New York: Pantheon, 1978.

Friedlander, Saul, ed. *Probing the Limits of Representation: Nazism and the "Final Solution".* Cambridge: Harvard UP, 1992.

Fritz, Mali. *Essig Gegen den Durst. 565 Tage in Auschwitz-Birkenau.* Wien: Verlag für Gesellschaftskritik, 1986.

Gallop, Jane. *Thinking through the Body.* New York: Cornell UP, 1988.

Haraway, Donna J. *Simians, Cyborgs, and Women: The Reinvention of Nature.* New York: Routledge, 1991.

Harvey, David. *The Condition of Postmodernity.* Oxford: Blackwell, 1989.

Hartman, Geoffrey H., ed. *Bitburg in Moral and Political Perspective.* Bloomington: Indiana UP, 1986.

Hutcheon, Linda. *The Politics of Postmodernism.* London: Routledge, 1989.

Huyssen, Andreas. *After the Great Divide: Modernism, Mass Culture, Postmodernism.* Bloomington: Indiana UP, 1986.

Jardine, Alice. "Of Bodies and Technologies." *Discussions in Contemporary Culture.* Ed. Hal Foster. Seattle: Bay, 1987. 151–58.

Kafka, Franz. *In der Strafkolonie und andere Prosa.* Stuttgart: Reclam, 1986.

Kroker, Arthur, and Marilouise Kroker, eds. *Body Invaders: Panic Sex in America.* New York: St. Martin's, 1987.

Levi, Primo. "The Memory of Offense." *Bitburg in Moral and Political Perspective.* Ed. Geoffrey H. Hartman. Bloomington: Indiana UP, 1986. 130–37.

McGee, Patrick. "Theory in Pain." *Genre* 20.1 (1987): 67–84.

Nicholson, Linda J., ed. *Feminism/Postmodernism.* New York: Routledge, 1990.

Perloff, Marjorie. *Postmodern Genres.* Norman: U of Oklahoma P, 1988.

Peters, Edward. *Torture.* Oxford: Blackwell, 1985.

Pfäfflin, Friedrich. "Jean Améry. Daten zu einer Bibliographie." *Jean Améry: Text + Kritik* 99 (1988). Ed. Heinz Ludwig Arnold.

Probyn, Elspeth. "Bodies and Anti-Bodies: Feminism and the Postmodern." *Cultural Studies* 1.3 (1987): 349–60.

Rosenberg, Alan, and Gerald E. Myers, eds. *Echoes from the Holocaust: Philosophical Reflections on a Dark Time.* Philadelphia: Temple UP, 1988.

Rosenfeld, Alvin H. *A Double Dying: Reflections on Holocaust Literature.* Bloomington: Indiana UP, 1980.

Santner, Eric L. *Stranded Objects: Mourning, Memory and Film in Postwar Germany.* Ithaca: Cornell UP, 1990.

Scarry, Elaine. *The Body in Pain: The Making and Unmaking of the World.* New York: Oxford UP, 1985.

———. "Consent and the Body: Injury, Departure, and Desire." *New Literary History* 21 (1990): 867–96.

———. Introduction. *Literature and the Body: Essays on Population and Persons.* Ed. Elaine Scarry. Baltimore: Johns Hopkins UP, 1988. vii–xxvii.

Shapiro, Gary, ed. *After the Future: Postmodern Times and Places.* New York: State U of New York P, 1990.

Smith-Rosenberg, Carroll. "The Body Politic." *Coming to Terms: Feminism, Theory, Politics.* Ed. Elizabeth Weed. London: Routledge, 1989. 101–21.

Spivak, Gayatri Chakravorty. *In Other Worlds: Essays in Cultural Politics.* New York: Methuen, 1987.

Suleiman, Susan Rubin. *Subversive Intent: Gender, Politics, and the Avant-Garde.* Cambridge: Harvard UP, 1990.

Treichler, Paula A. "AIDS, Homophobia and Biomedical Discourse: An Epidemic of Signification." *Cultural Studies* 1.3 (1987): 263–305.

Waugh, Patricia. *Feminine Fictions: Revisiting the Postmodern.* London: Routledge, 1989.

Young, James E. *Writing and Rewriting the Holocaust: Narrative and the Consequences of Interpretation.* Bloomington: Indiana UP, 1988.

15 | "Coming Home" on the Fourth of July

Constructing Immigrant Identities

Panivong Norindr

> The effect of mass migrations has been the creation of radically new types of human being: people who root themselves in ideas rather than places, in memories as much as in material things; people who have been obliged to define themselves—because they are so defined by others—by their otherness; people in whose deepest selves strange fusions occur, unprecedented unions between what they were and where they find themselves.
>
> —Salman Rushdie

On the front page of the *Southampton Press*,[1] dated July 5, 1979, amidst articles on the price of gas, tax reassessment, suits against the town, issues most characteristic of American politics, are two photographs. The most conspicuous one, in part because of its central placement and large size, is a photograph of veterans carrying the American flag, leading off the Fourth of July parade. The other is smaller, ex-centric, and represents two young Asian men in the process of mailing letters; in the background are the United States post office and its American flag.

These photographs, which appear to have no links, belong, in fact, to the same discursive field. They construct, and, at the same time, frame the space and social context of cultural representation. The Fourth of July photograph can be said to mediate the process by which the subject comes into being. It is the place of identification and of "potent symbolic and affective sources of cultural identity" (Bhabha, "DissemiNation" 292). Commemorating "Independence Day," it displays familiar and readily accessible cultural signs. Veterans in uniform—courageous, determined, and resilient men, who have faith in American values and the American way of life—hold American flags high above their heads. The spectators (mainly women and children) look on proudly; sunshine illuminates the scene.

There are, however, disturbing omissions. The photograph includes only white, middle-aged men, either World War II or Korean War veterans. There are no African-American or Hispanic veterans, no Vietnam veterans, no handicapped. Thus, the spectacle of the parade is perfectly staged to elicit an untroubled patriotism.[2] The *Southampton Press* photograph of the Fourth of July draws upon a stock of cultural images which invoke associations of heroism, chivalry, and pride to project them onto a political reality, repressed and displaced (as I will show) by the photograph of the two adolescents.[3] What is both represented and displaced by this "other" image is the history of American imperialism.

The picture of the two Asian adolescents who are, as we learn, threatened with deportation, must be read in relation to the Fourth of July photograph. Iconically, they are linked by the double inscription of the American flag. The "deportation" photograph functions as a kind of dangerous supplement[4] because it is added only to displace less palatable realities: the Vietnam war, racism, cultural colonization, the price of citizenship. The Fourth of July photograph, meanwhile, replaces these urgent and unresolved matters by substituting a contained and sanctioned image of America. Together, the two photographs, the accompanying text, and the (newspaper) site of their representation construct the problematic immigrant as an assimilable American subject. Central in this construction is the representation of the relationship between the new Asian immigrants and the myth of "America."

One of the founding myths of the United States is that of an immigrant nation: immigrants from Europe, we are told, "discovered" and settled the "New World," establishing an empire out of "nothing." What this myth masks and "forgets" is the violence done to the peoples who already lived here. It is this history of violence and forgetting that the new immigrants, especially those from Asia, are supplementing. Derrida's notion of the supplement is helpful here; he writes:

> It [the supplement] adds only to replace. It intervenes or insinuates itself *in-the-place-of*; if it fills, it is as if one fills a void. If it represents and makes an image, it is by the anterior default of a presence. Compensatory [*suppléant*] and vicarious, the supplement is an adjunct, a subaltern instance which *takes-(the) place [tient-lieu]*. As substitute, it is not simply added to the positivity of a presence, it produces no relief, its place is assigned in the structure by the mark of an emptiness. (145)

This essay seeks to illuminate the process whereby immigrant identities are constructed in the United States. It examines the tension between "ethnic identity" and "citizenship" by exploring the underlying premises behind the notion of "citizenship," a notion based on the assumption of a consensual, contractual relationship.[5] The Asian supplement I propose not only destroys the myth of the benevolent white man ("savior" and "civilizer"), but also replaces the bloody history that this myth has "a-voided." In the process, these new immigrants also remind us that the "founders of America," who came from Europe, came themselves as immigrants.

As Roland Barthes has demonstrated, the press photograph does not simply illustrate the article, but is of equal importance to the written text it supposedly illustrates. In fact, he concludes, the text which accompanies the press photograph merely functions to "sublimate, patheticize or rationalize the image" (204). In this case, the article about the two immigrants about to be deported reveals the hidden subtext, the "difference," obscured by the Fourth of July photograph to which it is linked as a supplement.

The urgency of the situation is conveyed by the dramatic headline: "Two Brothers Face Deportation to Laos." The setting—"Independence Day"—highlights the plight of two brothers who, the reader is told, are about to be sent back to Laos. The caption reads: "Their last hope: Dobby and Lang Norindr of Southampton mail letters appealing to President Carter and Congressman William Carney for help in their efforts to remain in the United States beyond July 29 deadline." At issue are the welfare and status of the two adolescents. Other issues also raised by the article are subsumed under the single goal of validating the claim that America is a land of asylum, a sanctuary. What is at stake, then, is less the fate of the protagonists, but the construction of an image of America, an America with the power to absorb and assimilate others, and transform them into Americans.

The caption gives more clues to the identity of the two brothers. They are "Dobby and Lang Norindr of Southampton." The place of origin to which they are assigned already claims them as Americans. When the title, which stresses "deportation to Laos" is opposed to the caption, the link between the two places becomes clear: Southampton, the American "home," is opposed to the foreign place, Laos. Together, caption and title establish an American identity that is territorially based: "Dobby and Lang Norindr *of Southampton.*"

Yet there are puzzling incongruities between the headline and the body of the text. The article begins with the seemingly irrelevant description of a traditional American rite of passage—high school graduation: "Sunday afternoon, June 24, was a great day for Southampton, as similar days at the end of June each year have been for more than eight decades." Like the photograph of the Fourth of July parade, this opening sentence operates first on the level of affect. A communal identity ("the class of 1979") is established within which individuals find their particular place. The next paragraph, however, begins with an ominous "but":

> But for one of the graduates, the exercises were bitter-sweet, and he looks at his future—which will be decided within the next few weeks—with grave apprehension. For before the end of July, unless a miracle somehow inter-

venes, his hopes and dreams for a bright future will be shattered. He and his
younger brother will be on their way to exile in a hostile country. . . .

The identity—that is, the name—of this graduate is deferred until the fourth
paragraph; he is as yet only identified as "one of the graduates." Finally we are
told who this member of the graduating class is:

> The graduate is Panivong Norindr, affectionately called "Dobby" by his
> classmates, a citizen of Laos who came to America two years ago by way of
> France on a tourist visa to spend his summer vacation with an older brother
> and his wife. His two-year visitor's visa will run out on July 29 and, to date,
> all of his appeals to the various federal agencies for permission to remain
> here beyond then have been rejected. He has been told that he and his
> brother must leave, get out, but go where?

Even though the patronymic identity (Panivong Norindr) and legal status ("a
citizen of Laos") of this person are now known, what is again stressed is his
affective identity ("affectionately called 'Dobby' by his classmates"). What is
more, in the remainder of the article, he will be referred to only by his "American" nickname, "Dobby," allegedly given to him by his classmates.

In short, the Laotian subject is erased. Moreover, it is suggested that
"Dobby" is Laotian not by choice but by accident (of birth). The reader is told
that "Dobby" cannot return or go back to Laos because it is communist ("a
hostile country"). No historical account, no mention of American involvement
and presence in Southeast Asia is supplied. To do so might remind the reader
of the Vietnam War, hardly an appropriate subject for a Fourth of July celebration. Instead, a personal narrative of oppression is provided which once again
operates on the level of affect. "Other members of his family have been sentenced to death by the Red regime there, or they have 'disappeared.' " Death
and disappearance, in other words, threaten the brothers if they return to Laos.
Two places, two systems are thus opposed: one bright and promising, ("America"), the other dark and menacing (the Asian "Red regime"). There is but one
alternative: "Dobby Norindr, member of the Southampton High School class
of 1979, wants desperately to become an American citizen."

The remainder of the article is devoted to legitimizing this desire and to
refashioning the Laotian subject as an American persona. And since what
makes an immigrant a good (assimilable) citizen is, above all, gratitude, the
article goes on to reconstruct and rewrite the history of the brothers in the
mode of the "exemplary" immigrant story, a narrative of persecution and re-
silience: "[They] were studying in Paris when the Communists took over their
Lao homeland. The Reds imprisoned his father's brother for 'plotting to restore the monarchy.' " The gravity of the situation is further conveyed by an
editorial, entitled "Let Them Stay," which reinforces the claims of the feature
article. The editorial makes it clear that the protagonists are considered

Southampton residents. It reiterates the fact that they will be "forced to leave the United States . . . for a foreign country which doesn't want them." This circuitous periphrasis conceals the fact that the country of destination, should they be deported, is actually not Laos, but France.[6] What is not mentioned at all is the fact that France had just rejected a bilateral law with Laos and would not allow the brothers to reenter. Yet neither international immigration treaties nor the problems of political refugees in the world are the focus here; what we are given is a human interest story.

The Immigration and Naturalization Service considers the two brothers Laotian citizens because they possess Laotian passports. But for the *Southampton Press*, they are both homeless and Americans. This paradox must be explained. To undo the logic of American immigration law which declares them, legally, Laotian citizens, the writer for the *Southampton Press* must convince the reader that the two adolescents are homeless. Moreover, it must redefine citizenship symbolically, as affective membership in a community. On these terms, the Laotian brothers are indeed Americans, for their deeds and "performance" since they have lived in Southampton demonstrate allegiance to the United States and not to communist Laos.

The editorial purports to speak for the community, to represent the "will of the people." In their name it plays the role of advocate and champion of the oppressed: "There is a chance that their story will have a happy ending, if only their appeals are answered on the merits and some way is found to cut through the government red tape which could mean, literally, the difference between life and death for them."

Gayatri Spivak's important distinction between two different but often complicit forms of representation—representation in the political sense and representation in the economic sense—are useful here ("Can the Subaltern Speak?"). In the absence of congressional representation, the *Southampton Press* takes the place of Representative Carney, the congressman who has not yet represented or spoken for the two brothers.[7] In that capacity, the *Press* denounces the ineptitude of federal agencies ("to cut through the governmental red tape") and contests their moral authority. The *Press* acts as a judicial review with the responsibility to annul legislative or executive acts which it considers morally in need of amendment.

As for representation in economic terms, the portrait drawn by the *Southampton Press* is unreservedly generous. The editorial rewrites the (American) history of the two brothers in terms of a prototypical American (immigrant) success story: "In the two years that they have lived in Southampton and attended the public school here, Dobby and Lang Norindr have been genuine assets both to the school and the community. Both are excellent, exceptional students; both have extraordinary promising futures. They would in no way impose any burden on the community." The Laotian brothers are used to retell the myth that those who are "hardworking, ambitious, smart" (Spivak, "Practical Politics") and believe in the puritan work ethic will succeed in America. At the same time, the economic metaphor ("genuine assets") inscribes them into a capitalistic market economy where they acquire quantifiable exchange value. They are said to belong (unproblematically) to a continuum of successful migrants. (How those—immigrants or "natives"—who are perceived to have little to give in exchange are treated within this economy is a question that remains open.)

The final paragraph of the editorial summarizes both what is at issue and what is at stake: the ideology and politics represented by the Fourth of July, the question of home and identity, and the relationship between citizens, refugees, and immigrants:

> It is not inappropriate that the Norindrs' appeal should be made on July 4, Independence Day, the birthday of the country which is still the symbol of freedom and hope for so many of the peoples of the world. Theirs is an appeal which should be granted; there is no reason whatsoever why it should not be. We urge the President and Rep. Carney to respond to the plea of two deserving Southampton residents for sanctuary here.

The denouement was, however, not in sight. Neither President Carter nor Representative Carney intervened. Nevertheless, the circulation of the newspaper provoked an extraordinary and unforeseeable set of events. Concrete political relief came from an unexpected place: Maryland. On July 27, 1979, less than a fortnight after the publication of the article, Senator Charles Mathias introduced, in the U.S. Senate, Bill S 1513 (For the relief of Panivong Norindr) and Bill S 1514 (For the relief of Panisouk Norindr), the first of which reads: "Be it enacted by the Senate and House of Representatives of the United States of America in Congress assembled, that for the purposes of the Immigration and Nationality Act, Panivong Norindr shall be held and considered to have been lawfully admitted to the United States for permanent residence as of the date of the enactment of this Act, upon payment of the required visa fee." These private relief bills prevented the Department of Justice and the Immigration and Nationalization Service from deporting the two brothers. How did this come about? Why did Senator Mathias from Maryland intervene? How did he learn about their predicament? Did their father, a former Laotian envoy to the United States, intercede?

The week the deportation article appeared, I was working as a gardener in a Southampton estate, literally and metaphorically sowing the seeds of my American roots. I was busy hoeing, trimming hedges—enacting the work ethic admired by many Americans—not realizing that Senator Mathias's wife (who was spending the Fourth of July weekend in Southampton) was observing me. Without revealing her identity, she came out to "assess"[8] for herself the immigrant's qualities exalted by the *Southampton Press*. A few moments spent conversing with me must have convinced her of the "authenticity" of the portrait drawn, since she brought the article back to her husband in Washington, D.C. On the merit of the newspaper's report and his wife's personal "knowledge" of the case, Senator Mathias introduced a private bill. The press had thus succeeded in inscribing myself and my brother into accessible and assimilable American cultural texts; texts of which Senator Mathias, to our great relief, was a generously responsive reader.

Thus, the "garden plot" thickens. But the question of "authenticity" remains: what made the immigrant so likable or authentic, so, as it were, American? An answer would have to deal not only with the role played by the newspaper article in fashioning and promoting a certain identity, but equally importantly with the active involvement of the immigrant protagonist himself—in short, with my negotiations with and manipulations of the power of the media in constructing that identity. The portrait privileged by the *Southampton Press* must be brought into relation, in other words, with the process of self-fashioning. For the article on my imminent deportation produced a "coherent" American subject by transforming a complex and composite identity collage into a readable "narrative of personal experience" (Said, "Yeats" 26). As information was collected and gleaned from various and quite different sources—a petition filed for political asylum and other INS forms, a personal interview, and word of mouth reputation—representation came together to impart what passed as "knowledge."

The conflation of different discourses (legal, journalistic) and the confusion between spoken, written, and pictorial texts defined the story told by the *Southampton Press*. But information revealed by the political asylum petition does not operate in the same register as the "facts" given in an oral interview. Knowledge obtained in an investigation may reinforce knowledge secured from other sources; it may also contradict it, or convey entirely different experiences. To make this case more compelling and thus more credible, the individual filing for political asylum writes and formulates his answers in such a way as to elicit a favorable response from the reader (in this case an immigration officer). As writing becomes a strategy for survival the boundary between truths and lies, legality and illegality is blurred.[9] Certain facts may have been glossed over and others emphasized (although none may be actually falsified). In many ways, the strategies used by an immigrant or refugee to "write" their (hi)story of oppression are similar to those used by the *Press* when it attempted to present a coherent and compelling figure of the immigrant.

The immigrant's agency in constructing his or her identity is critical. (Im)posturing can be used strategically to shift from liminal subaltern subject position to positions of (relative) authority within a system. What is problematic is the notion of an authentic immigrant experience as it is re-constructed by the press. In this scenario, the experiences of Asian Americans are often used as paradigms of success, as in the widely circulated press stories of the Vietnamese "boat person" who overcomes hardship and oppression to become the valedictorian of his or her class (and goes on to become a business or civic leader). As in the *Southampton Press* account, a certain reading is privileged, unpalatable questions and issues are left out or obscured in order to present yet another rags-to-riches story.

By focusing on the immigrant's experience and by narrating a personal story of the effects of the Vietnam War which shaped the life of an immigrant in the United States, I claim a place for myself. In doing so, I have reproduced, to a certain extent, the paradigms I set out to critique and unwittingly replicated the discursive marginalization of the Vietnam veteran. Yet because I rely on the logic of the supplement as a deconstructive tool to undermine the process whereby immigrant identity and American citizenship are constructed, I am not simply displacing the Vietnam veteran, but reinscribing him into the history that joins us. This essay challenges the accepted notion of Americanness by giving voice to the Laotian immigrant himself, providing, at the same time, a different perspective on American political history. That Laos has not been studied as much as Vietnam or Cambodia because its people have, allegedly, not been subjected to the same kind of genocidal violence and bloodshed as the Vietnamese or Cambodians, is in itself revealing.[10] The legacy of orientalism is at work here. To be worthy of scholarly interest, one has to be "exotic"—even if that means having been obliterated culturally.[11] I am convinced that a study of the political and cultural impact of the Vietnam War on the people of a "forgotten," peripheral Southeast Asian country can provide important new perspectives both on a cultural phenomenon as complex as "American citizenship" and on the history of American involvement in Southeast Asia. Toward that end I address the logic of the substitution of the immigrant story for that of the Vietnam veteran.

The absence of all reference to Vietnam in the July 4, 1979 issue of the *Southampton Press* is symptomatic of the deep cultural malaise in late-seventies America that the press came to label the "Vietnam syndrome." Less than five years after the fall of Saigon in 1975 and after nearly a decade of traumatic war images brought vividly home through the mediation of television,[12] U.S. involvement in Vietnam was considered by many to be a shameful "episode" that Americans needed to "put behind" them and forget. The *Southampton Press* article about two young Asian men reflects, in many ways, the contemporary mood of self-censure and political amnesia. The failure to represent the Vietnam veteran must therefore be inscribed within the larger context of the country's inability and refusal to come to terms with the specious anti-communist "logic" behind the imperialist U.S. foreign policies.[13] This logic is all too well known: it is predicated on unquestioned assumptions of the role of the United States as both benevolent liberator and cultural, political, and economic model to the "Third World," a role which assumes a moral and cultural authority over "backward" nations.

The coherent and idealized image of America as a stable community with one set of cultural assumptions and beliefs[14] was fractured by the Vietnam War. Nationwide anti-war activism refuted any remaining fantasy of a national, political consensus. The Vietnam veteran could not be represented in the July 4th issue of the *Southampton Press* in 1979 in part because he was a living reminder of this traumatic fracturing. He could not be represented because he was an unassimilable, perverted embodiment of the mythologized American soldier: no longer the patriotic and innocent adolescent who went to Vietnam to fight for his country, he returned home a dangerous outcast, a "baby killer," a "murderer."[15] Representations of the Vietnam veteran as rapist (in Elia Kazan's *The Visitors*), hitman (*The Stone Killer*), killer (*Welcome Home Soldier Boys*), and vigilante (*Rolling Thunder*) between 1972 and 1978 in popular B-movies reinforce the image of the dangerous vet, destroyer instead of savior.[16] Finally, Vietnam could not be mentioned because this war that had intruded so prominently into the life of Americans for over a decade had ended with the first military defeat in American history. The Communists, not the Americans, had won.[17] The elision of the Vietnam veteran from the *Southampton Press* front page, I suggest, is part of that much larger repression, the unwillingness to confront and address the ethics and "morality" of this war and the refusal to reflect on its consequences.[18]

In spite of the public's war-weariness and the culture industry's will to forget, a few original voices emerged that resisted the desire to erase all traces of the Vietnam War and its traumatic legacy. Two books in particular deserve to be mentioned here: Ron Kovic's *Born on the Fourth of July* and Michael Herr's *Dispatches*. Both Kovic and Herr did not represent the war in terms of simplistic dualities (good vs. evil, Vietnam vs. America, individual vs. collectivity, history vs. fiction, etc.) but tried to uncover, in their personal narratives, the complexity of the United States' involvement in Vietnam, and in the process come to terms with their own complicitous role in the war. The publication of these two influential books signaled an important turn in both the representation and perception of Vietnam vets from mad killers to victims of the war's madness. As one critic put it, "the paraplegic becomes the heroic victim . . . the paralysis symbolic of both the physical and the psychological maiming of our men" (Grant 24). *Coming Home*, the 1978 film directed by Hal Ashby, which featured the infamous "Hanoi Jane" as the married hospital volunteer who falls in love with a paraplegic veteran, reinforced the representation of the veteran as victim. The 1990 film adaptation of Kovic's *Born on the Fourth of July* further legitimized this theme and confirmed the now popular view of the veteran as a misunderstood and heroic figure who deserves our respect and compassion.

That no mention of the Vietnam War is made in the Fourth of July edition of the *Southampton Press*, just four years after the fall of Saigon, is in itself a remarkable and revealing repression. But in spite of all efforts to the contrary, Vietnam reappears in an uncanny fashion, not only as a ghost which haunts the body politic and the conscience of its people, but as a subtext which determines, in powerful ways, the logic behind the adoption and acceptance of the Southeast Asian immigrant in the late seventies. The generous "welcoming home" extended to two Laotian citizens in 1979 (Vietnam veterans would have to wait until 1985 for their homecoming[19]) worked to alleviate feelings of guilt for the destruction of three former French colonies, a ravage which continues today in the form of economic sanctions not yet lifted against these "Third World" countries who have resisted and successfully fought American military, cultural, and political domination. (Today, Western imperial ascendancy has been replaced by a Vietnamese military and cultural apparatus that has colonized much of Laos and Cambodia. But that is another story.)

Panivong, the Laotian citizen, is (re)born as Dobby, the Laotian-American teenager, in the space surrendered involuntarily by the Vietnam veteran. Dobby becomes part of the apparatus that displaces the Vietnam failure and guilt onto the Asian immigrant success/American benevolence story.[20] Assuredly, the constant and most immediate danger for the new immigrant lies in the assimilative power of a system that rewards homogeneity of thought and action, and scorns dissent and criticism as unpatriotic. This raises the question whether forgetting and the loss of cultural memory are prerequisites to becoming a "true American," a full-fledged member of the American polity. Recently, a writer in the *New Republic* declared that "the truly socially constructed identity is Americanism, not ethnicity." He went on to add that "Americanism is a continually evolving identity that changes with each new group that arrives—but only by insisting that all new groups share in its prerequisites" (Wolfe 30). These prerequisites, which he never defines other than in vague and general terms as "the memory of a struggle" by which the new immigrant transcends the conflicts and hostility that cultural and geographical displacements bring, determine, in his eyes, the essence of Americanness: the common bond that links all immigrants who have come to the United States.

But historical memory, as I have tried to show, is not impervious to repression and projection. The United States makes its "citizen" in its own image. To put it more concretely, the *Southampton Press* paints onto the still malleable figure of the Laotian immigrant American colors, symbols of American virtues and values which merely confirm what is already held to be "self-evident." Having overcome hardship to become a member of the ideal imagined (American) community, "Dobby" always already shares its values and assumptions. But how much paint covers this figure?

Social scientists have argued that identity is a socially constructed phenomenon, responsive to considerations of power, place, and circumstance. Like the article in the *Southampton Press*, my version of the story, my self-(re)presentation, is also circumscribed by institutional, disciplinary, and editorial constraints. I can be accused of appealing to the same images and symbols of Americanization (albeit negative ones) that I criticized earlier, and of reconstructing the experiences of the new immigrant as yet another, if more self-conscious, American success story. The beliefs and aspirations of the "new" immigrant, however, have changed. Unlike the (stereo)typical earlier immigrant, the new immigrant is no longer a passive recipient of the goodwill of the people, but an active character on the American stage. As Bharati Mukherjee puts it, "These new Americans are not willing to wait for a generation or two to establish themselves. They're working for themselves and their children of course, but they're not here to sacrifice themselves for the future's sake" (28).

There are still considerable pressures on the new immigrants to live up to the image of the hard-working and acquiescent petitioners for citizen membership who want, at all costs, to be accepted as Americans, just like their nineteenth-century European counterparts before them who yearned to become accepted into the community. The sentimentalization of the immigrants' experiences, of their difficult journey into mainstream America, have contributed to make the immigrant's story a cornerstone of American cultural mythology. But other stories are complicating and unsettling the premises of this tale. "America is not what it used to be." At the root of this lament, heard across the United States, is the changing demography of America, the result of recent immigration from Third World countries like Mexico, India, China, the Philippines, and Vietnam. Today's acrimonious debate about multi-culturalism must be linked to the changes brought by these new immigrants from "non-traditional" immigrant countries who are transfiguring not only the ethnic and racial composition of the American population but its customs and beliefs.[21] However, these groups of immigrants still tend to be subsumed under broad categories, like Hispanic and Asian, with little regard to their distinct cultural differences.

The category of Asian, for example, includes not only the peoples of China, Japan, and Korea, but also newly resettled immigrants from Southeast Asia, in particular, the Vietnamese, Cambodians, and Laotians displaced by the Vietnam War and its aftermath. This monolithic notion of Asians cannot convey adequately the differences between these peoples, their histories, traditions, and experiences. Today, there are thousands of Laotian refugees in the United States. The Laotian diaspora in the United States constitutes perhaps one-tenth of the total population of Laos (not to mention the large numbers of Laotian refugees in France and Canada). Yet even this diasporan community does not constitute a homogeneous group of "Laotians."[22]

In 1990 the *Milwaukee Journal* described in a three-part series "how the remnants of the Vietnam War continue to touch one of the largest concentrations of Hmong refugees in the world—the 27,000 who live in Wisconsin."[23] Leaders of the Hmong resistance who today are fighting the Communist Pathet Lao government as guerrillas of the United Lao National Liberation Front are former members of the 30,000-man secret Hmong army, armed and trained by the CIA to cut North Vietnamese supply lines and destroy their bases. The legacy of the Vietnam War thus continues, affecting the lives of thousands of Hmong in America who support the Lao war of liberation, financially and politically. Some even return periodically to Laos to engage the Pathet Lao forces backed by the Vietnamese government.

Although the *Milwaukee Journal* reporter can be lauded for making public the unending story of imperial powers' intervention in Southeast Asia, he depoliticized and neutralized it by ending on a predictable note with a story of cultural transformation and adaptation. Part III is devoted to the "New Generation [who] Shares American Dreams." The members of this generation are described as "Americans with American concerns and American goals."There is no mention of the painful acculturation process, of the behind-the-scenes negotiations which involve claiming another history as one's own, or rejecting native traditions and customs. Because of the focus on their successful attainment of "Americanness," assimilation is made to appear effortless.

Franklin Delano Roosevelt once described the essence of Americanness in the following terms: "The principle on which this country was founded and by which it has always been governed is that Americanism is a matter of the mind and heart; Americanism is not, and never was, a matter of race and ancestry" (qtd. in Wolfe 30). That FDR was making such a pronouncement in 1942, to justify the internment of Japanese-Americans in so-called "relocation camps," points to the ways Americanness has been defined "emotionally," articulated around a coercive demand for identification, and used politically.

The scope and tenor of discrimination against Asian Americans, nowhere as evident as in the enactment of American immigration laws, have recently been submitted to keen historical scrutiny (see Chan; Kim; Takaka; Karst; and Bishop). The spirit and legacy of these bills and executive orders can be found in the latest major immigration bill: the Immigration Reform and Control Act of 1986. This legislative bill had a dual function: to reform and control immigration, and to reconfigure the "illegal alien" into an "American subject." Thus it granted pardon to "aliens" who had been living in the United States legally or illegally, since 1982. For me, this meant that in order to become "a lawfully admitted resident of the United States," I would have to endure this "pardoning" process, since the private bill introduced by Senator Mathias passed the Senate but not the House. This radical change in subject position—from private bill beneficiary to illegal alien—was not simply a humbling experience. It taught me much about class privilege. I was no longer "Dobby" Norindr, "one of the graduates" of the Southampton class of '79, but one among millions of "illegal aliens" from working-class backgrounds applying for temporary residence in the United States. The Immigration Reform and Control Act inscribed me differently into the narrative of "foreignness" and "home"; I was now assessed strictly in legal, no longer in affective, terms.

The vicissitudes of the legalization process could be described at great length. This process, in which every facet of the applicant's private and personal life is scrutinized, is marked by a violence of its own kind. To illustrate this point, I will give but one example. Even though the "Immigration Reform and Control Act" was promoted as an amnesty bill, which meant that millions of illegal aliens were supposed to be "pardoned," individuals within certain categories were automatically denied temporary residence, the first step toward naturalization. Those denied residency include not only felons, "Nazi war criminals," and "drug traffickers," but also "members of or [those] affiliated with any communist party," "aliens afflicted with any dangerous contagious diseases" (that is, HIV-positive individuals), "aliens afflicted with sexual deviation" (that is, homosexuals). And the prospective applicant is warned that "Penalties for False Statements in Applications" result in "criminal prosecution and/or deportation." The restrictions not only institutionalize discrimination, they deny basic rights which protect every American citizen from discrimination because of mental or physical disabilities, sexual orientation, or political affiliation. The "alien" has no such rights. Two standards exist: one for "citizens," the other for "aliens."

What are the theoretical and political implications of this account, of making "myself" the "pre-text" of investigation. As the popular media, such as the *Southampton Press*, construct their sense of American cultural identity, individual subjects are written into an American (con)text that irons out their differences and weaves them into the fabric of Americanness represented symbolically by the American flag. The greatest challenge for many immigrants is to take issue with this process, to resist "riding on the hyphen" into the mainstream.[24] The subject is not simply a part of a patriotic body politic.[25]

I began this essay by examining the parade photograph as a privileged site of cultural signification and by unraveling, and to a certain degree reconstructing, the "authentic" immigrant story as it is represented in the press. My purpose was to examine the strategies deployed in the "production of an 'image' of identity and the transformation of the subject in assuming that image" (Bhabha, "Remembering Fanon" 139), that is to say, the making of an American. More than a decade after the publication of the *Southampton Press* article, I am not yet quite an American citizen. I am still negotiating between the various identities imposed on me—the one assigned to me by the press, the one defined by the Immigration and Naturalization Service, and the one associated with my profession.

In "supplementing" the absence of the Vietnam veteran with a narrative of some of the histories on which this repression is based, I hope to place myself in a "social-text" more complex than the *Southampton Press* made it to be. This contestatory gesture is not made to expose the "truth" or to recover a "true self." It is meant to render problematic the process by which a post-Vietnam era immigrant is both produced as an (American) citizen and effaced as a (Laotian) subject; in short, it is the ideological construction of otherness that Spivak describes well: "the epistemic violence that constituted/effaced a subject that was obliged to cathect (occupy in response to a desire) the space of the imperialist's self-consolidating other" (Spivak, "Introduction" 18).

Other stories by other Southeast Asian immigrants illuminate the complexity of this process.[26] My story is in itself rather banal. Therefore, rejecting all claims to be a "representative text" I prefer the identity I construct and deconstruct even as I write this essay: a fragmented and dislocated writing subject, alienated by the effects and repercussions of the United States—and I must add, French—involvement in Southeast Asia. A (post)colonial critic,[27] whose multiple cultural influences make him a cultural hybrid with contradictory and paradoxical allegiances: a Laotian citizen, born in France, and a resident of the United States, conscious of the dangers and pressures of assimilation, who refuses to be recuperated institutionally (as affirmative-action alibi or minority token) and who may have found a voice to write cultural difference and a "home" from which to speak and intervene.

Notes

I am grateful to Marina Pérez de Mendiola, Angelika Bammer, Roby Rajan, and Rey Chow for their comments on earlier drafts of this essay and to the participants of the conference on *Displacements: Cultural Identities in Question*, who have contributed to the discussion of this paper. I also wish to thank Carol Tennessen and Kathleen Woodward of the Center for Twentieth Century Studies, University of Wisconsin-Milwaukee, for their support. A fellowship at the Center enabled me to write a version of this essay in 1990–91.

1. The *Southampton Press*, founded in 1897, is a weekly newspaper published by the Southampton Press Publishing Company, of Southampton, New York. All subsequent references will refer to the Thursday, July 5, 1979, edition and to the article "Two Brothers Face Deportation to Laos" and editorial "Let Them Stay," by Portia Flanagan.

2. The American parade can be seen as a "text" which not only "encapsulates a culture," but attempts to "spell out a common social identity." See for example, Mary Ryan's "The American Parade."

3. As Susan Sontag has observed, "a photograph is both a pseudo-presence and a token of absence" (16).

4. Jacques Derrida discusses the concept of "dangerous supplement" in his *Of Grammatology* 141-64.

5. I thank Rey Chow and Angelika Bammer for helping me reformulate my arguments in these terms.

6. As the article explains: "Because he [Dobby] was studying in France when the Communists overran the legal Lao government and because his parents are still there, the U.S. government has informed him that that would be the place for him to go when his time here in America runs out."

7. Spivak elaborates further the differences between the two forms of representation (*Vertretung* and *Darstellung*) in "Practical Politics" 108-09.

8. To "assess," according to *The American Heritage Dictionary* (Boston: Houghton Mifflin, 1992), means "to estimate the value of (property) for taxation."

9. Using Bakhtin's concepts of "otherness" and "dialogic discourse," Robert F. Barsky examines the status of the immigrant as a legal subject in Canadian immigration proceedings in "Bakhtin and Otherness." I thank Angelika Bammer for bringing Barsky's study to my attention.

10. Stan Sesser's informative article on Laos tells a different story in "Forgotten Country."

11. Said examines this issue (among many others) in his *Orientalism*.

12. In "Losing Vietnam," Rick Berg examines the way Vietnam has become a prime commodity of the American culture industry, television in particular.

13. This point is driven home most polemically by Noam Chomsky in "Visions of Righteousness."

14. Benedict Anderson reformulates Hugh Seton-Watson's definition of a nation in the following fashion: "a nation exists when a significant number of a people in a community 'imagine themselves' to form a nation, or behave as if they formed one" (6). He goes on to add that "It is *imagined* because the members of even the smallest nation will never know most of their fellow-members, meet them or even hear them, yet in the minds of each lives the image of their communion" (6).

15. The reception and treatment of returning Vietnam veterans on college campuses needs to be studied in all its complexity. This includes both a critique of the self-righteous and smug indignation of students who opposed the war and blamed the veterans and a more sympathetic view of student anti-war militancy.

16. A number of studies have examined the representation of Vietnam veterans in Hollywood films. See Adair; Dittman and Michaud; and Jeffords.

17. Grant 23. In the period immediately following the withdrawal of American troops, fewer films on Vietnam were made than during the war. The publication of books on Vietnam also suffered the same fate, dropping to about a dozen titles a year.

18. Peter Marin examines the moral and political complacency of those who claimed to be against the war but continued to reelect officials who supported it and pay taxes which subsidized the war effort in "Coming to Terms with Vietnam."

19. Michael Clark writes movingly of the 25,000 middle-aged veterans who marched through the streets of New York ten years after the fall of Saigon ("Remembering Vietnam" 46-47).

20. I do not imply here that the Asian immigrant success story is always constructed in a positive light. Indeed, increasingly—particularly in the context of growing discontent over the Japanese "success story"—it is the object of scorn. One such example is the story of Tom Wu, a Vietnamese refugee, turned Florida real estate tycoon and "how-to-get-rich" evangelist. Wu, we are told, did not succeed "the old fashioned American way," through honest labor, but used manipulative and fraudulent strategies to deceive unsuspecting and naive (American) victims. A recent immigrant to the United States who speaks an accented English, Wu is accused of not playing by the rules. Thus, this too-successful Asian immigrant-entrepreneur becomes a threat to "legitimate Americans" (CBS news report, *48 Hours* 26 Jan. 1992).

21. A number of scholarly studies have been devoted to this complex question. See Fuchs; Portes and Rumbaut; and Waters.

22. The separate formation of the Hmong-American Association as distinct from the Lao-American Association is one concrete manifestation of this heterogeneity.

23. *Milwaukee Journal* 30 Sept. 1990–2 Oct. 1990. Series' reporter, Dennis R. Getto.

24. This is how the press has characterized the process by which the playright David Hwang, for example, the author of the Tony Award–winning play, *M. Butterfly*, is transforming himself into an "American" writer.

25. The press and immigration laws operate similarly in this regard. On a discursive level, both want to make the subject of investigation transparent and invisible in the sense that all marginality must disappear under scrutiny. On a practical level, they operate somewhat differently: the press tends to deny difference by emphasizing commonality; the Immigration Reform and Control Act attempts to eliminate difference by excluding those in designated categories.

26. Recently, John Tenhula collected the experiences of Southeast Asian refugees in his *Voices from Southeast Asia*.

27. Spivak discusses the notion of postcoloniality in "Poststructuralism"; Said in "Intellectuals."

Works Cited

Adair, Gilbert. *Vietnam on Film: From the Green Berets to Apocalypse Now*. New York: Proteus, 1981.

Alba, Richard D. *Ethnic Identity: The Transformation of White America*. New Haven: Yale UP, 1990.

Anderson, Benedict. *Imagined Communities*. London: Verso, 1991.

Barsky, Robert F. "Bakhtin and Otherness: The Destruction of the 'Subject' in Legal 'Hearings.' " ms.

Barthes, Roland. "The Photographic Message." *A Barthes Reader*. Ed. Susan Sontag. New York: Hill, 1982. 194–210.

Berg, Rick. "Losing Vietnam: Covering the War in an Age of Technology." *Cultural Critique* 3 (1986): 92–125.

Bhabha, Homi K. "DissemiNation: Time, Narrative, and the Margins of the Modern Nation." *Nation and Narration*. Ed. Homi K. Bhabha. London: Routledge, 1990. 291–322.

————. "Remembering Fanon: Self, Psyche, and the Colonial Condition." Kruger and Mariani. 131–48.

Bishop, Katherine. "Saving Voices of the Other Ellis Island." *New York Times* 11 Nov. 1990, sec. 1: 20.

Chan, Sucheng. *Asian Americans: An Interpretative History*. Boston: Twayne, 1991

Chomsky, Noam. "Visions of Righteousness." *Cultural Critique* 3 (1986): 10–43.

Clark, Michael. "Remembering Vietnam." *Cultural Critique* 3 (1986): 46–78.

Derrida, Jacques. *Of Grammatology*. Trans. Gayatri Chakravorty Spivak. Baltimore: Johns Hopkins UP, 1976.

Dittman, Linda, and Gene Michaud, eds. *From Hanoi to Hollywood*. New Brunswick: Rutgers UP, 1990.

Flanagan, Portia. "Let Them Stay." Editorial. *Southampton Press* 5 July 1979: 1, 20.

————. "Two Brothers Face Deportation to Laos." *Southampton Press* 5 July 1979: 6.

Fuchs, Lawrence H. *The American Kaleidoscope: Race, Ethnicity, and the Civic Culture*. Middletown: UP of New England, 1990.

Grant, Zalin. "Vietnam as Fable." *New Republic* 25 Mar. 1978: 21–24.

Herr, Michael. *Dispatches*. New York: Knopf, 1977.

Jeffords, Susan. *The Remasculinization of America*. Bloomington: Indiana UP, 1989.

Karst, Kenneth L. *Belonging to America: Equal Citizenship and the Constitution*. New Haven: Yale UP, 1989.

Kim, Elaine H. *Asian American Literature: An Introduction to the Writings and Their Social Context*. Philadelphia: Temple UP, 1982.

Kovic, Ron. *Born on the Fourth of July*. New York: McGraw-Hill, 1976.

Marin, Peter. "Coming to Terms with Vietnam: Settling our Moral Debts." *Harpers* Dec. 1990: 43–56.

Mukherjee, Bharati. "Immigrant Writing: Give Us Your Maximalists!" *New York Times Book Review* 28 Aug. 1988: 28.

Portes, Alejandro, and Rubén G. Rumbaut. *Immigrant America: A Portrait*. Berkeley: U of California P, 1990.

Rushdie, Salman. "The Location of *Brazil*." *Imaginary Homelands*. London: Penguin, 1991. 118–25.

Ryan, Mary. "The American Parade: Representations of the Nineteenth-Century Social Order." *The New Cultural History*. Ed. Lynn Hunt. Berkeley: U of California P, 1989. 131–53.

Said, Edward. "Intellectuals in the Post-Colonial World." *Salmagundi* 70–71 (1986): 44–64.

————. *Orientalism*. New York: Pantheon, 1978.

————. "Yeats and Decolonization." Kruger and Mariani. 3–29.

Sesser, Stan. "Forgotten Country." *The New Yorker* 20 Aug. 1990: 39–68.

Sontag, Susan. *On Photography*. New York: Farrar, 1973.

Spivak, Gayatri Chakravorty. "Can the Subaltern Speak?" *Marxism and the Interpretation of Culture*. Ed. Cary Nelson and Lawrence Grossberg. Urbana: U of Illinois P, 1988. 271–313.

————. Introduction. *Selected Subaltern Studies*. Ed. Gayatri Spivak. Oxford: Oxford UP, 1988.

————. "Poststructuralism, Marginality, Postcoloniality and Value." *Literary Theory Today*. Ed. Peter Collier and Helga Geyer-Ryan. Ithaca: Cornell UP, 1990. 219–44.

————. "Practical Politics of the Open End." *The Post-Colonial Critic: Interviews, Strategies, Dialogues*. Ed. Sarah Harasym. New York: Routledge, 1990. 95–112.

Takaka, Ronald. *Stranger from a Different Shore: A History of Asian Americans*. Boston: Little, 1989.

Tenhula, John. *Voices from Southeast Asia: The Refugee Experience in the United States.* New York: Holmes, 1991.

Waters, Mary C. *Ethnic Options: Choosing Identities in America.* U of California P, 1990.

Wolfe, Alan. "The Return of the Melting Pot: What the New Immigrants Can Learn from the Old." *The New Republic* 31 Dec. 1990: 27–34.

16 A Not-So-New Spelling of My Name

Notes toward (and against) a Politics of Equivocation

Elaine K. Chang

THE TITLE OF this essay brings together and corrupts the titles of Audre Lorde's biomythography, *Zami: A New Spelling of My Name* and Adrienne Rich's influential essay, "Notes toward a Politics of Location," in an attempt to problematize feminist strategies of naming and location while adhering to their critical significance. Equivocators, let me admit from the outset, like to have things both ways. I have taken the term by which feminists of many backgrounds and disciplinary persuasions have come to label a politics of accountability and critical self-knowledge and replaced it with a term connoting ambivalence and obscurantism. By this gesture, I mean to (im)pose equivocation, not as an alternative to "location," but as its literal re-placement in the ambiguous, historically shifting interstices of language. Equivocation exploits the self-unsettling properties of language; it is the deliberate mincing of available words. It is in this capacity, as an at once derivative and disruptive tactic within language use, that equivocation engages and provokes naming and location in current feminist discussion. For a "politics of equivocation," possibly lacking in fixed or incontrovertible convictions, suspects that no one has a "proper" name, nor can be assigned a "proper" place.

This essay takes issue with some of the key signifiers within contemporary feminist discourse as part of a larger, evaluative task made possible and necessary by the explosion of revisionary feminisms—and the concomitant erosion of women's and minorities' rights—during the last decade. I am led to equivocate over certain terms from my own location at what may well be another crossroads for Western feminist theory and practice. Concepts of naming, location, and coalition have become increasingly accepted as commonplaces of feminist discourse; the terms roll off some tongues as though they were ready-made axioms or accomplished facts. We are a full decade closer to "turning the century" than when Bernice Johnson Reagon coined the phrase, calling on potential coalition builders to give up the security and familiarity of "home," and take "some of the most dangerous work you can do" into the streets (359).

Many of us, indebted to activist feminists like Reagon, Lorde, and Rich, feel we have absorbed the lesson that not "all women" are created equally unequal.[1] And yet, perhaps wary of how such exalted terms as "multiculturalism" and "pluralism" have been manipulated within self-identified "progressive" academic institutions, we must ask: To what structural and strategic changes within feminist movement(s) do "coalition" and "location" actually refer? Has power among women, for example, been reconfigured or more equitably redistributed in their names?

At the same time, identity, location, and coalition cannot be read exclusively as mere rhetorical palliatives against inequities and marginalization. Rather, these concepts—which have helped to name the asymmetric racial, economic, and cultural relations mediating relations of gender—may serve as safeguards, at least in the immediate term, against the multiply corrosive and divisive effects of recession and backlash. Feminist cultural historians have shown that the notion of hierarchical differences between the sexes is most energetically defended in times of social instability and upheaval.[2] That the same holds true for the insistence on differences (in value and power) among economic classes and racial and ethnic groups has been amply demonstrated in the United States during the past decade of conservative rule.[3] If, as such varied examples suggest, social organizations tend to "close ranks" in times when their privileges are threatened—accentuating distinctions between uniformity and difference, between "us" and "them"—then feminism in the current political context faces a renewed threat of internal stratification; according to Chandra Talpade Mohanty, we are indeed witnessing "the second wave of white Western feminisms" ("Cartographies" 3). With such "fundamental" feminist issues as women's reproductive freedom now on the line, do the "specialized" struggles of non-white and non-Western women risk subsumption once again within the monolithic interest group, "all women"? Might redoubled emphasis on the delimited locations and identities that differently define us as women, and on the necessity of forming coalitions across these differences, alleviate such a risk?

In other words, what terms like "identity," "location," and "coalition" signify and what is at stake in their use vary according to shifting contextual and historical determinants: Who is using the terms, when, where, and for what purposes. The very use, abuse and/or disuse of the terms encode complex and multiply intersecting relations of power, both "within" feminism and "without." The equivocator is, for these reasons, neither satisfied with the existing terminology nor willing to give it up. As we shall see, the question, "What's in a name?" is for the equivocator neither purely rhetorical nor a tacit appeal to essential identities underlying variable appearances. To engage in a politics of location, as many participants acknowledge, means to engage in just this sort of paradox: to identify one's position on a temporal and spatial (historical and socio-geographical) grid while simultaneously critiquing the ideological construction of its coordinates (for example, gender, race, ethnicity, class, sexuality). This paradox and the challenges it poses are perhaps best expressed by Mohanty as "the complex *relationality* that shapes our social and political lives":

> ... it is possible to retain the idea of multiple, fluid structures of domination which intersect to locate women differently at particular historical conjunctures, while at the same time insisting on the dynamic oppositional agency of individuals and collectives and their engagement in "daily life." ("Cartographies" 13)

What I am calling a politics of equivocation is a politics of negotiating paradoxical or contradictory imperatives that orients itself by Mohanty's map of "a world which is definable only in *relational* terms . . . traversed with intersecting lines of power and resistance" ("Cartographies" 2). Such politics is also inspired by what Gayatri Chakravorty Spivak has called "the uneven many-strandedness of 'being,' " a condition marked by an equivocal, rather than strictly binary, relation between writing and reading. Evoking concepts of identity, position and location, Spivak writes:

> Writing is a position where the *absence* of the weaver from the web is structurally necessary. Reading is a position where I (or a group of us with whom I share an identificatory label) make this anonymous web my own, even as I find in it a guarantee of my existence as me, one of us. Between the two positions, there are displacements and consolidations, a disjunction in order to conjugate a representative self. (270)

The "conjugation of a representative self" at the intersections of power and resistance is the primary project of this paper. What follows is a series of critical and autobiographical reflections that proceeds by the (il)logic of equivocation, oscillating between some simultaneous and incompatible displacements and consolidations: between reading and writing, subject positions and object positions, "me" and "not-me," proper and improper names.

In what might be a *locus classicus* of feminist location politics, "Situated Knowledges," Donna Haraway seeks a relational, multi-stranded alternative to social constructionist and empiricist assumptions regarding the subjects and objects of knowledge. Calling for a revolutionary, feminist rewriting of "the curious and inescapable term objectivity," Haraway argues that all perspectives are dually partial, both biased and incomplete; knowledge claims are influenced and delimited by the never-disinterested observer or group of observers who advance and are accountable for them. To arrogate to oneself a privileged position of fixity or certitude outside the economy of partial perspectives is, according to Haraway, to be guilty of the "god-trick": "not just [the myth] . . . of seeing everything from nowhere, but to have put the myth into ordinary practice" (189). An interagency and coactivity of multiple subject-positions (not to be confused with certain social constructionist postulations of "a fully textualized and coded world" [185]) works to dispel and disempower this myth, facilitating the eradication of "alienating distance" between subjects and objects, the seers and the seen. A network of "situated and embodied knowledges" is one in which all participants equally are held and hold themselves responsible for their own positions. And this responsibility disqualifies bids not only for value-neutral perception, but also for the appropriation of subjugated vantage points—the privileging of the insight of the marginal "other" (190–91).

A significant contradiction (characteristic, I would argue, of location politics more generally) arises when Haraway attempts to configure this play and work of partial perspectives into something of an agenda for coalition politics, to reject relativism together with totalization in favor of a collective "doctrine and practice of objectivity that privileges contestation, deconstruction, passionate construction, webbed connections, and hope for transformation of systems of knowledge and ways of seeing" (191–92). The marshalling of pluralistic subjectivities, limited locations, and situated knowledges in a way that avoids "easy relativisms and holisms" is no uncomplicated matter, the tendency to relativize or totalize being influenced, as I have suggested, by the immediate and often unreflected exigencies of time and place. The problem is encoded in Haraway's suggestive and ambiguous phrase: "the privilege of partial perspective." Can "partial perspective"—as Haraway defines it, the aggregate product of specific social and historical constructions and contingencies—simply offer itself as "privilege"? From whose perspective, from where, does partial perspective appear as privilege? Ought not the ability to posit and to name privilege itself be interpreted as a kind of privilege?

How is it, furthermore, that some partial perspectives end up being more "privileged" than others? Haraway offers an important clue: "Vision is *always* a question of the power to see—and perhaps of the violence implicit in our visualizing practices" (192). Partial perspective, then, is a differential and differentiating privilege. It is also, in a manner of speaking, self-differentiated; the bifurcation of vision recurs across a range of texts as a trope of location politics. For Adrienne Rich, the partial perspective of the white Western feminist is a kind of visual dis-order or double vision: "a confusion between our claims to the white and Western eye and the woman-seeing eye, fear of losing the centrality of the one even as we claim the other" (219). For feminists for whom marginalization as women is compounded and possibly superseded by other marginalizations, the question of partial perspective is additionally complex, involving further fragmentations and multiplications of vision, and rendering the impulse to, in Rich's words, "name the ground we're coming from" at once necessary, empowering, and problematic. According to bell hooks, the experience of living "on the edge" endows the African-American feminist with the ability to view and comprehend reality from both margin and center.[4] For Gloria Anzaldúa's "new *mestiza*," inhabiting multiple cultural realms—locating oneself as the product of "racial, ideological, cultural and biological cross-pollination" (77)—engenders a kind of hybrid perception anchored in a hybrid subjective reality.

To read *Borderlands* within the conceptual framework of "situated knowledges," bracketing for the moment the generic distinctiveness of both works, is to conduct something of a formal exercise in double vision. Both Anzaldúa and Haraway pose models of plural or multiple consciousness against confining subject/object dualisms, but there the commonalities would appear to end. We might consider a striking passage in which Anzaldúa seems, at least rhetorically, to affect what Haraway calls the "god-trick":

> As a *mestiza* I have no country, my homeland cast me out; yet all countries are mine because I am every woman's sister or potential lover. (As a lesbian I have no race, my own people disclaim me; but I am all races because there is the queer of me in all races.) I am cultureless because, as a feminist, I challenge the collective cultural/religious male-derived beliefs of Indo-Hispanics and Anglos. (80–81)

Can this passage be interpreted as an act of "preferred positioning" on Anzaldúa's part, the assumption of a perspective which promises vision "both nowhere and everywhere" at once? To respond equivocally: yes and no. Anzaldúa posits *mestiza* consciousness as a synthetic element, literally "transcending" the duality between subject and object (80). Haraway critiques transcendent discourse for its refusal to acknowledge limits and responsibility: "Feminist objectivity is about limited location and situated knowledge, not about transcendence and splitting of subject and object. It allows us to become answerable for what we learn how to see" (190). Anzaldúa is, by her own admission, "not sure exactly how" the new *mestiza* has come to acquire an almost clairvoyant ability to resolve ambivalence (79); she has no answer.

The contested term here, "transcendence," serves to locate Haraway and Anzaldúa on different sides of the very subject-object hierarchy each writer critiques. From Haraway's perspective, transcendence appears as that which "alienates" subject from object. From Anzaldúa's perspective, transcendence involves "healing the split" between subject and object (80). Haraway chooses in this context to identify with the subject position; as the situated subject of knowledge, she resists transcendent discourse so as to concede and respect the equal agency of the "object" to be known. In this case, epistemological privilege and political privilege are coextensive and virtually interchangeable,[5] and "partial perspective," according to Haraway, carries with it the mandate to acknowledge this twofold "privilege" relative to others. The same (Aristotelian, patriarchal) subject-object duality from which Haraway admits to having benefitted[6] has kept Anzaldúa, on the other hand, "a prisoner" (80); the latter writes from and out of an object position—having been dually objectified, first as a member of the Mexican-American *mestizaje*, thereafter and specifically as a Chicana lesbian. *Borderlands* thus registers a disjunction between the epistemological and the political significances of privilege: Anzaldúa's claim to a transcendent viewpoint and understanding is formulated *without* the authorization or support of political privilege behind it. "God-tricks" might in context, then, serve certain strategic and enabling purposes; it may be a privilege to renounce those that not all women can afford.

Across what might be considered "purely semantic" discrepancies between Haraway and Anzaldúa, we confront a truism of location politics: that in the struggles to redistribute power within feminism, unequal power relations are reproduced. Owing to a variety of circumstances (which include access to language, education, and audience; and the polemical and disciplinary contexts in which individual writers operate) some women are more enabled than others to "locate" themselves definitively and self-critically, to determine exactly where they are and how (multiply) they see. Similarly, some women are more empowered to recognize, intervene into, and recreate their own conditions of visibility than are other women.

The equivocal operation of "privilege" among partial perspectives does not begin or end, however, with any simple rehearsal of differences by race, class, culture, or sexuality. According to Norma Alarcón, the subject who can "reach the moment of cognition of a situation for herself" is, in the prevailing political/epistemological climate, "always already" privileged: whether that subject is the "autonomous, self-making, self-determining subject" valorized by much Anglo-American feminist theory or the collectivist, multiple-voiced, contradictory subject given expression in texts like *This Bridge Called My Back*. Even while problematizing singular or unitary concepts of consciousness "by representing [consciousness] as a weave," oppositional theories of subjectivity formulated in works such as *Bridge* and *Borderlands* continue to "give credit to the subject of consciousness as the site of knowledge" (39). To name and locate individual or collective experience and knowledge—however much these practices have helped to open a more complex and multifaceted range of "subject-object" positionings—is to presuppose and reassert the privileges of a conscious subject, capable of "grasp[ing] or reclaim[ing] an identity" (37) in the first place. Naming and location are thus acquisitive or proprietary maneuvers, implicated in and bound by the political and epistemological hierarchies they would contest.

"Equivocation" cannot leverage anyone out of the pitfalls of consciousness attendant on naming and location. On the contrary, equivocation exacerbates binary divisions between the multiple "subjects" and "objects" of feminist theorizing in yet another bid to grasp or reclaim identity. Equivocation is the privileged, partial perspective of someone unwilling, though enabled, to focus her own "double vision" and who elects to name and locate herself by this default. As a self-identified subject/object constituted by multiple and at times countervailing oppressions and privileges, the equivocator reads the fine print and blank spaces of feminist location politics, in part, for the guidelines of her own participation. Reading Haraway in relation to Anzaldúa—exhortations to revise "objectivity" in connection with appeals to a "newer discourse" of subjectivity (31)—the equivocator finds it as difficult as has Chandra Mohanty, in another context, " . . . to define [her] place on the map" ("Feminist Encounters" 40). For not only is the equivocator wary of the (self-)centralizing privilege of consciousness, but she finds—in the process of reading feminist theory, literature, and the experience of her own life—that misnomers, mistaken identities, and dislocations are just as critical to the "conjugation of a representative self" as are perhaps more readily (re)claimable names and locations.

To better illustrate this point, I will devote the remainder of this paper to a reading of names and locations that, for a number of reasons, I have found difficult to (re)claim, but which serve nevertheless to define "my place on the map." Before doing so, however, I shall try to account for what will be a fairly conspicuous switch in pronouns and discursive modes. If the equivocator were aware of a truly relational, multi-stranded alternative to first person self-reference, she would probably use it. Her equivocation over "capital I" arises, not from a desire to exempt the speaking subject from the framework of current feminist discussion, to render such a subject unnamable and her knowledge unlocatable, but in recognition of the speaking subject's complicity in the problematics of self-representation on the one hand and her vulnerability to appropriation on the other.

Attentive to the multiple subject-object positionings encoded and elided by the "first-person" pronoun, Trinh Minh-ha has posited and rewritten "I" as an entity composed of "infinite layers," partially approximable "through such typographical conventions as I, i or I/i" (95): "I (the all-knowing subject)," "I/i (the plural, non-unitary subject)," and "i (the personal race- and gender-specific subject)" (9). The complexity of models like Trinh's has not, however, been fully extended throughout the institutional and political practices that mediate feminist theorizing. In fact, "the all-knowing subject" and "the plural, non-unitary subject" which Trinh defines as different dimensions of the same, infinitely layered "I" correspond rather well to Alarcón's distinction between the bourgeois individualist subject of Anglo-American feminism and the multiple voiced, heterogeneous subject of *Bridge*. Referring to Alarcón, Mohanty remarks a similar opposition between the subjects of "autobiographical" and "testimonial" life-narratives; whereas Anglo-American feminist writing has focussed "on the unfolding of a singular woman's consciousness (in the hege-monic tradition of European modernist autobiography)," the testimonials of Latin American women are "strikingly nonheroic and impersonal," reflecting a strategy of speaking "*from within* a collective" ("Cartographies" 37).

It is generic distinctions like these—which accurately describe the stratifi-cations among groups of women that make up the *Realpolitik* of feminist lo-cation discourse—that make coming forward as an "I" so risky. Which side of what dualism am "I" on? Just as the equivocator translates the "bifocality" of partial perspective as the mediation between more or less privileged eyes, so she mediates between differently privileged "I's" in her attempts both to locate herself and to write her "proper" name. What I want to underscore here, fi-nally, is the intermediary position of the equivocator in relation to categories that continue to define, and possibly reinscribe, the differences between white women and women of colour.[7] While the (epistemological/political) privilege of equivocation may not itself be racially marked (equivocation is basically a logic of comparison and contrast, a methodology of close reading, and a poli-tics of refusing to make up one's mind), I am led to name and locate myself as equivocator—to equivocate over naming and location—from the discontinu-ous locations I occupy as an Asian woman living and writing in North Amer-ica. Mitsuye Yamada has succinctly described the ambivalent position allocated to Asian Pacific women in relation to white women and women of colour: "I am weary . . . of hearing that among the women of color, Asian women are the least political, or the least oppressed, or the most polite" (71).

Like most Asian women, I have heard many things that weary me. And how I write my name is indelibly influenced by how I've read it, have heard it pronounced. I have been called many names which have compelled me to rec-ognize my "otherness" while forcing me to speechlessness. While I may not have heretofore answered to these names, I would now like to read my own silence for signs of resistance and complicity, against and in conversation with other silences—with those of Trinh Minh-ha, for example:

> Silence as a refusal to partake in the story does sometimes provide us with a means to gain a hearing. It is voice, a mode of uttering and a response in its own right. Without other silences, however, my silence goes unheard, unno-ticed; it is simply one voice less, one more point given to the silencers. (83)

Names like "chink," "gook," and "Jap" are probably self-explanatory terms of derision. Racism and name-calling: racist name-calling is interpella-tion in the Althusserian sense. Such terms, although they efface (and this is their strategy) one's identity as an autonomous person, interpellate the sub-ject—hailing the individual to assume the ideological space of the racial other. (Derisive terms such as "fag" and "dyke" similarly interpellate sexual others.) If interpellation by one's proper name can be considered already and simultaneously an act of subjection (Althusser) and an act of "originary" violence (Derrida),[8] to be called a "chink" or a "gook" is doubly subjecting and violent. Doubly subjecting in that the racial other is hailed as subject by and to one who is, according to Althusserian logic, himself or herself a subject: the name-caller, as "small-s" subject, interpellates a "smaller-s" subject. Doubly violent and violating in that the substitution of these epithets, or any one of their numerous permutations for the proper name—their suppression of the proper name—further dissociates the racial other from his or her (already problematic) "property and self-sameness."

To those who have called me by these names, I have appeared as a person of colour. The colour of my skin is named, while the colour of theirs is not. My colour is made to take priority over my proper name, and certain particularities are rejected as irrelevant. In retrospect, it has been at random moments in my life when I have been interpellated as a nondifferentiated person of colour that I have given the most serious thought to the privileges and problematics of naming and location. Being called a "chink" or a "Jap" would prompt crises of identity throughout my childhood: being Korean, I knew I was neither chink nor Jap, "properly" speaking—but such knowledge was no defense against the sting of the name directed at me. I could never think of an "appropriate" retort. Likewise, the familiar schoolyard taunt, "Chinese, Japanese, dirty-knees; look at these!"—ritually followed by the exposure of some taboo body part—always flabbergasted me into wondering who I really was, while causing me to despise, in silence, my physical resemblance to Chinese and Japanese people. For the resemblance was enough to make me a target.

When any Asian person is targeted as the object of racial hatred, he or she is very often a victim of misidentification. On June 23, 1982, in Detroit, a young Chinese American named Vincent Chin was bludgeoned to death by two white autoworkers armed with a baseball bat and a grudge against the Japanese auto industry. Ronald Ebens and Michael Nitz encountered Chin in a bar, called him a "Jap," and cursed "It's because of you motherfuckers that we're out of work." Ebens and Nitz then chased Chin out of the bar and crushed his skull. The murderers were eventually sentenced to three years of probation and fined $3,780 each; neither has served jail time (see Takaki 481–84). The only son of Lily and Hing Chin died in the hospital; his last words, often quoted in the years since his death, were "It isn't fair."

The brutal murder of Vincent Chin wasn't fair—clearly, not simply as a case of mistaken identity. Asians in North America have been and continue to be made scapegoats for economic decline, unemployment, and multiple other social ills; and in the context of the current recession, we are undergoing yet another "yellow peril" kind of marginalization. What Chin's story illustrates is that the victim of racial violence is always a surrogate for someone or something else, a target chronically deferred; the victim in his or her presence stands only for and as a collection of physical characteristics associated with the deferred target. Within such a context, certain particularities of identity recede into irrelevance. If all Asians can be mistaken for Korean merchants, Japanese executives, Vietnamese gang members, absentee Hong Kong landlords, or any other multipurpose villain with a yellow skin, then we might as well reclaim the label, "dirty-knees," as a sign of our solidarity and anger.

To equivocate over another name in another context: within the North American Asian community, I am sometimes called a banana. It has been said that I may have a yellow skin, but that I am white on the inside. I am considered ashamed of my yellowness, insofar as I supposedly aspire to master the language, culture, and ideology of white people. "*Banyukja*" is a name I have not been called, yet it is one I will invoke in this context. Literally "traitor" in Korean, it is not a term commonly used to express what is a powerful nationalist sentiment, perhaps so powerful as to be virtually unnamable. More commonly, it is a generation gap between immigrant parents (*ilse*, or first generation) and their Westernized children (*ise*, or second generation) that is remarked. The Korean who has "forgotten" her heritage, her language, a history that includes colonization both by the West and by other "yellow" peoples is quite possibly unspeakably traitorous. I cannot properly answer to such names, especially to and in a language I have virtually lost.

(My selection of the term *banyukja* is arbitrary and derivative; I have chosen it instead of the more available possibilities to name myself and my experience. I have chosen a Korean translation of the Spanish "*vendida*" out of admiration for Cherríe Moraga—an anglophone Chicana whose experience seems to bear some affinities with my own. Ironically, writing *banyukja* enables me to speak in Korean, while helping me to identify as a Korean with no palpable attachment to the nation that names me as such. *Banyukja*/banana: I kind of like the alliterative play. I am a *banyukja*-banana, I could say to myself—a synthesis or hybrid, an uneasy coalition of cultures, languages, and communities which also registers itself in my proper name. I have the surname my father inherited—or rather, its equivalent in English—and the Anglo first name my parents chose for me. Proper naming as originary and derivative violence: for four years under the Japanese occupation, Koreans were forced to adopt Japanese names. Under this edict, my father's family selected "Yama" as a last name—after the mountain upon which his family's burial ground had been located for centuries. Proper naming as outward compliance and covert resistance to colonial orders: in the ruler's lexicon my father learned to read his own name and history.)

I have read a few names which, for reasons I've tried to enumerate, I both own and disown—and which, more importantly, serve to name and locate me whether or not I (re)claim them. In my institutional practices as a "critic of colour," a "feminist of colour," and/or an "Asian feminist," I have found I equivocate, as many of us do, between the poles of donning "the enabling masks of [white critical] empowerment" (Gates 26) and painting myself "thick with authenticity" (Trinh 14). These competing imperatives, or so the quotations from Gates and Trinh suggest, involve costumery, imitation, and hidings. As I've attempted to demonstrate throughout this paper, the history of my particular equivocation between contradictory imperatives may have been a reduplicative series of imitations and hidings. I have engaged in a politics of identity and location primarily by rereading other people's words, trying to insert myself as I pilfer along. For someone like me to define her place on the map is, therefore, to trace the imitations and the hiding places and try to own up to them. I consider it now timely to write my proper name; once again, I write it as I have read it.

I had been a reader of "great Western literature" for many years without encountering my name in any of it. And so I was startled to find it in that bane and triumph of sophomore English majors, Joyce's *A Portrait of the Artist as a Young Man*:

> On the first line of the page appeared the title of the verses [Stephen Dedalus] was trying to write. To E_____ C_____. He knew it was right to begin so for he had seen similar titles in the collected poems of Lord Byron. . . . (71)

E_____ C_____: my initials, followed by blank spaces. Tracing my finger tentatively across the lines, I was seized with a temptation (probably influenced by Dedalus's adventures in sin and Christian guilt) to fill in the rest of my name. But could I really tamper with the text itself, possibly defacing great literature? Was even the idea a kind of sacrilege?

While I did not, finally, commit the deed, my mind was from that point forward to be contaminated with heretical ideas. Ideas about readerly identification, about how I'd learned how to read. From the cracked open blank spaces of Joyce's text emerged all sorts of disquieting truths: how "woman" (her name in this case literally immaterial, made to vanish in the intervening spaces between initials), for example, has been colonized as a site for male cultural production; how and to what extent someone like me both might and might not be this "woman."

I might not have known such things had I not read them as my own name.

Read against the grain, my proper name is a silent corruption of a Joycean text. That many of us read ourselves—for our own specifically located purposes—as deformations, mutations, or adaptations of "great Western" texts gives rise to certain considerations of identity. Adaptations of the Joycean gesture of Icarian revolt, significant revisions of Dedalus's grand mission "to forge in the smithy of [his] soul the uncreated conscience of [his] race" (253), range from Adrienne Rich[9] to Ralph Ellison. The English professor from whom Ellison's Invisible Man takes an Irish literature course, for example, literally and deliberately takes over Dedalus's project, reformulating it to apply to African Americans:

> Stephen's problem, like ours, was not actually one of creating the uncreated conscience of his race, but of creating the *uncreated features of his face*. Our task is that of making ourselves individuals who see, evaluate, record. . . . We create the race by creating ourselves. . . . (345–46)

I identify myself as E_____ C_____ partially out of semiparodic, semi-serious recognition of a commonplace of identity politics. To quote Caren Kaplan:

> Women have a history of reading and writing in the interstices of masculine culture, moving between use of the dominant language or form of expression and specific versions of experience based on their marginality. (187)

I also call on E_____ C_____ to help reprise my concern with the differential privileges reproduced throughout current feminist theorizing. Some women carry their histories of "reading and writing in the interstices of masculine culture" over into the vacant spaces, the malocclusions, and the aporiae of a feminist locational politics, where they still must equivocate between "dominant" and "marginal" voices and silences. Some women still lack a vocabulary with which they can or would want to declaratively claim their locations.

If I could rename myself, what name would I pick? Other writers have culled their national, iconographic, and imagistic repertories for models or representatives: Audre Lorde's *Zami* and Anzaldúa's *Coatlicue*[10] are but two examples. I think I would have to select a figure not female, not divine, not even human: the blue frog. My mother's story about the blue frog was my favorite childhood story. The blue frog never does anything his mother tells him to do; in fact he does precisely the opposite. I pestered my mother to tell the story over and over; each time she told it, the frog-mother's requests and the blue frog's responses seemed to become more outrageous. The ending, however, remained soberly the same. Loving and knowing her son, and knowing she is about to die, the frog-mother makes her last request. She asks the blue frog to bury her body in the river: thinking that her son, due to his contrary nature, will bury her in the ground. When his mother dies, however, the blue frog is so remorseful for his life-long disobedience that he chooses to observe her final wishes. So every time it rains, the blue frog cries, thinking that his mother's body is washing away in the river.

It wasn't until I was considerably older, and she had not told the story for years, that I asked my mother if she remembered the little blue frog. Confused at first, she remembered after I'd recapitulated the basic plot structure. Blushing, my mother informed me that the frog was not, in fact, blue; she had not yet "mastered" colours in English when she first told me the story. Old as I was, I was crushed by this information: it was all along just some ordinary green frog. What had compelled me about this particular frog—this frog whose story quite accurately resembled (perhaps still does) the story of my relationship with my mother—was his blueness. His blueness had made him special, even mythic, and had properly signified a sadness I had learned as a fledgling Western subject to colour-code as blue.

I would invoke the blue frog as my inspiration because of this coding and recoding of the colour of his skin; the ambiguity of his colour registers the sorts of small ironies that locate and characterize my experience as a Westernized child of immigrant parents. My mother shared with me a Korean folktale that acquired something else in its (mis)translation into English. For me, the blue frog remains blue; he is still and forever blue because his mother's body might be washing away. My mother's sense of inferiority, her embarrassment over a "mistake" made years ago, my unwillingness to distinguish the "original" fable from the "counterfeit" version, the corruption of the story that enhances it—all these and the things I cannot describe in this language intensify the blueness of this little blue frog. The blue frog is a (by-)product of cultural and linguistic cross-fertilization—a small and mundane one, to be sure, but one that I would take as my emblem. Do blue frogs have a place in feminist theorizing? (Am I blue? What's yellow and white and blue all over?)

As a Korean Canadian, middle-class, educated, feminist literary critical Anglophone straight woman, I equivocate between my privileges and my oppressions to the extent that I have sometimes wondered if they could—under pressure or hypothetically "ideal conditions"—nullify one another. Reading and writing: as Spivak suggests, a disjunction exists between the two practices "in order to conjugate a representative self." I had hoped to bridge the two— to write my readings—so as to question my place on the map. If I have succeeded, the approximation of a "representative self" that issues from and in this paper should appear a palimpsest, a composite derivation of names and locations. Hence the derivativeness of my title: a bid to entitle a derivative and equi-vocative self.

Do I/i finally come out of hiding only to say to you, "I am E_____ C_____, *pro tem* keeper of the interstice"? You might read the blanks for what they are, simultaneously and potentially something and nothing. Yet those of us who inhabit this kind of borderland between voices "central" and "marginal," who question every disconnected word, nevertheless participate in the discussion, perhaps by calling your attention to fine print and blank spaces.

Until such time that we may meet, I am

Yours sincerely,

E_____ C_____

In Memoriam V. C.

Notes

For their contributions to and careful readings of earlier versions of this paper, I would like to thank Kamala Visweswaran, Bill McPheron, Josie Saldaña, Heesok Chang, Beverly Allen, Mary Pratt and Trinh Minh-ha. I am especially indebted to Angelika Bammer, Shay Brawn, Lee Medovoi, and Brian Rourke for their extensive criticism and encouragement.

1. The category, "all women," is designated and interrogated by Adrienne Rich (219).

2. Sandra Harding makes such an argument regarding scientific justifications of female inferiority, which tend to emerge when "fundamental social changes between the genders were occurring or threatening to occur": "Overt misogynous expression is best thought of as masculine protest literature; after all, one does not bother to state what is obvious or to agitate for something one already has" (118). Thomas Laqueur makes a similar argument concerning the renewed appeal to gender politics attendant on liberalism's reformulation of the body within social discourse: "democracy [according to Tocqueville] had destroyed the old basis for patriarchal authority and . . . consequently it was necessary to trace anew and with great precision 'two clearly distinct lines of action for the two sexes.' In short, wherever boundaries were threatened arguments for fundamental sexual differences were shoved into the breach" (18).

3. Publicized examples of this are legion and include: the demonization of Manuel Noriega and Saddam Hussein; the acquittal of the Los Angeles police officers who beat Rodney King; the renewed hostility to Asian Americans that killed Detroit resident Vincent Chin in 1982 and denied Olympic gold medalist Kristi Yamaguchi product endorsements in 1992. These limited examples reflect the range of "justifiable" responses, and/or uses of force, that can be mounted against perceived threats to national security, urban order, and economic stability. I will be discussing Vincent Chin further later in the paper.

4. "Living as we did—on the edge—we developed a particular way of seeing reality. We looked both from the outside in and from the inside out. We focused our attention on the center as well as the margin. We understood both . . . " (i).

5. I thank Lee Medovoi for calling my attention to the two senses of "privilege" operating in Haraway and in Anzaldúa.

6. Haraway's resourceful and self-conscious use of diagrammatic binary oppositions is a defining feature of her work. As she puts it: "Noting [the] tradition [of binary analysis throughout Western history] does not invalidate its use; it *locates* its use and insists on its partiality and accountability. . . . Binaries, rather suspect for the feminists I know, can turn out to be nice little tools from time to time" (111).

7. I have opted to insist on the Anglicized spelling of the term "colour" throughout— as a minor, inaudible, and yet personally meaningful distinguishing mark of the "Canadian-ness" that informs my observations here. "You" say tomato; I say tomato. It's not simply that Canadians tend to obsess over what distinguishes them from Americans, no matter how trivial or silly, as a point of national solidarity and distinction. It also seems to me that as we venture and qualify our feminist "dreams of common languages," we continually come across this sort of unassimilable, at times barely perceptible, reminder or remainder of variation among us: things like the accents, however faint or residual, inflecting our speech; the often casual irruptions of "other" languages and dialects into our conversations; the specific frames of reference by which we perform our membership in certain communities and not in others. We are not always afforded opportunities to acknowledge these kinds of differences, much less to "locate" or "translate" them, but I take such an opportunity here. The spelling of the rest of this essay has been adjusted to Standard American English.

8. According to Derrida, the production of proper names is, in fact, their obliteration, severing "the proper from its property and its self-sameness." See, for more details than can appropriately be addressed here, "The Violence of the Letter," especially 109–12.

9. Rich, for example, makes reference to a name game played during her childhood in which "ever-widening" concentric circles are postulated around one's name: "Adrienne Rich/14 Edgevale Road/Baltimore, Maryland/. . . . The Earth/The Solar System/The Universe." Rich invokes the game (in a kind of "portrait of the artist as a young woman") as a concrete example of the notions of self-centered and self-centralizing subjectivity—the implied centrality of "home"—which a politics of location must abandon. As a schoolboy, Joyce's Dedalus plays the same game and is led to very similar reveries concerning the relation between self and universe. Where Rich and Dedalus diverge is in the recovery of decentralization and exile. For Rich, to destabilize one's presumptions about one's centrality is to discover one's own body and historical specificity. For Dedalus—who continues his odyssey into Joyce's *Ulysses*—the self is dissolved into and recreated as coherence by one's art; the decentered, exiled self is reintegrated into a medieval conception of the "book," and thereby transcends historical particularities and the mundaneness of the physical body. This is a mere outline for a much more complicated argument about "modernist" and "postmodernist," androcentric and feminist, conceptions of subjectivity, authorship and art than can be made here (see Rich 211–12; and Joyce 15–16).

10. Both *Zami* and *Coatlicue* are invoked and rewritten as bridge figures, within, across, and beyond specific cultural traditions. Lorde adopts "a Carriacou name for women who work together as friends and lovers" so as to name the years during which her life "had become increasingly a bridge and field of women" (*Zami* 255). Representing "duality in life, a synthesis of duality, and . . . something more than mere duality or a synthesis of duality," the goddess *Coatlicue* ("Serpent Skirt") encodes in her name and performs in her symbolic functions the kinds of contradictions and fusions that characterize Anzaldúa's borderlands. At the same time, Anzaldúa claims *Coatlicue* as one component of a larger amalgamation of names: "the entity that is the sum total of all my reincarnations, the godwoman in me I call *Antigua, mi Diosa*, the divine within, *Coatlicue-Cihuacoatl-Tlazolteotl-Tonantzin-Coatlalopeuh-Guadalupe*—they are one" *(Borderlands 46, 50)*.

Works Cited

Alarcón, Norma. "The Theoretical Subject(s) of *This Bridge Called My Back* and Anglo-American Feminism." *Criticism in the Borderlands: Studies in Chicano Literature, Culture, and Ideology.* Ed. Héctor Calderón and José David Saldívar. Durham: Duke UP, 1991. 28–39.

Althusser, Louis. "Ideology and Ideological State Apparatuses (Notes towards an Investigation)." *Lenin and Philosophy and Other Essays.* Trans. Ben Brewster. New York: Monthly Review, 1966. 127–86.

Anzaldúa, Gloria. *Borderlands/La Frontera: The New Mestiza.* San Francisco: Spinsters/Aunt Lute, 1987.

Derrida, Jacques. "The Violence of the Letter: From Lévi-Strauss to Rousseau." *Of Grammatology.* Trans. Gayatri Chakravorty Spivak. Baltimore: Johns Hopkins UP, 1976. 101–49.

Ellison, Ralph. *Invisible Man.* New York: Vintage, 1972.

Gates, Henry Louis, Jr. "Authority, (White) Power, and the (Black) Critic." *Cultural Critique* 7 (1987): 20–49.

Haraway, Donna. *Simians, Cyborgs, and Women: The Reinvention of Nature*. New York: Routledge, 1991.

Harding, Sandra. *The Science Question in Feminism*. Ithaca: Cornell UP, 1986.

hooks, bell. *Feminist Theory: From Margin to Center*. Boston: South End, 1984.

Joyce, James. *A Portrait of the Artist as a Young Man*. Harmondsworth: Penguin, 1982.

Kaplan, Caren. "Deterritorializations: The Rewriting of Home and Exile in Western Feminist Discourse." *Cultural Critique* 6 (1987): 187–98.

Laqueur, Thomas. "Orgasm, Generation, and the Politics of Reproductive Biology." *The Making of the Modern Body: Sexuality and Society in the Nineteenth Century*. Ed. Catherine Gallagher and Thomas Laqueur. Berkeley: U of California P, 1987. 1–41.

Lorde, Audre. *Zami: A New Spelling of My Name*. Trumansburg: Crossing, 1982.

Mohanty, Chandra Talpade. "Feminist Encounters: Locating the Politics of Experience." *Copyright* 1 (1987): 30–44.

——. "Sketching Cartographies of Struggle: Third World Women and the Politics of Feminism." *Third World Women and the Politics of Feminism*. Ed. Chandra Talpade Mohanty, Ann Russo, and Lourdes Torres. Bloomington: Indiana UP, 1991. 1–47.

Moraga, Cherríe. "From a Long Line of Vendidas: Chicanas and Feminism." *Feminist Studies/Critical Studies*. Ed. Teresa de Lauretis. Bloomington: Indiana UP, 1986. 173–90.

Reagon, Bernice Johnson. "Coalition Politics: Turning the Century." *Home Girls: A Black Feminist Anthology*. Ed. Barbara Smith. New York: Kitchen Table: Women of Color, 1983. 356–68.

Rich, Adrienne. "Notes toward a Politics of Location." *Blood, Bread, and Poetry: Selected Prose, 1979–85*. New York: Norton, 1986. 210–31.

Spivak, Gayatri Chakravorty. "Who Claims Alterity?" *Remaking History: Discussions in Contemporary Culture*. Ed. Barbara Kruger and Phil Mariani. Seattle: Bay, 1989. 269–92.

Takaki, Ronald. *Strangers from a Different Shore: A History of Asian Americans*. New York: Penguin, 1989.

This Bridge Called My Back: Writings by Radical Women of Color. Ed. Cherríe Moraga and Gloria Anzaldúa. New York: Kitchen Table: Women of Color, 1981.

Trinh T. Minh-ha. *Woman, Native, Other: Writing Postcoloniality and Feminism*. Bloomington: Indiana UP, 1989. 5–44.

Yamada, Mitsuye. "Asian Pacific American Women and Feminism." *This Bridge Called My Back*. 71–75.

Afterwords

17 | Frontlines/Borderposts
Homi K. Bhabha

THE POLITICS OF identity, the politics of difference, ethnic particularism, cultural pluralism, multiculturalism—as these terms proliferate both inside and outside the academy, there is the temptation of producing "a jargon of the minorities." Faced with major demographic shifts, educational, media, and governmental agencies both in the North and the South suffer crises of administrative and institutional "representability." Their response to this situation is either to generate anxiety around the threat to the canon, the national community, or the "common culture," or to "capitalize" on the changes by commodifying minority cultures into new disciplines and programs. Beyond the academy, and often in tension with it, there is a crisis of representation within minority communities around the knowledges that circulate in their name, and the "aid" agencies that are set up to legitimate their disadvantaged existence. Such circumstances may obfuscate our understanding of the profound changes that have occurred in our experience of contemporary cultural conflicts or the terms in which cultural consensus is negotiated amongst emergent or marginalized populations.

The move away from the singularities of "class" or "gender" as primary conceptual and organizational categories has resulted in a useful awareness of the multiple subject positions—of race, gender, generation, institutional location, geopolitical locale, sexual orientation—that inhabit any claim to identity in the (post)modern world. What is theoretically innovative, and politically crucial, is the necessity of thinking beyond initial categories and initiatory subjects and focusing on those *interstitial* moments or processes that are produced in the articulation of "differences." These spaces provide the terrain for elaborating strategies of selfhood and communal representations that generate new signs of cultural difference and innovative sites of collaboration and contestation. It is at the level of the interstices that the intersubjective and collective experiences of nationness, community interest, or cultural value are negotiated. How are subjects formed "in-between," or in excess of, the sum of the "parts" of difference (usually intoned as race/class/gender etc.)? What collective identifications become possible in the overlapping, or displacing, of domains of difference? How do strategies of representation or empowerment come to be formulated in the competing claims of communities where, despite shared histories of deprivation and discrimination, the exchange of values, meanings, and priorities may not be collaborative and dialogical, but profoundly antagonistic, conflictual, and even incommensurable?

The force of these questions is borne out by the "language" of recent social crises sparked by histories of cultural difference. Conflicts in South Central Los Angeles between Korean-Americans and African-Americans focus on the concept of "disrespect"—a term forged on the borderlines of ethnic deprivation that is, at once, the sign of racialized violence and the symptom of social victimage. In the aftermath of the Rushdie affair in Great Britain, black and Irish feminists, despite their different constituencies, have made common cause against the "racialization of religion" as the dominant discourse through which the state represents their conflicts and struggles, however secular or even "sexual" they may be. Terms of cultural engagement, whether antagonistic or affiliative, are produced performatively: "difference" is not so much a reflection of *pre-given* ethnic or cultural traits set in the tablets of a "fixed" tradition as it is a complex ongoing negotiation—against authorities, amongst minorities: the "right" to signify concerns, *not so much the teleologies of tradition as much as its powers of iteration, its forms of displacement and relocation, its ability to signify symbolic and social relations outside of the mimetic transmission of cultural contents.* The borderline engagements of cultural difference may as often be consensual as conflictual; they may confound our definitions of tradition and modernity; realign the customary boundary between the private and the public, high and low; and challenge normative expectations of development and progress.

What is at issue then, is the exploration of questions of historical agency and social temporality that constitute the borderposts and frontlines of cultural production and dissemination. By focusing on "events," "scenes," "memories that flash up in a moment of danger" we hope to maintain a sense of the enactment of meanings and practices involved in the regulation of policy and the formation of a politics, antagonistic or affiliative, that become the insignia of the interstices. These are the spaces through which minorities translate their dominant designations of difference—gender, ethnicity, class—into a solidarity that refuses both the binary politics of polarity, or the necessity of a homogeneous, unitary oppositional "bloc." The emphasis on the "event" as a performative matrix for discussing issues might unsettle that academic, inscriptive practice whereby incidents are seen as instances or examples of a more general, authoritative metalanguage. Indeed, a more productive discussion of the "event" is one that neither subsumes it into "theory" nor appropriates it by "practice," but allows it to maintain its own performative authority and interrogates the conditions under which knowledges, images, and discourses are socially and pedagogically authorized. By examining these agencies and ideologies of authentication, through such a notion of the event we might be able to attend to the various thematics and technologies that create the "public" sphere or dimension of a historical event.

By reconceptualizing culture as a category of translation,[1] as an analytic of "borderline" transformations, we might open up a range of questions that link the growing interdisciplinarity within the academy, with the global and the transnational nature of cultural transformations. These are just some of the questions that lie before us:

What are the changes within institutions and across disciplines that have made discourses of the "margin" or the "minority"—(post)colonial discourse, cultural studies, gay and lesbian studies, Chicano/a or Afro-American programs, black British cultural studies, Aboriginal literary studies—representative statements of a crisis in the concept of a common culture? Are the "canon-wars" in many Western institutions a distraction from the racism and discrimination meted out to minorities and migrant populations? Who are the constituents and the consumers of these areas of study? What, for instance, fuels the opposition to postcolonial theory from those locations—India, the Caribbean, Latin America—that are frequently represented within it?

As the migrant and the refugee become the "unhomely" inhabitants of the contemporary world, how do we rethink collective, communal concepts like homeland, the people, cultural exile, national cultures, interpretive communities? With the transfer of cultural technologies across metropolitan spaces, what new forms of cultural consumption and reproduction become visible? Do these transnational cultural movements make the binary distinction between East and West or North and South untenable?

Has the poststructuralist genealogy of "postcolonial" discourse, for instance, distracted attention from the economic and political determinism designated by terms such as neo-colonialism? Or does our theoretical attention to the forces of contingency and indeterminacy in social practices enable us to describe more clearly the uneven and unequal developments within social formations? Are we in a better position to grasp the avenging atavism of ethnicity in Eastern Europe by abandoning linear teleologies of progress? How does the Eurocentric experience of late capitalism and postmodernism look from other non-Eurocentric geographical and political sites?

Does the emphasis on the "interstitial" as a process of interpellation force us to reconsider our notion of the workings of ideology? Does it open up a space that is not merely theory, but not simply "experience"? Does this area of indeterminacy or "partial identification" within ideology make the place of desire, pleasure, and the affective body more critical to our understanding of the ambivalent mechanisms of social authority? Are we required to supplement our sense of social fantasy with an awareness of a situational ethics? What would be the ethical basis of such cultural practices? What would be the place of the intellectual within such forms of theory? How does the intellectual affiliate with political priorities that are to be found in the act of articulating, or contesting, differential political objectives—feminism, anti-racism, homophobia—rather than in the "objects" of difference themselves?

Notes

1. I have attempted to work out a theory of cultural translation in various essays to be found in my book *The Location of Culture*; see also "DissemiNation" and "Freedom's Basis."

Works Cited

Bhabha, Homi K. "DissemiNation: Time, Narrative, and the Margins of the Modern Nation." *Nation and Narration.* Ed. Homi K. Bhabha. New York: Routledge, 1990. 291–322.
———. "Freedom's Basis in the Indeterminate." *October* 61 (1992): 46–57.
———. *The Location of Culture.* New York: Routledge, 1993.

18 | Aller à la ligne

Theresa Hak Kyung Cha

Aller à la ligne   C'était le premier jour   point   Elle venait de loin   point ce soir au dîner   virgule   les familles demanderaient   virgule   ouvre les guillemets   Ça c'est bien passé le premier jour   point d'interrogation   ferme les guillemets   au moins   virgule   dire le moins possible   virgule   la réponse serait   virgule   ouvre les guillemets   Il n'y a qu'une chose   point ferme les guillemets   ouvre les guillemets   Il y a quelqu'une   point   loin point   ferme les guillemets

Open paragraph   It was the first day   period   She had come from afar period   tonight at dinner   comma   the families would ask   comma   open quotation marks   How was the first day   interrogation mark   close quotation marks   at least   comma   to say the least possible   comma   the answer would be   open quotation marks   there is but one thing   period close quotation marks   open quotation marks   There is someone   period From afar   period   close quotation marks

From *Dictée* (New York: Tanam, 1982) 1. Reprinted by permission of Richard Barnes.

Notes on Contributors

H. G. ADLER (1910-1988) was born in Prague and died in London. Raised in the ambience of Prague German Jewish culture, he studied literature, art, music, philosophy, and psychology and received a doctorate in German literature from Prague University. Between 1942 and 1945 he was interned in the concentration camps of Theresienstadt (where his parents died) and Buchenwald. After World War II he settled in London, where he lived as an independent scholar and writer. His work at once reflects on and documents the Holocaust in the context of German Jewish history. His scholarly works include *Theresienstadt, 1941-45: Das Antlitz einer Zwangsgemeinschaft* (1955; Theresienstadt, 1941-45: The Face of a Coerced Community) and its documentary sequel *Die verheimlichte Wahrheit: Theresienstädter Dokumente* (1958; The Silenced Truth: Theresienstadt Documents); *Die Juden in Deutschland: Von der Aufklärung bis zum Nationalsozialismus* (1960; Jews in Germany: From Enlightenment to National Socialism); and his magnum opus, *Der verwaltete Mensch: Studien zur Deportation der Juden aus Deutschland* (1974; The Administered Human Being: Studies on the Deportation of the Jews from Germany). JAMIE OWEN DANIEL teaches in the English Department at the University of Illinois-Chicago. She has published translations of several books and many essays, and is the author of an essay on Adorno and the concept of home in *New Formations*.

ANGELIKA BAMMER is Associate Professor of German Studies and Comparative literature and codirector of the Program in Culture, History, and Theory in the Graduate Institute of Liberal Arts at Emory University. She is the author of *Partial Visions: Feminism and Utopianism in the 1970s* and is currently working on issues of ethnic and gender identity in relation to national culture.

HOMI K. BHABHA teaches literature and cultural theory at the University of Sussex, England. He is the editor of *Nation and Narration* and *The Location of Culture*, as well as a *Critical Inquiry* special issue entitled *Frontlines and Borderposts* (forthcoming).

THERESA HAK KYUNG CHA was born in Pusan, Korea, in 1951. Her family emigrated to America in the early 1960s where she attended Catholic schools and later studied at the University of California at Berkeley and the Paris Film Institute. Her work includes video, film, installation, and poetry. In addition to the prose poem, *Dictée*, she was the editor/contributor of *Apparatus*, a film anthology, as well as a collection of essays contained in the book *Hotel*. Her work has been exhibited both in the United States and abroad, including a one-person show at the Whitney Museum of Art in New York in 1992. She died in New York in 1982. The University Art Museum at Berkeley has established an archive of her work and an endowment in her name.

ELAINE K. CHANG, a doctoral candidate in modern thought and literature at Stanford University, is completing a dissertation on the feminization of space in postcolonial and postmodern fiction. Her essays have appeared in the journal *Emergences* and in *Vancouver: Representing the Postmodern City* and *Designing Italy*.

REY CHOW was educated in Hong Kong and the United States. She is Associate Professor of Comparative Literature at the University of California at Irvine and the author of *Writing Diaspora: Tactics of Intervention in Contemporary Cultural Studies*; *Woman and Chinese Modernity*; and *Primitive Passions: Visuality, Sexuality, Ethnography, and Contemporary Chinese Cinema* (forthcoming). Her essays have appeared in a number of journals, including *Diaspora, Modern Chinese Literature, differences, Cinémas,* and *diacritics*.

JAMES CLIFFORD is the Director of the Center for Cultural Studies at the University of California, Santa Cruz. He is the author of *Person and Myth* and *The Predicament of Culture* and is coeditor of *Writing Culture*.

AMITAV GHOSH is a writer and ethnographer. Born in 1956 in Calcutta and educated in India and England, he has held visiting posts at several American universities and is currently affiliated with the Centre for Studies in Social Sciences in Calcutta. He has done extensive field work in rural Egypt. His novels include *The Circle of Reason, The Shadow Lines, Death of a Harvard Man,* and *In an Antique Land*.

MARIANNE HIRSCH is Dartmouth Professor of French and Comparative Literature at Dartmouth College. She is the author of *The Mother/Daughter Plot: Narrative, Psychoanalysis, Feminism* and coeditor of *Conflicts in Feminism* and *The Voyage In: Fictions of Female Development*.

ALICE YAEGER KAPLAN teaches in the Departments of Romance Studies and Literature at Duke University. She is the author of *French Lessons: A Memoir* and editor, with Philippe Roussin, of a special issue of *South Atlantic Quarterly* entitled *Céline, U.S.A.*

ABDELFATTAH KILITO's work bridges the gap between classical Arabic literature and modern literary theory. He has taught literature at Rabat University in Morocco and has held visiting posts at the École des Hautes Études and Collège de France. He is the author of studies focusing, among other things, on genre (*Les séances*), authorship (*L'Auteur et ses doubles*), and the *One Thousand and One*

Nights (L'Oeil et l'aiguille). ZIAD ELMARSAFY is Assistant Professor of French at Wellesley College.

DOREEN MASSEY is Professor of Geography at the Open University. She is the author of several books on the spatial structure of social relations, including *Spatial Divisions of Labor, Space, Place, and Gender,* and *High Tech Fantasies* (with Paul Quintas and David Wield).

KATHRYN MILUN is Assistant Professor in the Department of Anthropology at Rice University. She has published translations and essays in *Discourse, Surfaces,* the *Duke University Law Review,* and *Perilous States.* She is working with Pemina Yellow Bird on a book concerning the Indian reburial issue, forthcoming from University of Minnesota Press.

PANIVONG NORINDR, a Laotian citizen, was born in France and educated in the United States. He currently teaches at the University of Wisconsin–Milwaukee. He has published essays on French literature, architecture, and cinema, and has just completed a manuscript on the cultural topography of "Indo-China."

JULIO RAMOS teaches Latin American and Caribbean literatures at the University of California at Berkeley. He is the author of *Desencuentros de la modernidad: literatura y politica en el siglo XIX* and editor of *Amor y anarquia: Escritos de Luisa Capetillo.*

KAREN REMMLER is Assistant Professor of German Studies at Mount Holyoke College. Her research includes works in progress on Jewish identity and gender in the writing of Jewish women authors in post-unified Germany, the representation of the body in texts by Holocaust survivors, and structures of remembrance in texts by Ingeborg Bachmann and Walter Benjamin.

SHEILA ROBERTS, Professor of English at the University of Wisconsin–Milwaukee, was born in Johannesburg, South Africa. She is the author of three novels and three collections of short stories, including *Coming In.* She has published many essays on South African literature in American, Canadian, and South African journals.

BILL SCHWARZ is Principal Lecturer in Cultural Studies at the University of East London, where he also chairs the M. A. in cultural studies, history and theory. He is on the editorial collectives of *History Workshop Journal* and *Cultural Studies.*

SUSAN E. SHAPIRO teaches in the Department of Religion at Columbia University. She has published in the areas of post-Holocaust thought and the rhetorics of body and gender in Jewish philosophy. She is currently working on a manuscript, of which the essay "Écriture judaïque" forms a part, on the "Jewish uncanny."

PEMINA YELLOW BIRD is an enrolled member of the Three Affiliated Tribes (Madan, Hidatsa, and Arikara). She is a founding member of the North Dakota Reinterment Committee and has served as a board member of the North Dakota State Historical Society. She also serves on the National Congress of the American Indian's Religious Rights Committee, through which she has conducted workshops on the reburial issue. She is currently working, with Kathryn Milun, on a study of the Indian reburial issue, forthcoming from the University of Minnesota Press.

Index

Aboriginal literary studies, 271

Acculturation, 74, 85, 244

Adler, H. G.: *Der verwaltete Mensch: Studien zur Deportation der Juden aus Deutschland* (The Administered Human Being: A Study of the Deportation of the Jews from Germany), 205–215. *See also* Brüll, Ernst

Adolescence: as transition, 71–89 *passim*; and cultural displacement, 74; Carol Gilligan, 74–75; as emigration, 75

African National Congress, 175–80 *passim*; discussed in Joe Frederikse's *The Unbreakable Thread: Non Racialism in South Africa*, 177. *See also* Mandela, Nelson; Communism; Rivonia Trial

African: debate about term in South Africa, 178

Afro-American Studies, 271

Al-A^{c}jam, Ziyād, xxix

Al-Akhṭal, xxxn5

Alarcón, Norma: *This Bridge Called My Back*, 256; individualist and heterogeneous subjects, 257–58

Al-Azhar, 47

Algeria, 102, 134, 135, 136, 148n15, 162

Ali, Tariq, 159

Alienation: and displacement, xiii; and Eva Hoffman, 75; the Other, 143

Al-Jāḥiz: *The Book of Animals*, xxii; *The Book of Eloquence*, xxviii; origin of name, xxxn1

Alloula, Malek: *The Colonial Harem* critiqued, 134–44

Al-Sindī, Abū ^{c}Aṭā', xxix

Althusser, Louis: ideology in capitalism, 43n19; and naming, 258–59

An American Tail: 90–92, 104 *passim*; emigration in, 90; and Art Spiegelman, 92; and definition of family, 104

Améry, Jean, 216–27 *passim*; *At the Mind's Limits* (biography), 216–17; torture and the body, 217–25, 227; displacement through naming, 223; reclaiming body through words, 224; and Elaine Scarry, 224

Amritsar Massacre of 1919, 162–64 *passim*, 166

Anderson, Benedict, xix; *Imagined Communities* and imagining the nation, 41n9; family and nation, 106n6; reformulation of Seton-Watson's definition of nation, 247n14. *See also* Seton-Watson, Hugh

Anthropology, xiv, xviiin6, xxxn1, 10, 18, 27, 125, 131; and Argentina, 28, 34–36; discourse of, 27; anthropologist as flaneur, 35. *See also* Criminal anthropology; Archaeology; Lombroso, Cesare; Native American

Antisemitism: and Eva Hoffman, 77, 79; Lyotard's analysis, 182–99 *passim*. *See also* Améry, Jean; Brüll, Ernst; Fritz, Mali; Hoffman, Eva; Nazism and the Third Reich; Jew(ish)

Anzaldúa, Gloria: "borderlands" defined, 71; *Borderlands*, 255–56, 262; and lesbianism, 255–56; and Donna Haraway, 257

Apelfeld, Aharon, 78

Appadurai, Arjun, 137–38

Archaeology: and Native Americans, 4–21 *passim*; Bureau of American Ethnology, 13; Thomas Jefferson as collector, 13, 18; Antiquities Law of 1906, 14. *See also* Anthropology; Native American

Argentina, 25–40 *passim*; and language debates, 25–26; and war with the British, 159

Armstrong, Nancy, 133

"Asians"/"Asian Americans": as immigrants, 233–46 *passim*, 251–63 *passim*; stereotyping of, 233–34, 259–60; as model citizens, 240; targets for violence, 259–60 (*see also* Chin, Vincent)

Assimilation, 5, 15, 75, 77, 81, 85, 244, 246; and Richard Rodriguez, 61; avoided through